Martine Prange
Nietzsche, Wagner, Europe

Monographien und Texte zur Nietzsche-Forschung

Begründet von
Mazzino Montinari
Wolfgang Müller-Lauter
Heinz Wenzel

Herausgegeben von
Günter Abel, Berlin
Werner Stegmaier, Greifswald

Band 61

Martine Prange

Nietzsche, Wagner, Europe

—

DE GRUYTER

ISBN 978-3-11-048163-1
e-ISBN 978-3-11-031523-3
ISSN 1862-1260

Library of Congress Cataloging-in-Publication data
A CIP catalog record for this book has been applied for at the Library of Congress.

Bibliographic information published by the Deutsche Nationalbibliothek
The Deutsche Nationalbibliothek lists this publication in the Deutsche Nationalbibliografie;
detailed bibliographic data are available in the Internet at http://dnb.dnb.de.

© 2013 Walter de Gruyter GmbH, Berlin/Boston
Typesetting: PTP-Berlin Protago-T$_E$X-Production GmbH, www.ptp-berlin.de
Printing and binding: Hubert & Co. GmbH & Co. KG, Göttingen
♾ Printed on acid-free paper
Printed in Germany

www.degruyter.com

Acknowledgment

I thank Roger Stephenson, for his eminent, meticulous comments on this text and his deep-rooted trust in my project; Detlev Pätzold, for monitoring my German quotations and his unremitting support; my former colleagues at Groningen University and Maastricht University, especially Tsjalling Swierstra and Maaike Meijer, who helped me generate funds to edit the manuscript; my students from Groningen, Amsterdam, Maastricht, and Leiden, who helped me shape my ideas over the years; and my friends and family, particularly my father, to whom I dedicate this book. The textual editing (by R. Hanshe) was funded by the Faculty of Arts and Social Sciences, Maastricht University.

Abbreviations and translations

Nietzsche's works

All references to Nietzsche are made to the standard KSA or KSB editions, unless otherwise indicated. References to Nietzsche's published works appear in parentheses, using the standard English title acronyms indicated below, followed by chapter or aphorism number, KSA-volume number and page number. 'P' denotes the works' prefaces. References to *Thus Spoke Zarathustra* give the part number and chapter title, for example, Z IV 'Amongst the Daughters of the Desert' plus KSA-volume and page number. References to *Twilight of the Idols* and *Ecce Homo* give abbreviated chapter title and section number, for example, TI 'Ancients' 3, with KSA-volume and page number.

References to the notes include the number of the fragment, the number of the KSA-volume, and behind the full stop the page number for example, 11[10] (KSA 9.443–444) = notation 11[10] of volume 9, pages 443–444. Letters to Nietzsche are from the *Kritische Gesamtausgabe* (KGB) and are referred to with their volume and page number. For Nietzsche's notes (the *Nachlass*), I have used the KSA and *Kritische Gesamtwerke* (KGW) editions, and on one occasion the Beck edition of the early writings (*Frühe Schriften*, BAW).

References to published works

A	*The Antichrist*
AOM	*Assorted Opinions and Maxims*
ASC	*Attempt at Self-Criticism (1886 Preface to BT)*
BGE	*Beyond Good and Evil*
BT	*The Birth of Tragedy*
CW	*The Case of Wagner*
D	*Daybreak*
DS	*David Strauss*
EH	*Ecce Homo*
GM	*On the Genealogy of Morals*
GS	*The Gay Science*
GSJ	*Joke, Cunning, and Revenge (Prelude to GS)*
GSS	*Songs of Prince Vogelfrei (1887 Appendix to GS)*
HH I	*Human, All Too Human I*
HH II	*Human, All Too Human II*
HL	*On the Use and Disadvantage of History for Life*
IM	*Idylls from Messina*
NCW	*Nietzsche contra Wagner*

SE	*Schopenhauer as Educator*
TI	*Twilight of the Idols*
UM	*Untimely Meditations*
WB	*Richard Wagner in Bayreuth*
WS	*The Wanderer and His Shadow*
Z	*Thus Spoke Zarathustra*

References to essays and lectures from the notes

FP	*Five Prefaces to Five Unwritten Books*
HCPh	*Homer and Classical Philology*
PTAG	*Philosophy in the Tragic Age of the Greeks*
TL	*On Truth and Lies in a Non-moral Sense*

Works by Wagner, Schopenhauer, Goethe, and Schiller

For my analysis and discussion of Wagner's centenary 'Beethoven' essay, I have used Volume IX of Wagner's *Dichtungen und Schriften*, edited by Dieter Borchmeyer. The abbreviation used for the text of Beethoven is DS IX with page-number.

With regard to Schopenhauer, I made use of the English translation by Payne, i.e., the Dover edition. The abbreviations used are WWR I and WWR II for *The World as Will and Representation* volume I and II respectively.

For Goethe, I used the Hamburg and Munich editions (referred to as 'HA' and 'MA' with volume-number), and the Princeton University Press edition for English translations of *Italian Journey* and some aesthetic texts, such as *Simple Imitation, Manner, Style*. Other English translations are mine (e.g. *Maximen und Reflexionen*).

For Schiller, I used the *Nationalausgabe*. 'NA' with volume- and page-number refers to the *Nationalausgabe*. 'UNSD' refers to the essay 'Über naive und sentimentalische Dichtung'. For the English translation of UNSD, I used Helen Watanabe-O'Kelly's translation. Other English translations of Schiller are, except for one, my own.

HA	*Goethe. Werke. Hamburger Ausgabe.*
MA	*Johann Wolfgang Goethe.*
	Sämtliche Werke nach Epochen seines Schaffens. Münchner Ausgabe.
NA	*Schillers Werke. Nationalausgabe. Weimar.*
UNSD	*Schiller. Über naive und sentimentale Dichtung. Schriften und Briefe zur Ästhetik.*
	Schiller. On the Naive and Sentimental in Literature.
WWR I	*Schopenhauer. The World as Will and Representation Vol. 1*

WWR II   *Schopenhauer. The World as Will and Representation Vol. 2*
WWV 1   *Schopenhauer. Die Welt als Wille und Vorstellung Bd. 1*
WWV 2   *Schopenhauer. Die Welt als Wille und Vorstellung Bd. 2*
DS IX   *Wagner. Dichtungen und Schriften. Vol. IX*

Note on the translations and secondary literature

I have used the KSA edition for my interpretation of Nietzsche's philosophy. When available, I used existing English translations for the English quotations. However, many English quotations are my own translations of the German (and sometimes Dutch or French) originals – for example, from Nietzsche's *Nachlass* and Wagner's 'Beethoven' essay – unless mentioned otherwise. I quote the [German] original text where my critical focus is on textual detail. In other cases, I quote the English translation only. References to secondary literature are made with the name of the author and the year of publication.

Contents

Abbreviations and translations —— vi

General introduction —— 3

Part I
Aestheticization: Germany as saviour of Europe

Chapter 1
Was Nietzsche ever a true Wagnerian? —— 21

Chapter 2
Germanizing music and culture: Richard Wagner's 'Beethoven' essay —— 52

Chapter 3
Nietzsche's reception of Wagner's 'Beethoven' essay in the spirit
of Weimar Classicism —— 95

Chapter 4
The Birth of Tragedy out of Nietzsche's concern for Wagner's 'Graecization' —— 129

Part II
Dynamic interculturalism: De-Germanization and the
'Good European'

Chapter 5
Nietzsche's anti-Wagnerism in the light of his increasing cosmopolitanism —— 169

Chapter 6
'La Gaya Scienza' in music: Nietzsche's new musical aesthetics —— 199

Chapter 7
Goethe as model of the 'Good European' —— 228

Epilogue —— 258

Bibliography —— 265

Index —— 284

'Unser Zeitalter, so viel es von Ökonomie redet, ist ein Verschwender: es verschwendet das Kostbarste, den Geist'
(Nietzsche, *Morgenröthe* 179, KSA 3.158)

'Ein Deutscher ist grosser Dinge fähig, aber es ist unwahrscheinlich, dass er sie thut [...]'
(Nietzsche, *Morgenröthe* 207, KSA 3.185)

'[...] unsre Stolle ist die Deutsche Nachahmung des pane dolce di Genova'
(Nietzsche to his mother and sister in a letter from
21 December 1881, KSB 6.151)

'Ich habe nicht Kraft genug für den Norden [...] ich habe Geist genug für den Süden'
(Nietzsche, 12[181], KSA 9.607)

'Der Zweck des Lebens ist das Leben selbst'
(Goethe in a letter to J.H. Meyer, 8 February 1796)

General introduction

Europe today

Trade and economy have been the core 'business' of the European Union since 1955,[1] when representatives of Belgium, France, the Federal Republic of Germany, Italy, Luxembourg, and The Netherlands gathered to sign the 'Messina Declaration'. That declaration listed an agenda for the European formation, based on the aims

> to preserve the standing which she [Europe, MP] has in the world, to restore the influence and her prestige, and to improve steadily the living standard of the population.[2]

It further said that the signing countries 'are of the opinion that these objectives should be achieved first of all in the economic sphere' and

> believe that the establishment of a united Europe must be achieved through the development of common institutions, the progressive fusion of national economies, the creation of a common market, and the gradual harmonization of their social policies.

The Lisbon-strategy of 2000 sustained this economic conception of Europe by setting the EU the task of becoming 'the most competitive and dynamic knowledge-based economy in the world'.[3] This instrumentalist view of knowledge confirms Lyotard's analysis that knowledge 'is and will be produced in order to be sold' and is characteristic of a general trend, and one that informed the creation of the European Union.[4] Under the flag of liberal capitalism, Europe is propagated as a market, in which Europeans participate as consumers, and where cultural value is increasingly judged by its monetary gain. Anthony Pagden justifiably observed that ' "Europe" now exists as an economic, and increasingly political, entity. But this has no wider cultural or affective

---

1 The Treaty of Paris (1951) established the European Coal and Steel Community, the forerunner of the EU.

2 http://www.eurotreaties.com/messina.pdf.

3 http://www.europarl.europa.eu/summits/lis1_en.htm. The term 'Europe' stems from the Greek words meaning 'broad' ('*eurys*') and 'face' ('*ops*'). Some sources maintain that the name has a Semitic origin, from the Akkadian word '*gharoob*', '*erebu*', or '*ereb samsi*', which is supposed to mean 'sunset' (from a Middle East perspective, the sun sets over Europe). Likewise, 'Asia' is said to derive from the Akkadian word '*asu*', or '*wasa'u*' meaning 'sunrise'. In Greek mythology, Europa is the name of the daughter of Agenor, the Phoenician king of Tyre (Sidon). She was abducted by Zeus in the form of a white bull, to Crete, where she gave birth to three sons, Minos, Sarpedon, and Rhadamanthys. She gave her name to the continent. The Greeks already divided the world into Europe, foria, and Lybia (Africa). Cf. Gommers (2001), pp. 37–67.

4 Lyotard (2004), p. 4.

meaning.'[5] In addition, Thomas Docherty justly claimed that due to the trend of 'mercantilism', human freedom is 'reduced to a matter of "choice".'[6]

In the economic-political conception of Europe, European culture as formed by its artistic, historical, and scientific achievements is hardly taken into account as inherently meaningful. Such a view differs significantly from the pre-modern view, which held that art and knowledge were worthwhile for their own sake rather than because of their retail price.[7] Today, a new 'Golden Age' is anticipated for Europe, to result from a strong Euro, which, in turn, is strengthened and stabilized by up-to-date technological knowledge. Before the 1950s, however, 'Europe' resonated with a much broader meaning, and it is some of that echo that I want to make reverberate in this book by bringing out Friedrich Nietzsche's artistic view of Europe.[8] In so doing, I join in with Pagden and Docherty's cultural criticism, which stands in the Romantic tradition of criticizing the glorification of reason and technology at the expense of art and wisdom.[9] Nietzsche (1844–1900) applies this criticism particularly to the question concerning the future and unification of Europe, developing an artistic and aesthetic view of Europe and Europeans.

Nietzsche's artistic view of Europe

Nietzsche supported the unification of Europe and reflected on this like almost no other philosopher before or after him. Almost all his works are ultimately concerned with the present state and future of European culture and humanity. Already rather early, it was clear to Nietzsche that *'Europe wants to be one'* (BGE 256, p. 148/*'Europa eins werden will'*, KSA 5.201). However, to him the unification was not only an inevitable, future political reality, but he also developed a practical programme to

---

5 Pagden (2002), p. 33.
6 Docherty (2006), p. xiv.
7 For an analysis of the effect of the 'Knowledge Economy' on universities, see: Ferudi (2004). Succinctly, he states: 'Knowledge has become a branch embraced by virtually every significant institution. [...] Often knowledge is conceptualized as a ready-made digestible product that can be "delivered", "transmitted", "marketed", and "consumed". [...] The transformation of knowledge into a product deprives it of any intrinsic value or meaning, and the knowledge that is peddled by the merchants of the Knowledge Economy is in fact a mundane caricature' (Ferudi 2004, p. 7).
8 Compare also Mooij: 'Much more than the post-war conference [the Geneva conference of 1946, MP], did the conference of 1933 [the Parisian conference of writers, philosophers, and scientists of 1933, MP] focus on the purity of the mind, of the separation of the world of the mind from the political world' ('Veel meer dan het na-oorlogse congres [de Geneefse conferentie van 1946, MP] stond dat van 1933 [het Parijse schrijvers- en wetenschappers congres van 1933, MP] in het teken van de zuiverheid van de geest, van de gescheidenheid van de wereld van de geest van die van de politiek,' Mooij 2006, p. 31).
9 One of the most important, powerful, and inspiring criticisms of the instrumentalization of reason was given by Adorno and Horkheimer (1969).

help engender Europe's union.[10] Resisting the 'nationalist nonsense' ('*Nationalitäts-Wahnsinn*') and 'politics of dissolution' ('*auseinanderlösende Politik*') of his day, he advocated the birth of 'good Europeans' ('*guten Europäer*'), 'supra-national' individuals who shaped themselves into 'a mix of cultures' and promoted the 'amalgamation of nations' (HH I 475, pp. 174–175/'*Verschmelzung der Nationen*', KSA 2.309–311).[11]

However, he primarily conceived of Europe as a culture guided by art and not as a political or economic bond. To him, Europe drew its identity, unity, and height from its artistic spirit and productions, as exemplified by Greek Tragedy, Italian Renaissance painting, and (from 1881 on) Italian opera. This aesthetic view is characteristic of Nietzsche's Europeanism, and he explicitly contrasted it to the political-military nationalism and commercialism of his day. As he wrote to Rohde about his student house in Leipzig: 'to my comfort there is *hardly* any talk of politics, for I am not a ζῶν πολιτικόν, and I have a porcupine nature against such things'[12] and, in *Schopenhauer as Educator*, 'Humankind is only allowed that much culture as is in the interest of general profit and world traffic [...].'[13] Nietzsche's anti-political, anti-Christian, and artistic approach to Europe provides us with a methodological horizon, from which we may take a critical stance towards the current unification, which is inequitably based on economic and political views.

Admittedly, Nietzsche was also a notorious anti-Christian thinker, who repeatedly pointed to other cultural roots of Europe than the Christian ones – its Greek roots, specifically. He did that not only to show that Europe had always been more than a Christian society alone, but also to propose a new, post-Christian, European identity. When considering Europe's cultural identity, politicians today still often refer to Christianity as its main source. In so doing, they restrict the concept of culture to a religious and moral understanding, eliding the many non-Christian and non-religious influences on Europe's history and present. Nietzsche's philosophy offers a refreshing and helpful perspective in this regard too, for his 'good European' is a post-Christian

---

10 The inevitability of this must not be seen as teleological or natural determinism in the Kantian or Hegelian sense.

11 In WS 292, Nietzsche claims that one consequence of the democratization processes in Europe will be a European 'league of nations', in which foreign and domestic politics will become inseparable (WS 292, KSA 2.683–684). Cf. WS 393, KSA 2.685. Note that Nietzsche's ideal Europe as 'cultural concept' ('Cultur-Begriff') does not include all of geographical Europe, but 'only those nations and ethnic minorities who possess a common past in Greece, Rome, Judaism, and Christianity' (WS 215, p. 365/ 'nur alle jene Völker und Völkertheile, welche im Griechen-, Römer-, Juden- und Christenthum ihre gemeinsame Vergangenheit haben,' KSA 2.650), set against 'modern' Europe, which includes all of geographical Europe and the United States of America, as the 'daughterland' of Europe.

12 'Zu meinem Troste aber wird von Politik *fast* nicht gesprochen, da ich kein ζῶν πολιτικόν bin, und gegen derartige Dinge eine Stachelschweinnatur habe,' (Nietzsche to Rohde, 17 October 1868, KSB 2, p. 331).

13 'Dem Menschen wird nur soviel Kultur gestattet, als im Interesse des allgemeinen Erwerbs und des Weltverkehrs ist [...]' (SE 6, KSA 1.33).

and multi-cultural figure. This 'religious' motive is the least important in this book, yet contributes to the challenge to look at European identity and culture from a different, artistic, perspective.

This brings me to the last reason to analyze Nietzsche's artistic view of Europe, which derives from the current state of Nietzsche scholarship. With the growing interest in 'Europe', Nietzsche's views of Europe have been gaining more attention within international Nietzsche studies, especially in the last decade. These studies generally examine his concept of 'the good European', his diagnosis of the 'nihilism' modern Europe faces, and Nietzsche's (anti-) democratic, political views. None of these publications reflects on Nietzsche's aesthetic position with regard to Europe, or the relation between his music and European culture, as I do in the present study. Although all philosophers familiar with his work acknowledge that music was of vital importance to him and that he considered philosophy and life to be the same thing, the relationship between his musical aesthetics and philosophy of culture has yet to be taken as a starting-point for an understanding of his view of Europe.[14] In addition, whereas these studies generally concentrate on the later works, I focus on Nietzsche's cultural ideal of Europe as it comes to the fore from *The Birth of Tragedy* (1872) onwards. In delineating Nietzsche's artistic views of Europe by reconstructing the development of his musical aesthetics in relation to his philosophy of culture, I hope in the first place to make a substantial contribution to Nietzsche-scholarship.

Thus, until now scholars have principally reserved attention to Nietzsche's supposed political view of Europe or his moral critique of Christianity and European nihilism. Very little notion has been given to his artistic view of Europe, even though his concern for Europe was preponderantly with European culture and art. Müller-Warden justifiably stated:

> The valuation of the relationship of Nietzsche's philosophy with *politics* and with regard to the dominion of the *political* is due to a specific significance as to the question whether the field of the (critical) *present development of Europe* can be sufficiently described by means of political

---

14 Krökel (1929) and Visser (1933) were the first to systematically study Nietzsche's views of Europe. Only seventy years later, this subject became a topic of central interest in Nietzsche scholarship again. Krell and Bates (1997) contains beautiful photographs of places in Europe where Nietzsche used to live or vacation, but does not critically reflect on his philosophy of Europe. Kuhn (1992) and Witzler (2001) confine themselves to an analysis of European nihilism and leave out Nietzsche's reflections on art as the *sine qua non* of culture. None of the articles in Goedert and Nussbaumer-Benz (2002) addresses the question of the relevance of Nietzsche's artistic view of Europe. The same goes for Elbe (2003), although Elbe raises the question what might provide 'Europe' with meaning after 'the death of God' and answers that Europe should not create a new structure of meaning, but be responsive to the absence of meaning. See also: Riedel (1992), Martin (1995), Seubert (1999), Brusotti (2004, 2006), and D'Iorio and Merlio (2006). Kuhn (2002) and Brusotti (2004) raise the question of what kind of music would suit Nietzsche's view of Europe, but do not elaborate on it.

categories. If this is not the case, then new horizons should gradually be opened, that would have to be put forward as psychological, sociological, economic, or similar levels.

Die Bewertung des Verhältnisses der Philosophie Nietzsches zur Politik und zum Bereich des Politischen kommt eine besondere Bedeutung zu für die Frage, ob das Feld der [krisenhaften] aktuellen Entwicklung Europas in den Kategorien des Politischen umfassend beschrieben werden kann. Wäre dies nicht der Fall, so müßte methodisch gleichsam zu neuen Horizonten aufgebrochen werden, die dann darzulegen wären etwa als Ebenen des Psychologischen, des Soziologischen, des Ökonomischen oder vergleichbarer Gebiete. (Müller-Warden 1998, p. 123).

The category of 'the political' indeed does not suffice to grasp Nietzsche's view of Europe.[15] On the contrary, his reflections on Europe are best viewed from another 'horizon' (one that Müller-Warden does not mention), namely the horizon of aesthetics and art. Nietzsche expected cultural uplift from art only, and he trusted only art to fulfil his ideal of bringing Europe to new cultural heights in line with Ancient Greece and the Renaissance. With this goal in mind, he assigned himself the task of playing an active role in the process by writing books that called for the 'aestheticization' and 'dynamic interculturalism' of man and culture. This message was meant for his fellow Germans in the first place as they were seriously threatened by a 'distressing spiritual condition' ('*geistige Nothstände*')[16] due to their commercial outlook and their victory in the Franco-Prussian war:

Of all the evil consequences, however, which have followed the recent war with France, perhaps the words is a widespread, indeed universal, error: the error, committed by public opinion and by all who express their opinions publicly, that German culture too was victorious in that struggle [...]. This delusion is in the highest degree destructive [...] because it is capable of turning our victory into a defeat: *into the defeat, if not the extirpation, of the German spirit for the benefit of the "German Reich"* (DS 1, p. 3)

Von allen schlimmen Folgen aber, die der letzte mit Frankreich geführte Krieg hinter sich drein zieht, ist vielleicht die schlimmste ein weitverbreiteter, ja allgemeiner Irrthum: der Irrthum der öffentlichen Meinung, und aller öffentlich Meinenden, dass auch die deutsche Kultur in jenem Kampfe gesiegt habe [...]. Dieser Wahn ist höchst verderblich [...] weil er im Stande ist, unseren Sieg in eine völlige Niederlage zu verwandeln: *in die Niederlage, ja Exstirpation des deutschen Geistes zu Gunsten des "deutschen Reiches."* (DS 1, KSA 1.159–160)[17]

---

15 See also Stegmaier: 'Nietzsche stopped at the vision of Europe's unity. He barely made proposals for its political realization' ('Nietzsche hat es bei der Vision der Einheit Europa's belassen. Er hat kaum Vorschläge für seine politische Verfassung gemacht,' Stegmaier 2011, p. 347).

16 I would translate this as 'states of spiritual emergency'. These are due to the widespread desire to 'live well, by trade (that is to say, to try to buy as cheaply as possible from the producers and to sell as dearly as possible to the consumers, and thus to profit at the greatest possible expense of both,' WS 282, p. 379/'vom Handel leben und gut leben wollen [also dem Erzeugende die Preise möglichst zu verringern und dem Verzehrenden die Preise möglichst zu erhöhen suchen, um am möglichst grossen Schaden Beider den Vortheil zu haben],' KSA 2.677).

17 Cf. EH UM 1, p. 112/KSA 6.316; cf. Erich Heller (1988), p. 1.

Fifteen years later, he repeated in *Twilight of the Idols* that 'State' (*'Reich'*) and 'spirit' (*'Geist'*) are two decidedly different notions that should be kept as remote as possible from each other:

> German culture is in decline [...]. If you invest all your energy in economics, world commerce, parlaimentarism, military engagement, power and power politics, – if you take the quantum of intelligence, seriousness, will, and self-overcoming that you embody and expend it all in this *one* direction, then there won't be any left for the other direction. (TI 'What the Germans lack' 4, p. 188)

> die deutsche Cultur [geht] nieder. [...] Giebt man sich für Macht, für grosse Politik, für Wirthschaft, Weltverkehr, Parlamentarismus, Militär-Interessen aus, – giebt man das Quantum Verstand, Ernst, Wille, Selbstüberwindung, das man ist, nach *dieser* Seite weg, so fehlt es auf der andern Seite. (GD, 'Was Den Deutschen abgeht' 4, KSA 6.106)

That other direction is the direction of culture, which opposes the state:

> Culture and State – let us be honest with ourselves here – are advisories: 'Kultur-Staat' is just a modern idea. The one lives off the other, the one flourishes at the expense of the other. All the great ages of culture have been ages of political decline: anything great in the cultural sense is apolitical, even *anti-political*. (TI 'What the Germans lack' 4, p. 188)

> Die Cultur und der Staat – man betrüge sich hierüber nicht – sind Antagonisten: "Cultur-Staat" ist bloss eine moderne Idee. Das Eine lebt vom Andern, das Eine gedeiht auf Unkosten des Anderen. Alle grosse Zeiten der Cultur sind politische Niedergangs-Zeiten: was gross ist im Sinn der Cultur war unpolitisch, selbst *antipolitisch*. (GD, 'Was Den Deutschen abgeht' 4, KSA 6.106)

Nietzsche means that 'culture' and 'politics' exclude each other and that what is great in a culture (and that is always the artistic spirit of things, according to him) should be kept away from politics, because political powers repress cultural powers: 'In the history of European culture, the rise of the *"Reich"* means one thing above all else: *a shift in emphasis*' (TI 'What the Germans lack' 4, p. 189/'In der Geschichte der europäischen Cultur bedeutet die Heraufkunft des "Reichs" vor allem Eins: *eine Verlegung des Schwergewichts*', KSA 6.106).[18] The emphasis has shifted from 'what matters most (which is still culture)' (TI 'What the Germans lack' 4, p. 189) to politics and civil service. Hence, although one may claim that in reality politics and aesthetics are not antagonists but rather locked in a parasitical-reciprocal relationship, they exclude each other in Nietzsche's *ideal* of Europe. This view is supported by his call to 'free spirits' (the 'new philosophers' and 'good Europeans') not to meddle with politics,[19] his conviction that 'culture owes this [the highest moments possible, MP] above all to ages of political weakness' (HH I 465, p. 169/'Die Cultur verdankt das Allerhöchste den politisch geschwächten Zeiten', KSA 2.300), and his claim that he was 'the last anti-political

---

18 See also HH I 481 (pp. 177–178/KSA 2.314–316).
19 19[77], KSA 8.348.

German' ('der letzte antipolitische Deutsche', KSA 14.472).[20] One can ask, however, how this must be understood with regard to his call for 'great politics' ('*grosse Politik*'), by which term he labelled humanity's future cosmopolitan task of 'governing' the earth and establishing an 'world-government' ('*Erdregierung*') in order to overcome the 'petty politics' ('*kleine Politik*') of racist nationalism and democratic egalitarianism.[21]

'Aestheticization' and 'dynamic interculturalism'

Thus, Nietzsche held the idea that European culture was in decay and that this decay had to be interrupted by art. In addition, he claimed that, in order to interrupt Europe's artistic decay successfully, artists and philosophers (typically from 'sick' northern countries, such as Germany) had to 'Graecize' or 'southernize' first, meaning to purify their art works and aesthetics from corrupting elements, i.e., commercial, superficial, and 'idyllic' tendencies as well as expand their aesthetic capacities. For this, they needed to follow examples by engaging in a competition with them, in which they tried to learn from and then surpass them. These examples came typically from the healthy south, i.e., Ancient Greece and Italy – nations that are or were renowned for their artistic, anti-egalitarian, and life-affirming qualities. Nietzsche himself set this example by, first, instructing Wagner about this in The Birth of Tragedy and later journeying to Italy himself and introducing '*la gaya scienza*' in German life and music. That he was not the only one who had to go this southern road, is clarified by his call to all free spirits to follow his (and Goethe's!) example: 'What has happened to me [...] must happen to everyone in whom a *task* wants to become incarnate and "come into the world"' (HH I Preface 7, p. 10/'Wie es mir ergieng [...] muss es Jedem ergehn, in dem eine *Aufgabe* leibhaft werden und "zur Welt kommen" will', KSA 2.21).

The central thesis I defend concerning my historical investigation in this book is, therefore, Nietzsche propagated the 'aestheticization' by pleading for the 'Graecization' or 'southernization' of northern man, art, and culture throughout his life.

---

20 Cf. Terry Pinkard (2002), p. 3.
21 With this term, Nietzsche declares his 'war' against the so-called 'great politics' of Bismarck. Hence, he usese this term to ironize and empty out its original meaning of the term, thus turning Bismarck's 'great politics' into 'petty politics' (BGE 208, p. 102/'kleine Politik', KSA 5.140). Nietzsche rejects the 'great politics' that 'politicize' ('politisiren') people by stimulating their 'fatherlandishness' ('Vaterländerei') and devalue their 'cosmopolitanism' (BGE 241, pp. 132–133/'Ausländerei', KSA 5.180–182). Cf. HH I 481 (pp. 177–178/KSA 2.314ff); 26[451], KSA 11.270; EH Why I am a Destiny 1 (p. 144/KSA 6.366). Nietzsche underlines that his 'great politics' is not a war of peoples, but a war against the lies that have shaped human history for ages. It is the war supporting 'the will to life' against the 'vindictiveness against life' ('Rachsucht gegen das Leben', 25[1], KSA 13.637–638).

Whereas in his Basle years he associated 'the south' fully with Greece and Wagner, in the eighties, it became more and more 'Italian' and 'Goethean' for him.

The central thesis I defend with regard to Europe today is that it is in a crisis precisely because of its one-sided emphasis on economics and politics. Europe is in decay Nietzsche stated, because it lacks artistic spirit. In his footsteps, I claim that today Europe lacks a 'wider, cultural meaning'. To repair this, we need exactly the artistic spirit Nietzsche pointed to.[22]

I describe and analyze the historical development of Nietzsche's ideal of Europe by way of a reconstruction of his dramatically changing musical aesthetics. Both as an angry young man and mature 'free spirit', he converted his musical taste into a musical aesthetics, expanded it to an aesthetics of art in general and constructed a matching philosophy of culture. Nietzsche's reflections on music are the most appropriate starting point for my question in respect of his ideal Europe, because, as Renate Reschke justifiably argued, 'music and culture were all the same to him' ('die Musik war ihm gleichbedeutend mit der Kultur').[23] Hence, the rationale of my approach is to map Nietzsche's reflections on music and then to analyse his thoughts on culture on their basis. I am well aware that this scheme does not grasp the complexity of Nietzsche's philosophy of culture in its entirety. But I do believe that it is the best gateway to grasping Nietzsche's artistic *ideal* of Europe.

Below, I explain what the concepts 'music' and 'culture' stand for in Nietzsche's philosophy. Nietzsche does not give explicit definitions or definite descriptions of these important terms, so they take on a variety of meanings in his works. We need to have some idea of these terms first, however, in order to grasp Nietzsche's ideal of Europe.

Nietzsche's concept(s) of 'culture'

To Nietzsche the term 'culture' covers at least three meanings; first, it refers to the 'unity of style' (HL 10, KSA 1.334), i.e., the unifying artistic style of people that share a

---

22 In the sense that art is (serious) play, sports may certainly be regarded a part of it. I recognize sports as an important social field where inter-cultural relations are established. However, sports fall out of the scope of this book and will thus not be taken into account.

23 Reschke (2000), p. 214. Compare also: 'In music he found the medium in which he could exist. [...] So much so, that his reflections on music, to put it bluntly, become almost his philosophy, but in any case his aesthetics' ('In der Musik fand er das Medium, in dem er existieren konnte [...]. So sehr, daß seine Reflexionen über Musik, zugespitzt gesagt, fast seine Philosophie, sicher aber seine Ästhetik sind,' Reschke 2000, p. 208). Cf. Landerer and Schuster (2002): 'If there is a theme that runs like a thread through Nietzsche's total intellectual productivity, then this theme would be music' ('Wenn es ein Thema gibt, das sich wie ein roter Faden durch Nietzsches gesamte geistige Produktion zieht, dann ist dieses Thema die Musik,' p. 114).

common geographical ground and a basic view of the nature of life. Second, he uses it in the common sense of 'civilization', 'cultivation' as 'self-training' or 'refinement', that is as the artistic and moral cultivation or refinement (*'Bildung'*), in order for man to surmount his barbarism and gain control over his animalistic, violent, and instinctive nature. Third, the term is used to indicate the whole body of artistic, epistemological, moral, and religious symbols, productions, systems, and practices by which individuals or a united people attempt to give life meaning and give expression to their thoughts on humanity and its place in the world.

Nietzsche's interpretation of culture as a unity of style refers to the Romantic notion, which refers to a spirit (*'Volksgeist'*) that comes to expression in all traits, qualities, and actions of a people, holding them together. Nietzsche often sets 'culture' (*'Kultur'*) against 'civilization' (*'Zivilisation'*), the layer of manners, laws, and technical knowledge that covers human nature. Different cultural unities can share a civilization, but their culture will always differ, and culture determines one's identity.[24] But Nietzsche also stood in the 'Classical' tradition that subordinated culture to cultivation and regarded it with a more cosmopolitan spirit. Artistic and cultural superiority were not only a matter of natural bent, but also of learning from other developed cultures, in particular Ancient Greece. What one must learn is the aesthetic approach of life; To Nietzsche, culture depends on man's aesthetic answer to the ominous, 'Silenian' truth that life is senseless in the face of death.[25]

In sum, 'culture' stands for the acknowledgement that life in the face of human mortality is meaningless and the totality of symbols and practices by means of which humankind turns this tragic, pessimistic truth into aesthetic joy. The greatness of a man and a culture are determined by the ability to bear pain and the quality of the aesthetic transformation of this pain. In brief, the quality of 'joy' determines the 'health' of a culture.[26] This transformation is a matter of 'symbolization' and 'stylization' in the Goethean and Schillerean sense, as we shall see, leading to the building of a chain of 'great', 'eternal' moments, which binds humanity through thousands of years. That is the 'founding thought' of culture.[27]

---

24 Cf. Scruton (2003), p. 9ff.
25 See BT 3, pp. 22–23.
26 Cf. BGE 229 (pp. 120–121/KSA 5.165–167), in which Nietzsche defines 'high' (*'Hohe'*) respectively 'higher' (*'höhere'*) culture (*'Kultur'*) as the 'spiritualization' (*'Vergeistigung'*) and 'deepening' (*'Vertiefung'*) of cruelty (*'Grausamkeit'*).
27 FP 'Über das Pathos der Wahrheit' (KSA 1.756).

Nietzsche's concept(s) of 'music'

As said, to Nietzsche philosophy and music both were of vital importance and consequently his writings are permeated with musical allusions and metaphors. He reflected
on music incessantly, and these reflections often form the bottom-line of his philosophy of culture. Roughly, in his works the term takes on the following meanings:

'Music' denotes the art of sound based on melody, harmony, and rhythm. Of the
history of music, he mainly contemplates so-called European 'art music' (which we
now call 'classical music') and its Greek origin. Richard Wagner is the key figure in
these reflections, often in explicit contrast to Italian opera, thus building the conceptual context of German 'north' and Mediterranean (Italian, French) south in his philosophy of music and culture. This terminology is later, during his anti-Wagnerian period,
expanded with the terms 'sickness' and 'health', whereby Wagner's German music is
seen as 'sick' and the southern music of Bizet's *Carmen*, amongst others, as 'healthy'.

But 'music' also takes on the broader meaning of the 'spirit of music'. In this sense,
it primarily appears in his early, 'Romantic' or 'Wagnerian' period (1868–1876). By this,
he understands the anti-theoretical, artistic, tragic, and mythical spirit, which he also
subsumes under the term 'Dionysian'. In that manner, it is very reminiscent of the
Greek word '*musikè*', which has a much broader meaning than the current concept of
'music' and stands for art in general, as, for example, in the famous call in the *Phaedo*
to Socrates to 'make music'. But it also moves through history, in a competitive movement with the theoretical spirit, which expresses itself in words or concepts.

Nietzsche also reflected on music as a form of art that when combined with other
art forms (poetry, drama) could create a new form of art ('tragedy' or 'music drama').
Within such a constellation, music keeps its unique powers of immediacy and universality, exercising an empowering effect on drama. Drama, in its most successful form,
is the pictorial counterweight to music. He further contemplated the nature, effect,
and reception of music, thus its importance for culture, German and European culture
specifically.

Nietzsche reflected much more on 'music drama' than on instrumental music,
specifically Greek tragedy, Wagner's music drama, Italian opera, and Bizet,but also
the German Singspiel tradition, as we shall see in chapter 6. His main interest was, in
his early Wagnerian period, with the rejuvenation of the chorus and the restoration
of the balance of music and drama in Wagner's modern works. In his anti-Wagnerian
period, his focus changed to the 'Italianization' of German music, which means so
much as bringing 'la gaya scienza', lightness and the 'innocence of melody' in music.
This goal is opposed to the 'heaviness' of Wagner's music, which, Nietzsche claims, is
heavy because it is ridden with 'ideas', lacking stylistic restraining ('*Bändigung*'), and
neglecting musical form. The restraining of the will and passions are then key to his
aesthetics in general.

Thematic and conceptual structure of this book

In accordance with Nietzsche's 'Wagnerian' and 'anti-Wagnerian' period, the book is divided into two parts. The first part, 'Aestheticization: Germany as Europe's Saviour', concentrates on Nietzsche's early aesthetics and cultural ideal as influenced by and revolving around Richard Wagner. It argues that Nietzsche's ideal of Europe consists in its salvation from decadence by virtue of the process of 'aestheticization', the 'Graecization' ('*Gräcisierung*') or 'southernization' ('*Versüdlichung*'), which Wagner's music would bring about. The second part, 'Dynamic Interculturalism: De-Germanization and the "good European"', focuses on his search for new ways to fulfil this ideal, after his friendship with Wagner had turned into painful hostility and Nietzsche had left Basle to wander through Italy in the years 1876–1882. This part argues that Nietzsche's ideal of Europe still consisted in 'aestheticization' as 'southernization'. However, instead of equating this with the former 'Graecization', he then equated this with 'becoming Mediterranean' ('*méditerraniser*' as he put it in French). This idea of becoming Mediterranean was infused by Nietzsche's philosophical enthusiasm for Italian opera, next to the explicit call to travel to the south.

Nietzsche's new love of Italian opera is all the more remarkable, when we take into account that he, especially in *The Birth of Tragedy*, criticized Italian opera vehemently. Hence, his criticism of Italian opera in 1872, his embrace of it from 1881 onwards, and its influence on his philosophy of music, culture, and the idea of what philosophy must be, demarcate the starting-point of the Nietzsche-research in this book. My emphasis on Nietzsche's relation to Italian opera goes hand in hand with his embrace and then rejection of Wagner and his music. Hence, Nietzsche's praise of Wagner will be discussed in the context of his Italian opera-critique, and his praise of Italian opera will be examined in the context of his anti-Wagnerism, which he exposed from 1876 onwards without stinting. This simultaneous discussion of Wagner's music and Italian opera is done for three reasons: first, Nietzsche constantly sets the two musical forms against each other; second, Wagner and Italian opera are both praised on the same principle: their melodic and innocent aspects; third, Nietzsche regarded the existence and popularity of Wagner and Italian opera alike as 'signs' of a particular state of European culture, be it 'sick' or 'healthy', 'decadent' or flowering.[28]

Chapter 1 poses the question whether Nietzsche was ever a true Wagnerian at all, given his late turn to Wagner in November 1868 and his early doubt about Wagner, already expressed in February 1870. I have found it necessary to reassess the beginnings of Nietzsche's Wagnerism, because, first, the general idea still has it that Nietzsche was a Wagnerian from 1862 until 1876. Second, the claim that Nietzsche had serious doubts about Wagner as early as 1870 triggers the question how we then must under-

---

28 Compare ASC 1 (p. 4/KSA 1.12) and ASC 4 (pp. 7–8/KSA 1.16).

stand his explicit, even hyperbolic, Wagner-enthusiasm of *The Birth of Tragedy*. An answer to this question is given in chapter 4.

Chapter 2 discusses Wagner's philosophy of music and culture, as expounded in his centenary essay 'Beethoven' of 1870 by ways of detailed textual analysis. I examine this essay systematically and thoroughly with regard to (the development of) Nietzsche's early views of music and culture. Although it is recognized that Wagner's theories influenced Nietzsche, the depth and breadth of this influence has not been mapped out in detail until now. This is necessary, however, because Wagner was not only the centre of Nietzsche's early philosophy of music and culture, but as I argue, also a crucial theoretical source. Moreover, it will only be possible to examine the philosophical difficulties Nietzsche had with Wagner when his reception of Wagner's philosophy is scrutinized.

In order to determine Nietzsche's indebtedness to and difficulties with Wagnerian ideas, his reception of Wagner's 'Beethoven' essay is discussed in chapter 3. This leads to the conclusion that Wagner's aesthetic and 'tragic' spirit went hand in hand with a moral, 'idyllic' spirit, as Nietzsche understands Wagner's art with the help of Goethe's and Schiller's aesthetics. Moreover, it is shown that Nietzsche, rather than turning to Schopenhauer, forms his musical aesthetics by examining Wagner's 'Beethoven' essay with the help of Goethe's and Schiller's aesthetics.

Chapter 4 discusses the image Nietzsche draws of Wagner in *The Birth of Tragedy* as the saviour of European culture. This is done by discussing, first, what Nietzsche's 'aestheticism' amounts to and, second, relating this to his discussion of historical attempts to rejuvenate the Greek spirit. I argue that Nietzsche's support of Wagner is conditional and accompanied by a 'secret scepticism' of Wagner's ability to pursue the 'aestheticization' of Europe. This ability depends on his willingness to rid his music of all 'idyllic' and moral traits, which form a threat to the demands of aestheticization. Viewed in the light of the discussion pursued in chapters 1, 2, and 3, the Wagner-enthusiasm of *The Birth of Tragedy* is put into perspective. Nevertheless, I emphasize that Nietzsche's theoretical indebtedness to Wagner is greater than acknowledged until now. This leads me to the hypothesis that *The Birth of Tragedy* has a strange, double nature as a public defence of Wagner, which implicitly criticizes the composer. I propose to consider the historical analysis of the Greeks made in the first fifteen chapters of the book as a 'manual' addressed to Wagner as to how to 'Graecize', while the last ten chapters of the book describe what would happen if the composer would take Nietzsche's recipe for becoming Greek to heart.

Chapter 5 exposes how Nietzsche's hopes of Wagner, which despite his reservations prevailed in *The Birth of Tragedy*, but diminished under the influence of his growing cosmopolitanism. It argues that his aesthetic and cultural disagreement with Wagner was intensified when Nietzsche discovered that the Greeks were no 'autochthones', and had to conclude that Goethe's and Schiller's cosmopolitan spirit was more 'Greek' than Wagner's national focus. Furthermore, it is argued that Nietzsche's estrangement from Wagner was further provoked by his honest and 'cold' evaluation of the Bayreuth-project in early 1874. My analysis of Nietzsche's notes of 1872–1873 and early 1874 also suggests that his growing insight into the 'non-Greek' foundation of Greek superiority, hence into Greek 'cosmopolitanism' necessitated him to re-evaluate Greek identity and by implication his own ideas of Greek culture; and, as a result, his ideal of contemporary art and culture. Finally, I identify Nietzsche's 'cosmopolitanism' as what I call – inspired by Hoock-Demarle – a 'dynamic interculturalism' and his 'free spirit' books as 'travel-books'.[29]

Chapter 6, then, deals with Nietzsche's search for a new form and aesthetics of music. He finds this music in the 'European' or even 'supra-European' music of his new friend the composer Peter Gast (alias of Heinrich Köselitz), in Georges Bizet's *Carmen* and in the musical activities of Goethe. I argue that Nietzsche's new musical aesthetics must be seen as part of his general aim to 'de-Germanize' or 'Italianize'. I show that Nietzsche does so especially by following Goethe, also in his musical activities. In this context, I regard the 'prelude' *Joke, Cunning, and Revenge* as a libretto, with which Nietzsche tried to bring the Italian style into the German Singspiel. I also argue that Nietzsche's new musical aesthetics implies a renewed connection between the 'Dionysian' – as the continuing measure of 'good' music – and the 'idyllic', a relationship which we may identify as a 'binary synthesis' in his *Nachlass* notes of *The Birth of Tragedy*, a diametrical opposition in *The Birth of Tragedy*, and a synthesis held together by the term 'health' from *Human all too Human* onwards.

Chapter 7 investigates Goethe as Nietzsche's model of 'the good European'. The 'good European' is the figure that is a successful 'cosmopolitan' person. How the 'good European' relates to Nietzsche's continuing pleas for 'aestheticization' and 'dynamic interculturalism' and how we, in this new context, must understand Nietzsche's concept of the Dionysian (which becomes the central predicate to describe his *amor fati* philosophy) is illuminated in this chapter. Attention is also paid to the necessity of becoming 'supra-European' in order to be a 'good European' and the 'programme' for the 'good European' established in *The Gay Science*.

In the epilogue, I relate Nietzsche's ideal of Europe to the political-economic outlook of Europe today by way of asking what the relevance of Nietzsche's views of Europe may be for present discussions about Europe or the European Union. I am aware that Nietzsche asked different questions than most of us do today, when reflecting on Europe or the 'EU' (which obviously was not there during Nietzsche's life), but it is

---

29 I came to this term inspired by Marie-Claire Hoock-Demarle. She speaks of 'the dynamic process of interculturalism' ('der dynamische Prozeß der Interkulturalität') with regard to Goethe's *West-Östlicher Divan* (Hoock-Demarle 2002, p. 478). However, her use of this is also confined to that cycle of poems, while my conception of 'dynamic interculturalism' is much broader, pertaining to culture (Europe) in general and specifically understood as a special kind of purposeful way of travelling. This is not the case at all for Hoock-Demarle.

exactly this difference that I want to explore so as to open up a new perspective in the debate about Europe.[30]

Some final methodological remarks

A few methodological remarks remain to be made, before turning to our actual research. First, although music forms the central field of examination, I do not discuss Nietzsche's efforts as a composer. In general, Nietzsche was less conservative in his musical endeavours than in his musical aesthetics. In my view, an analysis of Nietzsche's musical compositions does not contribute to any substantial knowledge of his aesthetics and philosophy of culture. His musical compositions do not justify his musical aesthetics and are therefore inapt sources for a discussion of Nietzsche's philosophy of music; at times, his compositions attest to the contrary of his ideals, especially his demand of a unity of style. There are stylistically too chaotic to ascribe to them more than a biographical and musical merit.

Second, in discussing Nietzsche's ideal Europe from his musical aesthetics, the traditional division of his work in an 'early', 'middle', and 'late' period is not sufficient.[31] Dufour's division of Nietzsche's musical aesthetics as 'metaphysics of music' and 'physiology of music' is, for my purposes, equally ineffective.[32] If we feel the need to make a schematic, chronological division at all, then we may state, based on the research presented below, that Nietzsche was an anti-Wagnerian between 1858 and late 1868, a Wagnerian from late 1868 until the summer of 1876, and an anti-Wagnerian from the summer of 1876 until his mental break-down in January 1889. However, my claims that Nietzsche's Wagner-enthusiasm was soon undertoned by a serious, yet 'secret', scepticism of Wagner's theories and artistic practices, and that his cultural ideal for Europe was, despite the dramatic change in musical preference, constantly

---

30 Cf. Montinari (1982), p. 6.

31 Traditionally, Nietzsche's work is divided into an 'early', 'middle', and 'late' period. The early Nietzsche is the author of *The Birth of Tragedy* (1872) and the *Untimely Meditations* (1874–1876). The 'middle' Nietzsche is the writer of *Human, All Too Human I* (1878), *Assorted Opinions and Maxims* (1879) and *The Wanderer and his Shadow* (1880). The latter two were published as *Human, All Too Human II* in 1886. The other books of the 'middle' Nietzsche are *Daybreak* (1881) and *The Gay Science* (1882). The 'late' Nietzsche is the author of *Thus Spoke Zarathustra* (1883–1885), *Beyond Good and Evil* (1886), *The Genealogy of Morals* (1887), *The Case of Wagner* (1888), *Twilight of the Idols* (1889), and the following essays and poems written between August 1888 and January 1889: *The Anti-Christ, Ecce Homo, Dionysos-Dithyrambs*, and *Nietzsche contra Wagner*. Those were intended to be published on 2 January 1889, but did not appear before Nietzsche's collapse in Turin, between 3 and 10 January 1889.

32 Dufour (2001), p. 222ff. Note that Nietzsche's musical aesthetics was always more or less bodily, even the 'metaphysics of music' that infuses *The Birth of Tragedy*, where Nietzsche presents Dionysus and Apollo as 'physiological phenomena' (BT 1, p. 15/'*physiologische Erscheinungen*,' KSA 1.26).

the same, also overrule this time division, as does Nietzsche's constant search for 'Dionysian' and 'healthy' music. Hence, I amply refer to Nietzsche's later work when I come to discuss *The Gay Science* and his view of Goethe as 'good European' in the second part of my dissertation. However, I do not separately examine texts published later than this book, for Nietzsche's musical aesthetics do not substantially change from 1881 onwards.[33]

Third, my argumentation is built upon chronological and thematic close-readings of a selection of texts in order to delineate Nietzsche's musical aesthetics and their sources. I consider myself as working in the tradition of Nietzsche-scholarship as set by Colli and Montinari, which means that I consider every work by Nietzsche as a product of equal philosophical value, as part of a philosophical development (which we should not understand as a teleological process), which is only traceable by including the unpublished notes (*Nachlass*) in our researches and by meticulous reference to his intellectual sources for the benefit of the reconstruction of the genetic history ('*Entstehungsgeschichte*' and '*Quellenforschung*') of Nietzsche's works. Working in the Colli-Montinari tradition also implies working against the 'Weimar' tradition set by Elisabeth Förster-Nietzsche and Martin Heidegger, which claims that Nietzsche's published works were only a 'foreground' ('*Vordergrund*') to the 'real' work of *The Will to Power*.[34] Hence, I base my interpretations on the critical editions (KGW, KGB, KSA, and KSB) published by Colli and Montinari.

Fourth, regarding Nietzsche's concept and notes to the 'Will to Power', I confine myself to the position that a book with that title, written by Nietzsche, does not exist. All we have are notes and plans for a book with that title, which Nietzsche intended – as he did with all his books – as his 'main work' ('*Hauptwerk*'). The last notes suggest that he had rejected this title again, and probably even the whole book. From the start in 1885, the concept 'will to power' was a title for his understanding of reality as 'semblance' ('*Schein*'). Soon, from 1886 on, it became the name of Nietzsche's philosophy of 'revaluation of values' ('*Umwerthung aller Werte*').[35] Colli and Montinari conclude as follows, and I cite them in order to present my view in their words:

> The general conception [of the *Revaluation of all Values,* MP], remains the same: after the criticism of Christianity, morality, and philosophy, N[ietzsche] intends to proclaim his philosophy. This is the philosophy of Dionysus, the philosophy of the eternal return of the same. The *Revaluation of*

---

33 *The Gay Science* was first published in 1882 and then in 1887, completed with a preface, the fifth book *We Fearless Ones* (*Wir Furchtlosen*, comprising of aphorisms 343–383) and the Appendix *Songs of Prince Vogelfrei* (*Lieder des Prinzen Vogelfrei*).

34 Heidegger (1961, Vol. 1), p. 17. Cf. Diethe (2001), esp. pp. 122–153.

35 I agree fully with Colli and Montinari's analysis made of Nietzsche's notes of 1885–1888 in KSA 14.383–400. As Colli and Montinari rightly claim in the introductory remark to those volumes, their chronological presentation of Nietzsche's notes of 1885–1889 clarify that the compendium '*Wille zur Macht*', as edited by Peter Gast and Elisabeth Förster-Nietzsche is 'editorial untenable and intrinsically most questionable' ('editorisch unhaltbar und sachlich zutiefst fragwürdig', KSA 12.8).

all Values was similar to *The Will to Power* in one sense, as to *the content*, but simultaneously it was its *literary* renunciation. Or also: from the notes to *The Will to Power* emerged *Twilight of the Idols* and *The Antichrist*; the rest is – notes (KSA 14.400).

Die Gesamtkonzeption [der Umwertung aller Werte, MP] bleibt sich gleich: Nach der Kritik des Christentums, der Moral, der Philosophie, beabsichtigt N[ietzsche] die Verkündigung seiner Philosophie. Diese ist die Philosophie des Dionysos, die Philosophie der ewigen Wiederkunft des Gleichen. Inhaltlich gesehen war die Umwerthung aller Werte in einem gewissen Sinn dasselbe wie der Wille zur Macht, aber eben deshalb war sie dessen literarische Negation. Oder auch: Aus den Aufzeichnungen zum Willen zur Macht sind die Götzen-Dämmerung und Der Anti-Christ entstanden; der Rest ist – Nachlaß.

Or, as William Schaberg (1995) remarks in a telling manner:

what Elisabeth did is the literary and philosophical equivalent of trying to reconstruct Beethoven's *Tenth Symphony* from his sketchbooks – as was done recently with predictably disastrous results – and the resulting "Nietzsche book" is no more convincing than the phony Beethoven Symphony.[36]

---

36 Schaberg (1995), p. 186.

Part I
Aestheticization: Germany as saviour of Europe

Chapter 1
Was Nietzsche ever a true Wagnerian?

Introduction

The notion that Nietzsche was zealously supportive of Wagner from 1862 onwards is still persistent in Nietzsche scholarship. Recently, this view was repeated by Dieter Borchmeyer,[1] Manfred Eger[2] and Thomas Brobjer, who suggested:

> During 1861 and 62 his [Nietzsche's, MP] views changes profoundly [...] [and] the interests and influence of Krug becomes more and more visible. [...] Nietzsche very rarely refers to Wagner at this time, but his sister says that he and Krug played Wagner on the piano and sang to it for days on end with enthusiasm in 1862 [...]. Thus, already in 1862–1864 Nietzsche had a good knowledge of, and an enthusiasm for, Wagner. It seems as if this enthusiasm cools for some years, perhaps due to the influence of Otto Jahn (by whom Nietzsche read at least one book about music at this time and who was his teacher at Bonn) and Eduard Hanslick (1825–1904), a theoretician of music whom Nietzsche also read at this time, both critics of Wagner.[3]

My objections against this observation are the following: my first objection concerns the idea that Nietzsche's enthusiasm 'cools for some years, perhaps due to the influence of Otto Jahn [...] and Eduard Hanslick', which Nietzsche 'read at this time'. I contend that Nietzsche's 'enthusiasm' did not 'cool', because it was not there before 1868, and it certainly did not cool off under the influence of Hanslick and Jahn. Such a misperception is easily refuted by pointing to the years that Nietzsche actually read Hanslick (during the Easter of 1865) and Jahn (in the fall of 1868). This distinction is significant for two reasons. First, Nietzsche's (possible) reading of Hanslick is indeed a sign of his anti-Wagnerism and interest in musical formalism, and a confirmation of his love for the music of the so-called Leipzigian and Early-Romantic 'Old German School' (Robert and Clara Schumann, Johannes Brahms, Franz Schubert, and Felix Mendelssohn). Second, Nietzsche's reading of Jahn's essays fuelled rather than 'cooled' his Wagner enthusiasm in October 1868. Thus, there is a great discrepancy between Nietzsche's reception of Wagner in 1865 and 1868.

My second objection concerns the evidence on which Brobjer, like others before him, bases his conclusion that Nietzsche 'already in 1862–1864' had 'an enthusiasm for Wagner'. The idea depends mainly on Elisabeth Nietzsche's account that her brother knew Wagner's music and musical aesthetics in 1862, achieved through his friendship with Wagner fan Gustav Krug. However, Nietzsche's early knowledge of Wagner

---

1 Borchmeyer (2008) does not deviate from Borchmeyer and Salaquarda (1994) in this respect. Cf. Borchmeyer (2008), p. 75 and p. 97.
2 Eger (2001), p. 578.
3 Brobjer (2005), pp. 278–299, p. 296.

was not accompanied by the supposed enthusiasm. Nietzsche offers a late memory in *Ecce Homo*, stating that he loved Wagner 'from the moment he set his eyes on the *Tristan*-score'. However, as I argue below, this is refuted by numerous anti-Wagnerian utterances in the years prior to and following this event. For example, in a draft for an essay on the essence of music, written in 1861, Nietzsche defies Wagner and Wagnerians rather than supports the 'music of the future' when he writes that 'feeling is no criterion for music' ('[d]as Gefühl ist gar kein Maßstab für Musik').[4] This phrase is formalistic rather than Wagnerian. Moreover, he scorns the reaction of a Wagner fan (Krug?) in the same note: 'also about you and your common sense do some people shake their heads, when you, as if you're overwhelmed by the power of music, stand there before the passionate waves of *Tristan and Isolde*' ('[...] auch über dich und deinen Verstand schütteln manche Leute die Köpfe, wenn du wie niedergeschmettert von der Macht der Musik vor den leidenschaftl<ichen> Wogen Tristan und Isoldes dastehst').[5] In addition, the late memory must be placed in the right context, which many commentators neglect to do. I shall do so further on in this chapter, illustrating that Nietzsche's memory serves goals other than historical truth.

The fact that Nietzsche had psychological difficulties with Wagner already during the spring of 1871 also escapes Brobjer's attention, despite his mention of an article by Landerer and Schuster, which brings precisely this to the fore.[6] Brobjer's interpretation is in line with the dominant view in Nietzsche scholarship set by Elisabeth Nietzsche (1949), Janz (1972), Hollinrake (1982), and Borchmeyer/Salaquarda (1994), which holds that Nietzsche became a Wagnerian around 1862 and that Nietzsche's disappointment with Wagner during the first Bayreuth festival in the summer of 1876 occasioned their actual break – following his insult of Wagner in 1874, when he praised Johannes Brahms' *Triumph-Song* (*Triumphlied*), knowing all the while that 'the Master' held Brahms in contempt.[7] Further indications of the upcoming break are taken to be found in Nietzsche's fourth *Untimely Meditation* 'Richard Wagner in Bayreuth', which came out shortly before the first Bayreuth festival was held, in the summer of 1876.

Against the common view, I argue below that Nietzsche was only a true, that is, uncritical and unconditionally loyal Wagnerian between November 1868 and February 1870. I argue that definite proof of Wagner enthusiasm on Nietzsche's part is not traceable before November 1868 and that he already expresses doubt about Wagner in February 1870 in a letter to his close friend Erwin Rohde, which points to the conclusion that Nietzsche's unconditional Wagnerism lasted for fifteen months rather than

---

4 Nietzsche bases his expression on Fux and Albrechtsberger, two giants of musical classicism. In this passage, Nietzsche contrasts Wagner and Albrechtsberger, siding with the latter.

5 13[26] (KGW I/2, p. 474).

6 Landerer and Schuster (2002), pp. 114–133.

7 Holzer justifiably remarks that 'the analysis of the relationship [between Nietzsche and Wagner] and the comparison of their world views are still of interest' ('die Analyse der Beziehung und der Vergleich der Weltanschauung [sind] noch immer von Interesse [...],' Holzer 2010, p. 435).

for fourteen years. This is all the more important for the interpretation of *The Birth of Tragedy*, of which Richard Wagner is not only the centre but also a chief theoretical source.[8]

In the course of my interpretation, I substantiate theses put forward by Love, Silk and Stern, and Landerer and Schuster.[9] I develop my argument by analyzing Nietzsche's views on Wagner, Wagner's music, and the New German School of music, developed between 1858 and 1870. I focus on the reports of the Germania Society, Nietzsche's reception of Louis Ehlert's *Letters on Music*, Otto Jahn's *Essays on Music*, and Oswald Marbach's essay on the 'Rebirth of Drama in Music' ('Wiedergeburt der dramatischen Kunst durch die Kunst'). In doing so, I hope to illustrate that Marbach's lecture did not affect the content of Nietzsche's musical aesthetics and dramaturgy. This is important to clarify, because it fortifies Nietzsche's claim that Wagner's 'Beethoven' (1870) is the main source of *The Birth of Tragedy's* aesthetics and philosophy of culture – a thesis often neglected in Nietzsche scholarship. Moreover, I maintain that it was not only Wagnerian music and theories that turned Nietzsche from the 'Old German School' of music to the 'New German School', but also his ambition to enter Leipzig's higher society combined with his short-term status as a music journalist.

Then I turn my focus to February 1870, when Nietzsche expressed his first reservations concerning Wagner. In the conclusion, I briefly indicate the significance of Nietzsche's early Wagner-scepticism for our understanding of *The Birth of Tragedy*. This topic will be further discussed in chapter 4.

1858–1863: Nietzsche's classical taste versus Gustav Krug's Wagnerism

Despite his assertion that he was a 'Wagnerian' from the moment he set eyes on the *Tristan* score, during Easter 1861, Nietzsche as often as not exhibited an aversion to Wagner's 'music of the future' until November 1868.[10] In the context of the 'Clever' section of *Ecce Homo*, Nietzsche refers to his first encounter with *Tristan and Isolde* as a drug-experience, while he identifies it as an utterly non-German work, which liberated him from Germany. These remarks must be taken with the necessary reservation and irony. By claiming that he needed *Tristan and Isolde* as 'hashish' in order to free himself from the pressure of having been under the influence of Germans all his life, a negative connotation is attached to the composer's first truly 'Wagnerian' work. In

---

8 Cf. Prange (2007a), pp. 91–117.
9 Love, Young (1966), p. 2; Silk and Stern (1981), pp. 24–30 (esp. p. 24); Landerer and Schuster (2002); Landerer and Schuster (2005), pp. 246–255.
10 EH 'Clever' 6 (pp. 93–94/KSA 6.289).

Gay Science 86, Wagner's theatre is scorned as 'aping the high tide of the soul' ('eine Nachäffung der hohen Seelenfluth') and the need for spectacular theatre and extravagant music that underlies Wagnerian theatre is castigated as the 'hashish-smoking and betel-chewing of European man' ('das Haschisch-Rauchen und Betel-Kauen der Europäer'). Nietzsche even depicts Europe's history of art as 'the entire history of narcotics' ('die ganze Geschichte der Narcotica'), explaining that good art has often been measured by its capacity to induce oblivion and provide amusement rather than by its ability to give rise to the 'high tide of the soul'.[11] This oblivion, for Nietzsche, resembles the intoxication caused by narcotics and alcohol and he diametrically contrasts such 'Romantic' intoxication with 'Dionysian' intoxication, claiming that the former originates in the *'impoverishment of life'* (*'Verarmung des Lebens'*) and the latter in the *'superabundance of life'* (*'Ueberfülle des Lebens'*).[12] Abundant, Dionysian people do not need hashish, because they experience 'enough tragedy and comedy' in themselves – due to the abundance of passion and thought that incessantly stimulate their minds and bodies. By contrast, the Romantic person needs oblivion, because he or she desires redemption from inner emptiness, occasioned by a lack of passion and philosophical thought.

Further, by praising *Tristan and Isolde* as a non-German work of art, Nietzsche seeks to insult Wagner, who, in fact, tried to develop the German musical tradition of Bach, Beethoven, and Liszt, in explicit opposition to French and Italian music. Indeed, Wagner attempted to press German music forward, disputing the popularity of French and Italian music in Europe. Hence, by referring to *Tristan and Isolde* as non-German, to Wagner as 'the antidote *par excellence* for all things German' ('das Gegengift gegen alles Deutsche par excellence), and claiming admiration for Wagner as a *'foreign country'*, Nietzsche in fact scorns Wagner and Wagnerians, exploiting their nationalist narrow-mindedness.[13] In this manner, Nietzsche makes his denial of Germans and Wagner's (gradually more political) Germanism complete. Seen in the light of these remarks, the overstated praise of *Tristan and Isolde* as the piece of work that instantly converted him to Wagnerism turns out to be a harsh and ironic way to attack Wagner.

His sister's claim that her brother loved Wagner's music from autumn 1860 onwards is even more remote from the truth.[14] She calls her brother and his school friends Gustav Krug and Wilhelm Pinder 'the three enthusiastic Wagnerites', boosting her allegation with the pseudo-romantic hyperbole that the three boys 'by pooling their modest pocket money' purchased the piano score of *Tristan and Isolde*.[15] Contrary to Elisa-

---

11 GS 86 (pp. 86–87/KSA 3.443–444).
12 GS 370 (p. 234/KSA 3.620).
13 EH 'Clever' 5–6 (pp. 93–94/KSA 6.288–289).
14 Förster-Nietzsche (1949), p. 2.
15 Förster-Nietzsche (1949), pp. 1ff.

beth's assertion, of the three boys only Gustav Krug, who grew up in a musical family and who played the violin well, was an enthusiastic Wagnerian in those days. It had been his idea to acquire the *Tristan* arrangement. Nietzsche ascribed the society's financial sorrows to Krug's purchase of the *Tristan and Isolde* score. He even forced Krug to sign a contract in which he promised to abstain from any further purchases.[16]

By contrast, Nietzsche considered purchasing works of Schumann's, such as the oratorio 'Paradise and the Peri' ('Das Paradies und die Peri').[17] The planned lectures for the years 1861–1862 show that Krug dedicated most of his time to the new German school and Wagner specifically and that Nietzsche was focused on poetry, folk songs, and marches, especially the ones he had composed himself, such as the Autumn songs and the Hungarian sketches.[18] This was perfectly in accordance with his musical taste, which we find expressed in some fierce remarks in his early autobiography of 1858, 'From my Life' ('Aus meinem Leben'):

> I experienced [...] an inextinguishable hatred of all modern music and everything that was not classical. Mozart and Haidn [sic], Schubert and Mendelsohn Beethoven and Bach, they are the pillars on which genuine German music and I also are based.

> Ich empfing [...] einen unauslöschbaren Haß gegen alle moderne Musik und alles, was nicht klassisch war. Mozart und Haidn [sic], Schubert und Mendelsohn Beethoven und Bach das sind die Säulen auf die sich nur deutsche Musik u. ich gründete.[19]

Although we can hardly take the emotional expressions of a fourteen-year-old as seriously as the more theoretically substantiated positions of the elder Nietzsche, these articulations are indicative of his conservative taste and his determination to oppose the modernizations of German avant-garde music.[20] He simply abhorred the 'music of the future' of Liszt, Berlioz, and Wagner:

> Upon whom does not settle down a quieter and clearer peace when he hears the simple melodies of Haiden [sic]! The art of tones often speaks to us in tones that go deeper than poetry in words and grasps the most secret folds of the heart. [...] However, if the music is only used for amusement or to display oneself to the people, then music is sinful and damaging. Yet, precisely this is found so often, yes almost all modern music bears the traces of this. Another truly miserable phenomenon is that many newer composers attempt to write gloomily. However, it may be just these kinds of artistic periods, which delight the connoisseur, that leave the healthy human ear cold. Particularly the so-called music of the future of Liszt and Berlioz seeks something worthwhile in demonstrating passages as peculiar as possible.

---

16 13[23], KGW I 2.471 and 13[28] (KGW I/2, p. 477).
17 Cf. 11[71] and 11[74] (KGW I/2, p. 327–329).
18 See 13[28] (KGW I/2, pp. 480–483).
19 4[77] (KGW I/1, p. 298).
20 Compare also 4[13] (KGW I/1, p. 231), which enlists works by Mozart and Mendelssohn with the prices of the scores.

Ueber wen kommt nicht ein stiller, klarer Friede, wenn er die einfachen Melodien Haidnes [sic] hört! Die Tonkunst redet oft in Tönen eindringlicher als die Poesie in Worten zu uns u. ergreift die geheimsten Falten des Herzens. [...] Wird aber die Musik nur zur Belustigung gebraucht oder um sich sehen zu lassen vor den Menschen, so ist sie sündlich u. schädlich. Und doch findet man gerade dieses so häufig, ja fast die ganze moderne Musik trägt die Spuren davon. Eine andre rechte traurige Erscheinung ist daß viele neuere Componisten sich bemühen, dunkel zu schreiben. Aber gerade solche künstliche Perioden die vieleicht [sic] den Kenner entzücken, lassen das gesunde Menschenohr kalt. Vorzüglich diese sogennannte Zukunftsmusik eines Liszt, Berlioz, sucht etwas darin, so eigenthümliche Stellen wie nur möglich zu zeigen.[21]

Thus, whereas Gustav Krug already loved Wagner in his teens, Nietzsche rejected the music of the future in general. What did the third friend and Germania member Wilhelm Pinder think of Wagner and the music of the future? He was an explicit and ardent opponent of the music of the future. However, unlike Nietzsche (who expressed his contempt in his early autobiography out of emotion and an undeveloped taste), he attempted to sustain his rejection theoretically. In his lecture 'Music as the Daughter of Poetry' ('Musik als Tochter der Poesie'), held for the Germania Society at Christmas 1861, Pinder stated: 'the artwork of the future is and remains an ideal that will never be realized' ('das Kunstwerk der Zukunft ist und bleibt ein nie zu verwirklichendes Ideal').[22] In a written reaction to this lecture, Krug objected that Wagner had put his theory into practice with *Tristan and Isolde* and *The Ring of the Nibelung*, arguing that the artwork of the future carried out the old promise of opera to call in all arts. This promise was never fulfilled by opera before Wagner, according to Krug, because it drew music to the centre of the artwork instead of apportioning all aspects of it with equal attention.

Krug's report teaches us two things; First, Wagner's music was extensively discussed during the Germania meetings. Second, according to the records of the meetings, Nietzsche did not have any attribution worth mentioning in this respect. While Krug cites Pinder's essay extensively and gives comment on every detail, he has not recorded Nietzsche's position towards it. This indicates that Nietzsche did not participate in the particular discussion, or at least not with a significant and innovative contribution. It seems likely that, would he have advanced a pro-Wagnerian position, Krug would have reported this. However, Krug was all too familiar with Nietzsche's classical taste concerning music, because they used to discuss and play music together from the very beginnings of their friendship.[23]

---

21 4[77] (KGW I/1, p. 306).
22 BAW 2, pp. 339–443, p. 441.
23 See 4[77] (KGW I/1, p. 292).

Looking at the records of the other Germania lectures, Krug's ardent interest in Wagner's music stands out, yet so does the lack of Nietzsche's interest in the matter.[24] As someone who always wanted to prove his point, Krug might have been particularly interested in his own theses and arguments, or Nietzsche may not have found it worthwhile to oppose him, knowing that he could not win discussions with Krug.[25] However, had Nietzsche taken his side in the discussions with Pinder, especially because Nietzsche agreed with Pinder on issues in general, it seems likely that Krug would have noted it.[26]

1864: A positive note on Wagner and music drama

Since Nietzsche did not yet appreciate Wagner positively in 1862, the question remains as to when turned to the music of the future. Nietzsche's first recorded support of Wagner stems from 1864; hence after the Germania society had ceased to exist. In the spring of 1864, Nietzsche wrote a commentary on Sophocles's *Oedipus Rex* as an assignment for school.[27] In this essay, he opposes ancient Greek and modern German drama, arguing that the first evolved out of lyrical poetry and the second out of epic poetry. Nietzsche finds the explanation for the differences in character of ancient and modern drama in the different sources. Thus, here we find the seed of a basic idea proposed in *The Birth of Tragedy*, namely that Greek tragedy has a musical origin and that its decline should be sought in the augmentation of epic influences.[28] In the essay, Nietzsche noted that in Aeschylus's plays the chorus is the centre of the drama, while the interdialogues are short and function primarily to introduce new motives. He remarks that this relationship is turned around by modern German drama. In addition, he holds that the opera is characterised by an 'enormous imbalance between music and text' ('ungeheuerliches Mißverhältniß zwischen Musik und Text'). However, he makes an exception for 'the genius reformation plans and deeds of R. Wagner' ('die genialen Re-

---

24 Only in 1863, he plans to deliver two lectures on the demonic in music (15[16], KGW I/3, p. 143). Cf. 14[37] (KGW I/3, pp. 80–8). But even then, he listened mainly to Beethoven, Haydn, and Schubert (16[2], KGW I/3, p. 297).
25 Cf. Nietzsche's description of Krug in 'From my Life': 'In the meantime, this stubbornness of his sometimes went a bit too far. As a result, once he had formed an opinion, he could not let go, so that one tried in vain to convince him of his wrongness' ('Indessen ging diese Beharrlichkeit mitunter etwas zu weit; es entstand daraus, daß er von der einmal gefaßten Meinung nicht abließ sodaß man vergebens sich bemühte, ihn des Unrechts zu überzeugen,' 4[77], KGW I/1, p. 293).
26 Cf. 4[77] (KGW I/1, pp. 293–295). However, Nietzsche strongly criticized Pinder's poetical productions (15[15], KGW I/3, pp. 138–142).
27 17[1] (KGW I/3, pp. 329–364).
28 See also Reibnitz (1992), pp. 11–13.

formpläne und Thaten R. Wagners').[29] In the first public support with which he credits Wagner, Nietzsche states that his total artworks demonstrate a harmonic cooperation of art forms similar to Greek tragedy:

> From all annotations, one views a specific quality for the tragedians: not only that they were poets, but also that they were composers and even more than that: they were both in such a manner that the one went hand in hand with the other [...] thus we would have that which the newest musical school advances as the ideal of the 'artwork of the future' in their artworks [...].

> Aus allen Bemerkungen erkennt man einen den Tragikern eigenthümlichen Vorzug: nicht nur, daß sie Dichter waren, sie waren auch Komponisten und noch mehr, sie waren beides so, daß eins mit dem andern Hand in Hand gieng [...]: so hätten wir in ihren Kunstwerken das was die neuste musikalische Schule als das Ideal des 'Kunstwerks der Zukunft' aufstellt[...].[30]

This shows that Nietzsche understood the aims of the New German School of music in 1864 and that he sympathized with the idea to combine music and poetry. However, it is clear that he only supported this on the grounds that the chorus is the centre of the artwork and dialogues are kept to a minimum. Nietzsche sympathizes with *music drama* and rejects word drama. However, he does not refer to drama as the visual counterpart of music, a crucial view posited in *The Birth of Tragedy*, adopted from Wagner's 1870 'Beethoven' address and Schopenhauer's dream theory. But does Nietzsche's statement that Wagner's ideas and deeds are 'genius' not show more than theoretical sympathy alone? Notes from 1865 and 1866 confirm that he has not yet made the full turn to Wagner. They indicate, rather, that in those years Nietzsche opted for Hanslick's musical formalism.

1865–1866: A turn to Hanslickian musical formalism?

For the next three to four years, Nietzsche did not engage much with Wagner, music drama, or the New German School of Music. On the contrary, if anything, he was interested in Hanslick's formalistic theory of music. Two notes from Easter of 1865 insinuate that Nietzsche read Hanslick's influential *On the Musically Beautiful* (*Vom Musikalisch-Schönen*, 1854). Hanslick had written this treatise against the expressionist theory, claiming that music had no other content than its bare tones and that its meaning depended solely on its formal, tonal beauty.[31] As a proponent of musical formalism

---

29 17[1] (KGW I/3, p. 341).

30 17[1] (KGW I/3, p. 342).

31 Eduard Hanslick, *Vom musikalischen Schönen* [1854], Leipzig 1891. Landerer and Schuster (2002) argue in line with Carl Dahlhaus (1980) that Hanslick's aesthetic viewpoints dominate Nietzsche's musical reflections between 1870 and 1872. Although a challenging viewpoint, it is ultimately not convincing. Nietzsche even presents a restricted and ironic interpretation of Hanslick's standpoint in the only

and close friend of Johannes Brahms, Hanslick was not only the leading theoretician of German music, but also Wagner's main public enemy.[32]

In one note, Nietzsche listed the name 'Hanslick' among the names of books that he planned to read during the Easter holiday of 1865.[33] The second note is a longer reflection on the relation between poetry and music, possibly written in deliberation over Hanslick. The note says that 'music is analogous to feeling, not identical with it or the language of feeling' ('Die Musik ist analog dem Gefühl, nicht identisch oder Sprache des Gefühls') and that 'the purpose of music is to translate all moving things in nature into the movement of tones' ('Das Ziel der Musik, alles Bewegte in der Natur umzusetzen in die Bewegung der Töne').[34] Although this agrees with Hanslick's formalism, these expressions do not necessarily imply a preference on Nietzsche's part for Brahms and Hanslick. From the note, it is not clear whether Nietzsche adheres to Hanslick's view or just summarizes his position.

Even if he agreed with Hanslick, this did not stop Nietzsche from attending a matinée performance of 'music of the future' – in November of 1865.[35] He did not make the slightest mention of the effect the concert had on him, but exactly one year later, Nietzsche expressed obvious qualms about Wagner's music – in a letter to his friend Carl von Gersdorff:

> I brought along the piano score of Wagner's Valkyrie, with regard to which my feelings are so confused that I dare not venture an opinion on the subject. Great beauties and *virtutes* are offset by equally great shortcomings and positive ugliness.

> Dagegen hat mich der Klavierauszug der Walküre von Rich. Wagner begleitet, über die meine Empfindungen sehr gemischt sind, so daß ich kein Urtheil auszusprechen wage. Die großen Schönheiten und virtutes werden durch eben so große Häßlichkeiten und Mängel aufgewogen.[36]

---

note of 1871 in which he names him: 'Hanslick: can not find the content and is of the opinion that there is only form' ('Hanslick: findet den Inhalt nicht und meint es gebe nur Form,' 9[8], 7. 273). Love (1966), Janz (1988), and Dufour (1999) are more right to place Hanslick's authority in Nietzsche's early (1865) and later (from 1876 onwards) musical reflections.

32 According to Joachim Bergfeld, the hostility between Hanslick and Wagner grew from 23 November 1862 onwards, when Hanslick attended a lecture by Wagner in which he read his *Mastersingers* text. The character Beckmesser of *The Mastersingers* represents Hanslick and was originally called Hans Lick; Hanslick recognized himself in Beckmesser and turned his back on Wagner for good (Bergfeld, 1975, p. 209).

33 28[1] (KGW I/4, p. 50).

34 26[1] (KGW I/4, p. 32).

35 Nietzsche to Franziska und Elisabeth Nietzsche, around 12 November 1865 (KSB 2. 96).

36 Nietzsche to Carl von Gersdorff, 11 October 1866 (KSB 2. 174). Cf. note 43[1], entitled 'Richard Wagner's Valkyrie. Complete Piano Score by Karl Klindworth' ('Die Walküre von Richard Wagner. Vollständiger Klavierauszug von Karl Klindworth,' KGW I/4, p. 127f.)

Although Nietzsche renounces a final judgment about *The Valkyrie*, there is an obvious hint of dislike in the following passage drawn from the same letter:

> According to the newspapers, the same composer [Richard Wagner, MP] is working on an opera about the Hohenstaufen dynasty and allows the king [King Ludwig of Bavaria, MP], 'the devoted patron of his life' as the contribution has it, to visit him from time to time. Incidentally, it would not harm if the 'king would go with Wagner' ('go' in the boldest sense of the word), however, of course, with a decent annuity.

> Jetzt arbeitet derselbe Componist [Richard Wagner, MP] den Zeitungen nach an einer Hohenstaufenoper und läßt sich ab und zu vom König, 'dem holden Schirmherr seines Lebens', wie es in der Widmung heißt, besuchen. Es schadete übrigens nichts, wenn der König mit dem Wagner gienge,' (gehen in des Wortes verwegenster Bedeutung), natürlich aber mit anständiger Leibrente.[37]

The tone of this passage is highly sarcastic. By addressing Wagner ironically as 'the composer', Nietzsche distances himself from Wagner the person, intimating a simultaneous distancing from Wagner's music, too. At the same time, unmistakably, he dislikes the circus of which Wagner is the centre, and which is funded by the eccentric 'Fairy Tale' King Ludwig II of Bavaria (1845–1886). Nietzsche scoffs at the idea that Wagner is writing an opera in celebration of the king and suggests that it would not be a bad idea if the King would go and be bid farewell with a decent annuity.

What can we deduce from all this? First, in his school years, Nietzsche rejected the avant-garde music of Liszt and Wagner vehemently. Second, during the 'Germania' evenings in 1861–1863, he discussed modern music repeatedly with his friends Pinder and Krug. However, the evidence at hand makes clear that those discussions were particularly encouraged by Krug's zest for Wagner, not Nietzsche's, and pursued more by Krug and Pinder than by Nietzsche. Nietzsche shows more interest in poetry, folk songs, and marches, and he prefers Schumann and Beethoven's music. Third, Nietzsche's thesis on *Oedipus Rex* of 1864 testifies that Nietzsche understood the idea behind the 'artwork of the future'. It also displays a strong preference for *music drama* over word drama. It shows support for Wagner's *music drama* as a modern form of Greek tragedy. However, Nietzsche's 'ears' are not really 'warmed' by Wagner's music at that time. This is evidenced by his interest in Hanslick, his refusal to make a definitive judgment about the *Valkyrie*,[38] and his ironic expressions about Wagner in

---

37 KSB 2. 174.

38 As supportive of my claim that Nietzsche was not a Wagnerian before 1868, take note of Love remark that 'there is nothing whatever Wagnerian about' the songs Nietzsche composed between 1862 and 1865 (Love 1966, p. 28). Janz even states: 'As a composer, Nietzsche was never a Wagnerian' (Janz 1988, p. 103). Nietzsche's practice as a composer should not be taken as sufficient indication of his musical aesthetics, though.

October 1866, in particular with regard to his relationship to King Ludwig II of Bavaria. Nietzsche ridiculed this relationship and scorned its boastfulness.

Thus, despite his theoretical understanding of modern music, Nietzsche did not go along with Krug's zealous interest in Wagner.[39] His taste in music was still traditional and conservative rather than modern and progressive.[40] He was sceptical about the New German School. He found their innovative music dark, and its members 'braggarts', because they deliberately sought for obscurity and did not reach for higher pleasures than 'amusement'. Apart from this, he truly abhorred the eccentric Wagner circus under the command of 'Mad King' Ludwig of Bavaria.

This only changed when Nietzsche became part of the circus itself, in November 1868. Before this, he already had frequent contact with Wagner acolytes Franz Hüffer, Sophie Ritschl, and Ernst Windisch. The question is, whether and to what extent these contacts opened Nietzsche up to the music of the future, and Wagner in particular.

1867–1868: Franz Hüffer, Sophie Ritschl, and Louis Ehlert's Letters on Music

That Nietzsche's support for Wagner in 1864 was a unique incident, is substantiated by a note written between autumn 1867 and spring 1868. In 1867, Nietzsche and Wagner supporter Franz Hüffer, who he had met via his friend Heinrich Romundt (1845–1921), had frequent and passionate debates about Wagner.[41] In hindsight, Nietzsche puts Hüffer in the right:

> We always dashed at each other on the point of music; in particular, we did not tire of arguing about the meaning of Wagner. In hindsight, I now acknowledge that his musical judgment and perception were more delicately, at least more healthily developed than mine.

---

39 Cf. Werner Ross: 'Nietzsche was not a Wagnerian. [...] Even Gustav Krug, who had discovered the "Tristan" when he was still in school, could prompt only moderate interest in Nietzsche for it' ('Nietzsche war kein Wagnerianer. [...] Auch Gustav Krug, der als Primaner den "Tristan" entdeckt hatte, konnte dem Freund nur gemäßigtes Interesse dafür bringen,' Ross 1999, p. 168).

40 My view agrees with Frederick Love's: 'Despite all outward open-mindedness there are no real signs of weakening in his fundamentally conservative attitude until the spring and summer of 1868, only a few months before his encounter with Wagner' (Love 1966, p. 36).

41 Franz Hüffer (1845–1889) was the father of the well-known English Modernist writer Ford Maddox Ford (1873–1939). From 1869 onwards, he lived in London, where he became the secretary of the English Wagner Society, which was founded in 1873. As such, he organised a series of concerts for Wagner in the Albert Hall. In addition, he published several positive articles on his music. Hence, Wagner owed his fame in England in a large part to Franz Hüffer's preliminary work. In 1874, Hüffer published the essay 'Richard Wagner and the Music of the Future: History and Aesthetics'. In 1878, he became a musical critic for *The Times* and one of the most leading critics of his era. Hüffer was one of the few attending the ceremonial laying of the foundation stone of the Bayreuth theatre on 22 May 1872. Nietzsche was there, too. See: J. Rademacher (2002) and M. S. Asquith (2002), pp. 135–147.

> Wir lagen uns immer in den Haaren in musikalischen Punkten; vornehmlich über die Bedeutung Wagners gieng uns nie die Stimme und die Galle aus. Ich gebe ihm jetzt nachträglich zu, daß sein musikalisches Urtheilen und Empfinden feiner, vor allem gesünder entwickelt war als das meinige.[42]

This may seem to indicate that Nietzsche started to prefer modern music to more traditional classical music. It applies the same physiological terminology of 'health' and 'sickness' that Nietzsche used in 1858 to describe the ears of the man in the street and that he later used to describe humankind, art, philosophy, and culture. By terming Hüffer's defence of Wagner 'healthy', he seems to imply that his own classical taste is not healthy, but 'sick'. However, he does not say that Hüffer's *taste* was better than his was, but that Hüffer's 'judgement' (*'Urtheilen'*) and 'perception' (*'Empfinden'*) were well developed, while his was rather ill developed. This does not of necessity imply that Nietzsche agreed with or adopted Hüffer's Wagnerism, although it appears so.

With Hüffer, Nietzsche went to the theatre in Leipzig to hear music, and once he took him to pay the family Ritschl a visit in their home. Unfortunately, it has not been recorded whether music was discussed during that visit. It is likely, though, because it was under the active tutoring of Wagner devotee Sophie Ritschl, the wife of his former mentor and benefactor, that Nietzsche was further stimulated to reflect on the New Romantic School and the 'music of the future' in the summer of 1868. Sophie Ritschl gave him the essays *Letters on Music* by composer, music critic, and disciple of the New Romantic School, Louis Ehlert to read. In response, Nietzsche wrote Sophie that he suffered from the same 'problem' as Ehlert, regarding writing. In unison with Ehlert, he prefers the French writing style, the 'pariser Feuilleton' and 'Ragout' to German, academic prose and *'Rinderbraten'*. He further admits that he agrees with Ehlert, on the content that is.[43] This is interesting, because in Letter XVIII of *The Music of the Future*, Ehlert writes:

> What we do find to admire in this society of hypocritical would-be divinities [the composers associated with 'the music of the future', MP], this company of false prophets, who would force us to worship them, except their proper desire to accomplish something? [...] I agree with the fundamental principles which the musicians of the future profess, as to the power of our art to create a new world, of other appearance and different value. But I do not approve of their vouchers. [...] Wagner is remarkably inventive in orchestral coloring, and the scenic application of it; but it looks weak, to say the least, to place his instrumental and stage-managing talent in equal rank with his musical gifts. [...] When one reads the literature of the music of the future, one's feeling hesitates singularly between sympathy and sea-sickness.

---

42 60[1] (KGW I/4, p. 518). The note stems from somewhere between autumn of 1867 and spring of 1868.

43 To Sophie Ritschl, 2 July 1868 (KSB 2. 299). See Louis Ehlert, *Briefe über Musik an eine Freundin*, Berlin 1859. Louis Ehlert's style is indeed very pleasant, light, and essayistic, meandering from topic to topic, expressing apposite, compressed opinions.

Was soll diese gleißnerische Götterwirthschaft, dieses Prophetenthum, welches uns zum Anbeten zwingen will, wo wir doch nichts bewundern können als das sittliche Bemühen, etwas zu leisten? [...] Mit den Grundanschauungen, welche die Zukunftsmusiker von dem Allvermögen unsrer Kunst aufgestellt haben, eine neue Welt zu gebären, eine Welt mit anderen Erscheinungen und anderen Werthen, bin ich einverstanden. Nicht bin ich es mit ihren Belegen. [...] Wagner ist ein im Orchesterkolorit und in der scenischen Applikation bedeutend erfinderischer Kopf; aber sein Instrumentales und sein [R]egisseur-Talent in eine Reihe mit seiner musikalischen Begabung stellen zu wollen, das zeugt denn doch von einem sehr schwachen Gesicht. [...] wenn man die Literatur der Zukunftsmusik liest, so schwankt das Gefühl auf's seltsamste zwischen Theilnahme und Seekrankheit.[44]

If Nietzsche agreed with Ehlert, it implies that he (also) agreed with Ehlert's rejection of 'the music of the future' and his view that Wagner lacked musicality. In any case, Ehlert's descriptions remind us of Nietzsche's remarks in *The Case of Wagner* that Wagner's music dramas are more about ideas than about music, that they lack melody and that they make one sick. Ehlert admired Wagner as a librettist. In Letter X, *The Opera. – 'Lohengrin' and 'Tannhaüser'* [sic!], he reminds his friend how difficult it is for composers to find decent libretti, and exclaims: 'What an impression "Tannhaüser" [sic!] and "Lohengrin" must make on an enlightened public able to recall the history of the opera for the past twenty years! These are really opera-texts!' ('Welchen Eindruck mußten Tannhäuser und Lohengrin auf das gebildete Publikum machen, wenn man sich der Geschichte der Oper in den letzten 20 Jahren erinnert! Das sind wirklich Operntexte').[45] However, he criticized Wagner as a musician:

I willingly grant that 'Lohengrin' has an ideal superiority to 'Tannhaüser' [sic!]; but, in spite of myself, it produces in me a certain fatiguing tension, which arises from the restless, declamatory character of the music [...] I long for a passage of tranquil melody [...] for a melody during which the mind may draw breath, and repose for a moment [...] Wagner is not an original musical mind; but he is decidedly original in a dramaturgic sense.

Ich gebe dem Lohengrin gern den ideellen Vorzug vor dem Tannhäuser, aber es bemächtigt sich meiner doch zuweilen eine gewisse Abspannung, welche aus dem rastlos declamirenden Charakter der Musik entspringt. Ich bekomme eine wahre Sehnsucht nach einem Stück ruhiger Melodie [...] nach einer Melodie, bei welcher ich einmal tief Athem holen und ausruhen könnte. [...] Wagner ist kein origineller Kopf im musikalischen, sondern nur im dramaturgischen Verstande.[46]

---

44 Ehlert (1879), pp. 166–170. The German letters are numbered and do not have titles. Three of the twenty letters are devoted to Wagner and the 'music of the future': Letter X ('The Opera: Lohengrin and Tannhäuser'), Letter XVII ('Berlioz and Wagner') and Letter XVIII ('The Music of the Future'). The titles of the letters must have been added by the translator or editor of the English edition. Ehlert prefers by far the romantic music of Schumann and Berlioz (whom he considers the true founder of the 'new German school') to Wagner.

45 Ehlert (1879), p. 107/Ehlert (1859), p. 89.

46 Ehlert (1879), p. 110/Ehlert (1859), pp. 91 f.

This point of view is repeated in Letter XVII, *Berlioz and Wagner*: 'Wagner needs words, and also a situation. Only when these bear the musician onward is he excellent' ('Wagner braucht durchaus das Wort, ja mehr noch, die Situation. Nur wo diese den Musiker mit fortreißt, wird er erhaben').[47]

Apart from the stimulation of the *Germania* Society, Hanslick, Hüffer, Sophie Ritschl, and Ehlert's *Letters,* Nietzsche's taste of and theoretical reflections on music may have received an impulse from his friend Ernst Windisch and his new status of journalist and professional expert on music. I shall discuss this after my examination of the much-neglected relationship between Nietzsche and Oswald Marbach (1810–1890), Richard Wagner's brother-in-law. Marbach gave a lecture on Wagner's music drama at the Altenburg music festival in the summer of 1868, which Nietzsche attended. The lecture was called 'On the Rebirth of Drama in Music' ('Wiedergeburt der dramatischen Kunst durch die Musik'). Marbach published this lecture in his *Dramaturgy Papers*, which came out in 1870.[48]

Summer 1868: Oswald Marbach on the rebirth of drama in music

In the summer of 1868, Nietzsche visited the sixth Altenburg music festival, which took place from 19 until 23 July 1868 in Weimar at the Altenburg mansion – the residency of Franz Liszt and his mistress Princess Caroline Sayn-Wittgenstein. The Altenburg music festival was an annual festival organized by the General German Music Association ('Allgemeiner Deutscher Musikverein'), which was founded in 1861 by Franz Liszt and Franz Brendel. It was the most prominent institution in the promotion of avant-garde music.[49] On 29 July 1868, Nietzsche wrote to his mother and sister that Altenburg is 'very interesting'.[50]

---

47 Ehlert (1879), p. 182/Ehlert (1859), p. 157.
48 Brobjer (2005) is the only one who has taken the effort to look into Marbach's *Dramaturgy Papers*.
49 Nietzsche was probably a member too, given the fact that the ADMV archive contains his autograph. Franz Liszt lived at the Altenburg mansion with Princess Caroline Sayn-Wittgenstein from 1849 until 1861. He returned there in 1869.
50 KSB 2. 301. To Rohde, he also mentioned 'a lecture on The Mastersingers' (6 August 1868, KSB 2. 306). I presume that this reference is either to Marbach's lecture (even though Marbach does not mention *The Mastersingers* nor any other Wagnerian work) or to a lecture that is not mentioned in the written programme. Borchmeyer and Salaquarda interpret this record as a plan of Nietzsche to write an account on *The Mastersingers*, which he then only two months later delivers 'together with further expositions on Wagner' (Borchmeyer and Salaquarda 1994, vol. 2, p. 1224 f.). However, the letter of 8 October they refer to does not make mention of such writings at all and Nietzsche has never written an account on *The Mastersingers*. Raymond J. Benders and Stephan Oettermann refer to Marbach's lecture as the 'Rebirth of Dramatic Art in Music' ('Wiedergeburt der Dramatischen Kunst durch die Musik') and date it 19 July 1868 (2000, p. 178). Janz, although particularly interested in Nietzsche's musical de-

What may in particular have interested him in Altenburg is a lecture held by Oswald Marbach. The Altenburg festival programme shows that on 19 July, the first day of the festival, there were performances of works by Bach, Liszt, and Berlioz and that Oswald Marbach delivered his lecture 'On the Rebirth of Drama in Music' ('Ueber die Wiedergeburt der dramatischen Kunst durch die Musik').[51] Could Marbach's lecture have influenced Nietzsche's passion for Wagner, for example, by convincing Nietzsche of the composer's crucial importance for the salvation of (German or even European) culture – the thesis defended in chapters 16–25 of *The Birth of Tragedy*?[52]

An unambiguous answer concerning Marbach's exact influence would require an analysis of Nietzsche's reading of Marbach's *Dramaturgy Papers* copy. However, because Marbach's book is not available in Nietzsche's library anymore, it is not possible to uncover which passages he has read. Additionally, particularly of this period, relatively few notes have remained, which make it difficult to reveal Marbachian quotes and (para-) phrases. In the remaining letters of 1868–1870, he does not refer to Marbach.

However, looking at Marbach's lecture 'On the Rebirth of Drama in Music' shows that it bears remarkable similarities to *The Birth of Tragedy*. It treats the revival of Greek tragedy through a fresh mix of poetry and music in modern German music, which also forms the main topic of *The Birth of Tragedy*, specifically its last ten chapters. Right at the onset of Marbach's book, it is stated that drama requires a 'rebirth' (*'Wiedergeburt'*), meaning that contemporary theatre must imitate Greek drama in order to meet the rules of true drama. 'On the Rebirth of Drama in Music' states that drama should be re-united with music in order to facilitate this rebirth. Simultaneously, Marbach calls Greek drama a 'total artwork' (*'Gesamtkunstwerk'*), using Wagner's famous term. He also claims that the first steps of the renewal are taken by the New German School of Music, specifically by Wagner and Liszt.[53] These ideas also constitute the main thread of *The Birth of Tragedy*.[54]

---

velopment, mentions Nietzsche's visit to Altenburg remarkably briefly in his biography (Curt Paul Janz 1978a, vol. 1, p. 235).

51 I thank Dr. Irina Lucke-Kaminiarz, director of the Hochschularchiv/-Thüringisches Landesmusikarchiv in Weimar, for her help in retrieving the Altenburg Festival Programme of 1868.

52 On Richard Wagner's recommendation, Marbach sent his book to Nietzsche at the end of January or beginning of February 1870. The book is a collection of essays and lectures, amongst which is 'On the Rebirth of Drama in Music' (in: Oswald Marbach 1870, pp. 135–154). Marbach himself must have taken care of the publication and printing of his small-sized, two-hundred-fifty pages manuscript. For the letter Marbach sent to Nietzsche with the copy, see: KGB II/2, p. 132 f. (End of January beginning of February 1870). Cf. Cosima Wagner to Nietzsche, 31 January 1870 (KGB II/2, p. 131 f.).

53 Marbach (1870), p. 143 f.

54 Silk and Stern (1981) do not refer to Marbach as a possible source of Nietzsche's views on tragedy. They only point to Marbach's lecture as prefiguration of the title of Nietzsche's book (p. 417, footnote 111).

Marbach starts his essay by outlining a Herderian, organic view of cultural and musical decadence and blossoming, emphasizing his optimistic view for the future. The lecture's main purpose is to reveal the seeds from which the new future for dramatic music will be born. Like the young Nietzsche, Marbach has a Romantic outlook on life. He believes that maturity obstructs rather than promotes humanity, and that the goal for humanity is to become childlike again. Also in his consideration of drama, he turns out to be romantic-sentimental: we must look to drama's origins in order to determine what drama must be in the future.

Music, according to Marbach, is the highest of all the fine arts. However, in order to exert true power, music must be accompanied by language and drama. He drafts the ideal of the 'perfect dramatic artwork' based on the 'sympathetic cooperation' between music, poetry, and orchestra.[55] Greek drama demonstrated this sympathetic cooperation, especially in the works of Aeschylus, he further claims, adding that the separation of music, poetry, and drama causes the contemporary artistic decline and that opera demonstrates this in particular. Opera, he asserts, combines the different arts, but it remains on the level of 'artificiality' and does not achieve true art. The ideas of the libretti are poor, instrumental music forms opera's fundament instead of 'the shared human experience' (Marbach does not explain what kind of experience this is), and the singers focus on exposing their technical skills rather than on the expression of emotions. For these reasons, opera is an 'unfinished', 'decadent', and 'incomplete' art form.[56] Nevertheless, Marbach believes that opera has an enormous, yet unexplored, potential to express feelings. It just needs to focus more on the fusion of music with poetry and orchestra, he proposes.[57] Marbach expects that the New German School of Music (he names Liszt, Wagner, and von Bülow) will complete the revitalization of dramatic art by establishing a successful cooperation of the different arts.

The ideas advanced in the *Dramaturgy Papers* lack originality. Instead, they voice ideas that were quite common at that time. Like Nietzsche, Marbach perceives a collapse of drama that may be reversed by an overhaul of Greek tragedy. Yet, this idea was already seized upon by Schiller, Goethe, and Wagner as the starting-point of their artistic enterprises, long before Marbach's lecture in the summer of 1868. In addition, the interpretation of Greek tragedy as 'total artwork' and the New German School as the renewer of Greek tragedy were already established by Nietzsche in his Sophocles-essay of 1864, hence years before he had even heard of Marbach.[58] Furthermore, the idea of Wagner as a regenerator of Greek tragedy, which was crucial to Nietzsche's

---

55 Marbach (1870), pp. 140–142.
56 Marbach (1870), pp. 140–142.
57 Marbach (1870), pp. 145, p. 147, p. 149.
58 According to Love, the text of Marbach was never made available, which is obviously incorrect. Love bases his views on the summary of Marbach's lecture given by the review in *Die neue Zeitschrift für Musik* (1966, pp. 89 f.), which may have been a source of information for Nietzsche as well.

Wagner-understanding in *The Birth of Tragedy*, was not original either. This link was often made, also by Wagner himself.

Hence, the similarities in their views confirm the commonality of these views in nineteenth-century Germany rather than uncovering a direct theoretical link between Marbach and Nietzsche. In addition, the idea of a rebirth of tragedy has a long and rich lineage in the history of music, because exactly this idea spurred the *Camarata* around 1600 in Florence to configure the *dramma per musica*, which engendered the beginning of opera altogether. Wagner wanted to reform precisely this tradition, by building upon Beethoven's symphonic work. However, despite the fact that Marbach's *Dramaturgy Papers* lack originality and provide weak arguments and a lousy writing-style, it is interesting that Nietzsche ignored Marbach altogether, or pretended to do so. The least one may have expected from him is a sardonic remark about Marbach's writing-style to Erwin Rohde or Cosima Wagner. Perhaps Nietzsche considered Marbach as one of his 'too stupid brothers in Wagnero'?[59]

In a letter of 28 March 1870, Cosima Wagner asked Nietzsche to read Marbach's text on Hamlet in the *Dramaturgy Papers* 'in order to understand my dismay' ('um mein Entsetzen zu verstehen').[60] This not only suggests that Nietzsche might have at least been familiar with the book, but also that Cosima expected him to read Marbach's aesthetic and historical account with equal disdain. It may indeed seem unlikely that Nietzsche would have read Marbach's writings with real pleasure and serious interest, given its mediocre style and ideas, and the high regard he had for Cosima's taste. Yet again, there is no conclusive evidence either way.

The silence was only broken in 1874. On 3 March 1874, Marbach sent his translations of the Aeschylean plays *Oresteia* and *Prometheus* to Nietzsche, for which Nietzsche, on 14 June 1874, thanks Marbach, extensively complimenting him on the translation.[61] On 5 July 1874, Marbach responds to this letter, expressing sincere gratitude regarding Nietzsche's comprehension of his philology and aesthetics. He also confirms that Wagner puts these aesthetic insights into practice. Nietzsche does not refer to Marbach's 1870 text in this correspondence either, nor to any similarities in aesthetic views (despite Marbach's expressed thanks for Nietzsche's understanding in this matter). Nietzsche's remark in a letter to Wagner of 20 May 1874 that 'Aeschylus [...] has brought me together with Marbach now' ('Aeschylus [...] hat mich jetzt mit Oswald

---

59 Nietzsche to Erwin Rohde, 22/28 February 1869 (KSB 2. 378).

60 Cosima von Bülow to Nietzsche, 28 March 1870 (KGB I/2, p. 183). Cosima had a similar experience reading Marbach's *Proteus* in February 1869. She writes that Marbach has a deep view of things, yet advances them very perfunctorily (Cosima Wagner 1976–78, vol. 1, p. 52. Cf. 2 March 1869, vol. 1, p. 65, where she complains that Marbach wanted to make Shakespeare moral).

61 Marbach to Nietzsche, 3 March 1874 (KGB II/4, p. 398), and 5 July 1874 (KGB II/4, p. 505ff.). Nietzsche to Oswald Marbach, 14 June 1874 (KSB 4. 233f.). Marbach's satirical play *Shakespeare-Prometheus: phantastisch-satirisches Zauberspiel* (Leipzig 1874) is still in the Nietzsche-library (Campioni et. al. [eds.] 2003, pp. 376f.).

Marbach zusammengebracht') seems to indicate that there had not been any intellectual kinship before. However, Nietzsche is surprisingly positive about Marbach's philological qualities, here. He writes to Wagner that Marbach makes 'the deepest remarks' ('*die tiefsten Bermerkungen'*) in the commentary that goes with the translation, and he ends with the remark that Marbach is 'one of the very few persons, that hang onto ancient tragedy out of natural need and love' ('einer der ganz wenigen, welche mit einer natürlichen Noth und Liebe an der alten Tragödie hangen').[62]

In sum, it is unlikely that Marbach is responsible for Nietzsche's turn to Wagner in 1868. Thus, the question remains what and who may have pushed him in Wagner's direction? A much neglected, yet significant, moment in this respect is Nietzsche's short-term career move to music journalism.

Autumn 1868: Nietzsche's social ambition, musical journalism, and Otto Jahn

In October 1868, Nietzsche writes to Erwin Rohde a crucial letter in which he looks back at the year 1868 and reveals his good intentions for the new season in Leipzig. He remarks that all their acquaintances in Leipzig are already famous and that he needs to get an academic grade. He also intends to become a more social human being, and expresses that he especially wants to get to know Luise Brockhaus, Wagner's sister, because he has heard such astonishing things about her from his friend Ernst Windisch. Clearly, Nietzsche sets himself the task for the new academic year of climbing the social ladder.

He continues to say that he has read Otto Jahn's essays on music, including the critical essays on Wagner.[63] He writes that he agrees with Jahn's pejorative view that Wagner is 'the representative of a modern dilettantism that sucks up and digests all artistic interests' ('den Repräsentanten eines modernen, alle Kunstinteressen in sich aufsaugenden und verdauenden Dilettantismus'), but he also claims that Wagner's artistic talent is 'significant' ('*bedeutend'*) and 'versatile' ('*vielseitig'*), because it brings out an 'atmosphere of feeling' ('*Gefühlssphaere'*) that Jahn neglects. He describes this atmosphere famously as follows: 'I like about Wagner what I like about Schopenhauer, the ethical air, the Faustian smell, cross, death and grave' ('Mir behagt

---

62 Nietzsche to Richard Wagner, 20 May 1874 (KSB 4. 229f.).

63 Otto Jahn's *Gesammelte Aufsätze über Musik*, Leipzig 1866 (I use the reprint of 1969). The book contains thirteen essays, of which one is dedicated to *Tannhäuser* and one to *Lohengrin*. Jahn is very critical of Wagner in these essays. Similar to Ehlert and Schopenhauer, he first praises Wagner as a librettist, but then starts to show in detail the weaknesses of the poetic conception of *Tannhäuser*, claiming that these also affect the musical achievements negatively (Jahn 1969, p. 64ff.). Otto Jahn was a former teacher of Nietzsche in Bonn and a well-known Wagner-opponent. He also was the adversary of Nietzsche's tutor Ritschl.

an Wagner, was mir an Schopenhauer behagt, die ethische Luft, der faustische Duft, Kreuz, Tod, und Gruft etc.').[64] The letter thus shows that Nietzsche agrees with the criticism expressed by Ehlert and Jahn (and Schopenhauer!) that Wagner is not successful in meeting all the demands of the total artwork, especially the need of finding the balance between text and music. He praises the Schopenhauerian atmosphere of Wagner's total art works rather than the successful rejuvenation of Greek tragedy by way of the reconciliation of Dionysus and Apollo, or music, text, and visual means, as in *The Birth of Tragedy*.

An offer made by his landlord Otto Biedermann further stimulated Nietzsche's social ambitions and the development of a more serious and sophisticated attitude towards music. Biedermann asked Nietzsche to write musical and philological reviews for the daily *Deutsche Allgemeine*. From this ensued an intriguing yet overall neglected fact: as a journalist for this newspaper, and not as an amateur, Nietzsche visited the opening winter concert of the orchestra society Euterpe in Leipzig, in late October 1868. This fact should not be underestimated, because it seems to have made a significant impact on Nietzsche's self-perception. He suddenly listened and felt he had to listen to music with the ears of a professional critic instead of the ears of the 'amateurish man in the street'. It was, we might say, as if he was seen as someone who possessed Hüffer's healthy ears, well-developed judgement, and perception instead of an amateurish and ill-developed attitude towards music. His former explicit judgements about the music of the future were based on emotion (in 1858) or philological interests (in 1864). Now, he had to judge as a professional expert of music for a public medium. However, as a critic of music, Nietzsche was not able to take the necessary professional distance. His relation towards music was still emotional and amateurish – to his own amusement:

> Occasionally, I visit concerts and lectures as a representative of the *Deutsche Allgemeine*; they even offered me [to write] opera critiques. Tonight I went to the Euterpe [an orchestra society in Leipzig, MP], which started their winter concerts and entertained me with the prelude to *Tristan and Isolde* as well as with the overture to *The Mastersingers*. I do not have the heart to relate critically and coldly to this music; every fiber, every nerve in me twitches, and it has been a long time since I had such a continuous feeling of detachment as during the latter overture. Otherwise, my season ticket site is surrounded by critical spirits: immediately in front of me sits Bernsdorf, that signalled monster; next to me to the left is Dr. Paul, contemporary newspaper hero, two seats to

---

64 Nietzsche to Erwin Rohde, 8 October 1868 (KSB 2. 322). Nietzsche here ironizes the criticism expressed in Jahn's essay on Wagner's *Tannhäuser*. Jahn criticizes this opera for a 'wobbly' ('schwankend') treatment of ethics (Jahn, 1969, p. 65) and a lack of psychological foundation. On page 72, Jahn opposes dilettantism and art, pointing to Wagner's 'versatile talent for poetry, music, visual art' ('Wagner mit seinem vielseitigen Talent für Poesie, Musik, bildende Kunst') and claiming that Wagner is a representative of modern dilettantism. Naming Jahn 'Grenzbotenheld' is also ironic, because Jahn opposes the *Grenzboten* (a newspaper) and other newspapers that ascribe a historical meaning to the fact that there were three moderately visited performances of *Tannhäuser* in Leipzig, at the beginning of his essay on *Tannhäuser*.

the right is my friend Stade, who produces critical feelings for Brendel's music magazine [*Die neue Zeitschrift für Musik*, MP]. It is a sharp angle: and when the four of us shake our heads in phalanx, it means misfortune.

Gelegentlich gehe ich jetzt als Vertreter der Deutschen Allgemeinen in Conzerte und Vorlesungen; ja sogar die Kritik der Oper ist mir offerirt [...]. Heute Abend war ich in der Euterpe, die ihre Winterconzerte began und mich sowohl mit der Einleitung zu Tristan und Isolde, als auch mit der Ouvertüre zu den Meistersingern erquickte. Ich bringe es nicht übers Herz, mich dieser Musik gegenüber kritisch kühl zu verhalten; jede Faser, jeder Nerv zuckt an mir, und ich habe lange nicht ein solches andauerendes Gefühl der Entrücktheit gehabt als bei letztgenannter Ouvertüre. Sonst ist mein Abonnementsplatz umlagert von kritischen Geistern: unmittelbar vor mir sitzt Bernsdorf, jenes signalisirte Scheusal, links neben mir Dr. Paul, jetzt Tageblattheld, 2 Plätze rechts mein Freund Stade, der für die Brendelsche [Wagner-supportive, MP] Musikzeitung kritische Gefühle produziert: es ist eine scharfe Ecke: und wenn wir Vier einmüthig mit dem Kopfe schütteln, so bedeutet es ein Unglück.[65]

In spite of the fact that Nietzsche taunts the professionals, including himself, he identifies with them by describing his seat amongst them and next to one of the most famous journalists of the time, 'Dr. Paul'. Moreover, despite the fact that he borders off his emotional, warm approach to music from the critical and cold one he is supposed to have, it is remarkable that, now that he has become one of the 'connoisseurs' he detested in 'From my Life,' he, for the first time, appreciates modern music. It should be noted that he especially cheers *The Mastersingers* overture, one of Wagner's more 'classical', light, and 'un-Wagnerian' works.

Whether Nietzsche indeed wrote a review of the concert and whether it was ever published, is unknown.[66]

Nietzsche's first meeting with Wagner in November 1868

Nietzsche thus only became truly excited about Wagner's music when he visited the Euterpe concert as a journalist for the *Deutsche Allgemeine*. The Euterpe concert took place two weeks before he met Wagner via Sophie Ritschl. She was an acquaintance of Wagner's older sister Luise Brockhaus. Sophie told Wagner, while he was playing a song from *The Mastersingers* on the piano during a visit to his sister, that she knew the song already, because Friedrich Nietzsche had played it to her on the piano.[67] This made Wagner eager to meet the young philologist.

---

65 Nietzsche to Erwin Rohde, 27 October 1868 (KSB 2. 331f.). Cf. Nietzsche to Carl von Gersdorff, 18 January 1869 (KSB 2. 363f).

66 I was not able to discover whether Nietzsche actually ever wrote a musical review for the *Deutsche Allgemeine*.

67 It is unclear when Nietzsche had played this on the piano to Sophie Ritschl. Perhaps after the Euterpe concert, where he enjoyed *The Mastersingers'* overture so much? Wagner completed its compo-

Sophie Ritschl then arranged a meeting at the Brockhaus residence on Sunday evening, 8 November 1868. The whole thing was shrouded in secrecy, because the press was not allowed to know that the famous composer was in town (Nietzsche did not go there as a journalist either). This set the tone for the occult and intimate atmosphere Nietzsche appreciated so much when being with Wagner in a small circle of friends. In contrast, the big events, concerts, and festivals often made him feel uncomfortable.

Nietzsche came to the Brockhaus-Wagner family together with his friend Ernst Windisch. Soon, Wagner and Nietzsche engaged in a lively conversation about Wagner's music and Schopenhauer's philosophy, for which they shared a fondness. To Wagner, Schopenhauer was the only philosopher who understood music, while for Nietzsche Schopenhauer's pessimism was the modern version of the Greek view of life. Wagner also complained to Nietzsche that the university professors in philosophy did not understand his music, calling them 'philosophical servants'.[68] For convenience's sake, Wagner did not mention that Schopenhauer did not appreciate Wagner's music either.[69] The conversations were interrupted by performances of Wagner, who played and sang many instances of *The Mastersinger* to the small crowd. This evening made Nietzsche esteem Wagner's music as a 'Schopenhauerian sea of tones' ('*Schopenhauerische[s] Tonmeer*') and 'an amazing discovery of oneself' ('*ein staunendes Sichselbstfinden*').[70] The meeting with Wagner spurred Nietzsche to take the last step towards avant-garde music. From this day onwards, Nietzsche committed himself to Wagner without hardly any restraint, as is clearly shown by the letter he wrote to Erwin Rohde the following day. Nietzsche states that Wagner makes him feel 'idyllic-comfortable' ('*idyllisch-behaglich*'), which is a surprising choice of words in view of his later rejection of the idyllic in *The Birth of Tragedy*.

The idyll was continued in Switzerland, Tribschen in particular, from June 1869 onwards and lasted until July 1872, when the Wagners moved from Tribschen to Bayreuth. However, some cloudbanks drifted over the idyll as early as February 1870, I argue below, challenging Nietzsche's later overstated remark that 'no clouds ever darkened our skies'.[71]

---

sition in 1867. It is due to King Ludwig's financial help that Wagner could finish the score of this comic opera. *The Mastersingers* premiered 21 June 1868 at the Royal Court Theatre in Munich, but the overture already had its first public performance on 2 November 1862.

68 Nietzsche to Erwin Rohde, 9 November 1868 (KSB 2. 341).

69 When Wagner sent Schopenhauer his Nibelung libretto in 1854, Schopenhauer reacted pejoratively, telling Wagner's friend François Wille to bring Wagner the message that he would 'stay loyal to Rossini and Mozart,' because he considered Wagner a better poet than musician. See Karl Kropfinger (1991), p. 130.

70 Nietzsche to Erwin Rohde, 9 December 1868 (KSB 2. 352f.)

71 EH 'Clever' 5 (pp. 92–93/KSA 6.288).

Continuation of the friendship in 1869

After their first meeting in November 1868, Wagner and Nietzsche got in contact again only six months later. Aware of Wagner's grim anti-Semitism, Nietzsche blamed the 'forward pushing Judaism' (*'vordringliches Judenthum'*) – next to politics and inadequate philosophy – for the bad situation of the 'poor Germans', in his first Birthday letter to Wagner of 22 May 1869.[72] What was poor though was Nietzsche's attempt to flatter Wagner with views that may have been directly taken from Wagner's essay *Jewishness in Music* (*Das Judenthum in der Musik*).[73]

With remarkable similarity to the judgment of Italian music in his 'Beethoven' essay of 1870 (as we shall see in the next chapter), *Jewishness in Music* argues that Jewish musicians (specifically Mendelssohn and Meyerbeer) have a tendency to superficiality and are a threat to European culture. To this is added the cliché argument that Jews in general are led in life by a desire for money. The essay also argues that Jews should abstain from their own cultural identity in order to assimilate to German culture.[74] Nietzsche may have read Wagner's anti-Semitic essay, but it is not sure how this affected his early philosophy and judgment of Wagner, if it did.[75] In *The Birth of Tragedy*, for example, nothing is said about a possible Jewish source of philistinism and decadence, while Italian music is held largely responsible for the present decadent situation in Europe's musical culture.[76] Later, Nietzsche explicitly distanced himself from anti-Semitism and *'Deutschthümelei'*.[77] Then he also apologized for the fact that he had not completely succeeded in escaping this 'illness' either, in a perceptive

---

72 KSB 3, p. 9.

73 Wagner had published it first in 1850 in *Die Neue Zeitschrift für Musik* under the name 'K. Freigedank'. He re-published it under his own name in December 1869 (cf. Wagner to Nietzsche, 19 December 1869, KGB II/2, p. 96f). In spite of his public statement against Jewish influence in music and culture, Wagner had many Jewish friends with whom he worked together. Moreover, his favourite conductor was the Jew Hermann Levi.

74 See also Millington (1992), pp. 162–164. Millington refers to Bryan Magee, who has tried to point out that there was some truth in Wagner's essay, for Wagner offered 'explanations for what other people had not even noticed', but the logic of this escapes me.

75 One of the arguments in favour of his reading could be that Nietzsche, after the break with Wagner, blames him for the same superficiality and inclination to entertain the public as Wagner held against the Jews.

76 That arguing for an interpretation of Nietzsche's cultural war against philistinism as directed against Jews remains difficult is proven by Mittmann's highly speculative account (2002), p. 27. The only point at which this could be done more convincingly is with regard to chapter 9 of *The Birth of Tragedy*, where Nietzsche regards the Prometheus myth as 'Aryan' (BT 9, p. 50/KSA 1.69) and the Christian myth of the Fall of man as of 'Semitic' origin.

77 In a note from 1885–1886, Nietzsche wrote: 'was mir am fremdesten an ihm [Richard Wagner], die Deutschthümelei und Halbkirchlichkeit seiner letzten Jahre – – –' (2[34], KSA 12.81). Cf. 1[226], KSA 12.60 and 1[195, 196], KSA 12.54–55.

aphorism from *Beyond Good and Evil* that tries to explain German anti-Semitism. For instance, he states that 'prudence and politics are not really aimed at anti-Semitic sentiment in general, but instead at its dangerous excess, and especially at the outrageous and disgraceful expression of this excessive sentiment' ('so richtet sich doch auch diese Vorsicht und Politik nich etwa gegen die Gattung des [anti-semitischen] Gefühls selber, sondern nur gegen seine gefährliche Unmässigkeit, insbesondere gegen den abgeschmackten und schandbaren Austäuschen').[78]

Nonetheless, it is a fact that, while he regarded anti-Semitism and political nationalism as a stupid frigidity in later years, Nietzsche tried to flatter Wagner in the birthday letter with an anti-Semitic remark of equal stupidity and frigidity. In so doing, Nietzsche was – more in a clumsy than convincing way – keeping up the appearance of an anti-Semite, which was at odds with his intercultural interest. He made the same mistake when he read out his lecture *Socrates and Tragedy* and blamed the 'Jewish' press for being pray to 'Socratism' and blind to the possibilities of music drama.

Having read the lecture, Cosima advised Nietzsche not to make loose remarks on Jews anymore, until he would be ready to start the 'atrocious war' (*'grauenhaften Kampf'*).[79] He indeed barred the remark about the Jewish press from the manuscript and kept silent about the Jews and their Socratism since – which makes it hard to draw a definite conclusion about the truth and appearance of Nietzsche's anti-Semitism.[80] It is true that anti-Semitism was prevalent around him, and that their Wagner-enthusiasm stimulated anti-Semitism in his friends Heinrich Romundt, Paul Deussen, and Carl von Gersdorff. What is also true is that Nietzsche's expressions with regard to this

---

78 BGE 251, pp. 141/KSA 5.193. Cf. BGE 250 and other aphorisms of BGE chapter 8 'People and Fatherlands' ('Völker und Vaterländer'), which are testimony to Nietzsche's 'anti-anti-Semitism' and offer a sharp insight into the danger of German anti-Semitism. Very interesting in this context are also Nietzsche's letters to the editor of the *Antisemitischen Korrespondenz*, Theodor Fritsch, of 23 and 29 March 1887 (KSB 8. 45–46 and KSB 8. 51). Nietzsche scorned the anti-Semites openly. The letters also show that Nietzsche was well informed about the popularity and identity of German anti-Semitism, although he lived in the south of France; that he not only rejected anti-Semitism as such, but also the anti-Semitic willingness to submit themselves to authorities; and that Zarathustra, to Nietzsche, was an anti-anti-Semitic figure *par excellence*. In his letter to Franz Overbeck of 24 March 1887, Nietzsche reveals the 'comic' event that among radical parties (amongst which socialists, nihilists, anti-Semites, and Wagnerites), he has a 'curious and almost mysterious prestige' ('wunderlich und fast mysteriösen Ansehen,' KSB 8. 48). As he admits to Theodor Fritsch, he approaches this curiosity with irony, but, he says, he is not very patient with anti-Semites and Germans, and might become wrathful instead.
79 Cosima Wagner to Nietzsche, 5 February 1870 (KGB II/2, pp. 138–145). Cf. Richard Wagner to Nietzsche, 4 February 1870 (KGB II/2, pp. 137–138).
80 ST, KSA 1.533–549. See for the original end of ST: KSA 14.101. Cf. von Reibnitz (1992), pp. 38–40. Cf. 3[73], 7. 79–80 and 3[86], 7. 83. Also Nietzsche's overtly anti-Semitic friend and Wagnerite Carl von Gersdorff scorned the Jewish press, after reading *Das Judenthum in der Musik* (to Nietzsche, beginning of March 1870, KGB II/2, p. 164), to which Nietzsche responded on 11 and 17 March (KSB 3. 104–107).

appear rather inept, unnatural, and 'mild' when compared with what Gersdorff and Romundt have to say about this.[81]

A more intimate friendship with the Wagners only started in Switzerland in May 1869, after Nietzsche had moved to Basle to start his new job at the University. While, at the beginning of January 1869, Nietzsche had proposed to his friend Erwin Rohde to quit their philology study and sign up for chemistry, about a week later, his supervisor Professor Friedrich Ritschl recommended him for the vacant philology chair at the University of Basle.[82] Four weeks later, Nietzsche, then twenty-four years old, was officially appointed and another two months later, in April 1869, he said farewell to his student life in Leipzig to become (initially extra-ordinary) professor of classical philology at the University of Basle in Switzerland.

It took Nietzsche some time to find his feet in his new, Swiss life. Letters to his mother, sister, and friends show numerous accounts of his efforts to become accustomed to his life as a professor employed at a small university, surrounded by 'aristocratic, bigoted bourgeoisie' and cut off from his friends.[83] The organization of new housing and especially the endless social duties annoyed Nietzsche considerably and soon he started cancelling the dinner- and game-parties, to which his colleagues invited him. Indeed, the change of scenery from student life in Leipzig to a professional life in bourgeois Basle initially did not do him much good. 'I dearly miss a friend here,' Nietzsche informed his mother and sister only one week after his arrival in the Swiss city. The surplus of new things overwhelmed him, and several of these things and people fell short of his expectations. His lodgings did not please him and, of his colleagues, only the much older historian Jacob Burckhardt captivated him with his brightness.[84] Of all his friends Nietzsche missed Erwin Rohde the most. Rohde was on a sojourn in

---

81 Thomas Mittmann (2002, pp. 19–37) does not discriminate between negative expressions about *religious* criticism of Judaism and expressions about the Jewish press, Jews as people or Jewish individuals, nor when Nietzsche uses quotations marks for 'the Jews' by which he then means 'every individual that hates Wagner' (to Gersdorff, 11 March 1870, KSB 3. 105). This leads to a too black- and-white depiction of Nietzsche as an advocate of a war against the Jews, also because he refuses to discriminate between Nietzsche's 'soft' anti-Semitism and the frank, upsetting anti-Semitism of the Wagners and of his friends Erwin Rohde, Heinrich Romundt, and Carl von Gersdorff. They were all much ruder in their anti-Semitic expressions and sentiments than Nietzsche ever was, and Mittmann neglects to comment on that. It should also be noted that many German Jews in the music business venerated Wagner's music and attended *The Mastersingers* premiere, which shocked von Gersdorff, who tried to interpret the Jews as enemies of true art (in the spirit of Wagner).

82 To Erwin Rohde, 16 January 1869 (KSB 2. 358ff).

83 Besides, the firm wind that blew constantly through the city saddled Nietzsche with a troubling toothache, he claims (see Nietzsche to his mother, May 1869, KSB 3. 5).

84 Franz Overbeck (1837–1905), with whom Nietzsche developed a lifelong, close friendship, was not yet in Basle (Overbeck got appointed in Basle as a Professor of New Testament and old church history about one year after Nietzsche started his professorship there). Overbeck brought Nietzsche from Turin to Basle after his collapse in January 1889. Overbeck lived together with Nietzsche in the '*Baumanns-*

Continuation of the friendship in 1869 —— **45**

Italy, and Nietzsche thought of ways to get his dear friend employed at the University of Basle as well. The young professor, otherwise such a modest and friendly man,[85] even wished an aged colleague dead, so that Rohde might take his place. In addition, one year later, when he attempted to switch to philosophy, he wrote in his application letter how profoundly his life would be 'alleviated' if Rohde were to be commissioned as his successor for the philology chair.[86]

For lack of an intimate friend, Nietzsche focused his attention on the most interesting person near him, the German composer Richard Wagner. Wagner and his lover Cosima von Bülow, next to Jacob Burckhardt, were the only persons to exceed the mediocre people with whom Nietzsche's new life was crowded.[87] Wagner 'is really everything we expected him to be' ('ist wirklich alles, was wir von ihm gehofft haben'), Nietzsche wrote to Rohde in full admiration, after he had visited the family in Tribschen for the first time.[88] Yet Wagner was less keen, calling Nietzsche's second visit to Tribschen 'bearable' ('erträglich').[89] Nevertheless, many visits to Tribschen followed, twenty-three in total. Moreover, an intense and intimate correspondence started, especially between Nietzsche and Cosima. In Tribschen, Richard Wagner and Cosima von Bülow rented a villa near the lake Lucerne. The music, intellectual discussions, Cosima's warmth and loving interest, and the idyllic nature of the countryside that

---

Höhle,' named after their landholders Otto and Anne Baumann. With Overbeck, Heinrich Romundt (who came to live in the *'Baumanns-Höhle'* in 1872), Rohde, and von Gersdorff, Nietzsche formed a circle of friends, which they called the 'society of the hoping men' ('Gesellschaft der Hoffenden'). Cf. von Reibnitz (2000), p. ix.

85 Nietzsche's student T. Siegfried remembers his former teacher as a 'timid' and 'modest' person, 'who combined the highest wisdom with the most sophisticated manners, who had something dignified in his whole behaviour, yet approached his students only with kindness and correctly, so absolutely nothing of the Overman' ('der mit dem höchsten Wissen die feinsten Umgangsformen verband, der in seinem ganzen Auftreten etwas Vornehmes hatte und doch den Schülern mit lauter Güte und Wohlwollen begegnete, so gar nichts vom Uebermenschen.' Cited according to Benders and Oettermann 2000, p. 196).

86 To Wilhelm Vischer, January 1871 (KSB 3, pp. 174–178).

87 Cosima von Bülow was the daughter of Franz Liszt (1811–1886). She was still married to Hans von Bülow (a musical conductor, who often worked for Wagner), when she started living together with Richard Wagner. Richard and Cosima married on 25 August 1870. Nietzsche did not attend the wedding, because he was in France, serving the Prussian military service voluntarily as a paramedic.

88 29 May 1869 (KSB 3. 13). Cf. To Erwin Rohde, 16 June 1869 (KSB 3. 17).

89 Cosima Wagner, 5/6 June 1869 (1994, p. 24). German text after Borchmeyer/Salaquarda 1994, Vol. 2, p. 1149. Wagner's reaction is understandable given the fact that Nietzsche came to visit in the weekend that Siegfried was born (in the night of 5–6 June). Her condition did not keep Cosima from welcoming Nietzsche in her house, neither from writing in her diary on the 6th of June. Her report of that weekend gives the impression as if Siegfried's birth was just a small interruption of the daily routine.

pervaded his stays there, made Nietzsche find himself in an Epicurean dream.[90] In a letter to Erwin Rohde, who was on sojourn to Italy, he noted:

> In fact, I, like you, have my Italy as well, albeit that I can rescue myself there only on Saturdays and Sundays. It is called Tribschen and it is already like a real home to me [...]. My dearest friend, what I learn, see, hear, and understand there is beyond description. Schopenhauer and Goethe, Aeschylus and Pindar are still alive.[91]

> Übrigens habe ich auch mein Italien, wie Du; nur daß ich mich dahin immer nur die Sonnabende und Sonntage retten kann. Es heißt Tribschen und ist mir bereits ganz heimisch [...]. Liebster Freund, was ich dort lerne und schaue, höre und verstehe, ist unbeschreiblich. Schopenhauer und Goethe, Aeschylus und Pindar leben noch.

More than with his academic colleagues in Basle, Nietzsche found passionate, intellectual discussion with the Wagners. Wagner played parts of his music to him on the piano and gave him his theoretical writings to read, of which the treatises *On State and Religion* (*Über Staat und Religion*), *German Art and Politics* (*Deutsche Kunst und Politik*), *Opera and Drama* (*Oper und Drama*), *The Art-work of the Future* (*Das Kunstwerk der Zukunft*) and the celebration essay 'Beethoven' appealed strongly to the young professor.[92] Nietzsche was very impressed by their intellectual depth and amazed that Wagner's qualities were hardly noticed by German academics.[93] Moreover, he was overall pleasantly surprised with the 'entire synchronisation of our main interests' ('die völlige Gleichstimmung unsrer Hauptinteressen')[94] and Wagner's approval of his inaugural lecture on Homer's personality.[95]

That Wagner agreed totally with Nietzsche's views, as Cosima Wagner wrote,[96] is remarkable though, given that Wagner adhered to the Wolffian tradition that maintained the view that there is not one author of the *Iliad* and *Odyssey*, while Nietzsche challenged this view in his inaugural lecture. Perhaps, Nietzsche was too excited about the approval to notice the fact that his and Wagner's aesthetic ideas did not totally agree. He had his lecture printed and bounded in order to give it as a Christmas present to Cosima Wagner, complete with a personal dedication. Perhaps he just did not yet

---

90 Nietzsche cherished the dream of a Epicurean garden, where men would meet for intellectual discussion and friendship. See Janz (1978a), Volume 2, p. 265ff. The Tribschen-times formed one of Nietzsche's happiest memories, even in 1888, long after he had broken with Wagner (EH 'Clever' 5, p. 92/KSA 6.288f).
91 3 September 1869 (KSB 3. 52).
92 Nietzsche to Gustav Krug, 4 August 1869 (KSB 3. 37–39).
93 Cf. to Erwin Rohde, 15 August 1869 (KSB 3. 41–43).
94 Nietzsche to his mother, 23 August 1869 (KSB 3. 43–45, p. 45).
95 Nietzsche's inaugural lecture was originally called 'Homer's Personality' ('Die Persönlichkeit Homers'). Nietzsche re-baptized the lecture into 'Homer und die Klassische Philologie'.
96 Cosima Wagner to Nietzsche, 26 August 1869 (KGB II/2, p. 34), Cf. Nietzsche to Erwin Rohde, 3 September 1869 (KSB 3. 52).

fully comprehend how different Wagner's view of Greek culture in fact was. This, however, began to dawn upon Nietzsche in February 1870, after Wagner had come to Basle to hear him give the lecture *Socrates and Tragedy*.

February 1870: Nietzsche's diffidence vis-à-vis Wagner's favouritism

After hearing and re-reading the lecture *Socrates and Tragedy*, Richard Wagner wrote Nietzsche to tell him about his impressions. Cosima Wagner also wrote a particularly long letter with her response. Richard and Cosima urge Nietzsche to write a longer account on the 'current problem', which Nietzsche, referring to the 'grave problem for Germany' took up as a matter of aesthetics (and not as a matter of race and politics).[97] Wagner advises that Nietzsche should by all means continue his philological work to help him bring about the 'great Renaissance', describing this as the event in which 'Plato embraces Homer and Homer, filled with Plato's Ideas, only now truly becomes the greatest Homer' ('Platon den Homer umarmt, und Homer, von Platons Ideen erfüllt, nun erst recht der allergrösste Homer wird').[98] Nietzsche reacted with mixed feelings. He felt flattered, yet indicated that he also feared this enthusiasm, as transpires in the following letter to Erwin Rohde:

> I gave a lecture on Socrates and tragedy that has produced disquiet and misunderstanding. On the other hand, it has tied the bond with my friends from Tribschen even closer. If I do not watch out, I shall turn into walking hope: Richard Wagner gave me to understand in the most touching way, which fate he sees designated for me. This is all very frightening.

> Ich habe hier einen Vortrag über Socrates und die Tragödie gehalten, der Schrecken und Missverständnisse erregt hat. Dagegen hat sich durch ihn das Band mit meinen Tribschener Freunden noch enger geknüpft. Ich werde noch zur wandelnden Hoffnung: auch Richard Wagner hat mir in der rührendsten Weise zu erkennen gegeben, welche Bestimmung er mir vorgezeichnet sieht. Dies ist alles sehr beängstigend.[99]

However carefully this phrased, this remark displays a conflict with Wagner, and this for the first time since the beginning of their friendship.[100] His lecture caused disquiet

---

97 Richard Wagner to Nietzsche, 4 February 1870 (KGB II/2, p. 137f.) and around 12 February 1870 (KGB II/2, p. 145f); Cosima Wagner to Nietzsche, 5 February 1870 (KGB II/2, pp. 138–145); BT, pp. 13–14/1. 23f. Cf. Riedel (1995), pp. 45–61, pp. 53f.

98 Richard Wagner to Nietzsche, around 12 February 1870 (KGB II/2, p. 145f).

99 Nietzsche to Erwin Rohde, end of January and 15 February 1870 (KSB 3. 95). This part of the letter is written mid-February, in response to Wagner's letter of 12 February.

100 According to Landerer and Schuster (2005), the first chilliness in the Nietzsche-Wagner friendship is found in Cosima Wagner's diaries of May 1871, followed by a harsh remark in August 1871. In July 1871, she writes in reaction to a letter from Nietzsche (which has perished): 'Letter of Professor

and misunderstanding, but also strengthened the bond with Richard and Cosima. Nietzsche was touched, but also genuinely frightened by Richard Wagner's reaction.

Against the claim that Nietzsche may just be trying to attract attention, I want to state that Nietzsche's zealous support for Wagner was accompanied by an, albeit 'secret', scepticism, from this moment onwards. This implies that Nietzsche's true, unconditional Wagnerism only lasted from November 1868 until February 1870, and that, while the friendship was still fresh, it was already slowly on the wane. The 'misunderstanding' that the lecture has caused also points to Wagner's misunderstanding. Wagner had not understood the significance of Nietzsche's interpretation of Greek culture – as his definition of the 'great Renaissance', in which Plato and Homer embrace each other, shows. Against the radiant Olympic, and 'naive' Homeric world that German philosophers and artists in general held to be typically 'Greek', Nietzsche defended Greek art and culture as a 'tragic pessimistic' culture in *Socrates and Tragedy*. (Additionally, Wagner's definition of Homer is complicated and inapt, even without his misunderstanding of Nietzsche.) In addition, one of Nietzsche's central claims was that pre-Socratic culture was the high point of Greek culture. For that reason, he associated Wagner's art with that *tragic* culture, not with 'Homeric' or 'Socratic' cultures – which were, in Nietzsche's view, necessary stages in human history, but Apollonian cultures, of which the cultural decadence of Modernity was an upshot. To Wagner, apparently, it was all one kettle of fish.[101]

In the February letter to Rohde, Nietzsche also emphasizes his ambition to expand his philological horizons with art and philosophy, claiming his autonomy expressly.[102] Nietzsche was of the opinion that German philology should change from purely textual reconstruction to the reconstruction and historical description of ancient Greek philosophy. In addition, he understood that he wanted to speak his own mind, and

---

Nietzsche. Richard has spilled more love than he has received in this relationship too' ('Brief von Professor Nietzsche. Auch in dieser Lebensbeziehung hat Richard mehr Liebe verschwendet als er empfangen,' 15 July 1871, cited after Benders and Oettermann 2000, p. 245). Moreover, during a holiday with his sister and von Gersdorff in Gimmelwald, Nietzsche writes the poem 'To Melancholy' ('An die Melancholie'), which seems sign of a gradually growing critical attitude. Landerer and Schuster (2002) state that it is questionable whether Hanslick plays a role in this growing criticism, because Nietzsche's aesthetic insights still agree with Wagner (p. 253 f.). However, Nietzsche's aesthetic and cultural insights differ from Wagner's in 1871, not under the influence of Hanslick, but because of their different estimation of the Greeks. The musical problem originates mainly in Nietzsche's studies of Greek rhythmics, not in Hanslick's formalism.

101 His hesitancy notwithstanding, Nietzsche embarked on the 'Renaissance' project. He proposed to resign from the university to become the editor of the *Bayreuther Blätter*, which Wagner planned to publish as a means to propagate his music and philosophy. The first issue only came out in 1878 and Hans von Bülow was the editor. See for more information on the *Bayreuther Blätter* as ideological tool of anti-Semitism: Hein (1996).

102 To Wilhelm Vischer, January 1871 (KSB 3. 174–178).

voice others' (Wagner's, for example) only when his mind would be in unison with it. This awareness brought him to the following prophecy, in the same letter to Rohde:

> In contrast, when the time is there, I want to express myself as seriously and as candidly as possible. Science, art, and philosophy grow together in me so much now that in any case I shall give birth to centaurs one day.

> Dagegen will ich mich, wenn es Zeit ist, so Ernst und freimüthig äussern, wie nur möglich. Wissenschaft Kunst und Philosophie wachsen jetzt so sehr in mir zusammen, dass ich jedenfalls einmal Centauren gebären werde.[103]

It is remarkable that the first sign of Wagner-resistance is contextualized by the famous line 'I shall give birth to centaurs one day'. This triggers the question of whether the image of the centaur is an image that confirms or opposes Wagner as of a man of wisdom and art, an artist who expressed or failed to express the metaphysical, philosophical truth about life in his music.[104]

Nietzsche also wrote back to Cosima and Richard Wagner, besides visiting them on 12 and 13 February 1870. Unfortunately, this letter has not survived. It caused Cosima to note in her diary that she and Richard worried about Nietzsche's spirits, and to write to Nietzsche that his last visit had made her 'melancholic' ('*wehmütig*').[105] Richard Wagner ascribed Nietzsche's mood to Schopenhauer's 'bad influence' on young people. Remarkably, he stated that Schopenhauer's pessimism was 'a form of thought, of perception' ('eine Form des Denkens, der Anschauung') and the last thing young people had to do was take it as guiding principle of their personal lives.[106] In other words, the metaphysical depth Wagner sought to evoke in his music was *not* of the deeply felt Greek and Schopenhauerian tragic-pessimistic nature Nietzsche experienced and took personally. Nietzsche and Wagner thus not only differed in aesthetics, but also in metaphysics. Wagner appreciated Schopenhauer's defence of music as the highest of all fine arts, but did not draw all the consequences of his pessimism. Nietzsche's plea for the aestheticization of culture and Wagner's plea for culture's mythologization, therefore, had a different and unbridgeable outlook from the beginning, no matter how hard Nietzsche tried to bridge *and* cover up the gap, of which he was well aware.

---

103 End of January and 15 February 1870 (KSB 3. 95).

104 Strikingly similar passages can be found in a letter to Carl Fuchs of June 1878 (KSB 5.335) and in a letter to Mathilde Maier of 15 July 1878 (KSB 5. 338).

105 Cosima von Bülow to Nietzsche, 20 February 1870 (KGB II/2, p. 151).

106 17 February 1870, Borchmeyer and Salaquarda (1994), vol. 2, p. 1156; Benders and Oetermann (2000), p. 214.

Conclusion

Nietzsche's musical taste was long in favour of the 'Old German School' of Schubert, Schumann, Brahms, and Mendelssohn. His Wagner adherence and interest in the New German School of music only started in November 1868. A neglected, yet important, factor in Nietzsche's Wagnerian turn was his new status as musical 'connoisseur' and journalist, a position which made him look and listen with different, more professional eyes and ears while sitting in the theatre's press-gallery. Nietzsche's enthusiasm for the *Tristan* and *Mastersingers* overtures in October 1868 was stirred by this new VIP status. This new status fitted his ambition of climbing the social ladder in Leipzig well. His interest in Wagner and modern music was prepared by his friendships with Krug, Hüffer, Ernst Windisch, and Sophie Ritschl as well as by his encounter with Hanslick, Ehlert, Marbach, and Jahn. In his *Sophocles* essay of 1864, and in the letter of 8 October of 1868 to Rohde, Nietzsche had expressed regard for Wagner. This was first premissed on the view of Wagner as rejuvenator of Greek tragedy, and then on the Schopenhauerian ethics his music conveyed. However, only after meeting Wagner on 8 November 1868, did he show true adherence to Wagner. In February 1870, Nietzsche expressed doubt about Wagner, fuelled by the latter's misunderstanding of the Greeks and Nietzsche's desire for intellectual autonomy.

Nietzsche's late turn to Wagner and his subsequent early scepticism prompt the question whether Nietzsche was ever a 'true' Wagner devotee at all. If he ever was, then not for the fourteen years Nietzsche-scholars still often suppose, but for fifteen months at best, to wit from November 1868 until February 1870. From then on, his Wagnerism was not unconditional, but accompanied by a 'secret scepticism'. This has serious consequences for the interpretation of *The Birth of Tragedy*. If Nietzsche was much more sceptical of Wagner than acknowledged to date, the Wagner-enthusiasm of that book as well as its indebtedness to Wagner's 'Beethoven' essay must be reassessed. Hollinrake's remark that 'Beethoven's [that is, Wagner's centenary 'Beethoven' essay of 1870, MP] influence on *Die Geburt der Tragödie* was [...] less than Nietzsche diplomatically made it out to be'[107] is not sufficient, then. In fact, the theoretical influence of Wagner's 1870 'Beethoven' essay on *The Birth of Tragedy* is considerably larger than hitherto acknowledged. Yet, it is also true that Nietzsche was much more critical of Wagner in his debut-book than scholars have recognized until today – both of his musical theory and his musical achievements. *The Birth of Tragedy*, then, must be reexamined in view of its diagnosis of modern culture, the cultural powers ascribed to Wagner's music, and, specifically, the identification made between Wagner's music and Dionysus. The question must be raised whether Wagner's music dramas indeed

---

107 Hollinrake (1982), p. 174.

expressed the Greek, Dionysian, aesthetic view of art, science and life, according to Nietzsche, or that their 'Greek' nature was, in fact, not 'Greek' enough.

This will be done in chapter 4. First, I shall discuss Wagner's 'Beethoven' essay, in the next chapter, and Nietzsche's reception of this text, in chapter 3.

Chapter 2
Germanizing music and culture: Richard Wagner's 'Beethoven' essay

Introduction

In his 'Beethoven' essay, Richard Wagner not only advanced his own philosophy of music, but *the* philosophy of music, Nietzsche maintained.[1] Moreover, he considered it to be the book in which the cultural spirit that he envisaged for the future was outlined. As he wrote to Erwin Rohde:

> A book of Wagner's which recently appeared on 'Beethoven' will possibly indicate to you a lot about what I currently want from the future. Read it, it is a revelation of the spirit in which *we* – we! – shall live in the future.[2]

> Ein eben erschienenes Buch von Wagner über Beethoven wird Dir Vieles andeuten können, was ich jetzt von der Zukunft will. Lies es, es ist eine Offenbarung des Geistes, in dem wir – wir! – in der Zukunft leben werden.

Nietzsche made this remark in a letter, which largely centres on the idea of grounding a 'new, Greek academy'. Similar to Wagner's aim to break with institutionalized art, Nietzsche fantasized about setting up a new university ruled by the desire for art and truth instead of by bureaucracy and moneymaking.

Inspired by Wagner's 'Beethoven' essay, Nietzsche's view of the future for German culture was an optimistic one. It made him believe that Wagner was the 'pioneer in the jungle of a depraved paradise'. While Italian music and French philosophy had degraded the whole of European art with their moral and textual approaches, Wagner's German music would turn European decadence around by refocusing on the artistic expression of the tragic truth of life.[3] As I hope to show below, this line of thought, which dominates the last ten chapters of *The Birth of Tragedy*, is greatly indebted to Wagner's idea that Beethoven's *Ninth Symphony* saved European music from the 'Roman' tendency to superficiality, commercialism, fashion, and formalism.[4] His ability

---

1 To Richard Wagner, 10 November 1870 (KSB 3, pp. 156–157). See also Nietzsche to Carl von Gersdorff, 7 November 1870 (KSB 3, p. 154ff).

2 15 December 1870 (KSB 3, pp. 165–167).

3 See for example ASC 6 (p. 10/KSA 1.20); BT 20 (p. 95–97/KSA 1.129–131); WB 4 (KSA 1.446–453); GMD (KSA 1.531–532); EH BT 1 (p. 107–108/KSA 1.309); EH BT 4 (p. 110–111/KSA 1.313–314).

4 With his *Ninth Symphony*, the 'Choral' symphony, Beethoven reformed symphonic music, as he had previously done with the ossified sonata scheme. In the grand finale of Beethoven's Ninth, the chorus sings Friedrich Schiller's poem *Ode to Joy* (*An die Freude*). It was the first symphony in the history of music that inserted a chorus. In 1985, this finale (with the famous line 'Alle Menschen werden Brüder')

to descend to a greater depth and to express this in his music made Beethoven not only a 'genius' according to Wagner, but also a true 'German'. In order words, the ability to express the universal is a typically national, German trait, he claims.

This chapter delineates Wagner's intersecting philosophies of music and culture as expressed in his centenary 'Beethoven' essay, viewing them from the paradoxical relation of universalism and nationalism. Both Beethoven's *Ninth Symphony* and Wagner's symphonic music drama, with which Wagner aimed to preserve and continue Beethoven's musical legacy, must be seen in the light of the longer northern opposition to the Italian style. At the time that Beethoven composed his *Ninth Symphony*, between 1822 and 1824, Vienna was engrossed by Rossini and the Italian opera. Beethoven, and the members of the New German School in his footsteps, refused to bow to this trend. Wagner's art continues the resistance to the Italian fashion, and the 'philosophy of music' developed here harbours an important programme for the shaping of a national, German culture with larger, European impact. Both features were to an important extent incorporated by Nietzsche in *The Birth of Tragedy*, as I hope to show in chapter 4. In order to be able to demonstrate that Wagner was the book's primary theoretical source in that chapter, I discuss Wagner's 'Beethoven' essay below. I do so by way of a close reading, which starts from Wagner's concepts of 'paradise' and 'reformation'.

In focusing on these concepts, I deviate from previous studies on Wagner's musical theory. The great and insightful studies of Borchmeyer (1982) and Kropfinger (1991) already alerted us to Wagner's ideas concerning Greece as the main model of the ideal, mytho-poetic, and musical culture; his critique of Italian opera; his innovation that the drama is a visual 'projection' of the chorus; and, considering the productive genius of the artist, his idea that a musical experience stimulates the imagination (or 'dream-organ').[5] However, despite their concentration on Wagner's musical and dramatic aesthetics, Borchmeyer and Kropfinger neglect his cultural ideals and the image of future culture as a 'paradise' where man retrieves his 'original innocence'. Kropfinger does point to the fact that the serenity ('Heiterkeit') in Beethoven's works, as Wagner understands in his 'Beethoven' essay, has to do with 'innocence regained' and is bound up with Beethoven's belief in 'man's original goodness'.[6] However, he fails to see the cultural implications of this 'innocent melody'.

Furthermore, in his analysis of Wagner's view of history, Kropfinger advances the more or less dualistic view that Wagner was a cultural optimist with a revolutionary, utopian, and dialectical historical view, who with his essay *The Public and Popularity*

---

was chosen by European leaders as the national anthem of the European Union. This is an ironic choice with regard to Wagner's view of the major artistic and cultural importance of precisely this Beethoven symphony. Seen from a Wagnerian perspective, the choral finale the opposite of what the European Union at present establishes led by commercial and political interests rather than metaphysical and musical joy.

5 Wherever I speak of 'imagination' in this book, I mean imagination in its aesthetic modulation.

6 Kropfinger (1991), p. 66.

(*Publikum und Popularität*, 1878) turned into a cultural pessimist without faith in the revolution. Kropfinger thus ignores the historical view articulated in the 'Beethoven' essay. There, Wagner has substituted his revolutionary, dialectical view for a more moderate and 'reformatory' view of history, which is both optimistic and Romantic-utopian. Hence, whereas Borchmeyer and Kropfinger overlook Wagner's appreciation of 'paradise' and 'reformation', these terms will be central to my analysis below – alongside the framework built by the opposition of 'Germany' and 'depth' on the one hand and 'Italy', 'France', and 'superficiality' on the other.

To contextualize the term 'paradise' and to clarify the substance of Schopenhauer's influence on Wagner's philosophy of music, I first outline Schopenhauer's philosophical pessimism as a philosophy between 'hell' and 'paradise', and the philosophy of music that goes with this. In the Wagner studies Schopenhauer's influence on him is sometimes overstated or misrepresented.[7] As I show below, in his 'Beethoven' essay, Wagner cheered Schopenhauer mainly for his defence of music as the highest form of art. But whereas Schopenhauer's philosophy of music relies entirely on the tonal system, hailing Rossini's operas and the individual singer as musical highlights, Wagner precisely sought to uproot the classical tonal system, opposing Italian opera for its emphasis on the individual singer. And even though Wagner repeatedly states in his 'Beethoven' essay that music conveys the truth, it remains unclear what he means by this, and thus what the status of metaphysics and epistemology precisely are, in relation to art. This chapter claims that (rather than his metaphysics and philosophy of music), Wagner adopted Schopenhauer's concept of 'paradise' as 'childlike innocence', mixing this with Schopenhauer's theories of the genius, dreams, ghost-seeing, and clairvoyance so as to construct a new theory of the genius' creativity, expanding this with, amongst many other things, Rousseau's claim that humanity is 'originally good'. As we shall see in chapters three and four, it is precisely at this Rousseauian point that Nietzsche became sceptical of his hero.

Schopenhauer's philosophy between 'hell' and 'paradise'

In *The World as Will and Representation I* (*Die Welt als Wille und Vorstellung*, 1819),[8] Schopenhauer presents a metaphysics, which claims to successfully coalesce Plato's doctrine of the Ideas and Kant's ontological distinction between the 'things-in-themselves' (*'Dinge-an-sich'*) and the objects as they appear to us. It does so by identifying Kant's concept of the 'thing-in-itself' as 'Will' and squeezing the transcendent realm of

---

7 Magee tends to put his own 'feelings', 'suspicions', and 'experiences' forward as evidence of the closeness of Wagner's and Schopenhauer's aesthetics, which is, to say the least, unconvincing (Magee 2000, p. 128 and p. 184).
8 Henceforth WWR I/WWR II with paragraph- and page-number.

Platonic ideas in between the metaphysical and the phenomenal world. Unlike Kant, Schopenhauer thus states that the essence of things can be known and that it is the Will. The Will is a blind force and the motor of life, which by its nature always strives for satisfaction. And as soon as this is reached, the Will desires something else again. Hence, the Will's endless striving thus does not bring human life any further. Instead, it makes the World a living 'hell' and human life meaningless and painful. The only solution is to 'forget' the Will in aesthetic illusion or 'deny' it with the help of ascetic Buddhist training. With this pessimistic view of life and the calls for self-denial and passivity, Schopenhauer's philosophy opposes Kant, Hegel, Weimar Classicism, and Marx's optimism.

However, *The World as Will and Representation II*, published in 1844, reveals that Schopenhauer was not entirely insensitive to the Romantic views that seeped through Europe's intelligentsia. There, he recognizes the desire for paradise as a common desire of adults, claiming that the child 'knows', whereas the adult 'desires': '[...] childhood is the time of innocence and happiness, the paradise of life, the lost Eden, on which we look back longingly through the whole remaining course of our life' (WWR II 31, p. 394/'ist die Kindheit die Zeit der Unschuld und des Glückes, das Paradies des Lebens, das verlorene Eden, auf welches wir, unsern ganzen übrigen Lebensweg hindurch, sehnsüchtig zurückblicken,' p. 460). And: 'the basis of that [childlike, MP] happiness is that in childhood our whole existence lies much more in knowing than in willing,' (WWR II 31, p. 394/'Die Basis jenes Glückes aber ist, daß in der Kindheit unser ganzes Daseyn viel mehr im Erkennen, als im Wollen liegt,' p.460). Schopenhauer goes on to claim that children live in paradise, and adults can only return to the joy of childhood by way of aesthetic illusion. Adults can only experience paradise in the passing moment of aesthetic joy or 'artistic knowledge'. In that moment, they forget that they are willing and suffering beings. Instead, they achieve a deeper insight into the unity of all things, and enjoy the beauty of aesthetic semblance, soothing the pain caused by the endless striving of the Will. Schopenhauer quotes Goethe to underline his point: 'What in life does us annoy/we in picture do enjoy' (WWR II 30, p. 372; 'Was im Leben uns verdrießt,/Man im Bilde gern genießt', p. 433). Art comforts our pain, because it makes us forget.[9]

Goethe, Schiller, Schopenhauer, Wagner, and Nietzsche all regarded the transformation of pain into joy as the chief task of art. This is art understood as 'serious play'.[10] The four of them also hold to the achievement and expression of the 'objective' or 'sym-

---

9 However, that is not all: in order to enjoy oneself, every person strives for his objective representation: 'every person [...] needs to be apprehended only purely objectively, and made the object of a description or sketch [...] in order to appear interesting, delightful, and enviable [...]. Thus he [every person, MP] expects his life to take the form of an interesting work of fiction' (WWR II 30, p. 374).

10 'Greek serenity' ('Griechische Heiterkeit'), hence, is pain transformed into joyful play. That is what Greek tragedy is, or as Deleuze put it beautifully in his book on Nietzsche: '*the tragic* is the aesthetic form of joy' (Gilles Deleuze 1983, p. 17).

bolic' in art. In that sense, neither Schopenhauer, nor Wagner nor Nietzsche is 'Romantic', at least if we keep to Goethe's definition of it as the form of art that is unable to surpass the level of subjectivity. A true artist must strive for the objective or general in things, as Goethe articulated it to Eckermann.[11] He must bring out the general in the particular, the symbolic in daily life, with the purpose of expressing the truth (which is discursively inexpressible) and to posit himself as someone who strives for 'progress'. This ambition is mandatory, according to Goethe, so as not to fall back into subjectivity and artificiality, which are signs of 'weakness' and 'decadence'. 'Progress,' on the other hand, hints at 'energy' and a 'strong will'.[12]

Schopenhauer's concept of 'symbol' ('*Abbild*') expresses something similar. Calling music a 'symbol' of the Will, he considers music to be the representation of the objective and universal truth as opposed to the expression of particular and subjective feelings.[13] The artist that achieves this 'symbolic' level is considered a 'genius' by Schopenhauer: 'always to see the universal in the particular is precisely the fundamental characteristic of genius' (WWR II 31, p. 379; 'Im Einzelnen stets das Allgemeine zu sehen, ist gerade der Grundzug des Genies', p. 442), and: 'objectivity alone qualifies one for becoming an artist' (WWR II 30, p. 374; 'Nur die Objektivität befähigt zum Künstler', p. 435). In the state of objective perception, the genius forgets his pessimism, feeling serene and joyful instead. Nonetheless, this 'supra-earthly' ('überirdisch') serenity is united with melancholy: 'in tristitia hilaris, in hilaritate tristis' (WWR II 31, p. 383/ p. 443).

While adducing this ability of the genius to attain the level of 'objectivity', Wagner imports Schopenhauer's claim that a genius is 'serious' in a supernatural sense. This seriousness is characterized by its pursuit of the objective and theoretical: 'for such a seriousness of the individual, falling outside him in the objective, is something foreign to human nature, something unnatural, properly speaking supernatural' (WWR II 31, pp. 384–385; 'Denn ein solcher außerhalb des Individu, in das Objektive fallender Ernst desselben ist etwas der menschlichen Natur Fremdes, etwas Unnatürliches, eigentlich Uebernatürliches', p. 448). Such a genius, he continues, is a truly 'great man'. All others are destined to be only 'small' men. Small men may be talented, but they prefer to please their fellow men instead of finding the truth. A true genius never thinks of his own interest, but only of the interest of humankind. The genius 'sacrifices his personal welfare to the objective end; he simply cannot do otherwise, because

---

11 29 January 1826, MA 19, pp. 155–156. See for a more elaborative account on the similarities in the aesthetics of Weimar Classicsim, Schopenhauer, Wagner, and Nietzsche: Prange (2006-2).

12 29 January 1826, MA 19, pp. 155–156. Cf. 11 June 1825, MA 19, p. 144. Cf. Goethe's definition of 'style' ('Stil') in his essay 'Simple Imitation, Manner, Style' ('Einfache Nachahmung, Manier, Stil', 1789, HA XII, pp. 30–35, esp. pp. 32–34/*Collected Works* Vol. 3, 1986, pp. 71–74); See also R. H. Stephenson (2003), p. 82.

13 Confusion can be caused, because in this regard Schopenhauer uses 'representation' and 'expression' interchangeably.

there lies his seriousness' (WWR II 31 p. 385; 'sein persönliches Wohl opfert er dem objektiven Zweck: er kann eben nicht anders; weil dort sein Ernst liegt', p.448). In his concentration on the objective, the genius resembles the child, or, as Schopenhauer says: '[...] every child is to a certain extent a genius, and every genius to a certain extent a child' (WWR II 31, p. 395; 'Wirklich ist jedes Kind gewissermaßen ein Genie, und jedes Genie gewissermaßen ein Kind', p. 461). What they share is 'naiveté and sublime ingenuousness' (WWR II 31, p.395.; 'Naivetät und erhabenen Einfalt', p.461). As we shall see further on in this chapter, Wagner will adopt this characterization of the genius in his description of Beethoven.

Hence, Goethe and Schiller, and Schopenhauer, Wagner, and Nietzsche after them aim to gain a purchase on life by means of aesthetic appearance. At the very least, they appreciate aesthetic appearance rather than conceptual art and discursive thinking as the proper gateway towards reality, and, accordingly, as the suitable instrument to increase symbolic, artistic, epistemological and cultural powers. To understand life from the level of the symbolic is a precondition of great art, Nietzsche explicitly states, and modern decadence in art and (thus) culture is characterized by the lack of such understanding.[14] Interestingly, they all have special expectations of music, also Goethe and Schiller, whose interest in music, more specifically in the possibilities of opera, is generally underexposed. I shall come back to their interest in music several times in the course of this book. For now, I wish to remark that their appreciation of music is mainly directed at its possibilities for enhancing dramatic effect. On the other hand, Schopenhauer, Wagner, and Nietzsche attach a metaphysical, epistemological importance to music, by which they hoist it to the top of the fine arts.

How, according to Schopenhauer, does music express true knowledge and bring us the childlike happiness we all desire? What makes music surpass the other fine arts in symbolic and metaphysical powers? And is all music so powerful, or only certain types of music?

Schopenhauer's philosophy of music

Wagner understood Beethoven's music as Schopenhauerian philosophy set to music *avant la lettre*. But Schopenhauer did not like Wagner's music at all. For him, Rossini was the best composer. One day in 1854, Wagner sent his friend François Wille to Schopenhauer to bring him the *Nibelung* libretto, but Schopenhauer told Wagner's friend to bring the composer the message that he would 'stay loyal to Rossini and Mozart'. As so many adversaries of Wagner, he believed that Wagner was a better poet

---

14 'Understanding the world in "symbols" is the precondition of a great art' ('Verständniß der Welt in "Symbolen" ist die Voraussetzung einer großen Kunst', 9[92], KSA 7.308).

than musician.[15] Nevertheless, the composer stayed loyal to Schopenhauer. That is to say, he used Schopenhauer's philosophical justification of music as the highest fine art and as a matter of genius and truth to his own advantage. Until Mozart and Romanticism, music and composing were generally perceived as activities everybody practised, and a craft rather than an art.[16] An important aim of Wagner was to further music's emancipation as an art form, created by geniuses comparable to Leonardo da Vinci and Shakespeare. Geniuses should be allowed to create autonomously and not by royal commission. Using Schopenhauer to build this case, his music dramas produced results that were very different from what Schopenhauer had envisioned, however. What did he envision, exactly?

In *The World as Will and Representation I*, Schopenhauer enquires into the aesthetic effects that music imparts unto the beholder in order to reveal its universality and immediacy.[17] He also discusses the tonal system and the different musical forms to anchor the origin of music in the Will and the composer's unconscious. Problems turn up when Schopenhauer notes:

> Moreover, I regard it as necessary, in order that a man may assent with genuine conviction to the explanation of the significance of music here to be given, that he should often listen to music with constant reflection on this; and this again requires that he should be already very familiar with the whole thought which I expound. (WWR I 52, p. 257)

> Ueberdies halte ich es, um der hier zu gebenden Darstellung der Bedeutung der Musik mit ächter Ueberzeugung seinen Beifall geben zu können, für nothwendig, daß man oft mit anhalternder Reflexion auf dieselbe der Musik zuhöre, und hiezu wieder ist erforderlich, daß man mit dem ganzen von mir dargestellten Gedanken schon sehr vertraut sei. (WWR I 52, p. 340)

Obviously, the approach Schopenhauer suggests is inconsistent; it implies that music listeners have to abstain from the immediate effect of music in order to understand his theory of the immediacy of music. Nonetheless, let us proceed as the philosopher requires.

Schopenhauer assigns a *status aparte* to music in comparison to the other fine arts. He credits music with such a unique status for two reasons. The first reason is that the effect of music on 'man's innermost nature' is much stronger than that of all other art forms. The second reason is that music has an 'analogous' relationship to the world. Both reasons are strongly connected, for music owes its strong effect to this

---

15 Klaus Kropfinger (1991), p. 130.

16 Donelan (2008), pp. 24–30.

17 Although music plays a central role in Schopenhauer's system, he only dedicates § 52 of the first edition of his book to it. As the closing paragraph of book III, it returns to the beginning of the book, in which the Will was the key topic, and it prepares the transition to book IV, in which an ascetic ethics is advocated as most effective means for redeeming humankind from the Will. He continues his musical reflections in WWR II § 39.

special, analogous relationship to the world. According to Schopenhauer, the visual ('plastic') arts copy the 'ideas' of things, but music is itself an idea of the Will. Music 'never expresses the phenomenon, but only the inner nature, the in-itself, of every phenomenon, the Will itself' (WWR I 52, p. 261/'sie nie die Erscheinung, sondern allein das innere Wesen, das Ansich aller Erscheinung, den Willen selbst, ausspricht', p. 345). Music reveals the thing itself, whereas poetry and plastic arts divulge nothing but shadows, or the phenomena. Schopenhauer concludes: 'accordingly, we would just as well call the world embodied music as embodied will' (WWR I 52, pp. 262–263/'Man könnte demnach die Welt ebenso wohl verkörperte Musik, als verkörperten Willen nennen', p. 347). Therefore, the effect of music also strikes humankind deeper than the visual arts, for the latter only evoke pleasure. Music fills the inner being of man with 'profound pleasure' ('*innige Freude*') in revealing the deepest recesses of his nature. For this reason, music is much more than 'an unconscious exercise in arithmetic in which the mind does not know it is counting' (WWR I 52, pp. 262–263/*exercitium arithmeticae occultum nescientis se numerare animi*', p.347), as Leibniz defined it.[18] According to Schopenhauer, Leibniz's definition only defines the outer side of music, the 'Apollonian' or 'architectural' form as Nietzsche labels it in *The Birth of Tragedy*. It does not offer a satisfactory explanation for the 'joy' music confers.

Against Leibniz's definition, Schopenhauer defines music as 'an unconscious exercise in metaphysics in which the mind does not know it is philosophizing' (WWR I 52, p. 264/'*Musica est exercitium metaphysices occultum nescientis se philosophari animi*', p. 350) and philosophy as its conceptual counterpart: 'philosophy is nothing but a complete and accurate repetition and expression of the inner nature of the world in very general concepts' (WWR I 52, p. 264/'die Philosophie [ist] nichts Anderes [...], als eine vollständige und richtige Wiederholung und Aussprechung des Wesens der Welt, in sehr allgemeinen Begriffen', p. 349). Schopenhauer does not have a very high regard for the theoretical and creative qualities of philosophy: 'philosophy can never do more than interpret and explain what is present and at hand; it can never do more than bring to the distinct, abstract knowledge of the faculty of reason the inner nature of the world' (WWR I 53, p. 271/'Die Philosophie kann nirgends mehr thun, als das Vorhandene deuten und erklären, das Wesen der Welt, welches in concreto, d.h. als Gefühl, Jedem verständlich sich ausspricht, zur deutlichen, abstrakten Erkenntniß der Vernunft bringen', p. 358). But this is quite similar to how Wagner views the relation

---

18 Schopenhauer may also be drawing upon Schiller, especially Schiller's review of Matthison's poems (1794). There, Schiller distinguishes between the discursive and the musical aspects of poetry. By the latter term, he designates 'the power – shared in some measure by all the arts but possessed in supreme degree by music – of "symbolizing through analogical outer movements the inner movements of the psyche"' (Schiller 1982 [1967], p. xxviii/'Nun besteht aber der ganze Effekt der Musik (als schöner und nicht bloß angenehmer Kunst) darin, die innern Bewegungen des Gemüts durch analogische äußere zu begleiten und zu versinnlichen,' NA 22, pp. 265–283, p. 272).

between Beethoven's music and Schopenhauer's philosophy. The question is whether Nietzsche conceived his intellectual task in relation to Wagner's art in a similar way.

Schopenhauer on opera and melody

Hence, in Schopenhauer's view, music's uniqueness lies in its universality. Therefore, music should never 'stick too closely to the words', because in that case 'it is endeavouring to speak a language not its own'. Lyrical music such as opera could easily fall into this trap, but to Schopenhauer, the endeavours of opera composer Rossini are exemplary: 'no one has kept so [sic!] free from this mistake as Rossini; hence his music speaks its *own* language so distinctly and purely that it requires no words at all'.[19] In *The World as Will and Representation II*, he expands this view of Rossini's opera to opera in general: 'The music of an opera [...] has a wholly independent, separate [...] existence by itself [...]; it can therefore be completely effective even without the text'.[20]

According to Schopenhauer, music expresses nature, and the will that drives it. In the ground bass tones, the lowest gradations of nature are recognizable and the relationship between ground bass and the higher tones is analogous with the principle of nature that all bodies and organisms evolve out of the planet's mass. He sees the whole gamut of ideas, in which the Will objectifies itself, in harmony and melody. However, harmony does not possess the same 'sequence and continuity of progress' as the voice that sings the melody. In the melody, sang by the soprano's 'principal voice' in particular, one thought is developed from beginning to end. In this, the female singer even stands out against the most powerful orchestral accompaniment. The melody constitutes the unity of a piece of music, and it does so in analogy with the highest objectification of the Will, which for Schopenhauer, against instinct, is in humanity's ratio and the rational order of life. However, music in the end exceeds the rational side of life, because it is also the language of emotion. As such, melody portrays 'every movement of the will' including 'its satisfaction [...]'.[21] The melody expresses in symbols (hence, on a general level) desire and satisfaction, pain and lust. Their inner nature, their Will, is speaking in the melody. Therefore, in Schopenhauer's view, the melody stands for humanity. Schopenhauer argues that 'the four voices or parts of all harmony, that is, bass, tenor, alto, and soprano, or fundamental note, third, fifth, and octave, correspond to the four grades in the series of existences, hence to the mineral, plant, and animal kingdoms, and to man' (WWR II 39, p. 447/'Die vier Stimmen aller Harmonie, als Baß, Tenor, Alt, und Sopran, oder Grundton, Terz, Quinte und Oktave, entsprechen den vier Abstufungen in der Reihe der Wesen, also dem Mineralreich, Pflanzenreich,

---

19 WWR I 52, p. 262/p. 346.
20 WWR II 39, p. 449/pp. 522–523.
21 WWR I 52, pp. 259–260/pp. 342–344.

Thierreich und dem Menschen', p. 520). This kinship between (innocent) man and (innocent) melody is underwritten by Wagner and Nietzsche to such a degree that in their view the redemption of (European) culture depends in the end on 'innocent melody' as the dominant feature of music, as we shall see furtheron.

Instead of as three different element of music, as in his first book, Schopenhauer discusses rhythm and harmony as sub-elements of the melody in *The World as Will and Representation II*. He distinguishes a rhythmical and a harmonious element in melody, and describes the former as a 'quantitative' element that concerns the duration of the notes and the latter as 'qualitative', thus pointing to its 'pitch and depth'. Both, however, are subordinate to time, because the rhythmical element is about the relative duration, the second about the rapidity of the notes. This highly neglected differentiation in Schopenhauer will form the basis of Nietzsche's later understanding of rhythm, which accords Greek music with Wagnerian music. I shall come back to this in chapter 3.

Schopenhauer's view of tragedy

In *The World as Will and Representation* II, tragedy and opera are understood as 'sublime' art forms, at least Bellini's *Norma*.[22] Tragedy is sublime

> For, just as at the sight of the sublime in nature we turn away from the interest of the will, in order to behave in a purely perceptive way, so in the tragic catastrophe we turn away from the will-to-life itself. [...] At the moment of the tragic catastrophe, we become convinced more clearly than ever that life is a bad dream from which we awake. To this extent, the effect of the tragedy is analogous to that of the dynamically sublime, since [...] it raises us above the will and its interest, and puts us in such a mood that we find pleasure in the sight of what directly opposes the will. What gives to everything tragic, whatever the form in which it appears, the characteristic tendency to the sublime, is the dawning of the knowledge that the world and life can afford us no true satisfaction, and are therefore not worth our attachment to them. In this the tragic spirit consists; accordingly, it leads to resignation (WW II 37, pp. 433–434).

> Denn, wie wir beim Anblick des Erhabenen in der Natur uns vom Interesse des Willens abwenden, um uns rein anschauend zu verhalten; so wenden wir bei der tragischen Katastrophe uns vom Willen zum Leben selbst ab. [...] Im Augenblick der tragischen Katastrophe wird uns, deutlicher als jemals, die Ueberzeugung, daß das Leben ein schwerer Traum sei, aus dem wir zu erwachen haben. Insofern ist die Wirkung des Trauerspiels analog der des dynamisch Erhabenen, indem es [...] uns über den Willen und sein Iteresse hinaushebt und uns so umstimmt, daß wir am Anblick des ihm geradezu Widerstrebenden Gefallen finden. Was allem Tragischen, in welcher Gestalt es auch auftrete, den eigenthümlichen Schwung zur Erhebung giebt, ist das Aufgehen der Erkenntniß, daß die Welt, das Leben, kein wahres Genügen gewähren könne, mithin unsere

---

22 Cf. WWR II 37, pp. 433–437.

> Anhänglichkeit nicht werth sei: darin besteht der tragische Geist: er leitet demnach zur Resignation hin. (WWR II 37, p. 504)

The tragic spirit is only one step away from the saint, who, for Schopenhauer, symbolizes the denial of life. This view of the tragic is interesting to note, because Nietzsche holds to another view of the tragic, a view that confirms the purposelessness and absurdity of life, yet he nevertheless tries to affirm life rather than reject it. Nietzsche's view comes closer to *The World of Will and Representation I* than *II*. In the first edition, Schopenhauer claims that

> The true sense of the tragedy is the deeper insight that what the hero atones for is not his own particular sins, but original sin, in other words, the guilt of existence itself [...] "For man's greatest offence/Is that he has been born" (WWR I 51, p. 254)

> Der wahre Sinn des Trauerspiels ist die tiefere Einsicht, daß was der Held abbüßt nicht seine Partikularsünden sind, sondern die Erbsünde, d.h. die Schuld des Daseyns selbst: *Pues el delito mayor/Del hombre es haber nacido* [Da die größte Schuld des Menschen/Ist, daß er geboren ward]. (WWV I, p. 336)[23]

Another main difference between Schopenhauer and Nietzsche is that Schopenhauer values modern tragedy more than Greek tragedy. Furthermore, he recognizes the 'tragic tendency' of all tragedy, namely: its effect on the public as the wish for resignation.[24] According to Schopenhauer, the Greeks 'had not yet reached the summit and goal of tragedy, or indeed of the view of life generally' (WWR II 37, pp. 434–435/'weil die Alten noch nicht zum Gipfel und Ziel des Trauerspiels, ja, der Lebensansicht überhaupt, gelangt waren', p. 505), which is resignation. The turn away from human willing is the only answer to life and 'the true tendency of tragedy' (WWR II 37, p. 435/'die eigenthümliche Tendenz und Wirkung des Trauerspiels', p. 506).

In *The Birth of Tragedy*, Nietzsche declares that the Greeks were pessimists and that, in order to uplift culture, we must integrate their view of life. With this claim, he goes against Schopenhauer's idea that the Greeks did not have the right view of life and only the moderns had. To Nietzsche, the hero of Greek tragedy expresses the tragic view that man should never have been born, while modern tragedy and Italian opera are focused on individual heroes, who have achieved great deeds in human history. Nietzsche remains a real 'Graecomaniac', and his estimation of contemporary art depends on its 'Greek' spirit. Schopenhauer, on the other hand, prefers the popular works of Shakespeare and Rossini.

---

23 The sentence between brackets is quoted from Calderon's *La vida es bueno*.

24 Note the huge difference with Schiller's idea of the effect that beauty in drama has on the public. According to Schiller, it stimulates the public to take their lives in their own hands and strive for autonomy and freedom. While the effect on the public is resignation in Schopenhauer's view, for Nietzsche and Wagner the effect is redemption (although no Aristotelian catharsis), that is, life is made bearable. For Schiller, drama activates the public, meaning that it has an emancipatory effect.

Schopenhauer and Wagner

Although Schopenhauer's view of tragedy could not differ more from Nietzsche's, his view of opera could not differ more from Wagner's. The French *opéra comique* and the Italian *opera buffa*, of which Rossini was the master, polluted every form of purity and seriousness in Wagner's view. Wagner reserves the predicate 'sublime' for Beethoven's symphonies. However, the most striking difference concerns the technical basis of music: while Wagner attempted to put an end to the tonal system, Schopenhauer's metaphysics of music relies on the tonal system as *the* musical system, and this tonal system is projected into nature, i.e., the Will.

Schopenhauer's philosophy is not only indebted to Weimar Classicism and German Romanticism, but can also be viewed as a protest against the '*Graecomania*' that had been ruling German philosophy and art since the publication of Winckelmann's *Thoughts on the Imitation of Greek Works in Painting and Sculpture (Gedanken über die Nachahmung der griechischen Werke in Malerei und Bildhauerkunst)* in 1750, i.e., almost seventy years before *The World as Will and Representation* came out. Although Schopenhauer estimated the Greek plastic eye very highly, he dispensed with the idea that a return to paradisiacal Greece or the rejuvenation of the Greek spirit is possible by deeming every bit of hope, luck, pleasure, and joy as illusory. When art brings joy, innocence or salvation, Schopenhauer says, it does so only temporarily. No satisfaction abides; peace and harmony, the regain of the innocence, do not remain. The experience of 'Arcadia' is nothing more than the starting point of a new desire. Hence, happiness is in fact of a negative nature, for it does not transcend the satisfaction of a wish, the soothing of pain. All joy rests on a promise that will never be fulfilled. Paradise is lost forever, if it ever existed at all. Resignation, and the ascetic denial of the will, is all that remains.

In book IV of *The World as Will and Representation*, Schopenhauer therefore turns to a plea for an ascetic ethics, by means of which men try to become 'saints', a level that is not attainable by art. In Wagner's eyes, on the other hand, this level is reached by Beethoven's art (he even pretends to show his public 'a day in the life of a saint' in his 'Beethoven' essay). It is, we may say, exactly at this turn to the 'saint' that Nietzsche refuses to go along with Schopenhauer. While Schopenhauer flies into a practical resignation from the horror of life, Nietzsche will hold to an aesthetic answer to life's fundamental pain, inspired by Goethe as much as by Schopenhauer. Moreover, as I shall argue below, Wagner and Nietzsche sustain art as a means of redemption from pain by combining Schopenhauer's metaphysics with Schiller's historical view of human culture.

In his 'Beethoven' essay, Wagner offers a different argument. He states that Germans have the ultimate talent for understanding and telling the truth, because they are 'reformers'. Because Beethoven's music conveys this truth, he argues in his essay that Beethoven, although brought up a Catholic, had a reformatory spirit. Differently from Nietzsche, Wagner holds that 'Greece' is present only as the first culture in which this same musical and reformatory spirit was dominant. The question is how much survives of Schiller's 'Arcadia' and 'Elysium' in Nietzsche's and Wagner's view of culture and whether 'innocence' can be secured by music for more than an illusory moment.

Even though Wagner claimed to corroborate Schopenhauer's philosophy of music, he modified it from the start. Whereas Schopenhauer held to a hierarchical division of nature, the arts, and music, in which everything is a more or less adequate objectification of the Will, Wagner passed over this hierarchy. He maintained a view of the arts, which was much more dualistic than Schopenhauer's was. In essence, Schopenhauer claims, music represents the will, its satisfaction and dissatisfaction. This is confirmed by the existence of two general keys, the major and minor, which correspond to the mood of satisfaction, or pleasure, and dissatisfaction, or pain. Schopenhauer closes his account in the second volume with the remark that different nations show different preferences considering the general keys:

> With northern nations, whose life is subject to hard conditions, especially with the Russians, the minor prevails, even in church music. Allegro in the minor is very frequent in French music, and is characteristic; it is as if a man danced while his shoe pinched him. (WWR II 39, p. 456)

> Bei nordischen Völkern, deren Leben schweren Bedingungen unterliegt, namentlich bei den Russen, herrscht das Moll vor, sogar in der Kirchenmusik. – Allegro in Moll ist in der Französischen Musik sehr häufig und charakterisirt sie: es ist, wie wenn Einer tanzt, während ihn der Schuh drückt. (WWV I, p. 532)

As we shall see in the following, this distinction of 'northern nations' and 'southern nations', specifically Germany versus France and Italy, comprises the main framework within which Wagner unfolds his argument that Beethoven made truly German music, in 'Beethoven' (1870).

Wagner's 'Beethoven' essay

The address Wagner wrote as a commemoration for Beethoven's hundredth birthday in 1870 was not his first account of the great German composer: throughout his career, Wagner had reflected on Beethoven's music.[25] The essay of 1870, however, is not only an essay on Beethoven, but also an exposé of Wagner's own ideas on music and culture, and their intimate relation. It discloses the cultural importance Beethoven's music has for Germany and Europe and formulates the musical aesthetics Wagner sees embodied in Beethoven's oeuvre. In so doing, Wagner equally frames his view of what

---

25 In 1846, Wagner published his first account on Beethoven's *Ninth Symphony*. The essay discussed here is by far the most important one. The 1870 essay was conceived as a replacement for the planned festival, which was cancelled because of the outbreak of the Franco-Prussian war (see Vogel (1966), p. 114).

music is and should be with the objective of dissociating himself from the musical 'formalists', of which Eduard Hanslick was the commander-in-chief, and mapping out the criteria for the 'great Renaissance' of new mythical times he hoped to launch with his music dramas.[26] As it turns out in this essay, the 'Renaissance' needs a 'Reformation', of which Schopenhauer's musical aesthetics, Luther's reformatory spirit, and Beethoven's musical achievements form the cornerstones.[27]

Wagner's text is a long and dense text, which lacks a clear, thematic structure. It advances many ideas, often formulated in bold statements larded with deficient arguments. In that sense, Cosima could have said as much of her husband as she did of Marbach. Against Schopenhauer's avowal to his friend Wille that Wagner was a better poet than musician, I want to riposte that Wagner was a much better musician than writer, theorist, and philosopher. The fact that he wrote chaotically, imprecisely, and indeed 'gloomily', as Nietzsche had already epitomized the writing-style of the New German School in 1858, is mainly due to the fact that he thought chaotically, hastily, and without any critical self-reflection. The more one dives into the 'Beethoven' essay, the more one is startled by Nietzsche's praise of it. His enthusiasm must have been kindled by its themes rather than by Wagner's philosophical style.[28]

In what follows, therefore, I discuss Wagner's text according to a thematic division and examine several of his curious ideas, of which the attempt to prove the 'protestant', 'reformative' nature of Beethoven (who was a Catholic) tussles with the idea that Shakespeare was 'German' in oddity. Wagner's main issue is to show why Beethoven makes 'truly German' music. However, this proof ends up in a sophism,

---

26 In his commentary on Wagner's notes regarding the 'Beethoven' essay, Joachim Bergfeld writes: 'Wagner's performances equally served another goal: the discussion with his firmest opponent, the Viennese critic Eduard Hanslick' ('Wagners Ausführungen dienten aber zugleich einem weiteren Zweck: der Auseinandersetzung mit seinem entschiedensten Widersacher, dem Wiener Kritiker Eduard Hanslick,' Wagner/Bergfeld, 1975, p. 209). The final sentence of the draft-version of 'Beethoven' is said to be directed at Hanslick. It declares: 'What to think of a nation, in which a person [Hanslick, MP] who babbles such rubbish, is [...] as a consolation, promoted to a higher academic rank for this sickening stuff. Does Beethoven belong to this nation?' ('Was aber von einer Nation denken, in welcher derjenige [Hanslick, MP], der solch elendes Zeug schwatzt [...] für diese Kränkung sogleich zu einem höheren akademischen Grad als Tröstung, befördert wird. Gehört diesen Beethoven an?' Wagner/Bergfeld 1975, p. 211). This draft-version stems from about two months before the final essay and is entitled 'Beethoven u.d. deutsche Nation'. Here we find the central statement Wagner wanted to treat in this essay: 'Beeth.=Schopenhauer: his music put into concepts results in this philosophy' (Wagner/Bergfeld 1975, p. 210).

27 See, amongst others, HH I 237 (pp. 113–114/KSA 2.199–200), WS 214 (pp. 362–363/KSA 2.646–647), D 207 (pp. 127–129/KSA 3.185–188), GS 358 (pp. 221–223/KSA 3.602–605). Orsucci also discusses the opposition Nietzsche draws between the north, its Protestantism and Reformation and the south's Catholicism, Renaissance, and scepticism, referring to Lecky's influence (Orsucci 1996, pp. 281–287).

28 By contrast, in a later note, Nietzsche called Wagner's writing style: 'Muddy-German obscurity and embroidery' ('Sumpf-Deutsch der Unklarheit und Übertreibung', 41[2], KSA 11.676). Cf. 32[41], KSA 7.766 and 32[30], KSA 7.764.

asserting that a musician proves to be German when he produces sublime music, while the production of sublime art is reserved for German music only. The sophism becomes circular reasoning when it is added that music is 'sublime' whenever it is 'German'.

Despite such serious mistakes, diluted argumentation, and an abhorrent style, the text does contain some interesting and even elegant ideas, primarily in respect of the decadent state of present culture, the relation between music and text, and the genius' unconscious creativity. In addition, Wagner's resistance to the dominance of the commercial spirit is admirable, because this dominance has only become stronger since it has been institutionalized and supported officially by the European Union in the Messina declaration of 1955. His equation of Italian opera with decorative, amusing art may strike us as odd; however, today we witness similar events in the film industry, where art house movies are overpowered by the more commercial productions made in Hollywood, and music, where pop music has become an industry too.

In my analysis of Wagner's 'Beethoven' text, I work from the 'outside' to the 'inside'. I turn my focus first to the basic structuring and thematic frameworks we can derive. On those, I base my discussion of the contents, for not only do the frameworks outline an architectural form, so to speak, but they also reveal Wagner's basic thoughts. The key concept of my analysis is 'paradise'. Although the word is not mentioned that often, and is definitely not Wagner's focal point (he focuses on 'the genius of Beethoven'), it forms the horizon of the cultural ambition on display. The concepts 'paradise' and 'genius' intersect when Wagner argues that Beethoven's genius consists in the fact that he has succeeded in evoking the experience of paradise in his *Pastoral* and *Choral* symphonies.

The frameworks are distinguishable in several contrasting concepts and domains. The main frames are formed by the opposition Wagner draws between German and French culture and German instrumental and Italian vocal music. These oppositions transcend the aesthetic level and turn into an ethnic discussion, because Wagner regards artworks as the result of certain national features. The musical discussion is dominated, firstly, by the Schopenhauerian division between the art of music and the other fine arts. This yields the question whether the creative mind of the musician works differently from that of the painter or poet. Wagner makes a psychological analysis of Beethoven's creative genius including Schopenhauerian dream-theory, starting from a cliché depiction of Goethe and Schiller's creative geniuses. Schopenhauer's division between the arts gives Wagner reason to map the different powers of music and text or vision on to cultural history; he states that the French inclination for superficiality, for fleeting, ephemeral things and the general '*lexicomania*' of modern times, is the result of a process that started with the invention of printing techniques. When he subsequently regards Beethoven's achievements in terms of humanity's cultural history, he makes an analogy between Beethoven's musical and Luther's religious achievements. This analogy facilitates his argument that the achievements of both geniuses resulted from the same typically 'German', 'reformative' frame of mind.

Not only does Wagner connect a 'true' and 'false' or 'deep' and 'superficial' world to the aesthetic division of the arts, but he also makes a psychological difference between the awake, the sleeping, and dreaming brain. Within the sphere of this psychoanalytic account of the dreaming mind, he makes a comparison between Beethoven's and Shakespeare's creative genius, showing that Shakespeare was not so much the naive artist Schiller mistook him for as the genius artist described by Schopenhauer. This prompts the question as to how Wagner defines 'naive' and 'sublime' art, above all with regard to Beethoven, whom he addresses as a creator of 'sublime naiveté'. The comparison between Beethoven and Shakespeare entails the problematic thesis that Shakespeare was a 'German' artist. The comparison is mainly made to argue that Beethoven's music and Shakespeare's drama stem from the same musical impulse and in so doing contribute to Wagner's defence of his music dramas, in which drama is the pictorial form of the musical message. This argument, hence, is crucial in the Wagnerian history of ideas, because in the 'Beethoven' essay he says farewell to his former idea that the text should dominate the music (as defended in his 1851 essay *Opera and Drama*, which was adduced with the revolutionary élan following the 1848–1849 Dresden events, after which Wagner abandoned Germany and escaped to Zurich).

On the musical technical level, Wagner contrasts 'rhythmical' or 'world' music with 'melodic' or 'spiritual' music. Within rhythm as a musical element, he divides between rhythm as a construction of periods (*'Periodenbau'*) and as a sequence of time (*'Zeitfolge'*). Other elementary oppositions on the aesthetic and ethnographical level are the opposition between (German) 'seriousness' and (Italian) 'frivolity', (German) love of truth and (Italian) scepticism, the sublime versus pleasure in art, and 'guilt' against 'innocence'.

My primary focus in the discussion in all this is on the Rousseauian, ethical idea that Wagner attaches to his aesthetic conclusions, when he claims that the finale of Beethoven's *Ninth Symphony* is an expression of 'serenity' (*'Heiterkeit'*), of 'sublime naiveté', because it 'fills us with the ineffable joy of having attained paradise', the believe that 'man is good after all', and calls us to 'take part as a community in the ideal worship of God', that is a religious-artistic community consisting in a chorus of 'pure' human beings (contrary to any political or economic order). In my discussion of *The Birth of Tragedy*, in chapter 4, I shall argue that this 'idyllic' and 'moral' tendency of Wagner had not escaped Nietzsche's attention, a tendency that left its traces also on Wagner's perception of the Greeks.

French information society as a 'jungle of depraved paradise'

Wagner wrote his 'Beethoven' essay while Prussia and France were waging the Franco-Prussian War (1870–1871), and Prussia was close to victory. However, in Wagner's view, there was another war to be waged. Wagner hoped that the military victory would invoke cultural supremacy as well. France had been dominating European culture for about two hundred years; according to him, that had not done Europe much good. He abominated the dictation of the French, superficial taste in Europe, as it, to him, did not exhibit a truly cultural, but rather a pseudo-cultural and weakening influence.

A similar negative view of French art and culture had been ruling German aesthetics for decades by then. Goethe's and Schiller's 'cultural war' ('*Kulturkampf*') against 'dilettantism', which they fought in the decade marked by the year they met, 1794, and the year Schiller died, in 1805, consisted for an important part in the development of a theatrical aesthetics in opposition to French naturalistic theatre and the subjectivity of Romantic, lyrical poetry. Both art forms never reached the symbolic or general level of the 'objective', but remained on the level of the particular only, Goethe and Schiller charged. In *On the Naive and the Sentimental in Literature*, Schiller writes the French off as the nation 'which is gone farthest towards unnaturalness'.[29] In line with Goethe and Schiller's objection against the French and Romantic impotence to transcend the subjectivity of daily life, Wagner interpreted the French superficiality in Schopenhauerian terms as a matter of sticking to the empirical world of individuality and a lack of metaphysical depth and universal evocation. The popularity of French fashion and the growing influence of journalism confirmed for Wagner that France was a pseudo-culture, where also the arts were ruled by the commercial spirit and 'the principle of novelty'. Fashion, spectacular news, the latest trends were, according to him, more important to the French people than eternal truths and permanent quality. The Frenchman '[...] is entirely "modern" [...], totally "News"' ('[...] durch und durch "modern" [...] völlig "Journal", DS IX, p. 101). 'Modern' stands for 'false'. Seen in the light of its purpose to overcome this French modernity and falsity, Wagner's music can be regarded as 'un-modern' or 'post-modern', as 'overcoming modern traits'. Wagner traced the trendiness of French culture back to the decline in artistic taste that Europe had been suffering for several centuries already, caused by the augmenting influence of 'plasticity' in Western art since the invention of the printing machine by Gutenberg around 1450.[30]

With the gradual domination of the written word, Wagner argues, 'paradise' went lost, because the mythical spirit went lost. Before Modern times, i.e., before the art of printing was invented and spread over Europe, human art and culture were based on 'myth' or 'poetry', because humankind reflected its relationship to the world in myths, in the artistic creation of spoken-word stories, Wagner claims. With the 'textualization' of human society, the vivacity of language froze and poetry increasingly became a matter of rhetoric and dialectics, resulting eventually in the fact that modern, contemporary literature was created primarily in favour of readers.[31] The art of printing,

---

29 In the translation of Helen Watanabe-O'Kelly (1981), p. 34/NA 20, pp. 431–432.

30 The printing machine was invented by Gutenberg in 1436.

31 Nietzsche will attach the figure of 'Euripides' to the rhetorics mentioned here, and 'Socrates' to 'dialectics' in *The Birth of Tragedy*.

Wagner summarizes, created a *'lexicomania'* (*'Buchstaben-Krankheit'*, DS IX, p. 99). The increase of daily newspapers and popular magazines demonstrates to him that this 'craziness of letters' continues. He regards this as a threat to the human spirit, because, instead of narrating poetic myths that convey one deep truth supported by the whole community, the magazines are only interested in promoting public opinions. Hence, ephemeral and superficial public opinions, instead of truth, structure present society. Modern Western history, Wagner points out, is characterized by the '[...] shift of the poetic world in a newspaper-literary world' ('[...] Umwandlung der poetischen Welt in eine journal-literarische Welt,' DS IX, p. 99). Or, as Walter Benjamin, who also protested against the lack of truth and imagination in journalism, advocating the return of myth instead, wrote later:

> Every morning brings us the news of the globe, yet we are poor in noteworthy stories. This is because no event any longer comes to us without already being shot through with explanation. In other words, by now, almost nothing that happens benefits storytelling; almost everything benefits information.[32]

While 'the word', according to Wagner, owes its 'depth' and duration to its musical source, the story retains its power above all from keeping it free of information, so that room is left for the imagination of the beholder. Information does not leave much to the imagination, because the purpose of informing is exactly to tell what happened in as many details as possible so to rule out all illusion. This implies not only that the concept of 'truth' erodes into 'what really happened', but also that truth and illusion are reconfigured in an irreconcilable, excluding opposition of (good, informing) truth and (bad, deceiving) illusion. Thus, when Wagner advocates the return to paradise and the return of myth, he implicitly advocates the return of metaphysical truth and its intimate relationship to 'illusion' in terms of aesthetic semblance and imagination. In paradise, the human *'poiesis'* is 'poetry' (or *'musikè'*), and the world, thanks to the free dwelling of the imagination, is a colourful world, in which truth and illusion go hand in hand. 'Depraved paradise' or 'paradise lost', on the other hand, stands for the state, in which poetry is replaced with 'information' and 'truth' is equated with 'news'.

The primary cultural purpose of Wagner's art was to save Germany and Europe from the French 'principle of novelty', its *'lexicomania'*, its fascination with fashion, commerce, journalism, and sensationalism, in brief, from the separation of truth and art and from the modern conceptions of truth and illusion. Against the shallow, French spirit, he posed the German genius as salvation and safe harbour of art and truth, i.e., of culture. As Wagner expressed it: only 'an infinitely deeply established rebirth' (*'Neugeburt'*) of metaphysical or 'German' depth would be able to 'redeem' ('erlösen') Europe from the French cultural dominance. How could this rebirth be generated, according to Wagner?

---

32 Benjamin (1999), p. 89.

The model of Greek mythical society as paradise

The poetic world is not only 'mythical' and 'metaphysical' as opposed to 'theoretical' and 'conceptual', but also 'musical' and 'lyrical' against the modern 'verbal' or 'epic' culture. Based on poetic myths, the Greeks perceived the world as 'form and colour', whilst every form of spiritual depth is currently in danger. Wagner's model for his ideal, mythical society is Greek antiquity. Greek art had a divine, sublime quality, with which, Wagner argues, it gave a bearable form to human existence. Italian Renaissance art may give an indication of the Greek magnitude due to its Christian and musical spirit:

> The Christian spirit revived the spirit of music. She cleared the eye of the Italian painter, and inspired his power of observation. [...] Almost all these great painters were musicians, and it is the spirit of music, which makes us forget that we are *seeing*, as we sink into the view of their holy men and martyrs. (DS IX, pp. 104–105)

> Der Geist des Christentums war es, der die Seele der Musik neu wiederbelebte. Sie verklärte das Auge des italienischen Malers, und begeisterte seine Sehkraft [...]. Diese großen Maler waren fast alle Musiker, und der Geist der Musik ist es, der uns beim Versenken in den Anblick ihrer Heiligen und Märtyrer vergessen läßt, daß wir *sehen*.

This intimate view of the relationship between music and picture, in which music inspires the power of vision, is one of Wagner's richest and most convincing ideas.[33] It returns when he discusses Beethoven's genius in comparison to Shakespeare's. Music pervaded Greek art and civilization in flanking myth, Wagner says:

> It must seem to us that the music of the Greeks permeated the world of appearances intensely, and melted together with the laws of her visibility. The numbers of Pythagoras certainly are only in living terms understandable from music. The architect built after the rhythmic laws, the sculptor sculpted the human body after the laws of harmony, the laws of melody shaped the poet into a singer, and the drama projected itself from the chorus onto the stage. Everywhere we see how the inner law, which is understandable from the spirit of music, determines the outer law that orders the world of appearances: the real antique Doric state [...]. Indeed, the laws of music guided the war organization, the battle, with the same certainty as the dance – But this paradise was lost: the primal source of the world's movement dried up. (DS IX, p. 104)

> Uns muß es dünken, daß die Musik der Hellenen die Welt der Erscheinung selbst innig durchdrang, und mit den Gesetzen ihrer Wahrnehmbarkeit sich verschmolz. Die Zahlen des Pythagoras

---

33 'We know that the verses of the text-poet, even those of Goethe and Schiller, cannot determine the music; this can only be done by the *drama* [...] as visible counterpart of the music' ('Wir wissen, daß nicht die Verse des Textdichters, und wären es die Goethes und Schillers, die Musik bestimmen können; dies vermag allein das *Drama*, [...] als sichtbar gewordenes Gegenbild der Musik,' DS IX, p. 94). Music and poetry are two artistic expressions of the same metaphysical view, and there are most powerful when combined. Wagner speaks of music drama as 'das vollendetste Drama' (DS IX, p. 93). Music drama is therefore pressed forward as the better alternative to opera.

sind gewiß nur aus der Musik lebendig zu verstehen; nach den Gesetzen der Eurhythmie baute der Architekt, nach denen der Harmonie erfaßte der Bildner die menschliche Gestalt; die Regeln der Melodik machten den Dichter zum Sänger, und aus dem Chorgesange projizierte sich das Drama auf die Bühne, wir sehen überall das innere, nur aus dem Geiste der Musik zu verstehende Gesetz, das äußere, die Welt der Anschaulichkeit ordnende Gesetz bestimmen; den ächt antiken dorischen Staat [...] ja die Kriegsordnung, die Schlacht, leiteten die Gesetze der Musik mit der gleichen Sicherheit wie den Tanz. – Aber das Paradies ging verloren; der Urquell der Bewegung einer Welt versiechte.

This quotation demonstrates that Wagner indeed understood the Greek world as a paradise, and that he believed that the infusion of the world with music would lead back to this ideal, poetic state of humankind. Wagner notes that in history, several artistic periods attempted to lead humankind back to paradise, to mythical thought, and the innocence and serenity of life. However, only Italian Renaissance painting came close because of the musical spirit that intensified the paintings of Raphael and others. Italian opera, which also emerged during the Italian Renaissance, is, surprisingly, text-bound and unmusical according to Wagner, and accountable for the 'loss of soul' in European musical culture.

Despite his gloomy analysis of modernity, Wagner sustained hope for a better future to arise soon, a future based on the signs of musical depth he had experienced in Beethoven's music. Alongside the fashionable, decadent world, he therefore claimed, another world is coming into existence: 'Just as Christianity rose from Rome's universal civilization, so music rises out of the chaos of modern civilization in our days' ('Wie unter der römischen Universal-Zivilisation das Christentum hervortrat, so bricht jetzt aus dem Chaos der modernen Zivilisation die Musik hervor,' DS IX, p. 103). Similar to Christianity, Beethoven's music arose from the 'Essence', resisting the 'Roman' (French and Italian) tendency to superficiality in transcending everyday life:

> Let everyone for him experience how the complete, modern world of appearances [...] abruptly disappears in nothingness, the moment that he hears the first bars of one of these [Beethoven's, MP] divine symphonies. (DS IX, p. 103)

> Erfahre jeder an sich, wie die ganze moderne Erscheinungswelt, welche ihn überall zu seiner Verzweiflung undurchbrechbar einschließt, plötzlich in nichts vor ihm verschwindet, sobald ihm nur die ersten Takte einer jener göttlichen Symphonien ertönen.

Transcending everyday life means that modern society is overcome: 'music enhances it [modern society, MP], like daylight lifts up lamplight' ('die Musik hebt sie [unsere ganze moderne Zivilisation, MP] auf, wie das Tageslicht den Lampenschein,' DS IX, p. 104). This enormous, triumphal event is the triumph of nature over fashion, of depth over superficiality, according to Wagner, and best symbolized in the joyful lines and tones of the grand finale of Beethoven's *Ninth Symphony*: '*Deine Zauber binden wieder/*

Was die Mode frech geteilt'.[34] On this line, Wagner comments: 'We think we see before us *Luther* in his anger against the pope' ('Wir glauben Luther in seinem Zorne gegen den Papst vor uns zu sehen!' DS IX, p. 106). In making this analogy, Wagner expresses his fierce belief in the huge importance of Beethoven's music for Western culture and history. To him, Beethoven is the first person since Greek Antiquity and Luther to rescue Europe from the clutches of superficiality by animating culture with the deepest musical spirit. Moreover, the comparison of Beethoven with Luther also points to his conviction that the reanimation of modern culture is a typically German task, because he assumes that the German spirit contains a deeper understanding of life than any other nation in Europe. We shall return to this matter further on in this chapter when we come to speak of Beethoven as the composer of characteristically German music.

Beethoven's music as mirror of Schopenhauer's philosophy

Having pointed out the cultural context of Wagner's artistic vocation, the questions arise, what made Beethoven's music so universally powerful according to Wagner, and how did he assume Beethoven's reformative legacy in order to accomplish the '*Kulturkampf'*, started by Goethe and Schiller?

In order to answer these questions, Wagner not only tries to understand Beethoven's music from a technical viewpoint, but also attempts to pin down its metaphysical depth, of which the discerning technical structure gives an indication. Because the metaphysical depth of Beethoven's music is viewed as directly originating in Beethoven's personality, mind, and perceptive strength, Wagner also undertakes a psychoanalysis of Beethoven's 'creative genius' in comparison to the creative genius of Goethe, Schiller, and Shakespeare, with the purpose of delineating the musician's uniqueness in contrast to the poet. As it turns out in Wagner's analysis, musicians (or at least German and true musicians like Beethoven) create out of their unconscious, while poets (e.g., Goethe) create out of their conscious mind. In any event, Wagner understood Beethoven's music as the embodiment of Schopenhauerian metaphysics. While most musical works remained on the superficial level of beauty (that is, of imitation, visual perception, and empirical sense-reality), Beethoven's music is 'sublime', and thus, we may add, full of soul.

Wagner draws upon Schopenhauer's metaphysics of music by implementing the distinction between the Will and music on the one hand and the world of appearances and the other forms of art on the other. He addresses the phenomenal world as the 'world of light' ('*Die Lichtwelt'*) and the noumenal essence as the 'world of sounds' ('*Die Schallwelt'*), or also as a world of the eye and a world of the ear. In this (quite rigid) opposition, the 'eye' stands for appearances-without-any-depth, consciousness,

---

34 In his poem, Schiller writes '*streng geteilt'*. Beethoven substituted '*frech'* for '*streng'*.

and reasonable knowledge, while the 'ear' symbolizes nature's inner depth, the Will, and intuitive knowledge. The outward world of the 'eye' depends on appearances, and thus is a matter of illusion ('*Täuschung*'). According to Wagner, plastic arts use illusion deliberately to play upon the audience. Their purpose is to reveal the idea of a thing by playing with its characteristic deceiving power. In so doing, however, he maintains it conceals just as much as it reveals the idea of things. Plastic arts satisfy themselves with the pleasure sprung from beauty, which is a superficial kind of pleasure. Wagner contrarily valued 'deep' or 'inner' joy and the only aesthetic illusion or semblance he allowed was of Shakespeare's and his own drama, which, like Italian Renaissance painting, originated in true musicality.

Music, Wagner maintains with Schopenhauer, creates another kind of effect than that of the visual arts. It leads the beholder to something much more spiritual, namely the experience of the sublime. Whereas beauty means experiencing pleasure by looking at phenomena, the sublime is accomplished by insight into the deepest soul of all being, which connects nature, the art of music, and all living creatures. This soul, the Will, fills the beholder up, and brings him to, as Wagner puts it in a highly Romantic way of phrasing, 'the highest ecstasy of the consciousness of boundlessness' ('die höchste Ekstase des Bewußtseins der Schrankenlosigkeit,' DS IX, p. 56). This is the consciousness that in our innermost soul, on the deepest possible level of existence, limiting categories (as Wagner calls them with Schopenhauer) such as space and time – by help of which we achieve rational knowledge of the phenomenal world we live in – have no say. Exceeding every musical and phenomenal boundary, music thus reveals the absolute and eternal. Music, other than poetry and the plastic arts, is a source of true knowledge, just as Schopenhauer articulated the idea. It discloses the inner soul of life. Music expresses the knowledge that all things in nature, including humankind, stem from the same source, being the Will. Beethoven, anticipating Schopenhauer as it were, created music out of his inner vision of life's true being, that is, out of his vision of the universal Will, according to Wagner: 'his music itself is an Idea of the world, in which the world reveals its essence immediately' ('seine Musik selbst ist eine Idee der Welt, in welcher diese ihr Wesen unmittelbar darstellt,' DS IX, p. 50). Wagner's answer to the Faustian exclamation 'where do I grasp you, infinite Nature?' ('Wo fass' ich dich, unendliche Natur?' DS IX, p. 49) therefore runs as follows: in Beethoven's music. Beethoven's music is the embodiment of Schopenhauer's metaphysics of the Will.

Wagner attempts to understand how Beethoven created out of perception of the universal Will and especially what enables musicians to see life's essence, whereas poets, painters, and architects just cannot see the inner essence of things. In order to understand Beethoven's genius and creativity, Wagner takes a brief look at the creative acts of Goethe and Schiller. Although Wagner is clearly influenced by Goethe and Schiller, both in his aesthetics and his cultural analysis, he delivers some discomforting generalities about Schiller and his brother-in-arms Goethe, clichés which return in Nietzsche's *Birth of Tragedy*. However, the platitudes serve and legitimize his turn to Schopenhauer instead of to Goethe and Schiller's aesthetics for explaining Beethoven's musical genius, in showing that Goethe and Schiller fail to express musical brilliance. They 'lack musical spirit', as Nietzsche formulated it in several notes.

Looking at the two fathers of 'Weimar Classicism',[35] one may get hold of the conscious choices poets make for aesthetic forms, Wagner says, but it does not bring one much further in understanding the unconscious creative process. According to Wagner, Beethoven did not consciously choose his music, but the compositions were imposed upon him 'by his inner vision of the Idea' ('aus seiner inneren Anschauung der Idee,' DS IX, p. 42). This inner vision distinguishes the musician from the poet and the painter. Whereas the painter creates consciously, the musician creates unconsciously. The poet may create consciously, like Goethe, or unconsciously, like Schiller. In line with this, Wagner adds, Goethe was more a lover of 'the pleasing, plastic symmetry of art-music [...] by which the art of tone shows an analogy with architecture' ('das gefällige, plastisch symmetrische Element der Kunstmusik [...] durch welches die Tonkunst analogisch wiederum mit der Architektur eine Ähnlichkeit aufweist,' DS IX, p. 43). Schiller had a better understanding of the matter, considering his view that 'epos leans toward plastic art, the drama, on the contrary, toward music' ('daß das Epos der Plastik, das Drama dagegen der Musik sich zuneige', DS IX, p. 43). Wagner grounds his view of Goethe as a conscious poet in Goethe's prime wish to be a painter, and Schiller as an (almost) unconscious poet in his study of Kant's *'Ding-an-sich'*. Apart from advancing these clichés, Wagner points to Goethe's love of Italian music. This highly neglected yet interesting point will become a pillar of Nietzsche's identification of Goethe as his exemplary philosopher-artist in his later anti-Wagnerian period. I shall come back to Nietzsche's replacement of Wagner with Goethe in the second part of this book.

Wagner points to Goethe's love of Italian opera, the opera *buffa* especially, and combines this uncritically with Goethe's famous remark made to Eckermann that music is architecture in tones to justify his own distinction between 'rhythmical' and 'melodic', 'Italian' and 'German', 'untrue' and 'true' music. Nietzsche will adopt this conception of music and translate it as a distinction between 'Apollonian' and 'Dionysian' music, as we shall see in our discussion of *The Birth of Tragedy*. Wagner's remark reaches much deeper than notable at first glance. Goethe's preference for Italian music underlines the conscious, theoretical, or conceptual source of his art and dismisses him, implicitly, as a typically 'German' (Wagner) or 'tragic' (Nietzsche) artist,

---

35 By this, I especially point to the 'cultural war' (*'Kulturkampf'*) Goethe and Schiller undertook in collaboration between 1794 and 1805 (the year Schiller died) as part of the wider notion of 'German Classicism', which I prefer to periodize from Winckelmann's publications on Greek art of 1750 and 1764 to the death of Goethe in 1832. German and Weimar Classicism share their model of Greek art and society as an ideal of harmony and objectivity. Goethe and Schiller particularly emphasize the latter quality as a hallmark of art in their cultural struggle against dilettantism (see Bishop and Stephenson 2005, esp. pp. 4–16).

that is the artist who will bring mankind back to his European, paradisiacal roots, i.e., Ancient Greece.

Wagner puts an end to his critique with the obvious statement that Schiller felt happier as a dramatist than as a poet and that Goethe had a clear preference for the epic style. For understanding the musical, creative act Wagner then turns to Schopenhauer, because Schopenhauer distinguishes music from the visual arts and poetry by postulating music as 'Idea' of the Will. From this, he derives that the genius creates unconsciously, that is out of a direct relation to the Will. In addition, Wagner will compare Beethoven's creative act with Shakespeare's and, to some extent, with Bach and Palestrina, incidentally neglecting the fact that Palestrina was an Italian catholic. Against the French cultural dominance in Europe, against 'conceptual', conscious art, and against Italian music, Wagner advances the picture of Beethoven as a true 'German', an unconscious, creative genius, and a musical reformer, who was well on the way of saving Europe by returning to it the musical spirit that used to saturate Greek myth and culture.

Beethoven's German depth versus Italian superficiality

Despite his assertion that music reveals the infinite nature of life and, hence, speaks a universal language, Wagner says that nationality seems relevant to the quality and character of music. Musicians, like painters and poets, do express a national identity, according to Wagner. Turning an apparently exclusive opposition into an inclusion, he will argue that it is typically 'German' to compose universal, absolute music.[36] Wagner makes the distinction between 'German' and 'Italian' music to prove that Beethoven was a purely German composer of typically German music, which is Wagner's central claim together with the claim that Beethoven serves Germany and Europe by bringing us all back to paradise.[37] Wagner states, right at the beginning of his essay:

> Upon closer examination, we recognize that it is very possible to talk of German music in contradistinction to Italian music. For this distinction, a physiological, national predisposition may be taken into account [...]. The distinctive feature, by which means the musician is recognized as belonging to his nation, must in any case have a deeper foundation than the reasons that make us understand Goethe and Schiller as Germans, Rubens and Rembrandt as Dutch. (DS IX, pp. 39–40)

> Bei näherer Prüfung erkennen wir nun wohl, daß von einer deutschen Musik, im Unterschiede von einer italienischen, sehr wohl die Rede sein könne, und für diesen Unterschied darf noch

---

36 There are different definitions of 'absolute music'. Sometimes, the term refers to music, which is independent of other art forms (e.g., drama); on other occasions it indicates the experience or knowledge of the metaphysical Absolute. Here, I use it in the latter sense.
37 This point is overall disregarded in the literature, probably because the focus is commonly on Wagner's musical aesthetics rather than his philosophy of culture.

ein physiologischer nationaler Zug in Betracht genommen werden [...]. Der Zug der Eigentüm-
lichkeit, durch welchen der Musiker seiner Nation als angehörig erkannt wird, muß jedenfalls
tiefer begründet liegen, als der, durch welchen wir Goethe und Schiller als Deutsche, Rubens
und Rembrandt als Niederländer erkennen.

With this distinction between 'German' or 'northern' music and 'Italian' or 'southern'
music, Wagner places himself in the tradition of Romantic musical aesthetics invoked
by Jean-Jacques Rousseau (1712–1778). Rousseau's *Letter on French Music* (*Lettre sur la
musique française*, 1753) launched the discussion whether 'northern' or 'southern' art
is 'better', and developed the evaluation of music as a decoration in human life into a
high and fine art, which is highly significant for human culture. In this treatise, which
was the starting-point of French Romanticism, Rousseau distinguished between the
French language of northern origin, which is 'unmusical' because it cannot easily be
sung, and the musical, southern, Italian language, which can be easily sung. Wagner
repeats and modifies this idea by stating that German music revolves around the 'tone'
and Italian music around the 'voice'. Because the voice is tied to words and concepts,
Italian vocal music does not surpass the theoretical and empirical level, whereas German musicians, Wagner holds, due to their tonal focus, are able to reach an inward
genius, an unconscious look upon the truth and make music out of this deep knowledge.[38] This inwardness makes them unique, Wagner argues (again using platitudes);
whereas Italians and French are peoples of eyes and focused on outer vision (that is
on the perception of the empirical world that surrounds us), the German people form a
people of ears and inner hearing and vision, hence perception of the deep truth, which
is concealed in humanity's own inner nature. Based on this division, Wagner hopes to
prove that Beethoven makes typically 'German' music. From this, he adduces several
reasons of metaphysical, physiological, and religious natures. However, the central
idea that this representation of the truth in music was accomplished by Beethoven, because he is a German composer ends up in circular reasoning: concluding that German
music by nature possesses a metaphysical depth in reference to Beethoven's music, he
proves that Beethoven is German, because his music contains metaphysical depth. It
goes the same way in the case of Italian or French music; Wagner's view that music
from the 'south of the Alps' naturally lacks this metaphysical depth is used both as an
argument and as a conclusion.

That Italian music lacks depth, is a matter of natural bent, on the one hand, and
on the other fortified by the fact that Italy is a Catholic country, so Wagner. He further
argues that due to their Catholicism Italians are 'sceptical' – which Wagner strongly

---

38 This 'inwardness' was declared specifically 'German' by Franz Brendel, in a metaphorical sense. for
instance, because of their 'inwardness' the Hungarian Franz Liszt and the Frenchman Hector Berlioz
were considered part of New German School, not only because they, after the 'death of the symphony'
(occassioned by Beethoven's Ninth Symphony) continued Beethoven's legacy with their symphonic
poems (Liszt) and poetic symphony (Berlioz). See also Rehding (2006), pp. 167–172.

defines as 'hostility to the truth' rather than as doubting the possibility of a rational foundation of truth – and 'frivolous', by which he means that their love of decoration and spectacle prevails over the content:

> on the foundation of a falsified history, a falsified knowledge, and a falsified religion [Catholicism, MP], was a by nature joyful and happy people educated to a scepticism, which, because it must undermine the dedication to what is true, real, and free in the first place, had to manifest itself as frivolity. (DS IX, pp. 74–75)

> auf dem Boden einer gefälschten Geschichte, einer gefälschten Wissenschaft, einer gefälschten Religion [durch dem Katholizismus, MP], war eine von der Natur heiter und frohmütig angelegte Bevölkerung zu jenem Skeptizismus erzogen worden, welcher, da vor allem das Haften am Wahren, Ächten und Freien untergraben werden sollte, als wirkliche Frivolität sich zu erkennen geben mußte.

Scepticism, in Wagner's view, implies frivolity.[39] Alternatively, this characterization entails that when one is a 'protestant', one is 'German', a searcher after truth, a serious, yet joyful and happy person.

Having outlined the specific qualities of Germany and German music in contrast to France and Italy, the question remains how Beethoven has accomplished Europe's return to paradise. We have seen that his creativity is 'unconscious', contrary to Goethe's 'conscious' creativity. Expanding upon this assessment, Wagner explains that Beethoven's creativity amounts to a 'play with inner figures [*Gestalten*]', a (typically 'male') strength of instinct, dream-activity, and clairvoyance only equalled by Shakespeare and Homer, which make them supremely 'naive' artists. We shall examine this in the next two paragraphs, after which we shall turn to a discussion of the nature of Beethoven's, or rather German, music as a 'cheerful' ('*heiter*') and in a very specific way 'melodic' product of the night, which prompts the experience of the 'sublime' in the beholder.

Beethoven as 'dreamer' and 'clairvoyant'

In explaining Beethoven's creativity, Wagner appeals to Schopenhauer's dream-theory and the physiological phenomenon of clairvoyance, as expounded in his two-volume *Parerga und Paralipomena* (1851), a book in which longer essays on philosophy and the university intersperse with shorter articles and aphorisms about literature and psychology. Wagner mixes Schopenhauer's dream-theory with his philosophy of mu-

---

39 The scepticism and frivolity of his '*gaya scienza*', therefore, reinforce its 'Italian' and anti-Wagnerian nature.

sic, or, as Kropfinger accurately surmised, Wagner applies Schopenhauer to Schopenhauer.[40]

Wagner's argument develops along the distinction between seeing during daytime and seeing during nighttime. A serious problem, which arises out of this contention, is that the inner 'eye', which perceives the inner figures, is the base of the exceptional musical talent of Beethoven, while it is also argued that, for an accurate reception of music, the power of music must decrease (*'depotenzieren'*) the powers of sight in the beholder. Under the spell or magic (*'Zauber'*) of what he hears, then, the beholder turns his visual powers inward and perceives dream-like figures or forms, in the same manner as the composer, and in so doing partakes in the same joyful play with the inner forms as the composer. Although this argument seems to create a paradox, to say the very least, it accounts for the specific musical power Beethoven demonstrated even – or in Wagner's reasoning, primarily – in the time that he had become deaf. As we know, Beethoven was already deaf when he composed his later symphonies, and those, especially his last, the *Ninth Symphony* (composed in 1823), form the alpha and omega of Wagner's philosophy of music. Wagner thus faced the problem of explaining the genius of a deaf musician, who set the standard for all music to come. He found a solution in inserting Schopenhauer's theory of dreams in his theory of the genius. However problematic, this part of the treatise is probably the most personal and prosperous of Wagner's philosophy of music, in spite of the dubious examples with which he garnishes his theory of dreams.

Despite Wagner's objections against Italian music, he uses an experience in Venice (the city where he was to die in 1883) to illustrate the supposed 'dark' or 'night' side of music. By this means, he introduces his theory of dreams as the source of the musician's creativity. In his description of the occurrence in Venice, Wagner shows his highly Romantic nature. I quote a lengthy part of his memory to demonstrate his point:

> During a sleepless night, I stepped upon the balcony of my window that looked over the Grand Canal in Venice: like a deep dream, the fairy city of lagoons lay stretched in a shadow before me. Out of the breathless silence rose the piercing cry of a gondolier just woken on his barque; repeatedly his voice went forth into the night, until from the remotest distance its fellow-cry came answering down the midnight length of the canal: I recognized the antediluvian, glum melody to which the well-known lines of Tasso were also connected in his day [...]. After many a solemn pause the humming dialogue took quicker life, and seemed at last to melt in unison [...]. Whatever could sun-soaked, colour-piled Venice of the daylight tell me about itself, that sounding dream of night had not brought infinitely deeper, closer, to my consciousness? (DS IX, p. 52)

> Im schlafloser Nacht trat ich einst auf den Balkon meines Fensters am großen Kanal in Venedig: wie ein tiefer Traum lag die märchenhafte Lagunenstadt im Schatten vor mir ausgedehnt. Aus dem lautlosesten Schweigen erhob sich da der mächtige rauhe Klageruf eines soeben auf seiner Barke erwachten Gondoliers, mit welchen dieser in wiederholten Absätzen in die Nacht hineinrief, bis

---

40 Kropfinger (1975), p. 153.

aus weitester Ferne der gleiche Ruf dem nächtlichen Kanal entlang antwortete: ich erkannte die uralte schwermütige, melodische Phrase, welcher seinerzeit auch die bekannten Verse Tassos untergelegt worden [...]. Nach feierlichen Pausen belebte sich endlich der weithin tönende Dialog und schien sich im Einklang zu verschmelzen [...]. Was könnte mir das von der Sonne bestrahlte, bund durchwimmelte Venedig des Tages von sich sagen, das jener tönende Nachttraum mir nicht unendlich tiefer unmittelbar zum Bewußtsein gebracht gehabt hätte?

Apart from the fact that this experience bears remarkable resemblance to descriptions made of a similar experience by Goethe in his *Italian Journey*,[41] it is fairly interesting that this very typically 'Venetian' experience serves as a proof that the darkness of the night, the hours of sleep, dreams, and silence are typical elements of German art. The only light Wagner appreciates is the light of the 'clairvoyant', the bright light of inner knowledge, the light that does not surround us, but that lights things up, brings them to light before our own eyes. Beethoven puts his subjects in the silence of the night, he continues, from where he 'guides the light of the clairvoyant behind the image' ('das Licht des Hellsichtigen hinter das Bild leitet,' DS IX, p. 66).[42] Light, if I understand this passage correctly, thus does not burn in front of things, in order to have us see its shadows on the wall as in Plato's cave, but flames up from behind and makes the inner essence of things glow, in order for the beholders to grasp. This 'light from the clairvoyant' causes the 'spiritual vitality' in art, the metaphysical depth, which distinguishes Beethoven's music from the music composed by his predecessors: his is deeply spiritual, without being religious, in contrast to the music of his forerunners. Against Hanslick's formalism, Wagner propounds that technical skill and efficacy in form are not enough for music to deserve the name 'music', although these are the initial means by which an artist relates to his audience to make him understood. Technical skill and formal effectiveness are indeed what we discern when we listen to music soberly, that is uninspired. However, Beethoven's music inspires, enchants, and therefore 'everything becomes melody' ('alles wird Melodie,' DS IX, p.66) the moment Beethoven spreads his light, Wagner writes. Everything becomes an integral part of the melody, including silence and rhythm. The question is, however, how can the perception of music by daylight still be infused with the same strong spirit?

---

41 Goethe, *Italian Journey*, Venice, 6 October 1786 (1989, p. 72), 12 October 1786 (1989, p. 81), and the fragment 'Volksgesang. Venedig' [1789]. Nietzsche seems to argue against this musical understanding of Italy with his description of Genoese architecture as expression of the Italian spirit in GS 291 (pp. 164–165/KSA 3.531–532). See also EH 'Clever' 7 (p. 95/KSA 6.291).

42 Wagner adds to this: 'here this comes alive before us in wonderful expression, and a second world stands before us, of which even the greatest masterpiece of Raphael could not give us an idea' ('da lebt denn dieses in wundervoller Weise vor uns auf, und eine zweite Welt steht vor uns, von der uns auch das größte Meisterwerk eines Raphael keine Ahnung geben konnte,' DS IX, p. 66). This is interesting with regard to Nietzsche's interpretation of Raphael's *Transfiguration* in *The Birth of Tragedy*, which implies that Raphael *did* give an inkling of this.

Even though Wagner stresses darkness and the night, the 'dreamlike state' (that is required for the creation and reception of music) can also be prompted during the day. Hence, dreaming is not bound to the night, but rather to the decrease of outer vision, of eyesight, the weakened connection to the outer world. Wagner advances the example of the yodelling shepherd to illustrate this, an example again taken from his own experience, however this time reminiscent of 'The Shepherd on the Rock' ('Der Hirt auf dem Felsen'), a poem (probably by Wilhelm Müller) set to music by Franz Schubert (1797–1828):[43]

> It was in broad daylight when I heard coming from a high alpine meadow the shrill yodel of a cowherd, which he had sent forth across the vast valley; right away the same reckless cowherd-cry answered him from over there through the enormous silence: the echo of the towering mountain walls here mingled in; the seriously silent valley chimed cheerfully in the contest [...] this is the way [...] the angry groan of the thunder speaks to the contemplating man, over whom now comes the dreamlike state, in which he experiences that about which his sight kept him in the illusion of distraction, namely that his innermost Being is one with the inner Being of all things perceived, and that only in this perception also the Nature of things outside him is truly known.[44] (DS IX, pp. 52–53)

> Es war heller Tag, als ich von einer hohen Alpenweide zur Seite her den grell jauchzenden Reigen-ruf eines Sennen vernahm, den er über das weite Tal hinüber sandte; bald antwortete ihm von dort her durch das ungeheure Schweigen der gleiche übermütige Hirtenruf: hier mischte sich nun das Echo der ragenden Felswände hinein; im Wettkampfe ertönte lustig das ernst schweigsame Tal [...] so spricht [...] das Wutgeheul der Orkane zu dem sinnenden Manne, über den nun jener trau-martige Zustand kommt, in welchem er durch das Gehör das wahrnimmt, worüber ihn sein Sehen in der Täuschung der Zerstreutheit erhielt, nämlich daß sein innerstes Wesen mit dem innersten Wesen alles jenes Wahrgenommenen Eines ist, und daß nur in *dieser* Wahrnehmung auch das Wesen der Dinge außer ihm wirklich erkannt wird.

Sympathetic hearing plunges the beholder in a dream-like state, wherein the inner essence of the world becomes clear to him, through the ears towards his inner vision, whilst his eyesight is paralyzed by the music to such a degree that he, although his eyes are wide open, does not *see*. The dreamlike state is a state of hypnotic clairvoyance, and 'it is in this state alone that we immediately belong to the musician's world' ('es [ist] nur dieser Zustand daß wir der Welt des Musikers unmittelbar angehörig werden,' DS IX, p. 53). The decrease of visual powers is generated by the 'magic' ('Zauber') of music. It makes us dream the dream the musician had dreamt in deepest sleep. Under the spell of the musical magic, we not only find ourselves as in a dream, but also in a state of ecstasy. This is how Wagner defines the experience of the 'sublime':

---

43 In 1828 as D 965, opus 129.
44 My translation may not be optimal, but the translation-work is aggravated by Wagner's difficult style, which is at its worst when he stuffs his language with metaphysical and idealistic terminology. This also goes for the next quotation which brims over with redundant instances of '*an sich*'.

Music, that speaks to us solely through the fact that it breathes life into the most universal concept of the naturally speechless feeling in all imaginable gradations with greatest clarity for us, can in and for itself only be judged by nothing but the category of the sublime; for, as soon as it fills us, she engenders the highest ecstasy of consciousness of infinitude. (DS IX, p. 56)

Die Musik, welche einzig dadurch zu uns spricht, daß sie den allerallgemeinsten Begriff des an sich dunklen Gefühles in den erdenklichsten Abstufungen mit bestimmtester Deutlichkeit uns belebt, kann an und für sich einzig nach der Kategorie des *Erhabenen* beurteilt worden, da sie, sobald sie uns erfüllt, die höchste Ekstase des Bewußtseins der Schrankenlosigkeit erregt.

The aesthetic category of the 'sublime' is employed to hook onto the experience of infinity, an experience we have when the magic of music exceeds the boundaries of time and space and drags us in a state of ecstasy, wherein we, as in deep dreams, perceive the metaphysical truth via inner vision.

Shakespeare as the ultimate ghost-seer

An important part of the analysis of Beethoven's genius is comprised by Wagner's account of himself as a creator of music dramas. Having answered his question of the source of Beethoven's creativity, he turns his focus to the poet, asking whether it is possible for the poet to create out of the unconscious. For this, he turns to Shakespeare, not so much in order to understand his own creativity, but rather, as he claims, to put an end to all misunderstandings concerning the genius of Shakespeare. Whatever the case may be, both converge conveniently, as we shall see below.

Wagner argues that Shakespeare is the poetical counterpart to Beethoven, claiming that, while Beethoven was a 'clairvoyant', Shakespeare was a 'seer of spectres'. According to Wagner, the musician (Beethoven) and the dramatist (Shakespeare) are alike; hence, the clairvoyant, or 'dreaming sleepwalker', is the counterpart of the seer of ghosts. The sleepwalker dreams 'truth dreams' ('*Wahrträume*', DS IX, p. 91). The ghost seer sees a ghost projected before his inner eye, like the clairvoyant when he sees his visions, at the moment that their outer vision is decreased or paralyzed. For Wagner, Shakespeare therefore is 'a Beethoven, who goes on dreaming though awake' ('der im Wachen fortträumende Beethoven,' DS IX, p. 90). While the Will speaks to us through music in a world of tones, the inner vision or intuition ('*Anschauung*'[45]) speaks to us in drama, in the enlightened world of forms:

---

[45] I find the common English translation of the German '*Anschauung*' as 'intuition' problematic, because the word 'intuition' does not express the moment of visual perception incorporated in the '*schauung*' of '*Anschauung*'. Because of Wagner's definition of the musical creativity as a dream activity, I prefer to use 'inner vision' for '*innere Anschauung*'. Both 'intuition' and 'inner vision' do contain the moment of intuitive, inner knowledge, though.

> [...] what creates Beethoven's melodies also projects Shakespeare-spectres; and both will perme-
> ate the same substance together, when we let the musician, as he steps into the world of sounds,
> come into the world of light at the same time. (DS IX, p. 92)

> [...] was Beethovens Melodien hervorbringt, projiziert auch die Snakespeare-Geistergestalten;
> und beide werden sich gemeinschaftlich zu einem und demselben Wesen durchdringen, wenn
> wir den Musiker, indem er in die Klangwelt hervortritt, zugleich in die Lichtwelt eintreten lassen

In addition, Wagner explains:

> Shakespeare's spectres would be brought to make sound by the full awakening of the inner music-
> organ, or else, Beethoven's motives would inspire the diminished vision to clear sight of these
> forms embodied in which these moved before our now clairvoyant eye (DS IX, p. 92)

> Die Geistergestalten Shakespeares würden durch das völlige Wachwerden des inneren Musikor-
> ganes zum Ertönen gebracht werden, oder auch: Beethovens Motive würden das depotenzierte
> Gesicht zum deutlichen Gewahren jener Gestalten begeistern, in welchen verkörpert diese jetzt
> vor unserem hellsichtig gewordenen Auge sich bewegten.

Beethoven and Shakespeare both create out of 'inner vision'. Shakespeare builds a 'world of forms' in his dramas, and Beethoven builds a 'world of motives' in his music. Shakespeare's character Coriolanus, according to Wagner, is a proud character with supernatural power and in conflict with his own inner voice. In the prelude he wrote to *Coriolanus*, Beethoven presents the motives of pride and voice. Through his music, we feel the essence of both characters much better than could ever be explained in a rational way. Alongside the musical motives, we follow the drama, without missing anything of the dramatic performance. Shakespeare and Beethoven both knew how to present the drama in action immediately. The action 'there [in Shakespeare, MP] is so determined by the operating characters, as it was equal to natural powers op-erating characters, as here [in Beethoven, MP] by the operative, in essence identical motives of the musician in these characters' ('diese wurde dort [in Shakespeare, MP] durch die gleich Naturmächtigen [sic!] wirkenden Charaktere so bestimmt, wie hier [in Beethoven, MP] durch die in diesen Charakteren wirkenden, im innersten Wesen identischen Motive des Musikers,' DS IX, p. 89). The *dramatis personae* as well as the musical motives are immediate representations of natural powers, because the forms are deeply penetrated by the natural spirit. This makes the characters in the play and the motives in the music deeply vigorous, human, and recognizable, even for modern man, from Wagner's (again highly Romantic) point of view.

In explaining Shakespeare's creative kinship to Beethoven, Wagner, as a creator of music and drama, has explained the two expressions as stemming from the same vision. He will also argue that this creative vision lies at the heart of the 'reformatory' spirit, by which artistic and cultural change are generated, as we will see below.

Beethoven as a 'reformer' of music and 'saviour' of culture

The musical form people often think of when Beethoven's name is mentioned is, of course, the sonata. The German and Viennese composers Bach, Haydn, and Mozart made the originally Italian invention famous and Beethoven became its champion. With an amusing sonata, a pianist used to introduce him- or herself to the audience. The sonata was an expression of the formalism that, with the attenuation of religious music, gained ground. Wagner fully attributes this formalism to Catholicism and the Counter-Reformation, of which Italy and France are the home-countries. To him, opera arias and the sonata form analogies to the spirit-deadening (*'geisttötenden'*) laws of Jesuit architecture, the 'weakened and sweetened' Italian post-Renaissance painting, and 'classical' French poetry. All these forms of art are decadent forms of earlier, strong art forms such as Hellenistic architecture, Italian Renaissance painting, and Greek and Shakespearean drama. As Wagner understands the matter, a growing 'Roman', or 'Catholic' influence in Europe has produced an enormous effect on art by inventing all kind of forms, thereby neglecting the deepest, metaphysical spirit. Consequently, art became generally 'softer' and 'sweeter' than it used to be. The aria, the sonata, and French poetry, in short, everything 'Roman', are its sad, provisional pinnacles. However, Germany's religious and artistic Reformation saved Europe:

> We know that it was the 'over the mountains' [in Italy, MP] much feared and hated *'German spirit'*, which everywhere, also in the field of art, met the artistically conducted decadence of the spirit of European nations, in a redemptive manner. (DS IX, p. 63)

> Wir wissen, daß der "über den Bergen" so sehr gefürchtete und gehaßte "deutsche Geist" es war, welcher überall, so auch auf dem Gebiete der Kunst, dieser künstlich geleiteten Verderbnis des europäischen Völkergeistes erlösend entgegentrat.

The Italian and French Counter-Reformation triggered off the fall of art and religion, Wagner claims. However, due to German artists such as Lessing, Goethe, Schiller, and, above all, Beethoven, the European decadence was interrupted and European culture took a turn for the better. German art, Beethoven's music in particular, showed the way back to the true essence of art, away from mere amusement and beauty. With Beethoven, music returned to its very self, to its sublime innocence in style, its philosophical apprehension, and musical representation of the Will. It is herein, Wagner presumes, that the relationship between the great Beethoven and the German nation is grounded.

As an artistic reformer, Beethoven is the musical counterpart of Martin Luther, the great German religious reformer, Wagner claims. Naturally, it is quite odd to put a musician, who was raised a Catholic, on par with the father of Protestantism. Wagner, aware of this curiosity, tries to demonstrate that Beethoven, although coming from a Catholic family, nevertheless had a Protestant, reforming frame of mind. Beethoven's superiority, his argument runs, is not a matter of 'outer revolution', but of 'inner reformation'. This is made emphatically clear by his *Eighth Symphony*, Wagner argues in a remarkable fashion, as it is a highlight of

> German natural peculiarity, which is so internally, deeply and richly gifted that it knows how to impress every form upon its essence by transforming the form from within. This saves it from the necessity of outer revolution. That is the reason the German people are not of a revolutionary, but of a reformatory kind. (DS IX, pp. 64–65)

> die Eigentümlichkeit der deutschen Natur, welche so innerlich tief und reich begabt ist, daß sie jeder Form ihr Wesen einzuprägen weiß, indem sie diese von innen neu umbildet, und dadurch von der Nötigung zu ihrem äußerlichen Umsturz bewahrt wird. So ist der Deutsche nicht revolutionär, sondern reformatorisch.

The old revolutionist Wagner, who in the 1840s was a close friend of the illustrious Russian revolutionist Mikhail Bakunin, and who was banned from Prussia and exiled to Switzerland because of his revolutionary activities in the years 1848–1849, here condemns all revolutions. He compares artistic revolution with political revolution, and regards both as the result of the same revolutionary spirit. By reasoning so, he also holds the political and social Revolution in France responsible for the French artistic idea that poetic and musical forms should be destroyed so that a new, better form can rise spontaneously from their ruins. Wagner assumes this view erroneous. By contrast, he expounds the view that the Germans know how to work with different forms, because they do not replace forms with others, but rather seek to enrich them with the deep, German spirit:

> In this way, we took the classical form of Roman and Greek culture, imitated their language, their verses, succeeded in mastering the antique intuition, but only inasmuch we expressed our own spirit in them. Similarly, we inherited the music with all its forms owed to the Italians, and what we build into those is brought to us by the incredible works of Beethoven's genius. (DS IX, p. 65)

> So nahmen wir die klassische Form der römischen und griechischen Kultur zu uns, bildeten ihre Sprache, ihre Verse nach, wußten uns die antike Anschauung anzueignen, aber nur indem wir unseren eigenen innersten Geist in ihnen aussprachen. So auch überkamen wir die Musik mit allen ihren Formen von den Italienern, und was wir in diese einbildeten, das haben wir nun in den unbegreiflichen Werken des Beethovenschen Genius vor uns.

Artistic Reformation therefore amounts to the 'saturation of the [Italian] musical form with the [German] musical genius' ('Durchdringung der [Italienischen] musikalischen Form von dem [Germanischen] Genius der Musik', DS IX, p. 65).

The German spirit makes the difference and it is the German spirit to which the decline of spirit and taste in Europe bowed. German artists, such as Schiller and Goethe, already fought the Roman tendency for superficiality, but only recently has Beethoven's music overcome it, Wagner concludes. To summarize Wagner's position, Beethoven's music is a sign of possible victory over the French fashion, but it is only the beginning of the German Rebirth, of the victory of artistic taste over fashion, of mythical stories over news, and of Communitarianism over individualism.

Beethoven's 'sublime naiveté' and 'inner joy'

Wagner states that Beethoven's 'masculine power of his character' gave him the power to change German and Europe's musical culture. This character analysis forms the weakest and most cliché line of argumentation in the essay, especially for present-day readers, to whom the physiognomic declarations appear very outdated. Nevertheless, it retains a weighty place in the whole, because Wagner argues for Beethoven's 'naiveté' as based on masculinity. Hence, while Schiller assumed that Goethe's art was 'Greek', because it was 'naive', meaning in spontaneous harmony with nature, Wagner grounds naiveté in Beethoven's 'Germanhood' and masculinity.[46]

Wagner's aesthetics not only rest on ethnic or geographical grounds, but is also explicitly gender-based. Quite disturbingly, he uses his aesthetic, ethnic, geographical, physiognomic, and sexual terminology often quite literally. However, Wagner swings to a figural conception of these terms just as easily, when he wants to defend Palestrina (an Italian Catholic), Italian Renaissance painting (which then suddenly is 'Christian' and 'musical' rather than 'Catholic' and 'pictorial'), and the English playwright Shakespeare as endowed with a special *German* talent for unconscious creativity (while claiming that the *German* dramatists Goethe and Schiller lack exactly this talent). This uncritical use of concepts leads to a lack of nuance, a disturbing rigidness, and arbitrariness in Wagner's reasoning. Hence, the physiognomic argumentation, by which Wagner argues that Beethoven disliked 'beauty' and the outer world (incidentally, without remarking that Beethoven famously had a weakness for beau-

---

46 In *The Birth of Tragedy*, Nietzsche argues that the genius artist is *not* naive, but someone who finds the balance between the Dionysian (unrevealing, musical) and Apollonian (illusionary, pictorial) powers. On the other hand, the naive artist (Homer and Raphael form Nietzsche's examples) is dominated by Apollonian powers. In the Homeric stories the Silenian wisdom is reversed into the view that "the worst thing [...] was to die soon, the second worst ever to die at all"' (BT 3, p. 24). Homeric man clings to life so much that 'even his lament turns into a song in praise of being' (BT 3, p. 24). Nietzsche, thus, defines 'naiveté' as 'the complete victory of Apolline illusion' (BT 3, p. 25). He relativizes Schiller's definition of 'naiveté' explicitly: 'it must be said that this harmony, which modern men look on with such longing, this unity of man with nature, to which Schiller applied the now generally accepted art-word "naive", is by no means such a simple, so-to-speak inevitable condition which emerges of its own accord and which we would be *bound* to encounter at the threshold of every culture, as a human paradise [...]' (BT 3, p. 24). Nietzsche could just as well have said that he opposes Wagner's definition of 'naiveté'. To Wagner, the genius is naïve, although not in the Schillerian sense either. To Nietzsche, at the threshold of (Western) culture there was 'the realm of the Titans', which first had to be overthrown by Apollonian powers, 'monsters' to be killed, and 'a terrifyingly profound view of the world and the most acute sensitivity to suffering' (BT 3, p.24) to be overcome. In his view, this is overcome by the creation of the 'Olympian' world of gods by the naive artist Homer (± 800 B.C.). With the rise of Greek theatre, in the 6th Century B.C., a balance between the Dionysian horror and Apollonian beauty was found.

tiful women)[47] and the 'gender' issue, to use a contemporary term, weaken Wagner's text considerably. This becomes even worse, if possible, when he switches to grounding Beethoven's genius in his deafness. At a certain point, Wagner comes close to asserting that Beethoven would have preferred being blind to becoming deaf, but quite unexpectedly switches over to explaining, again in truisms, why Beethoven was actually blessed by his deafness.

The musical genius in general plays a charming game with the forms of his inner world. The inner eye becomes stronger the more one turns away from the phenomenal world. Accordingly, deafness helped Beethoven to sharpen his inner eye and thus his genius 'undisturbed by the noises of life, just listens to his inner harmonies' ('ungestört vom Geräusche des Lebens nun einzig noch den Harmonien seines Inneren lauscht,' DS IX, p. 72). Deaf 'is the genius redeemed from everything outside, totally with and in himself' ('von jedem Außer-sich befreit, ganz bei sich und in sich,' DS IX, p. 72). Thus living in the knowledge of the ideas, Beethoven was able to give his music a joy, which originated in inner depth. This particular joy characterizes Beethoven's *Pastoral*, the *Eight*, and the *Choral* symphony in particular. It is a *redeeming* joy, because it makes the world regain its childlike innocence:

> Even the lamentation, so intimately and authentically typical for all tones, calms down: the world regains its childlike innocence. "You shall be with me in Paradise today" – who would not hear this word of redemption calling to him, if he listened to the "Pastoral Symphony"? (DS IX, p. 72)

> Selbst die Klage, so innig ureigen allem Tönen, beschwichtigt sich zum Lächeln: die Welt gewinnt ihre Kindesunschuld wieder. "Mit mir seid heute im Paradiese" – wer hörte sich dieses Erlöserwort nicht zugerufen, wenn er der "Pastoral-Symphonie" lauschte?

Joy, laughter, and childlike innocence are, in Wagner's view, hallmarks of the genius.[48]

---

47 Beethoven was not looking for beauty, Wagner states, because he considered beauty to be something soft and the world of appearances did not fit or attract him at all. The world of the eye, Wagner argues, only distracted him from his inner world. 'That beauty and weakness meant the same to him, is expressed by his physiognomic constitution with already sufficient emphasis' ('Daß Schönheit und Weichlichkeit ihm für gleich gelten müßten, drückte seine physiognomische Konstitution sofort mit hinreißender Prägnanz aus,' DS IX, p. 69) is one of Wagner's weakest and non-philosophical arguments, perhaps written under the influence of Schopenhauer's cliché description of the face of the genius. A face's 'expression of genius', according to Schopenhauer, 'consists in the fact that a decided predominance of knowing over willing is visible in it, and hence that there is manifested in it a knowledge without any relation to a will [...], a pure knowing' (W I 36, p. 188). This is the same as the disinterested knowledge of the child, who spontaneously has its knowledge rule its will.

48 Wagner does not explain his use of the religious term 'guilt' in opposition to 'childlike innocence', nor does he define the terms 'joy' and 'laughter'. We may assume, though, that he follows Schopenhauer in this. In that case, laughter arises from the victory of intuitive knowledge over reason. 'Joy' (Wagner uses '*Heiterkeit*' and '*Freude*', whereas Schopenhauer uses '*Freude*' most of the time), is the great, vital jubilation, that originates in the delusion that a steady satisfaction of the will is reached and from the belief in the possibility of a new future.

The genius *knows* (his knowledge triumphs over his will)[49] and *enjoys* his play with the forms of his inner world (the *'Gestaltenspiel'*). Simultaneously, he laughs at himself, because he acknowledges the illusory, ephemeral character of his own existence.[50] Joy and laughter, then, restore the desired 'innocence' (*'Unschuld'*), and redeem the conscience of its 'guilt':

> The effect of this laughter on the beholder is in fact this redemption of all guilt, just as the effect on the long term is *the feeling of paradise lost*, by which we return to the world of appearances (DS IX, p. 73)[51]

> Die Wirkung hiervon auf den Hörer ist eben diese Befreiung von aller Schuld, wie die Nachwirkung das Gefühl des verscherzten Paradieses ist, mit welchem wir uns wieder der Welt der Erscheinung zukehren.

Joy includes, however, seriousness and truthfulness. Whenever Beethoven was composing, he played a joyful, but serious game, in which he would bring the world, as perceived inside of him, to life: 'the dance of the world itself: wild pleasure, agonising complaint, the ecstasy of love, highest satisfaction, pain, rage, lust, and suffering' ('der Tanz der Welt selbst: wilde Lust, schmerzliche Klage, Liebesentzücken, höchste Wonne, Jammer, Rasen, Wollust und Leid,' DS IX, p. 78).

Beethoven's music does not present his view of the world, but the world and life itself. Whether the joy thus originates in the Schopenhauerian, pessimistic knowledge of our transitory life and our dependent, limited nature is not discussed by Wagner. He generally speaks of the Will as the heart of life, yet without taking the logical consequence of 'pessimism' or life's absurdity, so it seems. He emphasizes the moment of redemption, joy, and unity at the expense of pondering the tragic side of life.

To sum up, Beethoven's music is testimony to true 'Germanhood' (*'Deutschtum'*), of earnestness, joy (both in contrast to Italian frivolity), religious optimism, inner vision, instinct, the sublime, innocence, reformation (contra revolution), nature itself, nobility, eternity, masculinity, and the search for and expression of the purely human. He created music out of his inner visions. He made his best music, while he was deaf. He spread the joy to he experienced while abiding between and playing with the inner

---

49 Wagner remarks that this art originates from philosophical investigation and knowledge, and not from money, like Haydn and Mozart's music. This is a curious remark when we take into account, that Beethoven composed several works on royal order (especially Russian royalty). Wagner's agitation against commercial art, his never-ending financial problems, and his envy of the Jews (whom he associated with financial richness and commercial art, besides moral decadency) are well-known facts. Rose (1992) compellingly argues that these facts had much more effect on Wagner's aesthetics and musical praxis than is generally assumed.

50 This idea of laughing at one's own ephemeral existence is a key idea of Nietzsche's anti-metaphysical philosophy, especially in *The Gay Science*.

51 My italics.

forms of his dream visions over the outer world (which is 'hell', *'discordia'*) to his audience. His goal was to find the archetype of innocence and by representing this, to make his beholders happy. This, says Wagner, is exactly the task of art. The *Pastoral Symphony* attests to this effect: 'everything outer shines with Beethoven's inner joy' when one listens to this work, according to Wagner. Exactly this effect should Germany have with regard to European culture; Europe should, we may say, shine with German, inner joy. There is only one piece of music that tops this joyful effect of Beethoven's *Pastoral*: his 'Choral' Symphony, or *'Ninth Symphony'*. The 'Ninth', Wagner claims, attests to the 'most sublime naiveté' (*'erhabenster Naivetät'*, DS IX, p. 78) and represents 'the good man', the 'primordial type of innocence' (*'Urtypus der Unschuld'*, DS IX, p. 79).

In proclaiming that it is the task of German art to encompass joy (*'beglücken'*) and thus to redeem, Wagner follows Schiller. In *On the Use of the Chorus in Tragedy* ('Ueber den Gebrauch des Chors in der Tragödie,' 1803), Schiller writes: 'all art is dedicated to joy, and there is no higher or more serious task than to make people happy' ('Alle Kunst ist der Freude gewidmet, und es gibt keine höhere und keine ernsthaftere Aufgabe, als die Menschen zu beglücken').[52] Theatre must empower people to decide to change their lives. Fantasy or the imagination must not be deployed to supply man 'an amusing delusion of the moment' ('ein gefälliger Wahn des Augenblicks').[53] To give joy means to 'put the public not only in a momentary dream of freedom, but to liberate them in reality and in fact' ('den Menschen nicht bloß in einen augenblicklichen Traum von Freiheit zu versetzen, sondern ihn wirklich und in der Tat frei zu machen').[54] In that sense, art is 'at the same moment totally ideal and yet in the deepest sense real' ('zugleich ganz ideell und doch im tiefsten Sinne reell').[55] It surpasses the mere imitation of empirical nature as in French naturalistic theatre (which carries man back to reality) without remaining in the pure semblance or appearance (*'Schein'*), on the level of the ideal, and the imagination. It combines reason and imagination, truth and appearance, seriousness and joy, reality and ideal, and becomes, in this way, symbolic and retains poetic freedom.

According to Wagner, music is best suited for this task, and this is especially proven by Beethoven's *Ninth Symphony*, the Choral symphony. Due to music's metaphysical powers, it reaches a joy and truthfulness that exceeds those of other forms of arts. Because only Beethoven (and Goethe's *Faust*)[56] succeeds in fulfilling this se-

---

52 NA 10, p. 8.
53 NA 10, p. 8.
54 NA 10, p. 8.
55 NA 10, p. 9.
56 In *Faust*, the spirit of plastic art and the spirit of music are both active, according to Wagner. The spirit of plastic art dictates the famous phrase 'Alles Vergängliche ist nur ein Gleichnis' and the spirit of music 'Das ewig Weibliche zieht uns hinan'. Unfortunately, the celebration essay does not leave room for expansion on his views of *Faust*. However, his applauding of it is particularly remarkable in view of his earlier denial of Goethe's *conscious* creative act. Perhaps, Wagner probably is no refer-

rious task, nothing can support this task more than the remembrance of Beethoven, who, much earlier than the German army in the Franco-Prussian War, turned against the 'freche Mode' and spread 'the new religion, the world-redeeming message of the most sublime innocence' ('die neue Religion, die welterlösende Verkündigung der erhabensten Unschuld,' DS IX, p. 109). Commemorating Beethoven's birthday, Wagner concludes, we celebrate the birthday of 'the great pioneer in the jungle of a depraved paradise' ('den großen Bahnbrecher in der Wildnis des entarteten Paradieses', DS IX, p. 109).

Now that we have reconstructed Wagner's explanation of Beethoven's genius and the value of his music for culture, the question remains which technical rules music must obey in order to be the right 'outer' form of the 'inner' truth? The remaining questions to be answered in this chapter thus are, 'how are "rhythm", "melody", and "harmony", ideally, organized?' and 'how does this relate to Wagner's music dramas?'

'*Zeitfolge*' and 'ennobling' melody

Once more Wagner comes back to Goethe's lack of music, proclaiming that music influences the latter's poetic practice only when measure and rhythm in music (its 'periodic syntax', '*Periodenbau*') are taken as examples of poetic proportion. Contrary to Goethe, Beethoven does not stick to the forms, Wagner argues. As we have seen, Beethoven infiltrated the essence of music in such manner that his music projects or spreads 'the light of the clairvoyant' over the world of appearances. He adds soul or 'spirit' to music. In this resides his 'reformation', the uniqueness of music as an art form. Such argues Wagner against Hanslick, who confines the meaning of music to its forms. But how does Wagner understand form? If the meaning of music lies in its evocation of the metaphysical, is the tonal system apt to convey this metaphysical meaning?

According to Wagner, the inner depth must determine the musical forms, the rhythm, harmonies, and melody. Every note on the musical score must serve the communication of the truth, and not one thing is allowed to serve the formal laws. The forms of music ensue from the fact that 'every note must tell', express the deeper, metaphysical truth of life, carry a 'message'. The forms must not divide the melody, the music must be fluent, one, and expressive at all times. There is, therefore, no room for formal repetition or for showing-off virtuosity of the individual singer. Every note in the musical part, and every movement and word in the drama must reveal the mythical truth of original, lost and restored paradise. This has serious consequences for Wagner's view of rhythm.

---

ring to Goethe's work, but to Liszt's *Faust* Symphony, which is a setting of the 'Chorus Mysticus' that concludes Goethe's *Faust*.

Because rhythm is subordinate to the category of time, according to Wagner, it is a non-metaphysical element in music, and thus an obstacle in music rather than an apt musical means. For this reason, Wagner proposes to understand rhythm not as '*Periodenbau*', as it is commonly understood, but as '*Zeitfolge*' – a term we could perhaps best translate as 'temporal sequence' to indicate a temporal sequence without measured units. The 'temporal sequence' is caused by gentle fluctuations of one 'ground-colour', the inner truth or inner light, on which all kinds of varied modulations range, tending to 'timelessness' and 'spacelessness'. Music ruled by '*Periodenbau*' is music stuck to the 'columnar ordering of rhythmic parts'. As rhythm is strongly connected with time, Wagner proclaims rhythmical music is a plastic art like architecture rather than true music.[57] He therefore calls rhythmical music 'architectural' music, arguing that by creating music out of rhythm, the musician leaves the inner, audible world and sets out for the outer, visible one. The musician exchanges the '*Schallwelt*', the world of sounds, for the '*Lichtwelt*', the world of light:

> For with *this* music one also wants to *see* something, and this seeing becomes the primary thing, as is shown clearly by the 'opera', where the spectacle, the ballet, etc., makes up the attraction and fascination. (DS IX, p. 60)

> Denn zu *dieser* Musik will man nun auch etwas *sehen*, und dieses Zusehende wird dabei zur Hauptsache, wie dies die "Oper" recht deutlich zeigt, wo das Spektakel, das Ballet usw. das Anziehende und Fesselnde ausmachen.

Hence, music based on rhythm (dance music and opera music) does not surpass the threshold of beauty. Instead, it is nothing but formal play. As a result, it remains entangled in appearances. Such music is '*entartet*', i.e., estranged, degenerated, false, and depraved, but also 'guilty' (as the reverse of 'innocent'), unmelodic, and short on spirit. This is 'worldly music', which has lost its spirituality, its soul, its 'sublime innocence'. Music composed following temporal sequence rather than a period 'syntax', with measurable units, is 'innocent'.

The '*Zeitfolge*' thus makes music not only highly spiritual, but also 'melodic' and 'innocent'. This leads to the suggestion that the restoration of the innocence in melody

---

57 Nietzsche inserts these different views or sorts of rhythm in *The Birth of Tragedy* when he divides between Apollonian music, in which rhythm as 'periodic syntax' ('*Periodenbau*') rules, and Dionysian music, in which rhythm is to be understood as harmony-based temporal sequence. I shall come back to this, when I discuss Nietzsche's 'discovery' of 'quantitative' rhythm in Greek music and poetry, in the next chapter, which is in line with Schopenhauer's demarcation of 'quantitave' rhythm in melody. This, as we have seen, concerns the duration of notes, and a harmonious element in melody, which is 'qualitative' and points to the 'pitch and depth' of melody. Both, however, are subordinate to time, in Schopenhauer. Nietzsche, contrarily (and even without mentioning Schopenhauer and Wagner altogether in this respect), discerns a quantitative rhythm, which is highly similar to Wagner's temporal sequence, thus tending to timelessness.

amounts to the uplift of music, musical culture, and thus culture in general. The success of Beethoven's reformation indeed consists in its restoration of the innocence in melody, according to Wagner. Beethoven's reformation occasioned the salvation or 'restoration' of European culture. Specifically, the salvation is instigated by the choral finale of the *Ninth Symphony*, according to Wagner, because in that piece of music the 'innocent melody', which rejuvenates man's original 'childlike innocence', is restored. In that finale, man is brought back to paradise, the experience of harmony with himself, humankind, and nature. There the 'purely human' reigns. To Wagner, this choral finale is therefore an expression of 'sublime naiveté'.

The kernel of true music, from a technical perspective, therefore lies in the art of 'ennobling melody'.[58] The *Ninth Symphony* owes its sublime naiveté to its success in ennobling the melody, i.e., returning the 'purest innocence' (*'reinste Unschuld'*, DS IX, p.60) to the melody, thereby finding the archetype of innocence, the 'good man' (*'den guten Menschen'*, DS IX, p. 78): 'melody has been emancipated by Beethoven from all influence of the Mode, of shifting taste, and elevated to an eternal purely-human type' ('die Melodie ist durch Beethoven von dem Einflusse der Mode und des wechselnden Geschmackes emanzipiert, zum ewig giltigen, rein menschlichen Typos erhoben worden', DS IX, p. 83). According to Wagner, Beethoven's search for the 'purely human' and optimistic, ethical belief in the good and innocent nature of man makes him 'divinely naive'. We shall see in chapter 4 that this view leads to the greatest theoretical problem Nietzsche has with Wagner's aesthetics. Whereas Wagner's aesthetics collapses in morality, Nietzsche strives for replacement of the moral view with the aesthetic view of art and life.

Conclusion

By interweaving a chorus in the *Ninth Symphony*, Beethoven indeed emancipated the symphony from its formal laws. In fact, he stated that music should be free to move and not be bound to formal laws, of which the law of repetition, reprise or *'da capo'*, was the most compromising of the content of music. Laws such as the *da capo* (in the aria) or reprise (of the overture) endowed music with frills, fulfilled the common expectations, took the road of least resistance, and did not add anything to the content of music. By

---

58 Wagner takes this as the starting point for his way of composing by means of the 'endless melody' (*'unendliche Melodie'*) and the *'Leitmotif'* (*'Leitmotive'*). 'Leitmotiv' is not a term invented by Wagner (who spoke of *'Grundthema'*), but by the critic F.W. Jähn (who used it first in 1871). The term is primarily associated with Wagner's music drama (although already used by composers before him as Carl Maria von Webern or Berlioz's *'idée fixe'*). A 'leitmotiv' is a returning theme in the musical composition, coupled to a particular idea or character. It usually exists of one accord or short melodic phrase. A famous Wagnerian 'leitmotiv' for example is the so-called 'Tristanchord' (made up of the notes F, B, D# and G).

crossing the formal symphonic borders, the *Ninth Symphony* in fact ushered in the end of the symphonic form, so at least the New German School of music diagnosed. This inspired Liszt to compose 'symphonic poems' and Wagner to create musical dramas with a strong symphonic streak, akin to Gluck, Berlioz, and Beethoven. Flexibility, movement, melody and (dramatic, emotional, and musical) expression replaced the tonal laws of measure and harmony, especially in Wagner's *Ring* cycle, which, according to Wagner, accomplished the development from Beethoven's symphonies (which themselves culminate from the rudimentary Third to a climax of sublime naiveté and innocence in the Ninth), via Liszt's symphonic poems into the music drama.[59]

In remarkable contrast to Schopenhauer, Wagner couples a strong nationalism with the universal, metaphysical, and melodic powers of music by stating – and this is the central idea of his essay – that *German* music saves European culture from its decadence. Contemporary Europe is decadent, he argues, because of its lack of 'depth', due to the popularity of the 'Roman tendency'. This manifests itself in the (Italian) preference for frivolity and formalism, (Catholic) scepticism (which Wagner defines as 'hostility to the truth'), and the popularity of fashion in France. Journalism, also popularized by France, is a threat, because it has a deformed concept of the truth; the truth is no longer defined as the metaphysical essence of life but rather as what has happened most recently, what is new. This brings about a general inflation of spirituality and imagination. A lively, productive imagination, however, is according to Wagner the root of 'a true paradise of productivity by the human mind' ('ein wahres Paradies von Produktivität des menschlichen Geistes', DS IX, p. 98). Therefore, he advocates the 'mythologization' of culture. The cultural task Wagner assigned himself was to renew paradise, to give Germany and Europe back its imagination and stories with his music dramas. Beethoven's *Sixth*, *Eighth*, and especially *Ninth Symphony* was his model, because it 'fills us with the ineffable joy at having attained paradise', and evokes the belief that 'man is good after all'. Beethoven's *Ninth Symphony* fulfilled, because of its 'ennoblement of melody', a truly 'German reformation' according to Wagner. It countered the French '*freche Mode*' and spread 'the new religion, the world-redeeming mes-

---

59 Around 1600, the Renaissance musicians of the Florentine Camarata, Jacopo Peri, Giulio Caccini, and Claudio Monteverdi produced the first *dramma per musica*. Their operas were intended as reconstructions of the Greek drama, in which the text was reinforced by the music. Wagner shares the aim to reinforce drama by way of music. Yet his programme is not to rejuvenate original Greek drama so much as to draw his own inspiration of Greek dramas, especially Aeschylus's *Prometheus* trilogy ('Prometheus' was a very popular figure in German Romantic art). The *dramma per musica* drifted away from its original musical programme, when it developed into Voice Theatre because of the hegemony the eunuch and soprano singers acquired in the seventeenth and eighteenth centuries. This development was facilitated especially by the typical style of Pietro Metastasio (1698–1782) of the 'Arcadic Academy' in Rome. The *Instituti della Ragunanza defli Arcadi*, of which Casanova and Mozart librettist Lorenzo da Ponte were also members, intended to liberate poetry from the complex and unnatural language of the Baroque by stressing the classical unities of time, place, and action.

sage of the most sublime innocence'. Beethoven had started a 'cultural war' against France and Italy, which Wagner intended to continue and win.

In his plea for the ennoblement of melody, Wagner deviates in important ways from Schopenhauer's philosophy of music. While holding to Schopenhauer's division of the arts into music and the visual arts, he does not adopt his hierarchal system of the musical elements and its analogies in nature, a system that solidly fixes the tonal system in the Will. Instead, he develops a view of music that breaks with the tonal system in attempting to transform every musical element into a significant part of the melody. Both Schopenhauer and Wagner, however, value the melody above the harmony and rhythm, and regard rhythm as the 'architectural' element of music, as it is bound to the category of time. To become 'timeless' (Nietzsche would say 'untimely'), therefore, becomes the highest task of art, according to Schopenhauer and Wagner. Wagner does not however embrace Schopenhauer's pessimism, in his 'Beethoven' essay; instead, he keeps to a moral optimism and a redemptive frame of mind. Whereas in Schopenhauer's view the experience of childlike innocence and paradise are just illusions, in Wagner's account these are visions of how the world actually could be. The 'innocence of melody' leads Europe to 'Elysium'.

The fight over melody in Italian versus French opera and French and Italian music versus German music forms the surprising core of the discussion about which path Europe has to take in order to find a better future, the 'northern' road, as Wagner advocated, or the 'southern' road, as Rousseau had defended long before Wagner? In *The Birth of Tragedy*, Nietzsche chooses the 'southern' road, arguing in his own typical way of 'binary synthesis', as Bishop and Stephenson termed it, that the 'southern' way is the 'northern' way.[60]

Before turning to *The Birth of Tragedy*, however, we shall have a close look at section 9 of KSA 7 (Notebook U I 4a). Section 9 is a collection of notes Nietzsche made in 1871, while he was working on *The Birth of Tragedy*.[61] In these notes, we can follow Nietzsche's adoption, modification, discussion, and problems with Wagner's 'Beethoven' essay in detail and more clearly than in *The Birth of Tragedy*, which tries to

---

60 Bishop and Stephenson define 'binary synthesis' as follows: 'In binary synthesis, the name of one element in a pair of antitheses is also applied to the synthesis, which thus represents both a richer concept, but one that tends towards on of the original antitheses in an ascending hierarchy' (p. 34). They show that 'binary synthesis' is a typically Weimarian mode of argumentation and that Nietzsche installs this especially in his use of the term 'semblance' ('*Schein*') in *The Birth of Tragedy* (2005, pp. 33–34). Cf. Stephenson, who refers to William James's explanation of this concept in this respect (2005, p. 579). The binary synthesis is a variation of the principle of *coniunction oppositorum* (2005, p 579), in which one term of the two, which form an opposition, soaks up the whole opposition. In so doing, that term, which is a *species*, becomes the *genus*, which roofs over both specific terms.

61 The genesis of *The Birth of Tragedy* is quite complicated, because the notes relevant to the book are spread out over fourteen different notebooks. See for more information: Silk and Stern (1981), pp. 41–52.

hide moments of scepticism towards Wagner's music and theory. Unmistakable, however, is the enormous theoretical influence Wagner exercised on Nietzsche's first book. This influence is deeper than Schopenhauer's and perhaps as important as Goethe's and Schiller's.

Chapter 3
Nietzsche's reception of Wagner's 'Beethoven' essay in the spirit of Weimar Classicism

Introduction

As we saw in chapter 1, Nietzsche became a Wagnerian only after he met the composer, in November 1868. We have also suggested that it was not only Wagner's music, but also his philosophy that turned him into a 'Wagner-*Jünger*'. However, this does not imply that Nietzsche approached Wagner's theoretical views uncritically. He diverged from Wagner concerning many subjects, for example on social equality, and the relation between art and politics.[1] The existence of slavery in Greek culture was reason enough for Wagner not to wish for a return to 'Arcadia', but to wish for an 'Elysium', a modern society based on social equality.[2] Nietzsche, however, expected cultural and social good from art but not from politics, because politics does not offer an honest answer to the tragedy of life, for it involves a manoeuvre *not* to have to face life's essentially tragic nature.[3] Nietzsche understood inequality as a necessary condition of the 'birth of the genius' ('Geburt des Genius').[4] As for his conception of culture, it implied that culture had 'the task to make [sic! MP] possible the context of understanding in which great men (geniuses) do not appear as strangers,' as Salim Kemal put it.[5] Perhaps we may rephrase it even more plainly into the idea that culture *is* the context in

---

1 Cf. López (1998–1), pp. 106–108.

2 In this 'equality' must be relativized, because Wagner's theoretical defence of 'equality' jars with his harsh anti-Semitism and also with his narrow view of women (as muses, artistic personage and wives only). See also Ruehl (2006), pp. 82–88.

3 Cf. Riedel (1995), p. 47.

4 Cf. 10[1], KSA 7.333–357 and FP 3 'The Greek State' ('Der Griechische Staat', KSA 1.764–777), which Nietzsche sent to Cosima Wagner for her birthday on 25 December 1872. However, it was originally written in early 1871. Ruehl considers 'The Greek State' to be 'the political "subtext" of Nietzsche's first book' (Ruehl 2004, p. 80), justifiably contending that: 'what an analysis of "The Greek State" shows is that beyond the biographical and the boudoir, Nietzsche's break with Wagner had an important political component' (Ruehl 2004, p. 81). However, Nietzsche never desired the *political* and *constitutional* realization of non-egalitarian society as the appropriate means to realize his own artistic and cultural ideals. Cf. Martin, who says that slavery is justified in Greek culture, because they were needed to produce great culture and that 'at times in his early writings Nietzsche appears to present this as a viable template for Europe's future development' (Ruehl, 2004, p. 47). Martin emphasizes rightly that 'however questionable Nietzsche's vision of the Greek state may be, both as history and as a model for a political theory, it is not racist [...]' (Ruehl, 2004, p.47) and that Nietzsche envisioned 'a vital role' for the Jews to perform in his 'Greek-inspired', 'new Europe' (Ruehl 2004, p. 48 and p. 50).

5 Kemal (1998), pp. 260–261.

which a genius does not appear as a stranger.[6] Nietzsche, therefore, posed the question as to how a culture could be created that would match Wagner's music, envisioning his and Germany's task as 'finding the culture to our music!' ('die Kultur zu unserer Musik zu finden!' 19[30], KSA 7.426).[7]

Goethe and Schiller were the precursors of this culture, and Wagner brought it to fruition. Whereas Wagner considered Beethoven the pioneer who would lead humankind away from and out of the jungle of 'a depraved paradise', Nietzsche regarded Wagner as the fulfiller of the 'cultural war' ('*Kulturkampf*'), which was started by Goethe and Schiller: 'Wagner fulfils what was initiated by Schiller and Goethe' ('Wagner vollendet was Schiller und Goethe begonnen haben,' 9[23], KSA 7.280). The Weimar friends had not been able to achieve their goals, because they had 'lacked music'. Their 'lack of music' notwithstanding, Nietzsche adopted the 'Weimar' aesthetic and cultural context to evaluate Wagner's 'Beethoven' essay. Remarkably, he did not employ Schopenhauer's philosophy to critically assess Wagner's musical aesthetics. Only later, in *The Birth of Tragedy* did he use Schopenhauer's metaphysics of music to fortify Wagner's views and enterprises. In this chapter, therefore, I delineate Nietzsche's reception of Wagner's 'Beethoven' essay with regard to his use of Weimar Classicist thought, asking which philosophical, cultural, and aesthetic views of Wagner Nietzsche adopted and rejected. I hope to answer this question in order to determine in more detail the exact nature of Nietzsche's early aesthetics and ideal of European culture, an ideal of which Wagner formed the centre and source.

Wagner's theoretical influence on Nietzsche's early philosophy can be detected by focusing on a series of notes collected in Section 9 of the KSA 7 (notebook U I 4 a). Those notes are the clearest evidence of Nietzsche's reception of Wagner's 'Beethoven' essay. They stem from the notes of 1871, when he worked on *The Birth of Tragedy*. I take them as a bridge between Wagner's 'Beethoven' essay and *The Birth of Tragedy*. In bridging the two treatises, the notes lean heavily on Goethe's and Schiller's aesthetics, especially Schiller's notion of the 'idyll'. Consequently, my focus in this chapter will be for the greater part on Nietzsche's examination of Wagner as a 'tragic-idyllic' composer – a highly remarkable understanding given Nietzsche's palpable rejection of Italian opera's 'idyllic tendencies' in *The Birth of Tragedy*.[8]

---

6 As Nietzsche expressed it, e.g., 'It is the task of a *culture* that a people's greatness does not appear as hermit, nor as exile' ('Es ist die Aufgabe einer *Kultur*, daß das Große in einem Volke nicht als Einsiedler erscheint, noch als Verbannter', 19[37], KSA 7.430).

7 In his later, anti-Wagnerian days, Nietzsche would turn this idea around: it was the modern, unartistic, typically 'German' culture that created Wagner's music. As he wrote: 'Modernity speaks its most *intimate* language in Wagner' (p. 234/'DurchWagner redet die Modernität ihre intimste Sprache,' KSA 6.12).

8 In *The Birth of Tragedy* Nietzsche scorns the idyllic tendencies of the figure of the shepherd (to which he opposes the satyr, chapter 7 and 8), Rousseau, Weimar Classicism (chapter 20) and, especially, Italian opera (chapter 21). I shall treat this more extensively in chapter 4, below. This is due to the fact

Preliminary methodological remarks

Before coming to the actual close-reading of KSA 7 section 9, I need to make some methodological remarks, first to account for my decision to read Nietzsche's notes separately, and second to position my work along the works of others who have discussed KSA 7 section 9 and Nietzsche's musical aesthetics.

There is a clear reason for examining the notes in a separate chapter. In order to determine the shifts and changes in Nietzsche's aesthetic and philosophical development in detail, I draw on the notes throughout this book. In my view, Nietzsche's published works should generally be valued above his unpublished essays and notes. One obvious reason for this is that Nietzsche chose other formulations and sometimes even other ideas in the definitive forms of his books. However, *The Birth of Tragedy* is not only written as a scholarly study. Nietzsche also hoped to flatter Richard Wagner with it and wrote it partly as a pamphlet for Wagner's artistic and cultural enterprises. In that sense, it can even be regarded as part of the range of pamphlets written by people of the Old German School (Johannes Brahms, Joachim, Clara and Robert Schumann, Felix Mendelssohn, Eduard Hanslick) and the New German School (Franz Liszt, Richard Wagner, and Franz Brendel). The propagandist character of the book, however, stimulated Nietzsche to rid the book of remarks that would be unwelcome to Wagner. The notes of the early seventies give us the opportunity to trace the development of Nietzsche's aesthetics and his Wagner-criticism more precisely, because they lack this propagandist and flattering character. Section 9 of KSA 7 contains a glossary of notes in which Nietzsche forms ideas on music and drama by contemplating Wagner's philosophy of music and drawing in Schopenhauerian, Schillerian, and Goethean views. More than *The Birth of Tragedy*, these notes point out the struggle he suffered to bring Greek tragedy and Wagnerian music drama together by invoking the help of Goethe and Schiller. These notes clearly show which specific Wagnerian ideas he experienced difficulties with, because he moved in a much freer and more critical way in them than in his book, which is compromised in part by his allegiance to Wagner. Hence, in order to decide more precisely upon Wagner's philosophical influence on Nietzsche, Nietzsche's early critique of his friend, and the content of Nietzsche's early aesthetics, these fragments, in my opinion, must be separately scrutinized.[9]

---

that Nietzsche there uses the term 'idyllic' more or less as an equation of 'moral' and 'moral optimism', while in his notes, he uses it also in the Schillerian understanding as the poetic representation of the unity between nature and reality (see 9[142], KSA 7.327).

9 Landerer and Schuster (2002) also state that, because 'Nietzsche's occasional scepticism had to be kept within a frame which would be acceptable to Wagner' ('Nietzsches gelegentliche Skepsis mußte freilich in einem für Wagner akzeptablen Rahmen gehalten werden,' p. 120) in *The Birth of Tragedy*, the notes that precede this book bear much more witness of Nietzsche's fluctuating views of music and tragedy: 'Nietzsche's factual dissident stance concerning pivotal points in Wagner's aesthetics is not so much to be reconstructed from *The Birth of Tragedy* but rather from unpublished sketches and

Venturelli (1989) and López (1995) have also made close examinations of section 9. López did so with regard to Nietzsche's study of Greek rhythmics and Venturelli in connection with Nietzsche's reading of the Goethe-Schiller correspondence. Both articles have been equally crucial to my interpretation of Nietzsche. To their important work in shedding light on Nietzsche's early aesthetics, I hope to contribute my view of the conflict Nietzsche experienced when he discovered in 1871 that Wagner was perhaps an idyllic composer. Venturelli points to Nietzsche's ponderings over the 'idyllic', yet does not discuss the major consequences this has for his view of Wagner.

It has been advanced by the established music scholar Carl Dahlhaus in his essay 'The Twofold Truth in Wagner's Aesthetics' (1980), and in his footsteps followed Bruse (1984) and Kropfinger (1985), that Nietzsche opposes Wagner's musical aesthetics as early as 1871. They pronounce that Nietzsche is 'all but a blind member of the party',[10] because Nietzsche criticizes the early, pre-Schopenhauerian Wagner. They do not mention, however, that the later, Schopenhauerian Wagner equally criticized that early Wagner, and that Nietzsche used the views of the later Wagner to criticize the early one. Instead, Dahlhaus points to parallels in Nietzsche's musical aesthetics and Hanslick's formalism. Basing his argument on the one phrase in fragment 12[1] (KSA 7.359–369) which is not at odds with Hanslick – in which it is said that music is not an expression of emotions – plus on Nietzsche's switch from Wagner's opposition to 'absolute music' in *Opera and Drama* (by which term Wagner referred to purely instrumental music and the idea that the value of music resides in the music itself), Dahlhaus concludes: 'The musical aesthetic Nietzsche outlined in the fragment 'On Music and Words' seems therefore [...] to be a covert argument on behalf of "absolute" music'.[11] Dahlhaus ends his argument with the thesis that:

> The historical significance of the fragment 'On Music and Words' is that Nietzsche, in an unconscious referral back to romanticism, formulated a comprehensive concept of 'absolute' music which reveals the latent unity of musical aesthetics in the nineteenth century.[12]

Kaufmann adorned the fragment 12[1] (originally without heading) with the title 'On Music and Words' and even labels it an 'essay'.[13] Consequently, Dahlhaus, while con-

---

some dispersed expressions in letters' ('Nietzsches tatsächliche Dissidentenhaltung in für Wagners Ästhetik wichtigen Punkten läßt sich daher weniger aus der *Geburt der Tragödie* als vielmehr aus unveröffentlichten Entwürfen und einigen verstreuten brieflichen Äußerungen rekonstruieren,' p. 121).

10 Kropfinger (1985), p. 4.

11 Dahlhaus (1980), p. 31.

12 Dahlhaus (1980), p. 39. Nietzsche's reference is not 'unconscious', because he was not unfamiliar with Romantic musical theory.

13 Dahlhaus (1980), p. 103. Kaufmann's translation is included as Appendix to Dahlhaus (1980).

fining his theoretical scope to the separation between composers of 'absolute music'[14] and its defender Eduard Hanslick on the one hand, and Romanticists such as E.T.A. Hoffmann,[15] programme musicians like Berlioz and Liszt, and Wagner's music drama on the other hand, interprets Nietzsche as a defender of 'absolute music' in the sense of Hanslickian formalism. In addition, he considers this fragment an important contribution to nineteenth century music theory. Janz (1988) also claims that after 1865 Nietzsche

> begins to move away from the Romantic conception of music, emerging as a philosophical pioneer of a formal aesthetic of music that finally, decades after Nietzsche, is completed in the serial constructions of Joseph Matthias Hauer and Arnold Schoenberg[16]

To perceive Nietzsche as a formalist as early as 1865 is a rather far-fetched idea, for which there is no substantive evidence. However, to turn him into a 'philosophical pioneer of a formal aesthetic of music' is completely out of order, especially when dating this to 1865 instead of 1878 (when he, in *Human All Too Human* criticizes his earlier views by confronting them with opposite views, amongst which – but not exclusively – formalist views). For now, let me bring in one counterargument against the idea that Nietzsche was an anti-Wagnerian, Hanslickian formalist as early as 1871. That his musical aesthetics was everything but Hanslickian in 1871 will become clear enough in the rest of this chapter.

Baptizing Nietzsche's early musical aesthetics as Hanslickian-formalistic triggers the question as to how we must reconcile his supposed formalist position with his zealous vindication of the chorus as the centre of the theatrical experience. Ignoring Nietzsche's preference for Wagner's music and Greek drama, Dahlhaus calls him essentially 'anti-theatrical', referring to his explanation in *Nietzsche contra Wagner* that 'you can see that my nature is intrinsically anti-theatrical, in the very depths of my soul I feel that profound contempt for the theatre, the mass art par excellence, that every artist feels today'.[17] But Dahlhaus divorces the remark from its historical context and consequently misses Nietzsche's point. In this late fragment (*Nietzsche contra Wagner* was written seventeen years later than 'On Music and Words'), Nietzsche combats

---

14 See also Dahlhaus (1978). The term 'absolute music' was brought into use by Wagner to indicate purely instrumental music, which originates only in the mechanical process of composing tones into melody.

15 Hoffmann's review of Beethoven's *Fifth Symphony*, which appeared in the *Allgemeine musikalische Zeitung* 12 in 1810, is a key text in Romantic musical aesthetics, chiefly because of its ensuing phrase: 'Music is the most romantic of all arts; one might even say that it alone is purely romantic. [...] Music unlocks for man an unfamiliar world having nothing in common with the external material world ['*Sinnenwelt*', the world of the senses, MP]' (1971, p. 151).

16 Janz (1988), p. 105. The biggest mistake of Janz's article is that in order to facilitate his claim, he ignores the theoretical impact of Nietzsche's intellectual friendship with Wagner completely.

17 Quoted from Dahlhaus (1980), p. 26.

exactly what he, together with Wagner, in earlier days had tried to fight, namely 'philistinism', the tendency to superficiality, and negation of the aesthetic. In this fragment, he does not despise the theatre in general (on the contrary, he often goes to Italian operas and Bizet's *Carmen*) so much as modern, German theatre, arguing that an artist worthy of the name 'artist', keeps remote from everything the German theatre has to offer. A true artistic person, according to Nietzsche, has enough 'tragedy and comedy in himself' (GS 86, p. 87/'[...] Tragödie und Komödie', KSA 3.444) and thus does not need the theatre as 'aping the high tide of the soul' (GS 86, p.87/'eine Nachäffung der hohen Seelenfluth', KSA 3.434–444), as an institution where the masses go to forget the emptiness of their own lives, and with the hope that the play will 'overwhelm the spectator with emotions' (GS 80, p. 80/'Ueberwältigung der Zuschauer durch Affecte', KSA 3.436). Dahlhaus thus overlooks the fact that Nietzsche disdains the modern theatre, specifically Wagner's music dramas in *Nietzsche contra Wagner* and not theatre in general.

Dahlhaus (1980) has a point in observing that Nietzsche is engaging a 'secret polemic' against Wagner; however, he is wrong in localizing this in the formalist camp of the Old German School. For that reason, his analysis that Nietzsche turns Wagner's 'twofold truth' into a dichotomy and that he does so, 'by adroit, selective emphasis', goes astray too.[18] Here, Dahlhaus projects his own way of arguing onto the philosopher. Dahlhaus is the one who searches for a secret polemic in the fragment by ascribing to Nietzsche a Hanslickian musical formalism and secret support to absolute music. In a forced and contradictory manner, Dahlhaus keeps to the idea that Wagner's 'Beethoven' essay is not meant as contradicting the twenty-year-old essay *Opera and Drama*, because the programme of defending music drama as the ultimate form of art is still the same.[19] However, this argument does not hold. With his 'Beethoven' essay, Wagner renounces *Opera and Drama* on the point of the relation between music and text. Wagner's 'Schopenhauerian' turn resides in the fact that he changes his view that music should serve the dramatic end (as *Opera and Drama* defended) to the view that music should dominate the text and the drama. This is not an alteration made by Nietzsche, but by Wagner himself, and the composer was clever enough to understand that this view made a defence of his music dramas problematic, because it made the balance between music and text very thin. Even Schopenhauer had already pointed to the problematic aspect of this in his defence of Rossini's operas as examples of per-

---

18 Dahlhaus (1980), p. 26. Cf. Dahlhaus (1980)., p. 27.

19 What seems odd, however, is the fact that Wagner agreed with re-issuing *Opera and Drama*, despite the fact that his view on the relation between text and music had changed since then. However, this change is a 'reformation' rather than a 'revolution', to use Wagner's terminology, and in that sense 'Beethoven' can be regarded as an essay that refines and deepens the aesthetic views of *Opera and Drama* rather than as an overall rejection of it. In the end, the theories of both essays suit *Tristan and Isolde*, a work finished in 1859 and first performed in 1865, albeit that 'Beethoven' would suit it more.

fect music in *The World as Will and Representation I* § 52, as we saw in the previous chapter. There we also saw that Wagner found an elegant solution in connecting the unconscious creativity of the musician (Beethoven) and the dramatist (Shakespeare). In 12[1], and in another three hundred something pages of notes from 1871, Nietzsche discusses Wagner's 'Beethoven' essay, but hardly *Opera and Drama*. Above all, in the alleged 'essay' on absolute music 12[1], the objective is to understand Schopenhauer's concept of the Will, especially its problematic relation to the idea (the problem resides above all in the question whether the 'idea' is the general form of an individual thing, and if so, in what sense the Will is present in the idea) rather than Hanslick.[20]

Recently, Christoph Landerer and Marc-Oliver Schuster (2002) also argued that Hanslick's aesthetic viewpoints dominated Nietzsche's musical reflections between 1870 and 1872. Although a challenging thesis, on the contrary, there is no evidence that supports this. Nietzsche names Hanslick three times in the notes of the early seventies. In the first note, he presents a restricted and ironic interpretation of Hanslick's standpoint in a note of 1871. Speaking of Hanslick's inability to find the content of music, Nietzsche ironizes the key notion of his theory that there was no other content than the music itself: 'Hanslick: cannot find the content and is of the opinion that there is only form' ('Hanslick: findet den Inhalt nicht und meint es gebe nur Form,' 9[8], KSA 7.273). In the second note, Nietzsche neutrally resumes Hanslick's differentiation between 'subjective', 'pathological' music and 'unpathological' music as pure form.[21] In the third note, he names Hanslick together with the club of philologists, Young Germany, the University of Strasbourg, Jahn, the daily newspaper Centralblatt, Leipzig, and about twenty other names and institutions as things under the headline 'to attack' ('*anzugreifen*').[22] In my view, Frederick Love (1966), Curt Paul Janz (1988), and Éric Dufour (1999) are more correct to place Hanslick's authority in Nietzsche's earlier (1865) and later (from 1876 onwards) musical reflections.[23]

It is more illuminating, justifiable, and logical to turn to Nietzsche's reception of Wagner's centenary essay 'Beethoven' than to regard Nietzsche's musical aesthetics as a discussion in favour of or against 'absolute music'. Wagner's 'Beethoven' essay forms the main theoretical source of Nietzsche's early musical aesthetics and philosophy of culture. None of the above-mentioned critics that are or have been involved with

---

20 Colli and Montinari refer to 12[1] as a pre-form of Nietzsche's lecture *Socrates and Greek Tragedy* (*Socrates und die griechische Tragödie*, KSA 14, p. 543). In my view, 12[1] is a fragment that Nietzsche wrote in April 1871 for the last ten chapters of *The Birth of Tragedy*, when he was trying to connect Greek tragedy to Wagnerian music drama by engendering it into Schopenhauer's metaphysical division of the arts.

21 9[98], KSA 7.310.

22 19[259], KSA 7.500–501. Cf. Nietzsche's mention of Hanslick in a negative context in a letter to Cosima Wagner of April 1873, KSB 4, pp. 143–144.

23 See chapter 1 of this book. I come back to Nietzsche's Hanslickian formalism when I discuss his later musical aesthetics in chapter 6, below.

Nietzsche's musical aesthetics have taken the pains to make a textual comparison of 'Beethoven' and *The Birth of Tragedy*, even though such research does more justice to Nietzsche and yields far more results than trying to prove Nietzsche's Hanslickian sympathy.[24] As we shall see in what follows, Nietzsche's 1871 reflections on music are dominated by '*the* philosophy of music', as Nietzsche ranked Wagner's musical aesthetics, and completed with Schopenhauerian metaphysics, Weimar aesthetics, and Weimar cultural theory.

Although I have strong sympathy for the attempt to relativize Nietzsche's Wagnerism, I do not believe the 'Hanslickian-formalistic' road is the course that should be taken. My study confirms Dahlhaus's thesis that Nietzsche is 'all but a blind member of the party'. However, it also shows that this is not because Nietzsche was secretly Hanslickian-formalistic in 1871. Rather it shows that Nietzsche's secret scepticism of Wagner resides in his view of the Greeks.[25] Part of his doubt was raised because of different musical insights, which are anything but 'absolute' in the Hanslickian sense (rather, they are 'absolute' in as far as they are metaphysical, holding to an absolute truth about life). As I argue below, and in chapter 4, the problems that Nietzsche experienced with Wagner in respect of his musical aesthetics are situated, first, in Wagner's 'idyllic' tendency; second, his reluctant use of the chorus; and third, in Wagner's view of rhythm. Genuinely secretly polemic, if I may put it so, is Nietzsche when he tries to understand Wagner as a 'radically idyllic' composer, a composer of 'tragic idylls', and having an 'idyllic tendency'.

Lastly, because we are dealing with a heap of fragments, I, once more, have to construe a thematic structure myself in the following discussion. As in the former chapter, I start from the cultural and musical-artistic opposition between Italy and Germany in order to move on towards a gradually more technical discussion of musical concepts. In my examination, I shall skip notes which have only little or nothing to add to my analysis of Nietzsche's historical roots or our thematic discussion, as well as notes which were not written for *The Birth of Tragedy*, but rather within the framework of his professorship or intended for lectures concerning the institutions of education in Germany, which Nietzsche delivered in 1872 and which are collected under the name *On the Future of Our Educational Institutions (Ueber die Zukunft unserer Bildungsanstalten)*, such as notes 9[60–70]. Obviously, wherever I find relevant or contradictory elements in those, I shall bring them into my discussion.

---

24 Nor have Sorgner, Birx, Knoepfler (2008).
25 Cf. Riedel (1995), p. 47ff.

Wagner's and Goethe and Schiller's ideal of a national theatre

Similar to Wagner's 'Beethoven', the notes assembled under '9' are framed by the opposition 'Germany' against 'Italy' and 'France'. However, Nietzsche assesses Wagner's
ideas by confronting them with the aesthetics and cultural theories of Goethe and
Schiller. The first three notes of section '9' are draft-titles for his début book and set the
tone for the rest of the discussion. The sketch 'opera and Greek tragedy' ('Die Oper und
die griechische Tragödie', 9[1], KSA 7.269) indicates that Nietzsche understood that the
whole tradition had to be regarded in the light of its original claim and purpose to rejuvenate Greek tragedy, while the other two, *'The Birth of Tragedy* out of Music' ('Die
Geburt der Tragoedie aus der Musik', 9[2], KSA 7.269), and *'The Birth of Tragedy* out
of the Spirit of Music' ('Die Geburt der Tragoedie aus dem Geiste der Musik' (9[3], KSA
7.269)) imply that he hoped to prove the musical origin of drama. This is confirmed by
note 9[5] (KSA 7.271–272), which shows that Nietzsche had studied, albeit rather modestly, the origins of Florentine opera, or *'dramma per musica'* (a term carefully avoided
by Wagner and Nietzsche). That Nietzsche read his two sources rather selectively is revealed by his focus on the 'unmusical' fact that the Florentine circle approached the
problem of the balance between music and text from the question how words should
be sung without making the words incomprehensible. This was a problem (church)
music in general faced at that time with regard to the Catholic scepticism of music.
Passages of Doni and Lindner are quoted to support Nietzsche's view of opera as being too 'textual' and focused on the recitative.[26] Because of its focus on the recitative,
Italian opera is claimed to be superficial, 'external' ('*veräußerlicht*', that is, in Schopenhauerian terms, focused on empirical reality), and 'craving for amusement' ('*zerstreu-
ungssüchtig*'). It is a form of art typical for modern times, and made by a typical modern
artist: that is to say, someone who is in fact incompetent for art ('*kunstohnmächtig*',
KSA 7.274). Moreover, it is made for an equally 'non-artistic' ('*unkünstlerisch*', 9[10],
KSA 7.275) public that sits in the theatre with a 'critical' mind instead of, as in pre-
modern times, unconsciously absorbed by the event. French opera is also rejected, yet
for the reason that it – leaving the pastoral image of paradise – celebrates the great
moments of human history. Rather than being 'pastoral', French opera is 'heroic' in
that it idealizes human virtue and not, we may add, humanity's original innocence.[27]
This makes it non-artistic too.

Wagner will end these non-artistic tendencies, Nietzsche believes. Wagner's greatest advantage over Italian opera was that he, instead of asking the question as to how

---

26 Nietzsche's sources are chapter one of Ernst Otto Lindner's, *Zur Tonkunst, Abhandlungen*. Berlin:
Guttentag, 1864 (chapter one is entitled 'Die Entstehung der Oper') and 'Doni *Tom. II* '.
27 Incidentally, Schiller's *The Robbers* (*Die Räuber*, his first play of 1783, which was made under the
spell of the French Revolution, MP) suffers from the same 'French' or 'Roman' spirit, Nietzsche ob-
serves. Cf. 9[123], KSA 7.319.

text can remain understandable when put to music, started from the music and understood words as mirrors of the musical tone. This was the core of Nietzsche's trust that
Wagner would accomplish Goethe and Schiller's project to reform German culture by
reforming its art, which until then was dominated by French and Italian, in short 'Roman' rules. In line with Wagner's praise of Beethoven for releasing Germany from the
superficial, Roman bent, Nietzsche cherishes Wagner for saving Germany from 'Ro-
manism' ('*Romanismus*', 9[147], KSA 7.329). In this context, he paraphrases Wagner's
proclamation that German music enriches Italian musical forms with depth: 'There-
with we note how the opera, as form of the Roman, non-artistic man, is deepened end-
lessly and lifted to art by the German tendency' ('Dabei bemerken wir, wie die Oper, als
die Form des romanischen unkünstlerischen Menschen, durch die germanische Tendenz unendlich vertieft und zur Kunst emporgehoben wird,' KSA 7.329). He then also
alludes to Wagner's view that the spirit of Schiller's *Ode to Joy* truly came to the fore
when put to music by Beethoven:

> We see, how the poet tries to transform his German, deep Dionysian impulse in images: how he,
> though, as a modern man can do nothing but stumble ineptly. When Beethoven then brings out
> the actual, Schillerian foundation, we have the infinitely higher, perfection. (9[10], KSA 7.275)

> Wir sehen, wie der Dichter sich seine germanisch tiefe dionysische Regung in Bildern zu deuten
> versucht: wie er aber, als moderner Mensch, nur schwerfällig zu stammeln weiß. Wenn jetzt
> Beethoven uns den eigentlich Schillerschen Untergrund darstellt, so haben wir das unendlich-
> Höhere und Vollkommene.

It was the enrichment of drama with music, 'his German, deep, Dionysian impulse',
which made Wagner the fulfiller of Goethe and Schiller's ideals. What defines 'modern' man, to Nietzsche, is exactly the lack of this musical, Dionysian impulse. And although Goethe and Schiller were great artists, they eventually were 'modern', because
they lacked the perfection of their art in music. This thought aligns with Schiller's own
ideas. He expected that drama would find its fulfilment in opera, exactly because it
would revive its fundamental 'Dionysian' element, the chorus. In so doing, Schiller
hoped, the drama would surpass the level of superficial outward appearance, of the
'real', and arrive at the symbolical level of the 'ideal':

> I always had a certain trust in opera, that out of it – as out of the choruses of the ancient festival
> of Bacchus – tragedy would develop into a nobler form. In opera, that servile imitation of nature
> is indeed remitted, and, although only under the name of indulgence, in this way the ideal could
> steal its way onto the stage. The opera attunes the heart to a more beautiful receptivity through the
> power of music and through a freer, harmonious excitation of the senses. Also in the pathos, there
> is a freer play, because music accompanies the play. And miraculousness, which will be tolerated
> here at last, is due to make [the audience] necessarily more indifferent towards the material.[28]

---

28 Schiller to Goethe, 29 December 1797 (MA 8/1, pp. 475–476).

Ich hatte immer ein gewisses Vertrauen zur Oper, daß aus ihr wie aus den Chören des alten Bacchusfestes das Trauerspiel in einer edlern Gestalt <sich> loswickeln sollte. In der Oper erläßt man wirklich jene servile NaturnacHHmung, und obgleich nur unter dem Namen von Indulgenz könnte sich auf diesem Wege das Ideale auf das Theater stehlen. Die Oper stimmt durch die Macht der Musik und durch eine freiere harmonische Reizung der Sinnlichkeit das Gemüt zu einer schönern Empfängnis, hier ist wirklich auch im Pathos selbst ein freieres Spiel, weil die Musik es begleitet, und das Wunderbare, welches hier einmal geduldet wird, müßte [das Publikum, MP] notwendig gegen den Stoff gleichgültiger machen.

Schopenhauer's, Wagner's, and Nietzsche's musical aesthetics are closely in agreement with the view Schiller advances here: music uplifts man above the common level of 'the real' to the more playful level of the 'ideal' by way of a miraculous experience (by Schopenhauer, Wagner, and Nietzsche referred to as 'the sublime' or 'magic', '*Zauber*'). According to Schiller, this theatrical and musical effect is the first step on man's way to change his life. In Schiller's dramaturgy, drama supplies man with the insight that he has the power and ability to improve his own life into a mature 'Elysium', where he is free. The miraculous experience of aesthetic freedom inspires him to realize his freedom in a political way. Schopenhauer, Wagner, and Nietzsche do not take this step to what Kant and Schiller called the Enlightenment way to 'maturity'. Their view of paradise comes down to the reinstitution of childlike innocence in a moment of illusionary, aesthetic freedom. They (Schopenhauer and Nietzsche more than Wagner) do not hold to the Enlightenment belief in self-realization through political emancipation. Instead, they maintain that the aesthetic moment in which we experience our original state of freedom in paradise – the childlike state of human history – is the only possible kind of human freedom. It is a negative form of freedom, which does not even liberate us from the things (the will) that hem us in, but only offers us a moment of forgetfulness of the fact that we are forever tied to the endless strivings of the will.

While Schiller has high hopes for opera, Wagner and Nietzsche contend that opera cannot fulfil Schiller's ideal, because opera uses music for its non-artistic end to amuse. Wagner's music drama was to solve this problem. The 'German tendency' for metaphysical depth and truth helps transform opera into true art:

We are completely unable to reach the naive even with the help of the Apollonian. However, we can explain the world in purely Dionysian terms and come to terms with the phenomenal world via music. In so doing, the least we accomplish is the artistic view of life, myth. Additionally we notice how opera, as the form of the roman, non-artistic man, is uplifted to *art* and deepened infinitely by the German tendency. (9[10], KSA 7.275)

Wir sind ganz unfähig, zum Naiven zu kommen und mit Hülfe des Apollinischen. Wohl aber können wir die Welt uns rein dionysisch auslegen und die Erscheinungswelt uns durch Musik deuten. Wir bekommen so wenigstens wieder die künstlerische Weltbetrachtung, den Mythus. Dabei bemerken wir, wie die Oper, als die Form des romanischen unkünstlerischen Menschen, durch die germanische Tendenz unendlich vertieft und zur *Kunst* emporgehoben wird.

The Dionysian power, which is typical for German artists (*and* Luther, according to Nietzsche) enables the artistic, mythical comprehension of the world. Like Wagner, he considers Beethoven's setting of Schiller's *Ode to Joy* as exemplary for the power of music:

> Schiller's *Ode to Joy* receives its deep, true artistic background only insofar [as the deepening effect of the German tendency, MP]. We see how the poet tries to express his German, deep, Dionysian sensitivity in pictures: how he as modern individual, however, can only stammer ineptly. When Beethoven then shows us the tangible Schillerian background, we hit on the infinitely higher and ideal (9[10], KSA 7.275)

> Schiller's Lied an die Freude bekommt insofern erst seinen tiefen, wahrhaft künstlerischen Hintergrund. Wir sehen, wie der Dichter sich seine germanisch tiefe dionysische Regung in Bildern zu deuten versucht: wie er aber als moderner Mensch, nur schwerfällig zu stammeln weiß. Wenn jetzt Beethoven uns den eigentlich Schillerschen Untergrund darstellt, so haben wir das Unendlich-Höhere und Vollkommene.

As in chapter 5 of *The Birth of Tragedy* (and Wagner had done likewise in 'Beethoven'), Nietzsche stresses Schiller's lyrical potency, his 'Dionysian sensitivity', yet he also points to the inability of words and pictures to express the level of the absolute or 'ideal'. As a German, Schiller by nature possessed the talent to bring man back into contact with his Dionysian provenance, in Nietzsche's eyes. However, 'as a modern man', meaning 'governed' by words, Schiller failed to express his Dionysian depth in the right mode. He heard a tone within him, but it led him to producing drama only instead of music *and* drama.[29] Nietzsche implies that Schiller suffers from exactly the 'fragmentation' of modern man Schiller claimed to fight. Only Beethoven's musical transmutation of the hymn reaches 'the infinitely higher and ideal', according to Nietzsche. Yet, he differs from Wagner on the kind and form of music, which reaches the level of infinity. According to Wagner, it is his melodic, orchestral, and dramatic elaboration of Beethoven's symphonic inheritance. In Nietzsche's view, however, the chorus, thus human voices singing *unisono*, should be the centre of musical theatre.

Nietzsche and Schiller on the chorus

Next to Wagner, Nietzsche himself tried to deliver a substantial contribution to the 'musicalization' of art and the implied ascent of culture, by reforming Schiller's theory of the chorus. According to him, Wagner 'abolished' ('beseitigt', 9[11], KSA 7.277) the cho-

---

29 Schiller, too, thought that the *Ode to Joy* was imperfect: 'The Joy is, according to my feeling now, truly flawed [...] because it met the flawed taste of that time, it has received the honour of becoming a national poem, to a certain extent' ('Die Freude ist nach meinem jetzigen Gefühl durchaus fehlerhaft [...] Weil sie aber einem fehlerhaften Geschmack der Zeit entgegen kam, so hat sie die Ehre erhalten, gewissermaßen ein Volksgedicht zu werden'). To Körner, 21 October 1800 (NA 30, p. 206).

rus. Although Wagner, under the influence of Schopenhauer, came to the 'parallelism' ('Parallelismus', 9[10], KSA 7.275) of music and drama and thus made his works 'genuine German' ('eigentlich Germanisch', 9[10], KSA 7.275), Wagner's music dramas are still in the danger-zone of falling back into his former, pre-Schopenhauerian aesthetics, Nietzsche claims. As long as he does not assign more space for the chorus as the Dionysian locus of truth and myth, Wagner will not have accomplished Goethe's and Schiller's reformation programme. Nietzsche continues that the chorus would be the most expressive and apt embodiment of Wagner's theory of unconscious creativity *and* his theory about the relationship between text and drama: '[…] *the chorus that has a vision and describes enthusiastically what it sees!* The Schillerian depiction deepened infinitely!' ('[…] *den Chor, der eine Vision hat und begeistert beschreibt was er schaut! Die Schillersche Vorstellung unendlich vertieft!* 9[11], KSA 7.277). The 'vision' of the chorus is the 'inner vision' Wagner ascribed to the genius in 'Beethoven'. By bestowing a greater responsibility upon the chorus, Nietzsche believes, Wagner's music dramas would not need the recitative and aria any longer (the dangerous elements of opera, as Schopenhauer had explained already), *and* amplify their musicality at the same time. Yet, what is the Schillerian depiction of the chorus that Wagner and Nietzsche deepen? Let us have a closer look at Schiller's theory of the chorus, as laid down in his essay 'On the Use of the Chorus in Tragedy' ('Ueber den Gebrauch des Chors in der Tragödie', 1803). As we shall see, this text paved the way for Nietzsche's critical stance towards Wagner.

Long before Nietzsche and Wagner, Schiller claimed that a tragic poem finds its completion in the performance: 'The tragic poem reaches perfection in the theatrical performance alone: the poem gives nothing but words; music and dance must be added to experience them' ('Das tragische Dichtwerk wird erst durch die theatralische Vorstellung zu einem Ganzen: Nur die Worte gibt der Dichter, Musik und Tanz müssen hinzukommen, sie zu beleben,' NA 10, p. 7). Play ('*Spiel*') and seriousness ('*Ernst*') must coincide, so as to become a 'poetic play' ('*poetisches Spiel*') and to 'ennoble' ('*veredlen*') the joy of the audience: 'All art is dedicated to joy, and there is no higher and no more serious task than making people happy' ('Alle Kunst ist der Freude gewidmet, und es gibt keine höhere und keine ernsthaftere Aufgabe, als die Menschen zu beglücken,' NA 10, p. 8). Against theatre, which offers nothing but 'an amusing delusion of the moment' ('*ein gefälliger Wahn des Augenblicks*'), 'a passing illusion' ('*eine vorübergehende Täuschung*'), Schiller stresses that 'true art does not aim at a passing play; it is a serious thing to true art[,] not to place people in a momentary dream of freedom, but indeed and actually to set them free' ('Die wahre Kunst […] hat es nicht bloß auf ein vorübergehendes Spiels abgesehen; es ist ihr ernst damit, den Menschen nicht bloß in einen augenblicklichen Traum von Freiheit zu versetzen, sondern ihn wirklich und in der Tat frei zu machen,' NA 10, p. 8). True art tries to appeal to a power in the beholder, which enables him to recreate the sensual world that he used to regard as 'a blind power' ('*eine blinde Macht*') and 'rude material' ('*roher Stoff*'). Through serious, poetic play, he experiences that he has the power to change the material world with his mind.[30] Therefore Schiller concluded, 'true art founds its ideal building on the truth itself, on the fixed and deep ground of nature' ('auf der Wahrheit selbst, auf dem festen und tiefen Grunde der Natur errichtet sie ihr ideales Gebäude,' NA 10, p. 9).[31] That is why art should be 'completely ideal and yet, in the deepest sense, real' (*'ganz ideell und doch im tiefsten Sinne reell'*). If art were to base itself on reality alone, then it would show nature as nothing more than mere appearance, without capturing the essence of reality (*'der Geist der Natur'*, NA 10, p. 9) and be nothing than a 'passing play'. Such art would be without true joy (*'Freude'*) and would be serious only in the sense of 'not enjoyable' (*'unerfreulich'*) and boring. According to Schiller, such art would be, for example, French naturalism.

On the other hand, art should not be a mere product of someone's fantasy. Such art, he thinks, would not be concerned with truth at all and would merely aim at surprising the audience: 'Just to link fantastic forms at random, does not mean to go into the ideal, and to represent reality by imitation does not mean to represent nature' ('Phantastische Gebilde willkürlich aneinanderreihen heißt nicht ins Ideale gehen, und das Wirkliche nachahmend wiederbringen heißt nicht die Natur darstellen', NA 10, p. 9). The aim of art should be 'to build and found something in the heart of the beholder' ('im Gemüt [des Zuschauers, MP] [etwas] erbauen und begründen', NA 10, p. 9) to surpass the level of empirical reality and penetrate something more substantial.[32] For this, art should unite truth and (aesthetic) illusion. What does Schiller mean by this, exactly?

---

30 Nietzsche speaks in *The Birth of Tragedy* of *'Formenspiel'* and *'Gestaltenspiel'* to distinguish between the Italian amusing and non-serious play with outer forms, and the genius's serious play with the figures (giants and other mythical beings, 'a crowd of spirits', BT 8, p. 43) of his inner imagination. The *Gestaltenspiel* is a play with the truth, while the form-play is unrelated to the truth.

31 The parallel between Schopenhauer and Schiller's view of the world as a 'blind power' is striking. However, for Schopenhauer, humanity is rather powerless in the face of this, while to Schiller humanity is powerful. As we shall see more clearly in chapter 4, an intimate relation between art and truth is a precondition for overcoming modernity and the return of the tragic, mythical age, to Nietzsche.

32 Here, I think, we should recall Goethe's important text 'Simple Imitation, Manner, Style' ('Einfache Nachahmung, Natur, Manier, Stil'), where 'imitation' (*'Nachahmung'*) is defined as the practical appropriation of a natural object; 'manner' (*'Manier'*) as the subjective appropriation of an object; and 'style' (*'Stil'*) as the truthful appropriation of an object, based on essential knowledge of it. As Goethe defines it, simple imitation 'depends on a tranquil and affectionate view of life' (p. 72/'beruht auf dem ruhigen Dasein und einer liebevollen Gegenwart', HA XII, p. 32), Manier is 'a reflection of the ease and competence with which the subject is treated' (p. 72/'eine Erscheinung mit einem leichten, fähigen Gemüt ergreift', HA XII, p. 32), and Stil rests 'on the most fundamental principle of cognition, on the essence of things – to the extent that it is granted to us to perceive this essence in visible and tangible form' (p. 72/'auf den tiefsten Grundfesten der Erkenntnis, auf dem Wesen der Dinge, in sofern uns erlaubt ist, es in sichtbaren und greiflichen Gestalten zu erkennen', HA XII, p. 32). Therefore, it was so important to Goethe that an artist (especially the painter) was a botanist as well. Art could not do without science, according to him. Again, we can imagine how Schopenhauer reflected on this matter. The genius then would be the artist who *knows* and generates *style* in his art.

Schiller clarifies this central thesis of his aesthetics by reference to French Naturalism, which has not understood the relation between truth and illusion, and therefore
was unable to capture the Greek spirit it sought to revive. French Naturalism interpreted the demand of unity of place and time purely empirically 'as if there was another
place here than the merely ideal space, and another time than the merely continuous
series of the action' ('als ob hier ein anderer Ort wäre als der bloß ideale Raum, und
eine andere Zeit als bloß die stetige Folge der Handlung,' NA 10, p. 10). Schiller, on the
other hand, states that the outward, visible dimension in the drama should not give
the illusion of empirical reality, but it should *symbolize* reality, that is: render the universal essence of life. This symbolic power depends, to Schiller, on the chorus. The introduction of the chorus in tragedy was a decisive step in art, in his view, because only
the chorus united illusion and truth. How does this work? As a 'living wall', the chorus isolates itself from empirical reality, preserving its original, poetic fundament and
raising tragedy to the symbolic level of the ideal. Simultaneously, it declares war on the
naturalist representation of empirical reality. Schiller holds that Greek tragedy ('as one
knows', he says, suggesting that this was common knowledge) sprang from the chorus,
and that the chorus was the natural result of the 'poetic' expression of human life.[33] In
modern times, the chorus is no longer a natural but an 'artificial organ', which helps
to call forth poetry. Schiller's distinction between ancient and modern life and art is
based on the modern aberration of the 'living word', the poetical times in which the
people formed a 'rude, living mass'. In modern times, the written word became dominant. As we recall, Wagner argued something similar, and the power of music resides
precisely in its capability of enlivening words and thus returning poetical or mythical times. Moreover, in modern times the 'living mass' has formed itself into a 'state',
which Schiller calls a 'skimmed concept' of the 'original' people. The poet has the task,
so Schiller, of bringing humankind back to its pre-modern, poetic situation by strip-
ping humanity of all artificiality and by its inner nature. At the same time, the poetical
power of the artwork is enhanced by dance and music, and by isolating reflection from
the action in the chorus. The chorus therefore brings life back into language; it augments the lyricism of the tragedy and forces the poet to enliven his material by supplying it with 'tragic greatness' ('*tragische Größe*'). On the other hand, the chorus, apart
from lyricism, renders peace ('*Ruhe*') to the whole, or as Schiller calls it – 'the beautiful
and high peace, in which the character of a noble artwork must consist' ('die schöne
und hohe Ruhe, die der Charakter eines edlen Kunstwerkes sein muß,' NA 10, p. 14).[34]

---

33 This idea returns in *The Birth of Tragedy*, when Nietzsche discusses the satyr chorus (chapter 7
and 8) and defines the satyr as 'genius of nature' (p. 42/'*Naturgenie*', KSA 1.59), because, he represents
the 'genuine truth of nature' (p. 41; '*Naturwahrheit*', KSA 1.58, which incidentally differs from Goethe's
'truth to nature'/'*Naturwahrheit*', GT 22, KSA 1.142). I come back to this in chapter 4.
34 Here, we see a sort of middle position between Winckelmann's 'edle Enfalt, stille Grosse' motto
and Nietzsche's focus on the Greek awareness of horror and tragedy.

This peace sees to it that 'the heart of the beholder [...] [will] retain his freedom, even in the most vehement passion' ('das Gemüt des Zuschauers [...] auch in der heftigsten Passion seine Freiheit behalten [kann],' NA 10, p. 10). This sort of freedom implies that the audience does not fall prey to emotive impression, to the 'violence of affects' ('*Gewalt der Affekte*') to 'mere illusion' ('*Täuschung*'). Instead, this freedom guarantees that the audience remains 'clear and cheerful' ('*klar und heiter*'), able to discriminate between 'heart' ('*Gemüth*') – and the emotions it undergoes – and 'mind'. In order to bring this about, the artist must build in the audience a balance between 'passivity' ('*Leiden*') and 'activity' ('*Aktivität*') by breaking the action in the chorus, which relieves the passion with reflection and distance:

> By separating the parts and stepping forward between the passions with its soothing reflection, the chorus gives us back our freedom, which was about to get lost in the storm of affections (NA 10, p. 10)

> Dadurch, daß der Chor die Teile auseinanderhält und zwischen die Passionen mit seiner beruhigenden Betrachtung tritt, gibt er uns unsre Freiheit zurück, die im Sturm der Affekte verloren gehen würde

The chorus constrains ('*bändigt*') the passion ('*Leidenschaft*'), which means it 'motivates the contemplation' ('motiviert die Besonnenheit', NA 10, p. 10).[35] At the same time, everyone, actors and chorus, act on a symbolic level. They are *ideal* persons, 'representations of their sort, giving voice to the depth of humanity' ('Repräsentanten ihrer Gattung, die das Tiefe der Menschheit aussprechen', NA 10, p. 10). What Schiller precisely means by this 'depth of humanity' is not totally clear. Is it humanity's insight into its own natural freedom and its freedom to form its freedom? Nietzsche and Wagner, under Schopenhauer's influence, understood it metaphysically. And although they agree in great part with Schiller, and – as he does – demand that art be symbolic, and – as Schiller – that tragedy be symbolic and musical, for them this level of symbolic depth has everything to do with a metaphysical conception of nature.

Wagner as mythical 'Greek'

Nietzsche drew heavily upon Schiller's theory of the chorus, yet he made some changes with three objectives in mind. First, it was important to him to show that Greek culture had *musical* roots; second, he intended to put forward a suggestion about how Wagner could get rid of the dramatic singer by extending the part of the chorus; and third, he

---

35 Nietzsche takes up this classical idea (posed against Romantic 'unbändigen' or 'unleashing') of constraining passions (he speaks more of constraining the will) in the aesthetics of his middle works, especially of HH, as we shall see in chapter 6 below.

wanted to show that Wagner, due to his enormous symbolic powers, was a true servant of Dionysus.

The chorus was, in Nietzsche's view, the only communicative body in drama, meaning the only element in drama that expresses the Will immediately. As the immediate representation of the Will the chorus is, by implication, the solely musical element of the whole drama. Therefore, it is in the chorus that the enrichment of words by music take place, just as we saw in Schiller. Wagner and Nietzsche adopted Schiller's hope, yet adjoined to it a Schoperhauerian, metaphysical, and 'tragic' content. Aligning with Schiller, Nietzsche advocated the re-institution of the chorus, protesting against the individual, dramatic singer. In his view, no instrument other than the tones of the singing chorus and a playing orchestra, supported only by dramatic acting,[36] could express the truth, and thus rejuvenate the Greek spirit, against French Naturalism and Italian opera. For this, Wagner had to give more room to the chorus than he had done until then; only 'the *music drama Tristan and Isolde*,' (9[11], KSA 7.277), gives some idea of what Nietzsche means.[37] Yet, what is the final end of his concern with the chorus? Similar to Schiller and Wagner, Nietzsche's aesthetics is motivated

---

36 Cf. Goethe, 'On Epic and Dramatic Poetry' ('Ueber epische und dramatische Dichtung,' 1797). Although written in 1797, the essay first appeared in *Über Kunst und Alterthum*, Vol. VI, 1827. It represents, along with 'The Collector and His Circle' (1799) and 'On Dillettantism' (1799) the collaborative aesthetics of Goethe and Schiller. In 'On Epic and Dramatic Poetry', Goethe tells between the epic writer or rhapsodist and dramatic writer or actor in discussing the nature of 'epos' and 'drama'. Both are poets, but the first recites before a 'quiet group of attentive listeners' (Vol. 3, p. 192/'ruhig horchenden [...] Kreise', HA XII, p. 249) and reads a subject which plays in the past, which makes him act as a wise man with overview. His aim is to bring peace ('Ruhe') over his audience: 'the rhapsodist himself should not appear as a higher being in his poem. It would be best for him to recite behind a curtain so that his audience will not associate any particular personality with what they hear and will imagine that they are listening only to the muses themselves' (Vol.3, p. 194/'Der Rhapsode sollte als ein höheres Wesen in seinem Gedicht nicht selbst erscheinen, er läse hinter einem Vorhange am allerbesten, so daß man von aller Persönlichkeit abstrahierte und nur die Stimme der Musen im allgemeinen zu hören glaubte', HA XII, p. 251). The actor in the play acts before an audience which is 'impatient both to watch and hear' (Vol. 3, p. 193/'ungeduldig schauend und hörend', HA XII, p. 249). He finds himself in a situation opposite to the one of the rhapsode. He places himself in front of the audience with his whole personality; the audience is part of his immediate environment. Therefore, he seeks direct contact with the public. While the rhapsodist speaks to the imagination of his audience, the actor searches contact through emotion, he wants his audience to be sensuously involved every single second. It is an absolute necessity that the audience be constantly engaged and not be allowed to assume a position of detached contemplation. The actor wants them to be passionately involved and their imagination completely inactive. Schiller responds to this in a letter to Goethe of 26 December 1797, in which he calls the opposition of rhapsode and mime 'a very strikingly chosen means to reflect the differences of both poetical forms [epos and drama, MP]' ('ein sehr glücklich gewältes Mittel, um der Verschiedenheit beider Dichtarten [epos and drama, MP] beizukommen', MA 8/1, p. 473).

37 In chapter 21 of *The Birth of Tragedy*, Nietzsche presents *Tristan and Isolde* as the perfect music-drama, in which 'Dionysos speaks the language of Apollo, but finally it is Apollo who speaks the language of Dionysos' (BT 21, p. 22; 'Dionysus redet die Sprache des Apollo, Apollo aber schliesslich die

by the desire for cultural change and depth. Rejuvenating the Greek spirit would have an enormous, fundamental, and deepening impact on culture, according to Nietzsche. He supposes that Wagner's art could be the starting point of a new period in which the tragic or Dionysian view of life would dominate German culture. This would entail the re-establishment of Germany's identity, its 'health' ('*Gesundheit*', 9[30], KSA 7.282), the 'return of the German spirit to itself' ('Rückkehr des germanischen Geistes zu sich selbst,' 9[31], KSA 7.283). He thus has extremely high hopes of Wagner, on the condition that he would indeed open up more space for the chorus: 'Wagnerian effects. Rebirth of tragedy out of music' (9[31], KSA 7.283), he writes, claiming that this would reanimate German culture as a whole: 'I recognize the only form of life in the Greek: and regard Wagner as the most sublime step towards its rebirth in the German soul' ('ich erkenne die einzige Lebensform in der griechischen: und betrachte Wagner als den erhabensten Schritt zu deren Wiedergeburt im deutschen Wesen,' 9[34], KSA 7.284). 'Greek' and 'German' become interchangeable predicates for Nietzsche. According to note 16[44] (KSA 7.408), he considered supplying his first book with the title 'The Rebirth of Greece out of the Rejuvenation of the German spirit' ('Die Wiedergeburt Griechenlands aus der Erneuerung des deutschen Geistes'). This title indicates how close he thought the bond between Greece and Germany was and had to be. The ideal culture would be the one in which 'our music' (Wagnerian music, obviously) would be understood. However, what, to Nietzsche's mind, is the specific merit of Wagner's music? What makes this music so different from other music, that present culture experienced difficulty in understanding it?

Note 9[36], provides the beginning of an answer and sheds some light on the question as to why Nietzsche aspired to a new culture at all. It opens with the remark that modern art lacks 'insight into the primordial phenomena' ('*Einblick in die Urphänomene*', KSA 7.284). Its subjects, instead, are 'artificially imitated models' ('*künstlerische nachgemachte Vorbilder*', KSA 7.284). Modern art offers nothing more than a shallow copy of Greek artworks, whereas it should originate from insight into the primordial. Only Richard Wagner, we read here, produces art out of such insight: 'Having seen the phenomenon of Wagner live, it has been explained to me, at first in a negative way, that we have not understood the Greek world yet' (KSA 7.284/'Für mich erläutert das leibhaft geschaute Phänomen Wagner's zuerst negativ, daß wir die griechische Welt bis jetzt nicht verstanden haben'). This note is somewhat enigmatic, specifically because of the phrase 'at first in a negative way' ('*zuerst negativ*'), but also because of its description of Wagner as a 'phenomenon' and the adverb 'live'. What to Nietzsche was first negative and then positive? Whom does he mean when he refers to the 'phenomenon Wagner live'? Is it his friend Wagner, whom he sees in the intimate setting of Tribschen, or is Nietzsche rather thinking of the public person and artist? Could or

---

Sprache des Dionysus', KSA 1.140). His only other example in his book is the third act of *The Valkyrie*, which famously opens with the *Valkyrie* chorus.

should such a division be made, anyway? Speaking of Wagner his friend, Nietzsche normally addressed him as 'Wagner', 'Richard Wagner', or 'der Meister'. This does not seem in accordance with the distant 'the phenomenon'. Moreover, the word 'live' seems to point to Wagner as a public figure, musician, artist, creator, director, and conductor. Nietzsche is, we may assume, speaking of Wagner as the public person and music. However, this still does not answer our question as to the nature of his negative judgement.

The phrase 'at first in a negative way' ('*zuerst negativ*') perhaps points to different things. First, it may be a further indication of Nietzsche's initial mistrust in Wagner's understanding of the Greeks, after the February 1870 letter.[38] 'Wagner' could be one of the 'we' that do not understand the Greeks. In that case, this note would prove that Nietzsche's mistrust in Wagner's understanding of the Greeks was a matter of the past. He mistrusted 'initially' ('*zuerst*'), but that, apparently, is no longer the case. However, this seems to be at odds with the distance Nietzsche allows himself here. He separates him from the 'we'. If so, it means that by looking at Wagner, the nature of the Greeks has become clear to Nietzsche, while before looking at Wagner (albeit 'negatively at first'), he, as part of the 'we' ('we philologists', 'we Germans', 'we modern people', or 'we all') was completely wrong about who the Greeks had been. In that sense the 'at first in a negative way' may be meant to refer to the time that he was negative about Wagnerian music.

Although it remains unclear to what exactly the comment 'at first in a negative way' refers, it is clear what Nietzsche wants to express; if we want to understand Wagner, we can do so by understanding the Greek world. The same applies the other way round: if we are to grasp Greek culture, we can attain understanding by going to the theatre to experience a performance of Wagner's music drama. Perhaps it is even stronger: as long as we have not understood Wagner, we have not understood the Greeks. And we can only get an idea of Wagner's genius, if we look at Greek tragedy. The tight relationship Nietzsche discerns here between the Greeks and Wagner becomes the cornerstone of *The Birth of Tragedy*: the (pre-Socratic and pre-Euripidean) Greeks and Wagner were ruled by the same 'Dionysian' spirit, or to put it more clearly, the same mythical truth and the same need to translate this truth into aesthetic joy. In other words, Wagner is a Greek. Nietzsche confirms this view in several other notes, for example in 14[3]:

> In world history, we have seen this enormous capacity for music reach the *creation of myths* twice: and we are so fortunate to experience this stunning process ourselves right now, in order to clarify analogously with our time the first time as well. (KSA 7.376)

---

38 See chapter 1, above.

> Dieses ungeheure Vermögen der Musik sahen wir zweimal bisher in der Weltgeschichte zur *Mythenschöpfung* kommen: und das eine Mal sind wir beglückt genug, diesen erstaunlichen Prozeß selbst zu erleben, um von hier aus auch jenes erste Mal uns analogisch zu verdeutlichen.

Through Wagner, Nietzsche achieves a better understanding of his beloved Greek culture and through Wagner, modern culture might actually become 'Greek' again, through him 'a German rebirth of the Hellenic world' ('eine deutsche Wiedergeburt der hellenischen Welt', 9[36], KSA 7.284) will take place, this note predicts, a rebirth – he comments in addition – 'to which we want to devote ourselves' ('der wir uns widmen wollen', 9[36], KSA 7.284).[39] Nietzsche imagines a Greek 'Man of the future' ('*Zukunftsmensch*', 9[24], KSA 7.280), meaning 'eccentric, energetic, warm, indefatigable, artistic' and an 'enemy of books' ('*Bucherfeind*', 9[24], KSA 7.280). This Greek 'Man of the future' is equally a 'Man of the past', for the coming of the tragic age involves a return to myth.

In our analysis of Wagner's 'Beethoven' text it became abundantly clear that the truth could only be expressed by 'myth', and that the metaphysical concept of truth deteriorated under the influence of journalism and fashion, which equalled 'truth' with 'news', and traded the eternal truth for the 'principle of novelty'. What attracted Wagner most in the Greeks was indeed their mythical culture. Nietzsche agrees on this, too. He claims that Wagner, contrary to modern opera, restores the place of myth in human life and thus deepens humanity with a tragic view of life (9[41], KSA 7.287–288). Against the tendency to abstract, conceptual thought and 'scholarship' ('*Wissenschaft*', 9[38], KSA 7.286–287) as the 'murderer' of tragedy, he posits myth as an expression of life's essence, its joy and sorrow (9[58], KSA 7.296–297). Myth, as 'interpretation of music' ('*Interpretation der Musik*', 9[125], KSA 7.320), is the textual representation of the truth as revealed in the innermost self, but also points to the pre-historical, 'poetical' period (as Schiller called it in contrast to the 'common' ['*gemeine*'] world), a period which refers to the ideal future, too. In the pre-historical period (that is 'pre-Socratic' to Nietzsche), human beings maintained a tragic view of life and were driven by the desire to express this artistically. Humanity, then, believed that it could only maintain *and* gain existence by the artistic transformation and softening of the destructive, Dionysian powers. Myth was a way of exploiting the powers of life, its deepest joys and sorrows, in an extraordinary extension of the human imagination. Compared to the artistic powers of ancient humanity, conceptual thought – which started with Socratic dialectics according to Nietzsche – in its will to control life with logical concepts, is not only poor in experience, but even hostile to life (what Wagner called 'scepticism' in the sense of 'hostile to the truth').

---

39 Compare with the preface to *The Birth of Tragedy* (pp. 13–14/KSA 1.24) and Nietzsche's letter to Richard Wagner of 24 January 1872 (KSB 3, p. 276).

In Nietzsche's view, myth is the highest symbolic form. Through the symbol, humanity relates to and gains life.[40] Myth contains symbolic powers, which lift humankind above empirical, individualized reality. The symbolic is the uniting force through which the individual understands himself as part of a community, as a person who shares his (way of) life with others, and this *tragic* way of life makes him human. The symbol speaks the language of the general (9[88], KSA 7.305), Nietzsche holds, yet *only* music can speak that general or universal language. Poetry can do that only insofar as it stems from the German, deep, Dionysian musical impulse. Yet art can only be truly great art when this level of the symbolic is attained: 'Understanding the world in "symbols" is the precondition of a great art' ('Verständnis der Welt in "Symbolen" ist die Voraussetzung einer großen Kunst', 9[92], KSA 7.308). Wagner recalls an 'artistic era' by utilising the original, symbolic character of music. Preserving the symbolic level of the 'universal', Wagner's music bridges different periods in history and different nations: '*Music as general-unnational-untimely form of art* is the *only blossoming form of art*. It represents for us the *entire* art and the artistic world. Therefore it redeems' (9[90], KSA 7.307; 'Die *Musik als allgemein-unnational-unzeitliche Kunst* ist die *einzig blühende*. Sie vertritt für uns die *ganze* Kunst und die künstlerische Welt. Darum erlöst sie').

Thus, grasping the world's and humanity's essence in symbols becomes Nietzsche's primary demand of art. In its symbolizing act, music creates an idyll, a 'Schillerian' world in which the reality and the ideal are united (9[142], KSA 7.327). Wagner's Siegfried[41] is such a Schillerian idyll, according to Nietzsche. Yet Wagner's view of na-

---

40 With 'symbolic form' I refer to Ernst Cassirer's *Philosophy of Symbolic Forms*, which he developed in the first half of the twentieth century. Cassirer objected 'to the nineteenth-century interpretation of myth as flawed attempt at scientific knowledge' (Louis Dupré, 2006, pp. 19), accentuating the 'participative' knowledge of myth vis-à-vis the 'differentiated knowledge of science' (Louis Dupré, 2006, pp. 19), meaning that the first 'lacks any awareness of a distinction between subject and object, between representation and reality' (Louis Dupré, 2006, pp. 19). Nietzsche and Wagner exactly strove for the destruction of the subject-object relationship in the experience of joyful unity, induced by art. See also Pätzold (2003).

41 It is not always clear whether Nietzsche refers to *Siegfried* (of which he copied the *Ur*-text of 1848) or to the *Siegfried-Idyll*. The original *Siegfried*, in any case, attests to the young Wagner's socialist ideas and socialism was, according to Nietzsche, also driven by an idyllic sentiment. Millington (1992) comments on the *Siegfried-Idyll*: 'in spite of the lyrical melodies and pastoral pedal-points, the work itself is in a broadly based (modified) sonata form, in which the subsidiary material is represented by the lullaby "Sleep, baby, sleep" [...]' (p. 311). The composition has, in any case, nothing to do with *Siegfried* or *Siegfrieds Tod* (*The Death of Siegfried*, later renamed *Götterdämmerung, Twilight of the Gods*), as second and third day respectively of *Der Ring der Nibelungen*. Even in his late autobiographic *Ecce Homo*, Nietzsche makes an exception for the *Siegfried-Idyll*: 'I shall never admit that a German *could* know what music is [...] there are three reasons why I shall make an exception for Wagner's *Siegfried Idyll*' (EH 'Clever' 7, p. 94/'Ich werde nie zulassen, dass ein Deutscher *wissen* könne, was Musik ist [...] ich nehme, aus drei Gründen, Wagner's Siegfried-Idyll aus,' KSA 6.290–291). Unfortunately, Nietzsche did not record the three reasons for this exception.

ture is tragic compared to Schiller's 'cheerful' ('*heiter*') understanding of nature. And it is precisely this insight into the tragic nature of an artist that makes an artist 'Greek' and thus a 'man of the future' – or not.

The 'idyllic tendency' of Italian opera

The 1870–1871 notes under discussion show that Nietzsche used Goethe's and Schiller's, rather than Schopenhauer's, aesthetics to understand Wagner, in spite of the fact that *The Birth of Tragedy* emphasizes the central importance of Schopenhauer's philosophy for understanding Wagner while brushing Goethe's and Schiller's 'word-drama' aside as failed imitations of Greek theatre.[42] In this 'Weimarian' context, Nietzsche also ponders Wagner as a composer of 'tragic-idyllic' works, such as *Tristan and Isolde* and *Siegfried*, a 'radically idyllic composer', and as having an 'idyllic tendency'. This is remarkable with regard to the book, where Wagner is presented as a 'tragic' artist who fiercely finishes with Italian opera's idyllic tendencies. It seems as if Nietzsche's attempt to reconcile the tragic and idyllic has failed, or was undesired after all, for in the book the two concepts emerge as an exclusive opposition, in which the tragic is embraced and the idyllic repudiated. In the notes, however, Nietzsche tries to think the idyllic and the tragic together in a way that reminds of the unity of Dionysus and Apollo, in *The Birth of Tragedy*. Accordingly, the idyllic is evaluated with much more ambiguity.

The 'idyllic' is so dominant in section '9' that it even dictates the 'tragic' and 'Dionysian'. As we shall see in chapter 4, the dichotomic opposition between the tragic and the idyllic also rules the last ten chapters of *The Birth of Tragedy*, where Nietzsche discusses Wagner. What role does 'the idyllic' play in Nietzsche's Wagner-reception, in section 9?

The first time that 'the idyll' is addressed, is in a note stemming from 1870 or 1871, numbered 7[126] (KSA 7.283–284). This note belongs to a group of long fragments, intended for *The Birth of Tragedy*. Nietzsche refers to Schiller's concept of the idyll as presented in *On the Naive and Sentimental in Literature*.[43] As we have seen at the beginning of the previous chapter, it is described there as the poetical depiction of humanity in the paradisiacal state of harmony and peace with itself and nature ('die poetische Darstellung unschuldiger und glücklicher Menschheit'). However, to Schiller,

---

42 Part of this section overlaps with Prange (2006-3).

43 The only systematic discussion of Nietzsche's relation to Schiller is made by Nicholas Martin (1996). However, his seminal study does not discuss the influence of Schiller's notion of the idyll on Nietzsche's aesthetics. My examination of this notion in Nietzsche's early reflections reinforces Martin's claims that 'Nietzsche's early writings owe more to Schiller than either Nietzsche or any commentator since wishes to admit' (1996, p. 5). In fact, I claim that it is exactly this Schillerian notion that connects Nietzsche's early 'tragic' and later 'heroic' aesthetics. See also Prange (2006-3).

the idyll was more than just a matter of poetic imagination. The idyll also indicated a situation at the beginning and at the end of human history, as in the Biblical Eden. Schiller calls the original state 'Arcadia' and the future state 'Elysium', while the latter represents the adoption of and victory over modern decadence. We may describe 'Elysium' as a culture, in which childlike innocence and mature conduct, play and seriousness, imagination and reason, nature and humankind are united in harmony, hence humankind is justified in its totality. In the same fragment, Nietzsche defines modern art as a 'sentimental' form of art, driven by the aim to create an 'idyll'.[44]

In note 8[29] (KSA 7.232–233), Nietzsche elaborates on the idea of modern art as 'idyllic' in connection with music. Although music in principle is 'Dionysian', modern opera is 'idyllic', Nietzsche states, because of the central role of the recitative, which is the attempt to restore the primordial language of humanity. The recitative confirms that a 'sentimental impulse into the idyllic' ('einen sentimentalischen Trieb ins Idyllische')[45], to wit the humanistic denial of the tragic sides of life, drives Italian opera to escapism 'in a fantastical primordial story of humanity' ('in eine phantastische Urgeschichte der Menschheit'), a prehistoric epoch of happiness, 'in the dreamt paradise of naive souls' ('in erträumtes Paradies naiver Wesen').

In note 9[123], Nietzsche proceeds to criticizing the idyll. He speaks of 'idyllic virtue-enthusiasm' ('idyllische Tugendschwärmerei') and scorns the moral feelings at which opera directs itself by transforming the desire for paradise into the idolization of the great, *moral* moments in human history. Fragment 9[126] explains this in more detail: the musical effect is lost because of the 'emotional effect' ('*Affektwirkung*'). The sentimental bent or idyllic tendency (Nietzsche puts them on par here) turns art into 'enticing emotions' ('*Affektwirkung*'). The public enjoys this form of art because of its 'morality' instead of for its aesthetic effect. To Nietzsche, this is a decisive insight, because it shows that the Greek world perished once humanity started to enjoy art for its moral optimism (9[129], KSA 7.322). It motivates *The Birth of Tragedy*'s aestheticism and its opposition to Italian opera. A strong objection against opera is its equally idyllic belief than one is an artist because of one's 'emotion' ('pathos'):

---

44 Nietzsche remarks on this in the context of his attempt to understand different artistic periods with the Schillerian terms 'naive' and 'sentimental'. In note 7[126], he develops his concepts of 'Apollonian' and 'naive' art as 'semblance of semblance' ('Schein des Scheins'). Because the 'sentimental' does not suffice to describe 'all non-naive art', he comes up with the 'Dionysian': 'Contrarily, I understand as the full opposite of the "naive" and the Apollonian the "Dionysian", that is all art that is not "semblance of semblance", but "semblance of Being", the reflection of the eternal original oneness' (7[126], KSA 7. 184/'Dagegen verstehe ich als den vollen Gegensatz des "Naiven" und des Apollinischen das "Dionysische" d.h. alle Kunst, die nicht "Schein des Scheins", sondern "Schein des Seins" ist, Wiederspiegelung des ewigen Ur-Einen'). See also 7[173], KSA 7.206.

45 Cf. 9[45], KSA 7.292, where Nietzsche speaks of a 'Re-discovery of the Ancient world' ('Wiederentdeckung des Alterthums') as a sign of a new idyllic tendency. He situates this in post-Raffaelite Italian Renaissance painting and the beginning of opera music.

'the idyllic belief, that in fact every simple, feeling person is an artist' ('der idyllis-che Glaube, daß eigentlich jeder einfach empfindende Mensch Künstler sei', 9[137], KSA 7.325). This pathological, emotional understanding of art attests in Nietzsche's view to the 'expression of amateurism in art' ('Ausdruck des Laienthums in der Kunst', 9[137], KSA 7.325). But the 'idyllic tendency' is widespread. Nietzsche even speaks of 'this idyllic feature of Modernity' ('dieser idyllische Zug der Neuzeit', 9[136], KSA 7.324), which one can also perceive in the simplicity Mozart sought to attain in mu-sic and his turn to the Italian folk comedy of the Italian *buffa* opera – which is ex-actly the kind of music that Nietzsche starts favouring in the 1880s, as we shall see in chapter 6.

In sum, the idyllic tendency implies that art is non-Dionysian, textual, moralistic, pathological, and amateurish. It weakens the musicality of an artwork, because of its moral and subjective aspects, and caused the end of the 'Greek', aesthetic response to life. The idyllic, in brief, is symptom and cause of Europe's artistic and cultural decadence.

Wagner as a 'radically idyllic' composer of 'tragic-idyllic' compositions

That the idyllic does nonetheless quite appeal to Nietzsche, while he is working on *The Birth of Tragedy*, is emphatically shown by the greater collection of notes that is clas-sified under number 9 of KSA 7 (Notizheft U I 41. 1871). These notes offer a counterbal-ance to Nietzsche's apparently one-sided, negative judgment of the 'idyllic tendency' of Italian opera. In the notes discussed below, Nietzsche's conception of the idyll is extended with a more specific analysis of its nature on the one hand, and complicated by the estimation of Wagner as a 'tragic-idyllic' musician, on the other.

Even though 9[40] starts with an opposition that suggests that Wagner returns to the saga, or myth, and therefore escapes the 'idyllic sheep- breeding' ('*idyllische Schäferei*', 7. 287), the same note defines Wagner's *Tristan and Isolde* as a 'tragic idyll'. In light of the foregoing, this union of the tragic and the idyll is highly remarkable. It either implies that Nietzsche finds the tendency to escapism 'in a fantastical primor-dial story of humanity' or that he values the idyll also positively, for example insofar as it does not reject but *embrace* the 'tragic', because that is what is strongly suggested here: the tragic and the idyllic can be united, in a musical drama that can be marked as 'tragic idyll'.

Fragment 9[48] (KSA 7.293) shows that Nietzsche planned to discuss the effect of opera on music and on 'true music' ('*die wahre Musik*'), followed by an explana-tion of the Dionysian spirit of music and the 'Kantian' and 'German' musical spirit in

Wagner.[46] This is elucidated as: 'in him [Wagner, MP] there is a terrifying intellectual struggle, to bring the opera-tendency to perfection: triumph' ('es giebt bei ihm einen furchtbaren intellektuellen Kampf, die Operntendenz zu vollenden: Überwindung'). It is not certain that Nietzsche means the escapism into paradisiacal fantasies or the humanistic optimism about humanity's original innocence and moral goodness with this 'opera-tendency', but even if he meant to indicate the recitative or some other opera feature, it seems at least strange to perceive Wagner as someone who was fighting a 'terrifying, intellectual struggle' to bring the opera-tendency to perfection in order to 'vindicate' opera. Had Wagner not consciously chosen to align with Beethoven's symphonic heritage and struggle *against* the 'Roman' tendency to superficiality, commercialism, fashion, frivolity, scepticism, and formalism? According to 9[90] (KSA 7.306–307), Wagner makes 'progression towards symphony' ('Fortschritt zur Symphonie') indeed, but there is 'perfection of the idyllic opera-tendency by Wagner' ('Die Vollendung der idyllischen Operntendenz durch Wagner'), at the same time. What could be meant by that? How can a composer of tragic music, who explicitly opposed Italian opera, be the one who *completes* the fundamental feature of Italian opera? How can the mirror of tragic depth mirror moral optimism in one stroke?

Nietzsche, too, seems to struggle with his own attempts to understand Wagner as a Greek-tragic artist on the one hand and as the creator of the ultimate idyll on the other: as, the creator of 'German music', music that is liberated from all Italian influences, and, in Nietzsche's words, 'as radically idyllic, as someone who accomplishes the Roman thought' ('als radikaler Idylliker, als Vollender des romanischen Gedanken, 9[135], KSA 7.324). His struggle seems to amount, however, to the technical side of his musical aesthetics. In other words, the liberation of the 'Roman yoke' ('vom romanischen Joche', 9[135], KSA 7.324) is a technical matter, which comes down to the liberation of the classical – Nietzsche calls them 'Roman' ('romanischen', 9[114], KSA 7.317) schemata, by way of 'unleashing the rhythm' ('Entfesselung des Rhythmus', 9[114], KSA 7.317) in the first place. By turning the rhythm into a so-called 'time-rhythm' ('Zeitrhythmus', 9[111], KSA 7.316), – a rhythm that turns against the mathematical beat in music – music will be liberated from its mathematical, abstract, and 'architectonic' clusters. The result will be a free, natural, intuitive, beatless music. This is all in accordance with Wagner's development of rhythm as *'Zeitfolge'*. However, in 9[116] (KSA 7.317–318) Wagner's 'beatless music' is called 'idyllic', because, as is explained with reference to *Siegfried* in 9[142] (KSA 7.327), it unites 'reality' and 'the ideal'. Wagner's music gives us 'the moral feeling of the sublime' ('die moralische Empfindung des Erhabenen', 9[106], KSA 7.314) by symbolization of the Will, because that is the 'paradise-intimating primordial situation' ('paradiesisch-ahnungsreicher Urzustand,' 9[106], KSA 7.313–314) of the idyll compared to the contemporary [deca-

---

46 Compare 7[127] (KSA 7.185–192), in which Nietzsche seemed to have carried out the first two steps of this plan.

dent, Modern, MP] situation. Here, Nietzsche holds on to an odd concept of the sublime, especially in light of his castigation of the Italians for polluting art with moral and pathological features. Towards the end of this collection, he even speaks of 'Richard Wagner, idyll of modern times' ('Richard Wagner das Idyll der Gegenwart', 9[149], KSA 7.329), declaring that Wagner 'has driven the prime tendency of opera, the idyllic, to its logical conclusion' ('hat die Urtendenz der Oper, die Idyllische bis zu ihren Consequenzen geführt [...]') in *Tristan and Isolde*, which, he claims, is not a 'symphony', but the expression of the radicalization of the idyllic tendencies in opera, thus of the recitative, the sentimental lust, the moral effect. *Tristan and Isolde* is an idyll, giving us 'primordial music' ('*Urmusik*'). *Tristan and Isolde* and *Siegfried* are, however, not only 'idyllic' because they recover the balance between nature and art, reality and ideal, but also because they evoke the belief in fundamental, human goodness – just as Italian opera attempts to do.

Nietzsche continues with the claim that Schiller's idea of 'the undivided person', 'the singing original man', is idyllic:

> I am thinking of the Schillerian ideas on a new idyll. [...] the undivided person. The singing original man. The orchestra is modern man, opposite the idyll. (9[149], KSA 7.329–330)

> Ich denke an den Schillerschen Gedanken über eine neue Idylle. [...] der ungetrennte Mensch. Der singende Urmensch. Das Orchester ist der moderne Mensch, der Idylle gegenüber.

It seems that Nietzsche here understands the idyll as the environment where man can be 'total' or 'undivided', and one with his environment, associating this man with the Rousseauian concept of the original man as the man that sings when he speaks. With this concept, Rousseau especially thinks of the man from the south, who lives happily, against the northern man, who lives in pain. Nietzsche's archetypical man is a southern person too, a Greek to be specific, yet he lives in pain and thus is characterized by a typical 'northern' feature. That the original or ideal man has a 'tragic' nature is made clear in the same note:

> *The tragic idyll:* the essence of things is not good and must expire, but people are so good and great, that their last breath strikes us deeply, because they feel incapable of such an ending. Siegfried the "person", we, on the other hand, the non-person without peace and objective. (9[149], KSA 7. 331)

> *Die tragische Idylle*: das Wesen der Dinge ist nicht gut und muß untergehen, aber die Menschen sind so gut und groß, daß uns ihr Vergehen am tiefsten ergreifen, weil sie fühlen für solche Vergehen unfähig zu sein. Siegfried der "Mensch", wir dagegen der Unmensch ohne Rast und Ziel.

The archetype of man is a hero, because he bears his inevitable loss of life with dignity, that is to say, peacefully. His attitude towards mortality (which is the essence of every human life; in *The Birth of Tragedy*, Nietzsche will articulate this by means of the Silenian myth) makes him truly human. Wagner is idyllic, because he strove for 'total' artworks:

> Idyllic tendency vis-à-vis art: he [Wagner, MP] notices the confusion of arts everywhere and believes he can rebuild the *one* art. The individuality of artforms appears to him as a mistake. The artist who is torn in pieces is condemned, the total artist, the artistic man that is, renovated. (9[149], KSA 7.133)

> Idyllische Tendenz der Kunst gegenüber: er sieht überall die Verirrung der Künste und glaubt die *eine* Kunst herzustellen. Der Individualismus der Künste erscheint ihm als Verirrung. Der in Stücke gerissene Künstler wird verurteilt, der Allkünstler d.h. der künstlerische Mensch restituiert.

In his *Letters on the Aesthetic Education of Man* (*Briefe über die ästhetische Erziehung des Menschen,* 1795), Schiller diagnosed the division and specialization in knowledge and art as a problem typical of modern times. For him, this led to an estrangement of man from himself, his fellow men, and nature, which should be avoided. In his *Letters,* as well as *On the Naive and Sentimental in Literature,* he pleaded for the integration of art and knowledge, of different art forms, different kinds of knowledge, and of reason and imagination in order for humanity to remain its humanity. The idylls that Schiller, Wagner, and Nietzsche dream of, agree when it comes to this important striving for totality via art. The disintegration of human talents and especially of reason and imagination leads to a loss of humanity. Schiller's, Wagner's, and Nietzsche's theses share opposition against the calculating mind at the expense of the aesthetic imagination. The calculating, abstract mind should be balanced by the imagination in order for human beings to experience themselves as *human,* and in order for societies to offer their inhabitants a space where they indeed are allowed, enabled, and even encouraged to exploit their human qualities as much as possible. Humanity, according to them, can only find its true soul when the muses or 'musical' spirit leads it.

Convinced of the agreement between Schiller and Wagner, Nietzsche writes in 9[145]:

> Motto for Wagner's tendency:

> Like after hopeless longing,/The bitter grief of long separation,/A child throws itself onto the heart of his mother/With burning tears of remorse:/That is how the song leads the fugitive back/From the strange customs of far foreign countries/To the hut of his youth, to the pure happiness/Of his innocence,/So that he warms himself in the reliable arms of Nature/From the cold rules.

> Motto für Wagner's Tendenz:

> Und wie nach hoffnungslosem Sehnen,/Nach langer Trennung bitterm Schmerz,/Ein Kind mit heißen Reuethränen/Sich stürzt an seiner Mutter Herz:/So führt zu seiner Jugend Hütten,/Zu seiner Unschuld reinem Glück,/Vom fernen Ausland fremder Sitten/Den Flüchtling der Gesang zurück,/In der Natur getreuen Armen Von kalten Regeln zu erwärmen.

The motto, by which Nietzsche describes Wagner's bucolic, idyllic tendency, is Schiller's poem 'The Power of Song' ('Die Macht des Gesanges', 1796). This poem depicts Wagner's idea that music brings a whole society of estranged men back to its roots, to nature and the pure happiness men experienced there. Nietzsche concludes this note with an assignment to himself: 'Afterwards, compare with the "Walk" ('Dann der "Spaziergang" zu vergleichen'). In 9[76] (KSA 7. 302), he refers to this poem of Schiller (first published in 1795 under the title *'Elegie'* in Schiller's magazine *Die Horen)*, because he wants to use it to explain the idyllic, which he characterizes as the 'embrace of nature', including nature's 'highest terror' ('höchster Schrecken').[47] Nietzsche emphasizes the horrific side of nature. Such is the 'German', tragic understanding of nature, which happens to be typically 'Greek' too, as *The Birth of Tragedy* teaches us. As a true, tragic-idyllic artist, who brings the estranged listener back to his original innocence (however accompanied by a deep layer of metaphysical pain), Wagner is the first to put the 'concept "classic"' (9[151], KSA 7.331) into practice, because he fulfills the '"sentimental"' movement (9[151], KSA 7.331). He is the first to fulfil the typically German 'Graecomaniac' sentimental longing, by making the true southern, Greek spirit accessible to the northern, German people.

Nietzsche will indeed present his friend Wagner in *The Birth of Tragedy* as the artist who succeeds where Goethe and Schiller have failed in rejuvenating the Greek spirit. There he abandons the terms 'sentimental' and 'classic', and also abandons the 'idyllic' to the camp of his enemies. Only the typical concepts of 'Apollonian', 'Dionysian' and 'tragic' survive. The 'tragic-idyllic' ideal of the future is still the cultural ideal attached to *The Birth of Tragedy's* aesthetics, yet, the ideal is no longer named 'tragic idyll'. Wagner is not called a composer of 'tragic idylls' anymore either, because Nietzsche identifies the 'idyllic' with a moral view of life (in chapter 19, just as in 8[29]) and Italian opera (just as in 9[123]), directed at 'emotional effect' ('Affektwirkung', 9[126, 129]) and 'pathological' (9[137]). Moreover, it is identified with 'rhythmical' music, whereas, as we shall see below, Nietzsche opposes 'idyllic' music and 'rhythmical' music in his notes of 1870–1871.

Nietzsche's studies of Greek rhythm

As we have seen, Nietzsche shrank back when Wagner exposed so much enthusiasm for his work, in February 1870, – especially because of Wagner's careless misunderstanding of his interpretation of the Greeks. Nevertheless, Nietzsche was a genuine and dedicated associate when it came to the ideal of enhancing European culture by deepening it through music. His interest in music and Greece also coincided, when

---

47 This bears a strong resemblance with Nietzsche's heroic doctrine of the *amor fati*, which he made public for the first time in GS 276 (p. 157/KSA 3.521).

Nietzsche started to reflect on Greek metrics and rhythmics, a subject he became focused on at the time he had to instruct his students about the matter. Nietzsche was
not convinced by the existing theories on Greek metrics, Rudolf Westphal's theory in
particular. Therefore, he formulated his own 'quantitative' theory of Greek rhythm.
This theory, I argue, combined Schopenhauer's distinction between 'quantitative' and
'qualitative' rhythm with Wagner's view of rhythm as 'time-sequence' ('*Zeitfolge*').
Nietzsche never referred to Schopenhauer or Wagner as sources of his theory, so there
is no empirical proof of any incorporation and combination of Schopenhauerian and
Wagnerian views of rhythm, and the application of this to Greek poetry. However, his
terms 'quantitative' and 'temporal rhythm' are suggestive enough to assume that there
had been such an influence. Moreover, because Wagner's 'idyllic tendency' confronted
him with the severe problem that Wagner did not understand the tragic view of life,
Nietzsche needed something else that could tie the composer to the Greeks. The theory
that Greek poetry was led by 'temporal sequence' rather than by 'pitch' would indeed
confirm that Wagner's 'melodic' music was on the right, Greek, track. Consequently,
Nietzsche's theory of Greek rhythm also facilitated the idea that Wagner made 'Greek'
music. This was at least a welcome side-effect of his philological work.

In *The World as Will and Representation II*, Schopenhauer discerned a rhythmical
and a harmonious element in melody, and regarded the former as a 'quantitative' element that concerned the duration of the notes and the latter as 'qualitative', pointing
at its 'pitch and depth'.[48] Both elements, however, were explained to be subordinate to
time, because the quantitative element is about the relative duration and the qualitative one about the rapidity or tempo of the notes. Possibly, Nietzsche modified this in
terms reminiscent of Wagner's 'temporal sequence' ('*Zeitfolge*'). The only indirect and
circumstantial pieces of evidence I have for my interpretation are that Nietzsche was
involved with Wagner's 'Beethoven' essay at the time that he developed his 'quantitative' theory, and the similarities in interpretation of the rhythmical element tenable in Schopenhauer's, Wagner's, and Nietzsche's understanding of rhythm. Wagner's idiom ('*Zeitfolge*') deviates from Schopenhauer, but agrees with Nietzsche's term
'*Zeitrhythmus*'. All three concepts, however, centre on the idea of melody built on du-

---

48 By making this distinction within rhythm, Schopenhauer united the different theories of '*Tak-
trhythmik*' that dominated German (musical) theory in the early 19th Century, which were adopted
by German philology. So did Nietzsche. The discussion of rhythm in music and the question as to what
rhythm was drew on Aristoxenos, the earliest Greek musical theorist. This implied a different conception of 'time' than the Newtonian idea that 'time' is an empty, homogenous medium. In Aristoxenos's
and Aristotle's definition, 'time' were 'times', measures of movements 'tempus mensura motus'. Cf.
Dahlhaus 1989, pp. 157–173, esp. p. 160. As empty, homogenous element, time *becomes* measure and
movement by rhythm ('Takt', 'Schlagfolge'), while in the Aristotelian sense time *was* measure and
movement.

ration instead of on beat – meaning on length of the tone instead of its strength of intonation.[49]

Yet, the most important thing is not that Nietzsche may have invented the term 'temporal rhythm' ('Zeitrhythmus'), but his idea that melody could be 'beatless'. This idea gave him a weapon to corroborate the divide between 'Apollonian', rhythmical or architectonic music on the one hand and 'Dionysian', 'melodic' music on the other, within the scope of the Schopenhauerian division between 'visual' ('Apollonian') arts and the ('Dionysian') art of music, which forms the onset of the aesthetics created in *The Birth of Tragedy*. This distinction enabled him to account for the rhythmical and epic music of the Greek rhapsodists on the one hand and for the melodic, lyrical music of the tragic satyr chorus on the other. Alternatively, this lays the foundation for the antagonism in chapter 19 of *The Birth of Tragedy* between individual voice-centred Italian opera and Wagner's choral music drama.

Nietzsche discovered that Greek rhythm was built up by 'time-quantities' instead of the '*ictus*', that is, a rhythm organized by strong and weak beats. His discovery was a great stimulation to him, as becomes clear from a letter to his friend Erwin Rohde:

> If you want to believe me, then I can tell you that there is a new metrics that I have discovered which, compared to the whole new development of metrics by G. Hermann to Westphal or Schmidt, is off track. Laugh or ridicule as you like – to me the case is very astonishing. There is a lot to do, but I swallow dust with pleasure, because this time I have the greatest confidence and I am able to give the fundamental idea an ever-greater depth.[50]

> Wenn du mir glauben willst, so kann ich dir erzahlen, dass es eine neue Metrik gibt, die ich entdeckt habe, der gegenüber die ganze neuere Entwicklung der Metrik von G. Hermann bis Westphal oder Schmidt eine Verirrung ist. Lache oder hohne, wie du willst – mir selber ist die Sache sehr erstaunlich. Es gibt sehr viel zu arbeiten, aber ich schlucke Staub mit Lust, weil ich diesmal die schönste Zuversicht habe und dem Grundgedanken eine immer grössere Tiefe geben kann.

Nietzsche's 'quantitative' metrics departs from the units of time and their relations, considering these as of long or short duration: 'So we must give up the *rhythm. Ictus* totally and keep ourselves to Aristoxenus, who only knows the *time rhythm*. The Greeks and Romans recited their verses with word accents, but with the sharpest feeling for equal time' ('Wir haben also ganz den rhythm. ictus aufzugeben und uns an Aristoxenus zu halten, der nur den *Zeitrhytmus* kennt. Die Griechen und Romer recitirten ihre

---

49 The issue of 'rhythm' in Nietzsche is also studied by Bornmann (1989), in view of Nietzsche's studies of Greek metrics, and López (1995) and Porter (2000), in regard of *The Birth of Tragedy*. They remark that Nietzsche's view of Greek rhythm is guided by his knowledge of modern music, Wagner in particular. However, they do not point at Wagner's notion of '*Zeitfolge*' nor do they make the claim that this offered Nietzsche evidence to prove Wagner's 'Greek spirit'.

50 November 1870 (KSB 3, p. 159). He repeats this judgment in a late letter to Carl Fuchs (April 1886, KSB 7, p. 178). Cf. Nietzsche to Carl Fuchs, July 1877 (KSB 5, pp. 260–263) and Nietzsche to Carl Fuchs, end of August 1888 (KSB 8, pp. 403–405).

Verse mit den Wortaccenten, aber mit scharfstem Gefühl fur gleiche Zeiten').[51] With this hypothesis, Nietzsche questioned von Westphals theory that stated that the rhythm depended on the intensity or strength ('*arsis*' and '*thesis*', going up and going down) of a tone and not on its duration.[52]

Not only did Nietzsche deny the theory of *ictus*-based rhythm, he also combined Schopenhauer's metaphysics with the view of duration based rhythm: 'Rhythm is an attempt at individuation. [...] Rhythm is the form of becoming, anyhow the form of the world of appearance' ('Der Rhythmus ist ein Versuch der Individuation. [...] Rhythmus ist die Form des Werdens, überhaupt die Form der Erscheinungswelt').[53] As such, he repeated his criticism of the *Takt* and accorded Greek music with Wagner's '*unendliche Melodie*'. This, at least seems to be the case when we have a look, once again, at 9[111] and 9[116] of KSA 7. In 9[111], Nietzsche writes:

> Greek music is therefore the most ideal, in that it does not bother at all about stressing words. It does not even know the musical accent in the slightest way: the effect relies in *time-rhythm and the melody*, not in the *strenght* of rhythm. Rhythm is just *experienced*, and not expressed by stress [...]. Height and depth of notes, thesis or arsis in the beat do not have anything to do with Greek rhythm. On the other hand, the feeling for *tonal scales* and *time-rhythms* were very sophisticated. (KSA 7.316)

> Die griechische Musik darin die idealste, daß sie auf Wortbetonung [...] gar keine Rücksicht nimmt. Sie kennt überhaupt das musikalische Accentuiren nicht: die Wirkung beruht im *Zeitrhyhmus und der Melodie*, nicht im Rhythmus der *Stärken*. Der Rhythmus wurde nur *empfunden*, er kam nicht durch die *Betonung* zum Ausdruck. [...] Höhe und Tiefe der Note, These oder Arse des Taktes hatten mit ihm nichts zu thun. Dagegen war das Gefühl für die *Tonleitern* und die *Zeitrhythmen* auf das Feinste entwickelt.

---

51 Cited by Bornmann (1989), p. 484. Aristoxenus of Tarantum (364–304 BC) was a student of Aristotle. Fragments of his books *Elements of Rhythm* and *Elements of Harmony* as well as on the dithyrambic poets are important sources concerning Greek music and its practice. The Peripatetics were the first to make scholarly enquiries into the development of Greek music and poetry (for example Sappho's poetry), and to record and discuss different views of music in Greece

52 Éric Dufour (2001) comments to this: 'All the scholars [next to Von Westphal, Schmidt, and Hermann, MP] lack historical sense, because they assimilate rhythm as it exists today with Greek rhythm. Therefore, they believe that Greek rhythm is based on the accentuation, on the intonation [...]' ('Tous ces theoriens [next to Von Westphal, Schmidt and Hermann, MP] manquent de sens historique, car ils assimilent le rythme tel qu'il existe aujourd'hui au rythme grec. Ainsi pensent-ils que le rythme grec etait fonde sur l'accentuation, sur l'intonation [...]', p. 227). Cf. Bornmann (1989), p. 478. Nietzsche does so too, but he leans on Wagner (while others lean on Bach, Mozart, Beethoven).

53 Cited by Bornmann (1989), p. 484. Hans-Gerd von Seggern (2003) claims that 'making language more rhythmical and inserting the chorus in the word drama were perceived by Nietzsche as preliminary stages of Wagner's music drama [...]' ('Rhythmisierung der Sprache und Einfuhrung des Chors im Wortdrama erscheinen Nietzsche als Vorstufen zum Musikdrama Wagners [...],' p. 202). Von Seggern neglects Nietzsche's problem with rhythm: instead of 'rhythmisierung', Nietzsche (and Wagner of course) preferred 'de-rhythmisierung', thus the *liberation* or unchaining of rhythm ('Entfesselung des Rhythmus') to culminate into a beatless and 'timeless' rhythm.

He refers to the Greek excellence in dancing and takes this as an argument for his theory, which is remarkable in the light of Wagner's strong opposition to dance-music. What might make this idea defensible is that the Greek way of dancing is in perfect accordance with natural sound, while beat-music is seen as un-natural or un-true, as it is attached to the empirical, and not to the metaphysical world. In Wagner's argumentation, dance-music is based on rhythm and beat (*'Takt'*) and therefore superficial, i.e., lacking metaphysical depth. Here, indeed, Nietzsche, due to his research, is able to take another stance; not all dance-music is superficial, because there are different kinds of rhythms. His argument, however, implies that the Greek *'Zeitrhythmus'* is not the same as Wagner's stretching of the 'Takt', the time or beat. Nietzsche supported Wagner's attempts to uproot the traditional, rhythmical borders and open up space for the immediate effect of musical depth, for example in 9[114], KSA 7.317, where he speaks of *'liberation of the symphony from its Roman schematism. Unleashing of rhythm'* (*'Befreiung der Symphonie von ihrem romanischen Schematismus. Entfesselung des Rhythmus'*). However, after counting parts of *Tristan* and *Mastersingers*, he found that Wagner 'cheated' with rhythms:

> I remembered that I, during my study of antique rhythmics [in] 1870, hunted after 5- and 7-time measures and counted the *Mastersingers* and *Tristan:* during which some things about W<agner>'s rhythmics dawned upon me. He is so inclined against the mathematical, strictly symmetrical [...] that he fancies to *decelerate* 4-beat times into 5-beat times, the 6-beat times in 7-beats [...]. One of the most dangerous after-effects of W <agner>'s seems to me 'to enliven at any cost': because this turns very easily into a trick, a technique.[54]

> Mir fiel ein, daß ich, beim Studium der antiken Rhythmik, 1870 auf der Jagd nach 5- und 7-taktigen Perioden war und die Meistersinger und Tristan durchzählte: wobei mir einiges über W<agner>'s Rhythmik aufgieng. Er ist nämlich so abgeneigt gegen das Mathematische, streng Symmetrische [...] daß er mit Vorliebe die 4-taktigen Perioden in 5-taktige *verzögert*, die 6-taktigen in 7-taktige [...]. Unter den gefährlichen Nachwirkungen W<agner>'s scheint mir "das Lebendig-machen-wollen um jeden Preis" eine der gefährlichsten: denn blitzschnell wird's Manier, Handgriff.

While Nietzsche's reflections on the 'idyllic' nature of Wagner led to doubts about the latter's ability to understand, let alone rejuvenate, the Greek spirit, his studies of Greek rhythm resulted in openly Wagner-friendly conclusions. They supplied him with the hope that Wagner was on the right, 'Greek' track. While he condemned Wagner's deliberate play with rhythmical expectations in this letter of 1877, pointing to the threat of an artificial vitality, he applauded it in 1871.

Moreover, it provided him with a tool to parry an upcoming serious threat to his hopes of Wagner's music, because he was able to identify Wagner's melodic, beatless

---

54 To Carl Fuchs, 29 July 1877 (KSB 5, pp. 261–262).

music as 'Dionysian' music.[55] However, as we shall see in the next chapter, the picture of Wagner as a 'Dionysian' artist implied the elimination of all idyllic tendencies. Concerning 'harmony', 'melody', and 'rhythm', Nietzsche delivered himself to Schopenhauerian and Wagnerian definitions, while calling in the aid of the Greek division into 'flute' and 'guitar' music. He gave a definition of the tragic of which he thought that Wagner had to adopt it. Wagner applied the right, 'Greek' musical techniques, but he had to prove, still, that his view of nature was deeply tragic, and not tragic-idyllic, after all.

Conclusion

Despite extolling Wagner's 1870 essay on Beethoven to the skies, Nietzsche took a perspective which conflicted with the musical aesthetics and anthropological claims advanced in that very essay. Wagner's search for the morally 'good man', which is echoed or anticipated in the restoration of paradisiacal innocence by 'sublime-naive' music, places Nietzsche's purely aesthetic view of art in an especially problematic position.[56]

Nietzsche regarded Wagner as the fulfiller of Goethe and Schiller's project to establish a national, German theatre to revitalize German and European culture against the dissipation of art and metaphysical depth, caused by Italian opera. According to Nietzsche, Wagner had a 'tragic' view of nature, which saved him from the 'idyllic sheep-breeding' ('idyllische Schäferei') other 'Graecomaniac' German artists before him were guilty of. Wagner's 'tragic' view went, however, indeed together with an 'idyllic', Schillerian view of humanity as 'undivided', of art as representing the unity of 'ideal' and 'reality' (in *Tristan and Isolde* and *Siegfried*), a Rousseauian view of humanity as originally good, and the Romantic, idyllic view of art as based on feelings (the 'Affektwirkung' of Wagner's works). Hence, Nietzsche coined Wagner a 'radically idyllic' and 'tragic-idyllic' composer of 'tragic idylls', suffering from the same 'idyllic tendency' as the one that made Italian opera 'moral' and 'superficial'. In *The Birth of Tragedy*, as we shall see in the next chapter, Nietzsche neglects Wagner's idyllic side, claiming that he is a tragic, rather than a 'tragic-idyllic' composer, who saves Europe from all idyllicism – then mainly understood as Rousseauian, moral optimism. This chapter has shown, however, that Nietzsche was well aware of Wagner's own idyllicism and thus of his lack of 'Greek', tragic awareness.

---

55 However important it was to Wagner to be considered the heir of Beethoven, this was important to Nietzsche only in so far he could coin this activity 'Dionysian'. Whether or not he was a Dionysian composer, was not relevant to Wagner.

56 One can argue whether Nietzsche's view of art and life is purely aesthetic, and even if it is at all possible to view things purely aesthetically, but at least it is Nietzsche's ambition to do so and I shall not discuss this matter at this point. Let me just say that I agree with van Tongeren's claim that there is 'an unmistakably strong moral pathos' in Nietzsche's philosophy (2006, p. 389).

Nietzsche's technical discussion of music centred on the contrast between 'melodic', 'beatless' ('*Taktlos*') music and 'rhythmical' music. Combining his remarks in this section of his notes with the results of his studies of Greek rhythmics at the end of 1870, it followed that Nietzsche, when he formed his new 'quantitative' theory of Greek rhythmics, in fact tried to renew the existing philological research on Greek meter and rhythm by adducing Schopenhauerian and Wagnerian views – the same strategy he used to explain the nature of Greek tragedy in *The Birth of Tragedy*. Equally, it functions as a defence of Wagner's artistic endeavours, just like in the book. This difficult marriage between Greek and Wagnerian music may have been motivated by Nietzsche's insight that he could only account for Wagner's 'Greek' nature if the technical side of the argument was satisfactory.

There were more differences between Nietzsche and Wagner, besides their idyllicism and tragicism.

While Wagner tried to fortify Beethoven's 'reformative' frame of mind by engaging in Luther's battle against Catholicism, in 'Beethoven', Nietzsche said farewell to Christianity in general, turning to pre-Socratic, Greek culture. Additionally, rather than agreeing with Wagner's attempt to follow Beethoven's pioneering symphonic work in the composition of his specific melodic music, he sought to prove that Greek music was melodic and that Wagner's melodic music was 'Greek'. To corroborate the 'Greek' character of Wagner's music drama, he encouraged Wagner to give the chorus more space within his works. The mythical inspiration Wagner found in Aeschylus's *Oresteia* for his *Ring* cycle notwithstanding, Nietzsche's philosophy of music and culture were much more 'Graecomaniac' than Wagner.

Furthermore, rather than blaming other European cultures (or the Jews) for bestowing the superficial tendency upon the North, like Wagner, in *The Birth of Tragedy* Nietzsche held the Germans themselves accountable for keeping to the wrong interpretation of Greek nature. With Wagner, in several notes he indeed regarded the Italian and French tendency to superficiality and the idyllic, moral tendency as reprobate, considering the 'deep, Dionysian impulse' typically 'German'. However, before curing the whole of Europe, Germany had to cure itself – Nietzsche advanced against Wagner's too optimistic, one-sided, and uncritical view of Germany's artistic and cultural perfection. Nietzsche's far more 'Greek' and 'supra-national' focus was, I argue in what follows, responsible for the main differences in Nietzsche's and Wagner's aesthetics and anthropology. In my view, Nietzsche was aware of this, and this awareness led him to pair his Wagner-enthusiasm with a 'secret scepticism', which questioned Wagner's alleged 'Greekness'.

Chapter 4
The Birth of Tragedy out of Nietzsche's concern for Wagner's 'Graecization'

Introduction

During the last weeks that he spent in Leipzig before moving to Basle, in April 1869, Nietzsche became increasingly popular with the Wagnerians who lived in the musical capital. Since Nietzsche came out with his views on the music of the future, its supporters were curious to meet him. He was even invited to a private dinner in the Hotel de Pologne with Franz Liszt. However, despite his desire to ascend on Leipzig's social scale, Nietzsche did not intend to become part of the Wagner-circle. 'As it happens, they wish that I participate in their interest in a literary way, yet I on my part do not feel at all like overtly clucking like a hen straight away' ('Sie wünschen nämlich, daß ich mich litterarisch in Ihrem Interesse betheilige, ich aber für mein Theil habe nicht die geringste Lust, wie eine Henne gleich öffentlich zu gackern'), he informed Rohde.[1]

With *The Birth of Tragedy*, which came out 2 January 1872, Nietzsche still partook in the interest of the New German School and their doctrinaire activities.[2] In that context, the book can even be regarded as part of the series of pamphlets written by members of the Old German School (Johannes Brahms, Clara and Robert Schumann, Felix Mendelssohn, Eduard Hanslick) and the New German School (Franz Liszt, Richard Wagner, and Franz Brendel), published in magazines such as the *Neue Zeitschrift für Musik* and the *Berliner Musikzeitung*.[3] The question is what made Nietzsche change his mind? Despite his personal allegiance to Wagner since their meeting in November 1868, he never felt like grouping together like a bunch of scouts around their

---

1 22/28 February 1869 (KSB 2. 377). For a more detailed account on the problematic aspects of the terms 'Old' and 'New' German School, see Altenburg (2006).

2 Schaberg (1995) reports that the printing was completed by 29 December 1871, that the book arrived on New Year's Day in Basle, and that the copies went on sale on 2 January 1872. By then, Nietzsche's philological master Ritschl had already read the book and noted in his diary: 'an inspired waste of energy' (cited by Schaberg 1995, p. 25).

3 *Die neue Zeitschrift für Musik* was founded by Robert Schumann (1810–1856) in 1834, who was also a teacher at the conservatorium in Leipzig, which Felix Mendelssohn-Bartholdy had founded. Directing also the *Gewandhaus* concerts, Mendelssohn turned Leipzig in one of the leading cities in music in the German-speaking world. Mendelssohn and Schumann tried to preserve and continue the inheritance of Bach, Beethoven, Weber, and Schubert. In 1844, Franz Brendel took over the editing of the *Neue Zeitschrift*, at which point the magazine started to develop into the pulpit of Liszt and Wagner. Brendel was also a teacher at Leipzig conservatorium, but was dismissed after the publication of Wagner's essay *Jewishness in Music* (*Das Judenthum in der Musik*), in 1850. Wagner had published this essay under the pseudonym 'K. Freigedank'. He re-published it with his own name, in 1869.

leader. Yet, the reason why he initially refused to join in with other Wagnerians perhaps turned into one of the motives for Nietzsche to write *The Birth of Tragedy* after all. For in his view, his 'gentlemen brothers in Wagnero' were 'too stupid' and wrote 'horribly' ('*ekelhaft*').[4] The reason for this, he explained, was that 'principally, they are absolutely unrelated to this genius, they do not have an eye for depth but only for the surface' ('sie sind im Grunde mit jenem Genius schlechterdings nicht verwandt und haben keinen Blick für die Tiefe, sondern nur für die Oberfläche'). Nietzsche assumed he had to reveal Wagner's genius in *The Birth of Tragedy*, because he was the only one who grasped the depth of his music. In other words, if he would not do it, Europe would never hear about the 'depth' Germany had in store. His explanation of Wagner was therefore of utmost cultural importance.

However, Wagner's idea of depth was not entirely congruent with Nietzsche's tragic-pessimistic view of it. In making the Greek connection with his music dramas, Wagner linked his ambition as easily to Homer as to Plato and Aeschylus. Without differentiation, they all represented the same, Mythical Age to him. In addition, according to his 1870 'Beethoven' essay, 'the truth' that needed to be expressed by music turned out to be the belief in humanity's original goodness instead of the tragic and Schopenhauerian awareness of the vanity and 'hell' of life. Indeed, in pigeonholing Beethoven's 'sublime' music as an expression of the belief that 'man is good after all,' Wagner mixed up aesthetics and morality, the 'tragic' and the 'idyllic', according to the notes Nietzsche when he read 'Beethoven'. This raises the question as to how we can rhyme Nietzsche's endorsement of Wagner in *The Birth of Tragedy* with the 'aestheticist' claim made in the same book.

Below, I argue that *The Birth of Tragedy* evolves around this problem and therefore has a 'double nature', because Nietzsche's explicit 'Wagner enthusiasm' is escorted and restrained by a 'secret Wagner scepticism'. I claim that the scepticism is logically implied in Nietzsche's radical rejection of any kind of idyllic tendency in his début-book.[5] Different from his attempt to combine the tragic and the idyllic, in the notes of 1871, by branding Wagner a composer of 'tragic-idyllic' music and a 'radical idyllicist,' he presents him as a composer of purely tragic music in *The Birth of Tragedy*. The strong dichotomy of the tragic and the idyllic even outranks the central pair of Apollo and Dionysus in the last ten chapters of the book, where Nietzsche reflects upon the rebirth of the tragic in Wagner's music dramas. My analysis of these chapters brings me to the suspicion that, despite Nietzsche's public declaration that Wagner would return Germany to its original, Greek roots of tragic pessimism and metaphysical depth,

---

4 To Erwin Rohde, 22/28 February 1869 (KSB 2, p. 378).

5 Ruehl concluded something similar, on the basis of a *political* reading of *The Birth of Tragedy*: 'While officially propagating Wagner's cause, Nietzsche had in fact already begun to tread new paths that would soon lead him away from Bayreuth and the artwork of the future' (2006, p. 88).

and thus redeem European musical culture from its shallowness, his personal belief that this would indeed happen was restricted.

In addition, I maintain that Nietzsche's implicit criticism of Wagner's idyllic tendencies was meant to familiarize the composer with the tragic, Greek spirit and to instruct him on the path of 'Graecization': how to create artworks by re-awakening Greek tragedy's aesthetics and Silenian wisdom, and how to supersede the moral view of art and life with a purely aesthetic one. Hence, *The Birth of Tragedy* was not only intended as a book to help bring about the 'great Renaissance' in explaining Wagner's music as the contemporary version of Greek tragedy to the general and academic public, but it was also intended as a 'manual,' which would teach Wagner what 'Greekness' was and how he could become 'more Greek'. *The Birth of Tragedy* thus was written out of Nietzsche's concern for Wagner's 'Graecization'. Indeed, Nietzsche regarded his book in this way too, as he explained in retrospect:

> While the thunders of the Battle of Worth rolled away over baffled Europe – I, in some corner of the Alps, wrote down this book's [*The Birth of Tragedy*, MP] decisive thoughts: in essence, not so much for me as for Richard Wagner, for whose Graecization and southernization until then no one had really cared.[6]

> Während die Donner der Schlacht von Wörth über das erstaunte Europa weggiengen – schrieb ich in irgend einem Winkel der Alpen die entscheidenden Gedanken dieses Buches nieder: im Grunde nicht viel für mich, sondern für Richard Wagner, um dessen Gräcisierung und Versüdlichung sich bis dahin Niemand sonderlich Mühe gegeben hatte.

A note from 1874 confirms that Nietzsche was aware of Wagner's idyllicism, i.e., his Rousseauian view of nature and mankind as inherently and originally good: 'He [Richard Wagner, MP] discharges his weaknesses by ascribing them to modernity: natural belief in the goodness of nature, as long as nature dwells freely' ('Er [Richard Wagner, MP] entladet sich seiner Schwächen, dadurch dass er sie der modernen Zeit zuschiebt: natürlicher Glaube an die Güte der Natur, wenn sie frei waltet').[7] Hence, while Wagner was a more important theoretical source of Nietzsche's early philosophy than generally acknowledged – principally in the philosophy of culture – there were also crucially different views in philosophical anthropology and aesthetics, which made the break between the philosopher and composer inevitable.

Let me start my argument by explaining Nietzsche's radical aestheticism, which revolves around the rigid exclusion of morality in art. This helps achieve a better appreciation of his wholesale rejection of the idyll, be it in a Schillerian, Rousseauian, Italian, or Wagnerian form.

---

6 In the first version of the 'Attempt at Self-Criticism' (KSA 14.45).
7 In the first version of the 'Attempt at Self-Criticism' (KSA 14.45).
Cf. 32[33], KSA 7.765. I come back to Nietzsche's Wagner criticism in the *Nachlass* notes of 1874 in chapter 5.

Nietzsche's aestheticism

Daniel Came recently argued that *The Birth of Tragedy* 'presents a fundamental op-position between moral and aesthetic value' and that 'this opposition forms the basis framework of BT'.[8] However true this claim may be, it could be even stronger consid-ering that it mainly rests on texts that do not stem from *The Birth of Tragedy*. This chapter can, amongst other things, be regarded as a substantiation of Came's argu-ment, because it provides evidence for his claim from *The Birth of Tragedy* itself, analyzing it from the perspective of Nietzsche's resistance to the 'idyll'. Came, how-ever, misses the anti-moral component involved in this, ignoring the forming role of the idyll in Nietzsche's early aesthetics altogether. And, even though he argues that Nietzsche's retrospective assessments of his published works contain important in-terpretative value (especially the *Attempt at Self-Criticism*), he also misses Nietzsche's declaration that he had written the book 'out of concern with Wagner's "Graecization" and "southernization"', made in the first version of this *Attempt*. In his defence, it must be remarked that Came does not focus on Nietzsche's interaction with Wagner, but on the logics of the 'theodicy' implied in the famous remark that 'life can *only* be justified aesthetically'.[9]

In this famous remark, Nietzsche's aestheticism and underlying admiration of the Greek capacity to translate even the most tragic events into joyful works of art, come to-gether.[10] It sums up his artistic and cultural ideal to restore this capacity by way of wag-ing a 'cultural war'. The *Foreword to Richard Wagner*, which heralded the 1872-edition of *The Birth of Tragedy*, indicates that Nietzsche hoped to combat the cultural war against France together with his friend the composer Richard Wagner.[11] In it, Nietzsche claims that 'while conceiving these thoughts, he [the author] was conversing with you constantly, as if you had been present and as if he could only write down things which were appropriate in your presence' (BT Foreword, p. 13/'ebenfalls dass er, bei allem, was er sich erdachte, mit Ihnen wie mit einem Gegenwärtigen verkehrte und nur etwas

---

8 Came (2004), p. 38. See also Came (2006), which is a shorter version of his 2004 article. Compare Bishop and Stephenson (2005), p. 25.

9 He also rightly concludes that Nietzsche is less Schopenhauerian than is often thought, in that he does share Schopenhauer's pessimism concerning the tragic and absurdity of life (the 'hell' that the will only returns to itself), but does not go along with Schopenhauer's ethical and ascetic conclusion of self-denial. However, I do not agree with Came's remark that 'it would not have furthered Nietzsche's friendship with Richard Wagner, who bought into Schopenhauer's philosophy wholesale, to draw at-tention in BT to these pernicious moral foundations of Schopenhauer's pessimism' (2004, p. 46). Not only would Wagner have agreed with Nietzsche's refusal to buy Schopenhauer's pessimism 'whole-sale' on various grounds, but he also blamed Nietzsche's bad mood to Schopenhauer's 'bad influence' on young people.

10 I come back to this Goethean insight further on in this chapter, in the section *Aesthetic Play and the Child at Play*.

11 Nietzsche had written the foreword on 22 February 1871 in Lugano, i.e., on Schopenhauer's birthday.

dieser Gegenwart Entsprechendes niederschreiben durfte', GT Vorwort, KSA 1.23). In his 'Beethoven' essay, Wagner had articulated the view that an artistic and cultural war had to be waged with France and Italy in order to secure Germany's place in Europe. In referring to the Franco-Prussian war of 1870–1871 and stating that 'we' [Nietzsche himself and Richard Wagner, MP] wrote 'Beethoven' and *The Birth of Tragedy* out of concern with a 'grave problem for Germany' (p. 13/'ernsthaft deutsches Problem', KSA 1.24), Nietzsche linked the two books ideologically. Yet, his book contains a crucial difference in comparison to Wagner's. While Wagner simply extolled Germany's unique qualifications for saving European culture, Nietzsche interwove a critical perspective of Germany into his book. Contrary to Wagner (who made a strict, exclusive opposition between the 'bad' cultural impact of France and Italy and the 'good' cultural impact of Germany on Europe), Nietzsche criticized Germany for accommodating cultural power to military-political power, for adopting Rousseau's moral, optimistic, and 'idyllic' view of humanity, and for following Winckelmann's serene view of the Greeks.[12] In his first untimely meditation *David Strauss, The Confessor and Writer* (1873), he emphasized that the military victory of Germany over France should not be appreciated as a cultural victory: '*Geist*' and '*Reich*', 'spirit' and 'state', should not be mistaken for the same thing.[13] The cultural war between Germany and France is still to be waged, Nietzsche argues, claiming that 'a great victory is a great danger' ('ein grosser Sieg ist eine grosse Gefahr').[14] The great danger is that people mix up military and cultural power, and turn art and aesthetics into a target of (militant) politics.[15]

---

[12] Nietzsche shared his rejection of Rousseau's doctrine with Jacob Burckhardt. See for more information: Ruehl (2006), pp. 88–92. Compare also e.g., WS 221 (p. 367/KSA 2.654).

[13] By way of which Nietzsche also distances himself from his former belief in a possible 'spiritual' interpretation of the Franco-Prussian war. Compare 7[88], KSA 7.158: 'I could imagine that on the German side the war was fought to liberate the Venus [the Venus of Milo, MP] from the Louvre, for a second Helena. This would be the spiritual interpretation of this war. The beautiful ancient rigidity of existence is inaugurated by means of this war – there begins the time of earnestness – we believe that it will also become the time of *art*' (translation by Bishop and Stephenson 2005, p. 58/'Ich könnte mir einbilden, man habe deutscher Seite den Krieg geführt, um die Venus aus dem Louvre zu befreien, als eine zweite Helena. Dies wäre die pneumatische Auslegung dieses Krieges. Die schöne Antike Starrheit des Daseins durch diesen Krieg inaugurirt – es beginnt die Zeit des Ernstes – wir glauben daß es auch die der *Kunst* sein wird'). This self-critical turn is traceable to a letter to Carl von Gersdorff, in which Nietzsche admitted: 'My worries about the current state of culture are big [...]; in confidence, I regard present-day Prussia as an enormous powerful threat for culture' ('Vor dem bevorstehenden Culturzustande habe ich die größten Besorgnisse [...] Im Vertrauen: ich halte das jetzige Preußen für eine der Cultur höchst gefährliche Macht', 7 November 1870, KSB 3, p. 155).

[14] DS 1, p. 3/KSA 1.159.

[15] Nietzsche repeated this in *Nietzsche contra Wagner*, lecturing Italy's Prime Minister Francesco Crispi for believing in the triple alliance: 'an intelligent people can only enter into a *mésalliance* with the "*Reich*"...' (NW, p. 265/'mit dem "Reich" macht ein intelligentes Volk immer nur eine mésalliance...', KSA 6.415). See also Janz III (1988), pp. 26–27.

Hence, in Nietzsche's view, art only can uplift German culture. Equalizing spirit and state is the clear-cut expression of the 'philistinism' or cultural 'decadence', Nietzsche contends.[16] 'Philistinism' in his sense is 'the absolute negation of the aesthetic', Malcolm Bull explains, adding that 'read in the light of Nietzsche's subsequent attack on Strauss, *The Birth of Tragedy* emerges as an account not just of *The Birth of Tragedy* from the spirit of music, but also of the birth of philistinism from the spirit of rationality.'[17] However, Nietzsche's cultural war is not only directed against the philistine idea that 'state' and 'culture' are one. It also aims to contend the moral interpretation of art. Contrary to what is still widely assumed, Nietzsche's amoral, aesthetic view of life (life as 'beyond good and evil') did not begin with *Human All Too Human* or *Daybreak*, nor with his '*amor fati* philosophy' or with *Beyond Good and Evil* (published in 1886).[18] Daniel Came is certainly right when he states that the clash between moral and aesthetic value forms the axis of *The Birth of Tragedy*.

What does Nietzsche's 'aestheticism' or 'aestheticist claim' amount to? The aesthetic view Nietzsche proposes is not simply the plea to go 'beyond good and evil', nor the warning to keep state and culture separate. His 'immoralism'[19] is too closely related to the view of art as the sole creator of culture and promoter of life to sustain such an interpretation. Indeed, in stating famously and somewhat enigmatically that 'art ist the highest task and the true metaphysical activity of this life' (p. 14/'Kunst [ist] die höchste Aufgabe und der eigentlich metaphysischen Thätigkeit dieses Lebens', KSA 1.24)[20], Nietzsche claims the field of aesthetics as the only field in which humanity can realize its true nature. For Nietzsche, this entails 'to look at science through the prism of the artist, but also to look at art through the prism of life' (ASC 2, p. 5/'die Wissenschaft unter der Optik des Künstlers zu sehn, die Kunst aber unter der des Lebens...', KSA 1.14). According to him, humanity's mission is to spread the aesthetic view to all directions of life and to create a culture united by 'style'.[21]

---

16 The others are Socratism, French naturalism (French naturalistic theatre), (Hanslickian) musical formalism, humanism, and scientific optimism.

17 Bull (2002), p. 51 and p. 62.

18 This misunderstanding is mainly due to Nietzsche's own evocative expression about *Daybreak* in *Ecce Homo*: 'My campaign against *morality* begins with this book' (EH, D 1, p. 120/'Mit diesem Buche beginnt mein Feldzug gegen die *Moral*', EH, M 1, KSA 6.329). In D 190, Nietzsche understands the 'thirst for appearing morally *excited* at all costs' as a characteristic of German philosophers and aesthetics in general and blames this tendency for Germany's wrong interpretation of the Greeks (D 190, pp. 111–112/KSA 3.162–164). Nietzsche makes an exception for Goethe, however.

19 Nietzsche generally uses the German '*Immoralismus*' to indicate the amoral view of things. For example, his assertion 'I am the first *immoralist*' (EH, UO 2, p. 114/EH, UB 2, 'Ich bin der erste *Immoralist*', KSA 6.319) and 'Nietzsche, the first *immoralist*' (EH, HH 6, p. 120/'Nietzsche, der erste *Immoralist*', EH, MA 6, KSA 6.328).

20 See also ASC 5 (p. 8/KSA 1.17), BT 5 (p. 33/KSA 1.47), and BT 24 (p. 113/KSA 1.152).

21 Barbarism is then 'lack of style or a chaotic jumble of styles' (DS 1, p. 6/KSA 1.163), in the first place.

Nietzsche, therefore, maintains a 'broad' conception of aestheticism, as Rebecca Bamford (2003) expressed: 'Nietzsche's own version of aestheticism is constituted in the deliberate application of aesthetic concerns to non[-] aesthetic situations and are- nas'.[22] We may add to this that it includes the protection of the aesthetic sphere against non-aesthetic (moral, dialectical, and political) intrusion and pollution. We should also consider that it implies the (Kantian and Schillerian) idea that our faculty of aes- thetic judgment must be cultivated, for the simple reason that 'art and developed judg- ment are inseparable', as Andrew Bowie stated, explaining that

> [...] the abolition of the aesthetic into the attitude of 'well, it's what I like' is the swiftest path to a consumerism which has no resources for resisting the manipulation of taste by multinational corporations and reactionary political interests.[23]

It is this philistine, consumerist attitude to art and life that Nietzsche and Wagner fought. But Nietzsche did so from the aestheticist position that holds that the aesthetic realm must be protected from non-aesthetic influences and the non-aesthetic must be viewed from an aesthetic perspective. Wagner lacked this firm aestheticist vantage- point.

The aesthetic realm is the sole realm of culture, because it is the only place where humankind is natural and free from moral judgements. It is the realm in which human- ity regains its 'childlike innocence'. The question is justified to what extent this child- like innocence resembles the Schillerian naiveté (which Nietzsche explicitly rejects in chapter 3 of *The Birth of Tragedy*), and thus to what extent it actually nears Schiller's definition of the 'idyll' as the unity of the 'ideal' and the 'real', as well as Schiller's famous dictum that 'man only plays when he is in the fullest sense of the word a hu- man being, and he is *only fully a human being when he plays*' ('der Mensch spielt nur, wo er in voller Bedeutung des Worts Mensch ist, und *er ist nur da ganz Mensch, wo er spielt*').[24] If so, then we have another strange doubleness in the book. Then it might be rightfully claimed that Nietzsche explicitly rejects Schiller, but lets him in through the backdoor in the context of his defence of the childlike realm of innocence, dreams, and poetic freedom. This entails further that he covers up not only Wagner's idyllic tendencies but also his own.

---

22 Bamford (2003), p. 66. She comes to this definition inspired by Megill, who defines 'aestheticism' as the 'attempt to expand the aesthetic to embrace the whole of reality' (1985, p. 2).
23 Bowie (2002–2), p. 91.
24 In letter XV of *Letters on the Aesthetic Education of Mankind* (Schiller 1982, pp. 106–107). Cf. Martin (1996), p. 9.

Homer, myth, and the symbol

With such a broad conception of aestheticism, culture becomes the space where art, artists and aesthetic experiences are saved, protected, stored, and explored. This means that culture creates a context 'in which great men (geniuses) do not appear as strangers'. Such a context can only grow with the return of myth: 'Without myth [...] all cultures lose their healthy, creative, natural energy; only a horizon surrounded by myths encloses and unifies a cultural movement (BT 23, p. 108/'Ohne Mythus [...] geht jede Cultur ihrer gesunden schöpferischen Naturkraft verlustig: erst ein mit Mythen umstellter Horizont schliesst eine ganze Culturbewegung zur Einheit ab, KSA 1.145').[25] But what does it mean for a culture to become 'mythical' so that geniuses are understood? It means, to put it in Schillerian terms, that culture should move on the level of the 'ideal' rather than the real or 'common' and of the 'general' rather than the 'particular'. It means that the public understands (and longs for) the *Gestaltenspiel* rather than the *Formenspiel*. It means that culture is there where daily life is 'ennobled' by 'Dionysian depth', 'with *wider* or *affective* meaning'. To enrich Europe with wider, cultural meaning thus requires the uplift of common reality as ruled by political, instrumental, and economic rationality – to unite it with 'the ideal' of the tragic experience as the truth of life.

Myth (other than journalism or any kind of prosaic writing, which merges from every day reality alone, lacking in imagination) moves in the sphere of the Schillerian 'ideal'. There the imagination – instead of technological reason – rules. The 'ideal' sphere is 'a true paradise of productivity by the human mind' ('ein wahres Paradies von Produktivität des menschlichen Geistes'), as Wagner formulated it (DS IX, p. 98). It is the free streaming '*melos*' upon which fantasy floats, dreaming its dreams. If I am right in associating Nietzsche's appreciation of 'myth' with the Schillerian 'ideal', then 'myth' takes on two meanings. First, 'myth' stands for the creative space, where stories incessantly float around (because the telling of the stories continues, as Benjamin pointed out. A story only exists in its being told and re-told). And second, 'myth' stands for the story itself. That story is necessary for two reasons. First, in order to channel the creative energy: 'only by myth can all the energies of fantasy and Apolline dream be saved from aimless meandering' (BT 23, p. 108/'Alle Kräfte der Phantasie und des apollinischen Traumes werden erst durch den Mythus aus ihrem wahllosen Herumschweifen gerettet', KSA 1.145) and second, to purvey meaning, that is to say: to reveal the truth of life that life is meaningless due to humanity's finitude, and thus enhance the meaning of human life – again in binary synthesis.

Nietzsche does not advocate myth or mythical culture for its own sake. He promotes mythical culture as a culture with enhanced meaning, because it makes way for

---

25 Cf. 'Only where the radiance of the myth falls is the life of the Greeks bright [...]' (HH I 261, p. 122/ 'Nur wohin der Strahl des Mythus fällt, da leuchtet das Leben der Griechen [...]', KSA 2.214).

the imagination and dreams. His campaign for myth is a call for dreaming, for playing with the dreamy 'forms' ('*Gestaltenspiel*' not '*Formenspiel*' – which is what Italian
opera plays in its music[26]) – of which Homer was the champion. Homer was, Nietzsche
holds, 'a dreaming Greek', and the dreaming Greeks were 'Homers' (BT 2, p. 20/KSA
1.31). Homer knew how to transform human life into fiction with fantasy (thus not by
recounting in chronological order the 'real facts', as is the order of the day in modern
times).[27] As Schopenhauer stated, following Goethe:

> Every state or condition, every person, every scene of life, needs to be apprehended only purely
> objectively, and made the object of a description or sketch, whether with brush or with words, in
> order to appear interesting, delightful, and enviable [...]. (WWR II 30, p. 372)

> Jeder Zustand, jeder Mensch, jede Scene des Lebens, braucht nur rein objektiv aufgefaßt und zum
> Gegenstand einer Schilderung, sei es mit Pinsel oder mit Worten, gemacht zu werden, um inter-
> essant, allerliebst, beneidenswerth zu erscheinen [...]. (WWV II 30, p. 433)

Mythical culture harbours and cherishes the symbol, which is necessary to be able to
bear the excruciating, Silenian truth and to celebrate and justify life.[28] Nietzsche's aestheticism, we may therefore deduce, evolves around the mythologicization and sym-

---

26 Wagner's art and Italian opera are both playful art forms; however, Italian opera plays with outer
forms, while Wagner plays with figures of his '*Wahrträume*'. The latter stem from metaphysical depth
whilst the former precisely lack this metaphysical depth and are devoid of epistemological, symbolic,
and mythical quality. Thinking this through, it seems that Nietzsche deliberately does not mention
that the dream-*impulse* has Dionysian content here, in the sense that Homer's dreams contain or originate in metaphysical truth. Homer's shortcoming was thus rather the epic, rhapsodic *style* he gave
to the Dionysian content. One may wonder, however, if this does not mean that Homer was the most
Dionysian artist, given that the power of Apollo is equal to the power of Dionysus, and Homer's Apollonian nature did not result in Socratism.
27 Especially on Twitter and comparable websites. Even fictitious persons are nothing but masks of
common people. People invent characters, news, and events, however all without true mythical fantasy, without reaching the level of symbolic meaning.
28 Daniel Came goes too far when he states that 'Nietzsche's point is not simply that the world was
justified for the Greeks *in spite of* its problematic aspects it is rather, that they saw life as good precisely
because of its problematic aspects' (2004, p. 56). The only thing that justifies life is life, there is no
reason, also not in spite of or because of whatever problem humanity may experience. The tragic Greek
knows that life is good *and* that life is not good, precisely because he or she does not long for an
appreciation of life as good '*from our human perspective*', as Came desires (2004, p. 58). The only
thing he or she longs for is the *aesthetic* view (transformation) of life. Incidentally, we do not find the
more positive formulation that 'life is good' in *The Birth of Tragedy*, but in chapter 5 of *Human All Too
Human I*, when Nietzsche, maintains that Goethe's 'Greek' art and aesthetic approach to life is 'Greek'
and 'aesthetic' precisely because it is ruled by the motto 'life, however it may be, is good!' (HH I 222,
p. 105/'wie es auch sei, das Leben, es ist gut', KSA 2.185). This is notably a more positive formulation of
Nietzsche's former attempt to *bear* life with the help of the aesthetic, in keeping with Goethe's poem
'The Groom' ('Der Bräutigam'). That poem ends with the confirmation that life is good, independent
of what the future brings.

bolization of human experience. However, this mythologicization and symbolization requires a specific artistic input and style. Apollonian stylization based on dreaming (even if that is a *'Gestaltenspiel'*) is not enough, as becomes obvious from Nietzsche's remarks on Homer. His art is, although 'sublime naive', optimistic in its assertion that, contrary to the Silenian truth that life is unbearable, life is worth living. The Homeric man thus lives by the reversion of Silenian truth that 'the very worst thing for them was to die soon, the second worst ever to die at all' (BT 3, p. 24/'das Allerschlimmste sei für sie, bald zu sterben, das Zweitschlimmste, überhaupt einmal zu sterben', KSA 1.36). In order to achieve the level of the symbol, however, the story must be accompanied by music, for 'in the Dionysiac dithyramb [the choral song as part of the Dionysus cult, MP] man is stimulated to the highest intensification of his symbolic powers' (BT 2, p. 21/'im dionysischen Dithyrambus wird der Mensch zur höchsten Steigerung aller seiner symbolischen Fähigkeiten gereizt,' KSA 1.33).[29] For that reason, Nietzsche prefers tragedy, with its chorus, song, and dance, to the epic story, in which the text rules over the lyre music and individual song of the rhapsodist. In this 'total' artwork, the truth is expressed in a way that the public understands it *and* can cope with it. This total artwork elevates the public, bringing it deep joy in its musical and dramatic mirroring of the *Gestaltenspiel*, originally played by the genius artist in his dreams. Hence, the theatre creates a truly aesthetic experience, where metaphysical truth, aesthetic play, joy, and the tragic, *Lust und Unlust*, artist and public, unite.

Aesthetic play and the child at play

What appealed most to Nietzsche was the idea that the Greeks were aesthetes out of instinct. It provided him with a powerful tool to baptize Greek culture the ideal culture, without falling into the Classicist trap of a too humanistic, optimistic, idyllic view of the Greeks.[30] The Greeks were, according to Nietzsche, 'tragic pessimists', in

---

29 He also says that only in music does the 'complete unchaining of all symbolic powers' (BT 2, p. 21/ 'Gesammtentfesselung aller symbolischen Kräfte', KSA 1.34) happen.

30 I come back to this further on, when I discuss the 'failure' ascribed to German Classicism in BT 20. Nietzsche's concern for Wagner's 'Graecization' was closely related to the question what the 'alleged "cheerfulness" of the Greeks' (BT 'Attempt', p. 3/GT 'Versuch', KSA 1.11) was. His initial question was, 'how does the world of the Olympian gods relate to this piece of popular wisdom?' (BT 3, p. 23/ 'wie verhält sich zu dieser Volksweisheit die olympische Götterwelt?' KSA 1.35). This 'popular wisdom' is the pessimistic truth of life narrated by the Silenian myth. Nietzsche asks, how this deeply pessimistic knowledge can be united with the 'inexplicably serene existence' (BT 3, p. 22/'unerklärlicher Heiterkeit', KSA 1.35) of the Olympian Gods. He suggests that Greek pessimism was perhaps a sign of strength and health rather than of weakness and sickness. This possibility makes him place a question mark over the alleged Greek harmonic, peaceful, and quiet nature, an image created by Winckelmann and adopted by German aesthetics and philology.

the sense that they considered life to be tragic and absurd. This is evidenced by the so-called 'Silenian' or 'popular' wisdom that says that 'the very best thing is utterly beyond your reach [:] not to have been born, not to *be*, to be *nothing*. However, the second best thing for you is: to die soon' (BT 3, p. 23/'Das Allerbeste ist für dich gänzlich unerreichbar: nicht geboren zu sein, nicht zu *sein*, *nichts* zu sein. Das Zweitbeste aber ist für dich – bald zu sterben', KSA 1.35). What separated Greek pessimism from Schopenhauer's was the response to this tragic truth.[31] While Schopenhauer fled into a Buddhist, ascetic renunciation of life, in order to create consecrated moments of will-lessness, the Greeks gave the tragic truth an aesthetic style and enjoyable form in tragedy. Against Schopenhauer, who believed that modern tragedy was a much more sophisticated form of theatre, Nietzsche defended the superiority and sophistication of the Greek theatre, commending the deep, tragic content of Greek 'serenity' or 'joy' ('*Heiterkeit*'). According to him, the Greeks (and after them Beethoven's *Ode to Joy* and Wagner's *Tristan and Isolde*) had championed the transformation of the tragic into a joyful experience, in accordance with Goethe's phrase: 'what in life does us annoy, we in picture do enjoy' ('Was im Leben uns verdrießt,/Man im Bilde gern genießt').[32] This was, in his understanding, the effect of 'Dionysian magic'.[33]

Nietzsche owed the insight that the aesthetic view of life is a typically 'Greek' view of things to Goethe, a source often overlooked in this respect:[34]

> He [Goethe] says, 'I have never succeeded in treating any tragic situation artistically without some lively pathological interest, and I have therefore chosen to avoid them rather than seek them out. Could it be yet another of the merits of the ancients that even subjects of the most intense pathos were merely aesthetic play for them, since in our case truth to nature must be involved if a work of this kind is to be produced?'[35]

> 'Ohne ein lebhaftes pathologisches Interesse', sagt er [Goethe, MP], 'ist es auch mir niemals gelungen, irgend eine tragische Situation zu bearbeiten, und ich habe sie daher lieber vermieden als aufgesucht. Sollte es wohl auch einer von den Vorzügen der Alten gewesen sein, dass das höchste Pathetische auch nur aesthetisches Spiel bei ihnen Gewesen wäre, da bei uns die Naturwahrheit mitwirken muss, um ein solches Werk hervorzubringen?' (KSA 1.142)

In this fragment, Goethe admits to Schiller that he has a lot of trouble coming to the level of the 'symbolic' in his art (or as he articulates it here, to overcome the 'pathological' level) and thus achieve the 'naiveté' that Schiller ascribed to him – and for which

---

31 Interestingly, Nietzsche later claims that Schopenhauer was a pessimist 'as a Good European', and not 'as a German' (GS 357, pp. 217–221/KSA 3.597–602). See also: Stegmaier (2011), pp. 375–377.
32 WWR II 30 (p. 372/p. 433).
33 Recall that Wagner also spoke of 'magic' ('*Zauber*') in this respect, although not of Dionysus.
34 Also by Came, cf. Came (2004), p. 55, where he quotes Nietzsche on this without mentioning Goethe.
35 Goethe to Schiller, 9 December 1797 (MA 8/1, p. 462).

reason he put Goethe on a par with Homer and regarded him as 'Greek'. Nietzsche adopted Goethe's view of the 'ancients', the Greeks as an aesthetic, powerful people on the one hand, and on the other, held his confession against Goethe. It brought Nietzsche to the view that the cultural war, the 'aestheticization' of modern culture, necessitates a 'Graecization', yet it also gave him the idea that the tragic can only be expressed by music. In other words, without music the metaphysical, tragic truth of life cannot be successfully transformed into aesthetic joy. Modern culture needs music *and* the Greek aesthetic view of art and life, according to Nietzsche, meaning music drama, understood as the combination of music and aesthetic play.

With this view, Goethe had taught Nietzsche one of the most vital lessons of his intellectual development, which remained fundamental to him at all times. Overcoming the tragic truth in discharging pain in aesthetic, joyful play was what Greek tragedy had been all about. Greek culture was unique in human history, for it possessed the aesthetic and symbolic powers to carry this out.[36] It is for this reason, too, that Nietzsche regarded Goethe in his later anti-Wagnerian years as the philosopher-poet who came closest to the Greeks of all Germans, and, therefore, was 'not a German event but a European one,'[37] a true free spirit and philosopher of *amor fati*, because 'he does not negate any more...'.[38] He had avoided such justification in *The Birth of Tragedy*. As part of the heroic advertisement campaign for Wagner, Nietzsche chose to underline the failure of Goethe and Schiller's aesthetics and art (to which I return shortly) and present Wagner as a 'European event' instead.

The 'joy' of Beethoven's *Ode to Joy* is a product of Dionysian magic, because it changes the tragic into joy, returning to humankind its childlike innocence. Hence, the transformation of the tragic into joy, of pain into aesthetic play and pleasure is also the event of humanity regaining its original innocence, of adults experiencing what it is to be a child. Although he does not call this 'idyllic', Nietzsche still seems to keep to some sort of concept of paradise here, one that resembles Schopenhauer and Wagner's concepts of paradise. However, while it led Schopenhauer to the ideal of the 'saint' on the ethical path to will-lessness, it led Nietzsche to the figure of the child on

---

36 BT 22 (p. 106/KSA 1.142).

37 TI Skirmishes 49 (p. 222/'kein deutsches Ereigniss, sondern ein europäisches', KSA 6.151). Goethe, Nietzsche concluded at that time, had been the best student of the Greeks: he wanted to learn from the Greeks, *and* he wanted to learn from them *how* one can learn from the past and from other cultures. Cf. WS 125, where Goethe is praised as 'not only a good and great human being but a culture' (p. 340/'nicht nur ein guter und grosser Mensch, sondern eine Cultur', KSA 2.607) for the fact that he had always tried to learn with the intention to overcome himself and create new norms.

38 TI Skirmishes 49 (p. 223/'*er verneint nicht mehr...*', 6. 152). Cf. BGE 256 (pp. 148–150/KSA 5.201–204). Nietzsche even justified Goethe's amoral, 'pagan' understanding of nature, which he explained as 'a *coming-towards*' (TI Skirmishes 48, p. 221/'ein Hinaufkommen', KSA 6.150) nature, and explicitly opposed to Rousseau's moral 'return to nature' (TI Skirmishes 48/'*Rückkehr zur Natur*', KSA 6.150).

the one hand and the satyr on the other. 'I would rather be a satyr than a saint,'[39] he admitted later in *Ecce Homo*. The child and the satyr are both negations of Schopenhauer's 'saint'. They are not will-denying figures, but figures that are able to play with the (multiple) will and to enjoy the (contradictory) will (-impulses). Nietzsche connects Goethe's term 'aesthetic play' to Heraclitus's imagery of the playing child[40] so as to explain that the world of semblance is a matter of

> playful construction and demolition of the world of individuality as an outpouring of primal pleasure and delight, a process quite similar to Heraclitus the Obscure's comparison of the force that shapes the world to a playing child who sets down stones here, there, and the next place, and who builds up piles of sand only to knock them down again (BT 24, p. 114)

> das spielende Aufbauen und Zertrümmern der Individualwelt als den Ausfluss einer Urlust [...], in einer ähnlichen Weise, wie wenn von Heraklit dem Dunklen die weltbildende Kraft einem Kinde verglichen wird, das spielend Steine hin und her setzt und Sandhaufen aufbaut und wieder einwirft, [...] (KSA 1.153)

I want to underline that the child 'is not a moral agent'.[41] 'Playing' is certainly not 'carrying out decisions'.[42] Daniel Came, like Julian Young[43] and others, misses the symbolic meaning of Nietzsche's child as a symbol of creativity, fantasy, imagination. Nor is the child 'based on the Kantian-Schopenhauerian model of the experience of an individuated human subject' as Came suggests, but rather on Schopenhauer's depiction of childlike innocence as human paradise. The innocent child is Nietzsche's symbol of the aesthetic realm. It does not negate the will, but is nevertheless 'Will-less' ('Willenlos').[44] 'Aesthetic' then means 'will-less' as in the Kantian sense of 'without interest' ('interesselos'). The child, as I understand Nietzsche's description, symbolizes *being as being*, and nothing more than that. It symbolizes the liberation or transcendence from the moral and dialectical interpretation of the world, the moment in which humanity is finally able to let life be, and let it be *in* the world instead of being locked up in a subject-object relationship to it. Hence, the child symbolizes the moment in which humankind has stopped judging, and plays, subsisting in one endless realm of imagination and fantasy. The child, thus, represents the moment of transcendence of common, daily life and of immanence or unity insofar as it is *in* the world, in a way that transcends the common involvement with reality (therefore it is stronger than be-

---

39 EH Preface 2 (p. 71/'Ich zöge vor, eher noch ein Satyr zu sein als ein Heiliger,' KSA 6.258).
40 Diels-Kranz fragment 22 (B 52), which says 'eternal life is a child, is at play like a child with boardcheckers; mastery belongs to a child'. Cited from Bishop and Stephenson (2005), p. 52 fn 8. Compare BT 24 (p. 114/KSA 1.153).
41 Came (2004), p. 55.
42 Came (2004), p. 59.
43 Young (1994), pp. 58–60.
44 See BT 22 (p. 104/KSA 1.140).

ing 'part' of the world or 'to partake in being'). The imagery of the child symbolizes Schiller's famous adage in his education letters that 'man only plays when he is in the fullest sense of the word a human being, and he is *only fully a human being when he plays*' ('der Mensch spielt nur, wo er in voller Bedeutung des Worts Mensch ist, und *er ist nur da ganz Mensch, wo er spielt*'). It is *beauty* as 'living form' with which man plays: 'with beauty man shall *only play*, and it is *with beauty only* that he shall play' ('der Mensch soll mit der Schönheit *nur spielen*, und er soll *nur mit der Schönheit* spielen').[45] In Nietzsche's aesthetics, Schiller's 'play-drive' is a musical drive or impulse, which needs the discharge of pain and the transformation of dreamlike figures in outer forms. These outer forms then shine with inner joy.

The child does not 'see' in the sense Daniel Came wants us to believe when he describes the child's perspective as an experience of the world as 'an aesthetically pleasing spectacle,'[46] thus intimating that the child subsists in a subject-object relation with the world. However, the child is not watching a scary movie. Neither is it the child in Schopenhauer's description of Raphael's 'Madonna with child', in which the child's face expresses both fear and the moment in which that fear is overcome, or the hope to overcome that fear.[47] The child is one with the world, for it does not experience individuation, but harmony. Therefore, it does not *see* the world, it *is* the world. The child symbolizes the 'return to home and origin' (BT 22, p. 105/'*Rückkehr zur Urheimat*', KSA 1.141), 'a supreme, artistic, primal joy in the womb of Primordial Unity' (BT 22, p. 105/ 'eine höchste künstlerische Urfreude im Schoosse des Ur-Einen', KSA 1.141). The child also symbolizes the typical Greek, as emerges from the following passage:

> [...] the Greeks are eternal children, and in the tragic art, too, they are mere children who do not know what sublime toy has been created – and smashed – by their hands (BT 17, p. 82)

> Die Griechen sind [...] die ewigen Kinder, und auch in der tragischen Kunst nur die Kinder, welche nicht wissen, welches erhabene Spielzeug unter ihren Händen entstanden ist und – zertrümmert wird (KSA 1.110).

The question is, how does this naive, innocent, Greek child relate to that other amoral figure and counter-image of Schopenhauer's saint, the satyr – a follower of Dionysus? What is the relationship between childlike innocence and the destructive wildness of the satyr?[48] And if the child represents the 'ideal' sphere, because it has returned to the Primordial Unity, then in what sense does this child *not* indicate the idyllic experience of paradise? Nietzsche does not answer or even raise these questions, although we need to get this clear in order to get a full picture of his concept of 'Greekness'.

---

45 See BT 22 (p. 104/KSA 1.140).
46 BT 22, p. 59.
47 Compare Schopenhauer, *Sämtliche Werke* V ('Einige Verse'), p. 564.
48 Both are at least signs of 'health' (compare BT 1, p. 18/KSA 1.29).

From Socratic to tragic-aesthetic culture: signs of upcoming success

The emergence of the new tragic-aesthetic age, in which humanity will return to itself, its Dionysian origin, with the help of Wagner's art, is discussed most poignantly in chapter 18 of *The Birth of Tragedy*.

To Nietzsche, Modernity is the age in which the Gordian knot of Greek culture is untied, and Modernity should indeed be overcome. However, rather than the printing machine, Socrates untied the Gordian knot of Greek culture, according to Nietzsche. Modernity began already with Socrates's trust in human reason and rejection of art as communicator of truth. Thus, rather than equating Modernity with the emergence of the information society, Nietzsche understands Modernity as the moment that three things happened; first, art and knowledge were separated; second, the truth become a matter of logical deduction; third, art was judged morally. To Nietzsche, Socrates personalizes this moment where the tragic age of the Greeks ended, and he therefore baptizes 'Modernity' 'Socratism'. Inversely, we may deduce that the 'tragic' age was the age in which art and truth were united, and the truth was not something obtainable by logical deduction, but only by *artistic* or *aesthetic* revelation. Moreover, in the tragic age, art was judged *purely aesthetically*. Information society, to Nietzsche, is the last convulsion of the long reign of 'Socratic' culture.[49] But in agreement with Wagner, he sees signs that a new artistic age is coming. According to Nietzsche, the first signs to overcome Socratism are found in Kant's *Kritik der reinen Vernunft*, because it tried to nail down the limits of reason, in Goethe's *Faust*, because it is the poetical expression of the idea that human reason and conceptual knowledge are limited, and Schopenhauer, who put the genius perception and art above the intellectual perception and theoretical knowledge in his *World as Will and Representation* (*Die Welt als Wille und Vorstellung I*, 1818 and *II*, 1841). In so doing, he continued and fulfilled the 'tragic' tendencies of Kant and Goethe.

Hence, Modernity (Wagner) and 'Socratism' (Nietzsche) stand for 'the discordance of art and truth'.[50] The characteristic of Modernity then is 'aesthetic alienation', meaning the dismissal of art from the centre to the borders of society and the forbiddance for art (-ists) to participate in the truth. Socratism, more specifically, starts with Plato's *Republic*, in which the truth is installed as society's foundation, while at the same time this truth is made the domain of philosophical (dialectical) reason, and artists are considered 'strangers'. Thus, when Nietzsche searches for a culture in which the genius is no longer a stranger, he searches for an anti-Platonic *Republic*, a 'tragic' culture, in which art and truth, imagination and reason are re-united.

---

49 This is 'Socratic' serenity, the serenity of the 'theoretical' person that threatens all true art. The present state of Socratism is in fact 'simply the red flush across the evening sky' (BT ASC 1, p. 4/'eine Abendröthe', GT Versuch einer Selbstkritik 1, KSA 1.12).

50 Bernstein (1992), p. 1. Bernstein explains Modernity as constituted by the 'aesthetic alienation' too.

Nietzsche derives his trust that a tragic age will come also from Socrates self. He perceives a tragic tendency in Socrates, although he is the counter-example of the tragic-aesthetic. Nietzsche argues that there will always come a moment when even the theoretical optimist feels 'the need for art', and starts looking at life with a 'tragic perception'. He considers Socrates's attempt to put Aesop's fables to rhyme, after being ordered to do so in a dream, as metaphor for the scientific need for art:

> The words spoken by the figure who appeared to Socrates in dream are the only hint of any scruples in him about the limits of logical nature; perhaps, he must have told himself, things which I do not understand are not automatically unreasonable. Perhaps there is a kingdom of wisdom from which the logician is banished? Perhaps art may even be a necessary correlative and supplement of science? (BT 14, p. 71)

> Jenes Wort der sokratischen Traumerscheinung ist das einzige Zeichen einer Bedenklichkeit über die Grenzen der logischen Natur: vielleicht – so musste er sich fragen – ist das mir Nichtverständliche doch nicht auch sofort das Unverständliche? Vielleicht giebt es ein Reich der Weisheit, aus dem der Logiker verbannt ist? Vielleicht ist die Kunst sogar ein nothwendiges Correlativum und Supplement der Wissenschaft? (GT 14, KSA 1.96)

This famous story from Plato's *Phaedo* even becomes an allegory of modern culture for Nietzsche. Nietzsche takes on the role of the demon of contemporary culture: he is the voice that orders modern Man to 'aestheticize', to interchange his logical understanding and moral view of life with aesthetic perception and the need for art. Man, thus, has to become a hybrid being of Apollonian and Dionysian powers, a 'centaur', which unites knowledge and art, just as Socrates united them on the last day of his life.

By way of 'aestheticization' or 'Graecization', tragic culture will come to perfection in the near future of European culture, as I understand the matter, in the more sophisticated form of a tragic-aesthetic culture. That the tragic has already begun to gain ground is visible in three signs for Nietzsche: first, Kant's critical philosophy; second, Goethe's *Faust*; and third, Schopenhauer's pessimism and view of art as locus of the truth.[51] In confronting human reason with its limits, Kant's critique subdued scientific optimism. Nietzsche interprets *Faust* as the literary depiction of the changeover from Socratism to tragic culture. However, tragic culture is still in its infancy and has not yet come to full blossoming. Although humanity has reached its epistemological limits, it has not found a fitting art, 'a new form of art, the art of metaphysical solace' (BT 18, p. 88/'eine neue Kunst, die Kunst des metaphysischen Trostes', KSA 1.119). Conceived in this way, Socratic culture is on its way to collapse. In fact, Nietzsche even helps Socratic culture passing to tragic culture by explaining what tragic is, so that his readers – Wagner in the first place – learn what tragic pessimism and aestheticism are.

---

51 See BT 18 (p. 87–88/KSA 1.118–119).

Failures and successes in 'Graecization' and 'aestheticization'

Failure #1: The failure of German Classicism

Against this background, we may safely state that Nietzsche understood Wagner's art as having the potentiality to 'aestheticize' culture, to make art the centre of knowledge and culture again, to fulfil the work of Goethe, Kant, and Schopenhauer (the latter two seem to have taken Schiller's place as forerunners of Wagner's project). Of crucial importance, yet highly neglected in the secondary literature, is Nietzsche's discussion of Italian opera and German Classicism as failing attempts to 'Graecize' art and culture. In my view, Nietzsche does this not only with the intention to make Wagner come out better, but also, and perhaps in the first place, to point out what must be done and what not when a modern art-form or culture turns to the Greeks. By this, I mean that he wanted to distil what can be learned from the Greeks and how this lesson should be put into practice. It is obvious that Nietzsche highly estimated the fact that people have seriously tried to interact with the past and to come closer to the high moments of human history. In this perspective, his reflections on Italian opera and German Classicism should be seen as his own attempt to learn from the past what can be learned from it. At the same time they function as an imperative for Wagner ('learn from the past!'). Therefore, when I speak of 'failing', we should relativize that with Goethe, to whom Nietzsche refers later in *Assorted Opinions and Maxims* (1879) aphorism 227, which is called 'Goethe's errors' ('Goethe's Irrungen').[52] Interestingly enough, in this (long) aphorism, he regards Goethe as a Greek, but for a different reason than Nietzsche considered Wagner to be Greek in *The Birth of Tragedy*. He considers Goethe a Greek here, because he was a searcher, who in order to learn about himself 'experimented' with his life. This search, however, was always directed at attaining the higher, that is: to come to a new norm. Goethe's search was always a self-overcoming as form of self-education:

> Without this *digression through error* he would not have become Goethe: that is to say, the only German literary artist who has not yet become antiquated – because he desired to be a writer by profession just as little as he desired to be a German by profession (p. 271)

> Ohne die *Umschweife des Irrthums* wäre er nicht Goethe geworden: das heißt, der einzige deutsche Künstler der Schrift, der jetzt noch nicht veraltet ist, – weil er eben so wenig Schriftsteller als Deutscher von Beruf sein wollte. (KSA 2.483)

In brief, we can still learn from Goethe, because he was always busy learning. This is relevant for our case because, in Nietzsche's view, a 'cultural war' is not just simply a matter of fighting Italian opera and 'word-drama'. A cultural war distinguishes itself

---

52 AOM 227 (p. 271/KSA 2.282–283).

from a mere military campaign because it involves *learning* and *competition* (also with oneself). This is perhaps more palpable in the works after *The Birth of Tragedy*, but an important point of perception in Nietzsche's début book too:

> Some day the attempt might be made to weigh up, under the gaze of an impartial judge, at what period and through which men the German spirit had striven most vigorously to learn from the Greeks; and if we may confidently assume that this unique praise must be accorded to the noblest struggles for self-cultivation of Goethe, Schiller, and Winckelmann, we would also have to add that, since those days and the immediate effects of their struggle, the striving to reach the Greeks and to achieve self-cultivation by the same route has become, for incomprehensible reasons, weaker and weaker. (pp. 95–96)

> Es möchte einmal, unter den Augen eines unbestochenen Richters, abgewogen werden, in welcher Zeit und in welchen Männern bisher der deutsche Geist von den Griechen zu lernen am kräftigsten gerungen hat; und wenn wir mit Zuversicht annehmen, dass dem edelsten Bildungskampfe Goethes, Schillers und Winckelmanns dieses einzige Lob zugesprochen werden müsste, so wäre jedenfalls hinzuzufügen, dass seit jener Zeit und den nächsten Einwirkungen jenes Kampfes, das Streben auf einer gleichen Bahn zur Bildung und zu den Griechen zu kommen, in unbegreiflicher Weise schwächer und schwächer geworden ist. (KSA 1.129)

Nietzsche positively values the openness to learning from the Greeks in German Classicism, observing that the will to learn from the Greeks was never as high in German culture. Before actually starting to learn from the Greeks, one must learn how to learn from the Greeks. To apply this to Wagner: Wagner must become an excellent student of the Greek way of learning in order to be able to understand and then rejuvenate Greek tragedy – which is the precondition to his cultural success. However, it is not just about rejuvenating, but also about going into competition with the great examples of the past, and to try to make even more striking, wonderful, and beautiful things than they had.[53]

The problem with German Classicism was not so much the fact that they turned to the Greeks, but that they misinterpreted the Greeks, and thus learned something from them, which was not entirely 'Greek'. There had been too much projection and wishful thinking in Winckelmann's idyllic perception of the Greeks. To Wagner's fortune, he had a better, the best, teacher he could have in this respect: Nietzsche. The young and very talented professor in classics could tell him all about Greek philosophy, music, and 'music drama'. Seen in this way, Nietzsche's Wagner-enthusiasm or Wagner-trust in this book is partly based on his confidence in his teaching skills.

Despite their will to learn from the Greeks, German Classicists had failed 'to penetrate to the essential core of Hellenism' (p. 96/'in den Kern des hellenischen Wesens einzudringen', KSA 1.129). Nietzsche underlines that Winckelmann's 'noble' interpretation of the Greek world has occasioned an enduring misunderstanding about the Greeks, because it is not in accordance with the monstrous worlds that the Greeks

---

53 I come back to this in chapter 5, p. 225ff.

called to life in many of their myths. Instead of being optimistic, elegant, and 'cheer-ful', the Greeks were pessimists, Nietzsche claims. Thus, while Nietzsche turned to Goethe and Schiller's aesthetics to get an understanding of Wagner's aesthetics, he simultaneously criticized their moralism and optimism. A note of 1871 avers that only the end of Goethe's *Faust I* and *Egmont* came close to his artistic ideal.[54] However, it was the idyllic tendency in Goethe, which drove him away from his musical lyricism and to producing works like *Tarquato Tasso* and *Iphigenia*. In one of the most striking passages of *The Birth of Tragedy*, and what may be considered the axis of its last ten chapters, he of all uses a scene from Goethe's *Iphigenia auf Tauris* to show the failure of German Classicism:

> If such heroes as Goethe and Schiller were not granted the ability to break open the enchanted gateway leading into the Hellenic magic mountain, if the furthest reach of their most courageous struggle was that wistful gaze which Goethe's Iphigeneia sends homewards across the sea from the barbaric land of the Taurians,[55] what was left to the epigones of such heroes to hope for, if the gate did not open of its own accord, suddenly, in a quite different place, as yet untouched by all the previous exertions of culture – to the mystical sound of the re-awakened music of tragedy? Let no one seek to diminish our belief in the impending rebirth of Hellenic Antiquity, for this alone allows us to hope for a renewal and purification of the German spirit through the fire-magic of music.[56] (BT 20, p. 97)

> Wenn es solchen Helden, wie Schiller und Goethe, nicht gelingen durfte, jene verzauberte Pforte zu erbrechen, die in den hellenischen Zauberberg führt, wenn es bei ihrem muthigsten Ringen nicht weiter gekommen ist als bis zu jenem sehnsüchtigen Blick, den die Goethische Iphigenie vom barbarischen Tauris aus nach der Heimat über das Meer hin sendet, was bliebe den Epigo-nen solcher Helden zu hoffen, wenn sich ihnen nicht plötzlich, an einer ganz anderen, von allen Bemühungen der bisherigen Cultur unberührten Seite die Pforte von selbst aufthäte – unter dem mystischen Klange der wiedererweckten Tragödienmusik. Möge uns Niemand unsern Glauben an eine noch bevorstehende Wiedergeburt des hellenischen Alterthums zu verkümmern suchen; denn in ihm finden wir allein unsre Hoffnung für eine Erneuerung und Läuterung, des deutschen Geistes durch den Feuerzauber der Musik. (KSA 1.131)

Although all signs of contemporary culture[57] – also within classical philology, which was dominated by discussions about language – pointed towards the opposite direc-

---

54 9[146], KSA 7.328.
55 Goethe, *Iphigenie auf Tauris*, Act I, scene I.
56 Here Nietzsche alludes to the 'magic fire music' in act III of Wagner's *Valkyrie*.
57 Nietzsche speaks of 'the growing sterility and exhaustion of present-day culture' (p. 97/'Verö-dung und Ermattung der jetzigen Cultur', KSA 1.131) and 'the wilderness of our tired culture' (p. 97/ 'Wilderniss unserer ermüdeten Cultur', KSA 1.131). The term 'wilderniss' is opposed to Nietzsche's def-inition of culture as 'unity of style' (in DS 1: 'Kultur ist vor allem Einheit des künstlerischen Stiles in allen Lebensäusserungen eines Volkes', KSA 1.163). Wilderness suggests that stylization is needed in order to bind (Nietzsche often speaks of '*bändigen*' in this respect) the fragmented, chaotic life into a unity of style. This (artistic) style, in turn, is called forward by the dominant perception of life (e.g., the 'tragic' view of life).

tion, Nietzsche nevertheless believed in a rebirth of old times, referring to the 'fire music' in the third act of *The Valkyrie*. Wagner's *Valkyrie* and *Tristan* are more effective than *Iphigenia, Faust* and *Egmont*. Goethe had made frantic efforts to reach 'the gateway leading into the Hellenic magic mountain', but did not surpass the 'atrium', as he would express it himself. A 'lack of music' and 'idyllic tendencies' obstructed Goethe and Schiller from bridging the gap between exemplary Greece and imitative, 'epigone' Germany. Schiller and Goethe may have possessed a hint of a 'musical drive' (*'musikalischen Antrieb'*), but they never really produced music, thus failed to articulate in practice what they had grasped in theory. In the end, both Weimarians suffered from what Nietzsche dubbed in his notes a 'lack of music' (*'Mangel an Musik'*)[58], and 'idyllic sheep-breeding' (*'idyllische Schäferei'*), let alone that they were able to pass on the 'Dionysian magic' that the magic fire music of *The Valkyrie* incites, and in which the 'impudent fashion' (*'freche Mode'*) is resisted.[59]

Failure #2: The failure of Italian opera

One expression of this 'impudent fashion' is Italian opera, discussed in chapter 19. Nietzsche first contrasts Palestrina with the new form of opera, the *drama per musica* that came into existence in the sixteenth century in Italy. He finds it remarkable that such different forms of music came into being in the same age. However, this is not that remarkable, because Palestrina, employed in Rome and the great artist of the Contra-reformation, and the Italian opera, which started in Florence, both emerged from the madrigal tradition, in the context of the debate about the understanding of the words sung by the chorus in the church. Both the Roman and Lutheran churches have always been afraid that the joy of music would tower over the message of the words. What Nietzsche rejects is not so much that words are understood, but that they are not really sung anymore, but spoken, in order to be understood by the public, thereby releasing themselves from music. On top of this, they make the claims that with this invention of the recitative, Greek music is being rejuvenated. Nietzsche calls it a typically 'Socratic' tendency. Indeed, Florentines like Jacopo Peri and his circle tried to return to the Greek roots of music, imagining that the *stilo rappresentativo* and the recitative paved the way back to the paradisiacal, original state of humankind, the 'magic mountain' of Hellenism, which they located in the Homeric world. Their music was as mighty and innocent as Homer's world. This implies, however, that their desire for Greek music is 'idyllic', based on the belief in an original, noble, and artistic man. This artistic man did not speak as we do, but sang, like singers in the newly founded Italian opera, so they presumed:

---

58 8[47], KSA 7.241.
59 Cf. BT 1 (p. 18/KSA 1.29).

Recitative was thought to be the rediscovered language of those original humans, and opera to be the rediscovered land of that idyllic or heroic good being who follows a natural artistic drive in all his actions; who, whenever he speaks, at least sings a little; and who promptly bursts into full song at the slightest stirring of emotion (BT 19, p. 90)

Das Recitativ galt als die wiederentdeckte Sprache jenes Urmenschen; die Oper als das wieder-aufgefundene Land jenes idyllisch oder heroisch guten Wesens, das zugleich in allen seinen Handlungen einem natürlichen Kunsttriebe folgt, das bei allem, was es zu sagen hat, wenigstens etwas singt, um, bei der leisesten Gefühlserregung, sofort mit voller Stimme zu singen. (KSA 1.122)

To the preliminary notes, chapter 19 adds the assertion that opera is founded on the same Socratic and theoretical principles as 'Alexandrian' culture.[60] Nietzsche describes the idyllic tendency of opera as the 'gay optimism' of the theoretical man. Simultaneously, he remarks that this idyllic tendency must be understood in the Schillerian way. Here more explicitly than anywhere else, Nietzsche distances himself from Schiller's aesthetics and his ideas concerning the way culture is to be led back to Greek Antiquity and to true humanity. According to Nietzsche, Italian opera starts from the idea of an idyllic reality, in which nature and the ideal come together, a primordial moment in which humanity 'lay at the heart of nature', a state of paradise and an ultimately artistic state at the same time. Opera reintroduced this idyllic image in history by means of the singing herdsman, who expresses 'the cheerfulness of eternal re-discovery' (p. 92/'*Heiterkeit des ewigen Wiederfindens*', KSA 1.125) against the elegiac suffering on account of an eternal loss. This serenity ('*Heiterkeit*') is identified here as 'Alexandrian'. For Nietzsche, however, the (best representation of) true man is the satyr and not the idyllic shepherd, and the true artist hence should be 'satirical' rather than idyllic. Nietzsche resists the Alexandrian serenity of opera, saying expressly: 'Anyone who wants to destroy opera must take up arms against that Alexandrian cheerfulness' (p. 93/'Wer die Oper vernichten will, muss den Kampf gegen jene alexandrinische Heiterkeit aufnehmen', KSA 1.125) – incidentally alluding to Schiller's expression that 'war' was needed to conquer French Naturalism. What art should do, Nietzsche argues, is redeem us from the agitation of the will in aesthetic semblance, in '*schöner Schein*'. This vital task of art, however, is threatened under the influences of the idyllic temptations of merely Apollonian, or even Socratic, art-forms, in which music is obscured as the mirror of truth. The 'war' that Nietzsche declares against the 'typical music of modern, non-artistic man' – opera – is also a call to Wagner to fight the idyllic tendencies of his historic examples, thus the belief that 'man is good', an 'eternally singing or flute-playing shepherd' (p. 92/'ewig flötende oder singende Schäfer', KSA 1.125).

---

60 Nietzsche does not give an adequate account of Italian opera. His critique of Italian music rather functions as part of his attempt to show the merit and 'Dionysian' spirit of Wagner's music.

Nietzsche had more serious objections against Italian opera than against German Classicism. At least Winckelmann, Goethe, and Schiller are 'heroes' for having tried to come to terms with Greek art. Their interest was artistic, while the interest of Italian opera was moral.[61] While he agreed with Goethe and Schiller's attempt to reach for the 'objective' or 'symbolic' level of 'style', he simultaneously claimed that they did not reach that level, but remained 'on the surface' of subjective lyricism, suggesting that they themselves were the 'Romantics' they repudiated. Only *Faust* attests to a tragic sense, thus escaping the idyllic tendency characteristic for Goethe's *Iphigenia*.

Between success and failure: Beethoven's 'Ode to Joy'

As noted above, Kant's critical philosophy and Schopenhauer's pessimism marked 'the beginning of a culture' (BT 18, p. 87/'*eine Cultur [ist] eingeleitet*', KSA 1.118), which Nietzsche described 'as a tragic culture' (BT 18, p. 87/'*als eine tragische [Cultur]* ', KSA 1.118), while Goethe's *Faust* expressed the despair humanity experienced because of its limited powers of reason. However, the despair of *Faust* apparently lacked something. Somehow, it was not 'Greek' enough. Winckelmann, Goethe, nor Schiller – including Goethe's *Faust* – had not thrived 'to penetrate to the essential core of Hellenism and to create a lasting bond of love between German and Greek culture' (BT 20, p. 96/'in den Kern des hellenischen Wesens einzudringen und einen dauernden Liebesbund zwischen der deutschen und der griechischen Cultur herzustellen', KSA 1.129). They did not create the 'aesthetic public' (BT 7, p. 38/'*aesthetisches Publicum*', KSA 1.53)[62] that could grasp the tragic situation of humanity: its finitude and therefore utter powerlessness. What would create an 'aesthetic public'?

Wagner suggested, referring to *Faust*, that the 'infinite nature' was grasped by Beethoven's music and that this was the intrinsic and unique merit of music. Especially the finale of Beethoven's *Ode to Joy* had been successful in restoring humanity's unity with nature. Nietzsche writes of such restoration too, suggesting that the 'rebirth

---

61 Nietzsche's critique of the 'idyllic tendency' of Italian opera re-voices the critique Goethe uttered against Romantic art to Eckermann: 'I call the classic *healthy*, the romantic *sickly*. In this sense, the *Nibelungenlied* is as classic as the *Iliad*, for both are vigorous and healthy. Most modern productions are romantic – not because they are new; but because they are weak, morbid, and sickly. And the antique is classic – not because it is old; but because it is strong, fresh, joyous, and healthy' 29 January 1826 in: Eckermann (1986)/MA 19, pp. 155–156. See also Goethe/Eckermann, 29 January 1829 and MR 1032: 'The classical is what is healthy, the romantic that what is sick' ('Klassisch ist das Gesunde, romantisch das Kranke'). Cf. WS 217 (pp. 100–101/KSA 2.652) and Bishop (2004). Compare also with their conversation of 11 June 1825 and Goethe's definition of 'style' in art in his essay 'Simple Imitation of Nature, Manner, Style' (1788).

62 See also 'aesthetic listener' (BT 22, p. 105/'ästhetische Zuhörer, KSA 1.141), who Nietzsche opposes to the Socratic- critical audience, that judges art on its *moral* qualities and not on its *aesthetic* merits.

of tragedy' (BT 19, p. 95/'*Wiedergeburt der Tragödie*', KSA 1.129) will accomplish the 'blissful reunion with its own being', however

> [...] provided, of course, that [he] [the German spirit] goes on learning, unceasingly, from the Greeks, for the ability to learn from this people is in itself a matter of lofty fame and distinguishing rarity (BT 19, p. 95)

> [...] wenn er [der deutsche Geist, MP] nur von einem Volke unentwegt zu lernen versteht, von dem überhaupt lernen zu können schon ein hoher Ruhm und eine auszeichnende Seltenheit ist, von den Griechen, (KSA 1.129)

The creation and accomplishment of tragic culture is a matter of incessantly learning from the Greeks. If one cannot assent to such dedication, the project of fulfilling the artistic task of creating a culture in which one is actually 'capable of conversing about Beethoven and Shakespeare' fails (BT 23, p. 107/'im Stande [...], sich über Beethoven und Shakespeare zu unterhalten', KSA 1.144).

Here lies a task for German music, since it has a 'Dionysiac ground' (BT 19, p. 94/ '*dionysischen Grund*', KSA 1.127). As we saw in chapter 3, Nietzsche had noted in his *Nachlass* that Schiller's poem *Ode to Joy* was testimony to a specifically German talent for the Dionysian, however only Beethoven's musical setting perfected the *Ode to Joy*.[63] In *The Birth of Tragedy*, the *Ode to Joy* is considered as a part of the 'mighty, brilliant course' (BT 19, p. 94/'*mächtigen Sonnenlaufe*', KSA 1.127) that runs from Bach to Beethoven and from Beethoven to Wagner. Nietzsche also reviews the *Pastoral* Symphony, stating that 'even when a musician speaks in images about a composition, as when he describes a symphony as "pastoral", calling one movement a "scene by a stream" and another a "merry gathering of country folk", these too are merely symbolic representations born out of the music' (BT 6, p. 35/'Ja selbst wenn der Tondichter in Bildern über eine Composition geredet hat, etwa wenn er eine Symphonie als pastorale und einen Satz als "Scene am Bach", einem anderen als "lustiges Zusammensein der Landleute" bezeichnet, so sind das ebenfalls nur gleichnissartige, aus der Musik geborne Vorstellungen', KSA 1.50). This is so because Beethoven's words are the result of the discharge of music in images. The relation between music and text or image is not one of mere imitative expression or analogous representation, but 'symbolic'. This means that the image or word 'speaks' music, as Wagner said of the Italian Renaissance painters in his essay Beethoven.[64]

However, there is one thing Beethoven's music lacks. It contains the Dionysian magic, but it does not contain Apollonian semblance. It mirrors Dionysus, but its music

---

63 9[10], KSA 7.275. Compare BT 5, in which Nietzsche defends Schiller's lyrical strength pointing to his avowal that he wrote poetry from a '*musical mood*' (BT 5, p. 29/'*musikalische Stimmung*', KSA 1.43).
64 Nietzsche does not refer to Wagner's claim that the *Pastoral* Symphony's success is in its representation of the original goodness of humanity.

still seeks fulfilment and expression in semblance too. While Goethe and Schiller's word dramas lack music, Beethoven's music lacks drama, i.e., there is no discharge of music in image and text. As Nietzsche pointed out in referring to Raphael's painting *Transfiguration*, Apollo and Dionysus are in a mutually dependent relationship.[65] 'The primordial unity' (which is 'eternal suffering and contradictory') aims at 'release and redemption':[66]

> If one were to transform Beethoven's jubilant "Hymn [Ode, MP] to Joy" into a painting and place no constraints on one's imagination as the millions sink into the dust, shivering in awe, then one could begin to approach the Dionysiac', Nietzsche writes (BT 1, p. 18)

> Man verwandele das Beethoven'sche Jubellied der "Freude" in ein Gemälde und bleibe mit seiner Einbildungskraft nicht zurück, wenn die Millionen schauervoll in den Staub sinken: so kann man sich dem Dionysischen nähern. (KSA 1.29)

Wagner indeed tried to transform music into the pictorial in order to stretch the powers of imagination, to seek and cross the limits of artistic imagination – an imagination that is, contrary to human reason, unlimited. In so doing, he approached the Dionysian in his works. He came closer to true 'health' (BT 6, p. 35/'*Gesundheit*', KSA 1.50), the 'universal harmony' (BT 6, p. 35; '*Evangelium der Weltenharmonie*', KSA 1.50) than Beethoven, while Beethoven came closer to 'health' than Goethe. 'Health' is the term that Nietzsche uses instead of Schopenhauer's and Wagner's 'paradise'. It is the renewal of 'the bond between human beings' (BT 6, p. 35/'der Bund zwischen Mensch und Mensch', KSA 1.50), and the 'festival of reconciliation' (BT 6, p. 35/'*Versöhnungsfest*', KSA 1.50) of nature 'with her lost son, humankind' (BT 6, p. 35/'mit ihrem verlorenen Sohne, dem Menschen', KSA 1.50).

Paradise lost has become paradise regained. The bond between art and knowledge, man and nature, which was disrupted in Socratic culture, is restored by tragic culture, and tragic culture, that is the culture in which knowledge and art are united in the tragic wisdom and the redemption of this gruesome wisdom in aesthetic play. It is the renewal of paradise and innocence. However, Nietzsche calls it 'health', because 'paradise' as 'naive', harmonic unity of man with nature at the 'threshold of every culture' sounds too 'idyllic', too Rousseauian.[67] Paradise has no room for the satyr. Only in *On the Use and Disadvantage of History for Life*, does Nietzsche publicly put both terms on par, speaking of a 'paradise of health' ('*Paradies der Gesundheit*', KSA 1.329).

True health is only gained in tragedy or music drama, because the aesthetic people (who inhibit, preserve, continue, and create tragic culture) can only be created by truly aesthetic play. Nietzsche stated that a tragic culture needed an art, which provided

---

65 BT 4 (p. 26–27/KSA 1.39).
66 BT 4 (pp. 25–26/KSA 1.38–39).
67 Cf. BT 3 (p. 24/KSA 1.37).

metaphysical comfort. This now can only be supplied by the Apollonian semblance, i.e., aesthetic play. Wagner's music drama, specifically *Tristan and Isolde* as we shall see next, therefore is the ideal art-form for a tragic culture. Nietzsche regards it as the fulfilment of the cycle starting with Bach and ending in Wagner via Beethoven.[68]

As we have seen, Schopenhauer provided a philosophical justification of music as the highest artform, however, not of music drama. Wagner then came to a justification by combining Schopenhauer's philosophy of music with his dream theory. Nietzsche adopts this account, and even uses it to explain Greek tragedy as the reconciliation of Apollo and Dionysus. This leads to the suggestion that *Tristan and Isolde* is the rejuvenation of Greek tragedy.

Successful Graecization: Wagner's *Tristan and Isolde*

While Nietzsche reflects on Greek music and the tragic chorus in the first eight chapters of the book within the dialectics of Apollo (symbolizing music based on rhythm and form) and Dionysus (who symbolizes melodic music, which seeks to break the forms open), he discusses (although in a rather oblique way) Wagner's music drama in the last ten chapters of the book within the exclusive opposition of the tragic and the idyllic. The tragic is smoothly equated with the Dionysian, while the idyllic could be circumscribed as the extreme, Socratic or 'Alexandrian' (as Nietzsche calls Italian opera in chapter 19), overshooting Apollonian music, thus music which focuses entirely on text, formal virtuosity, rhythm, and amusement.

As we have seen, Nietzsche rejects the outer form play (*'Formenspiel'*) to the advantage of the play with the figures produced by the imagination (*'Gestaltenspiel'*). Stretched to its extremes by musical inspiration, the imagination becomes 'larger than life'. The genius' creativity knows no boundaries and creates one supra-human figure after the other. It is, however, in this realm of 'poetic freedom' that Nietzsche localizes the experience of being human. Here, humanity is undivided.

With this view of art, Nietzsche is rather Schillerian in *The Birth of Tragedy*. While criticizing Schiller's view of a theatre as a 'moral institute', he nevertheless adopts a substantial amount of ideas that Schiller developed in his essay 'The Stage regarded as a Moral Institute' ('Die Schaubühne als eine moralische Anstalt betrachtet', 1784). Art had an emancipatory function, according to Schiller, in the sense that it would urge humanity to stand up for its rights, along the line of the Enlightenment motto *'sapere aude'*. Yet, with Goethe, and – a hundred years later – Wagner and Nietzsche, Schiller had vested his hopes in a 'national theatre' (*'Nationaltheater'*), which would establish German culture as a serious cultural power within Europe. Crucial in Schiller's

---

68 This suggests that Nietzsche sees his own book as the fulfilment of the line running from Kant's critical philosophy to Schopenhauer's pessimism and aesthetics.

dramaturgy is the insight that 'visible account' ('*sichtbare Darstellung*') has a much stronger effect on the public than 'dead letter and cold storytelling' ('toter Buchstab und kalte Erzählung'),[69] and that theatre can affect people in a deeper way than moral laws: 'when morality is not being taught anymore, when religion finds no belief anymore, when law is not found anymore, then Medea would still make me shiver,' ('wenn keine Moral mehr gelehrt wird, keine Religion mehr Glauben findet, wenn kein Gesetz mehr vorhanden ist, wird uns Medea noch anschauern'), Schiller wrote tellingly:

> The stage is the establishment where pleasure unites with instruction, enjoyment with education [...] in this artistic world we dream the real one away, we are given back to ourselves, our sensitivity awakes, healing passions shake our slumbering nature and drive our blood in fresher impulses [...] a victory for nature! [...] a resurrecting nature![70]

> Die Schaubühne ist die Stiftung, wo sich Vergnügen mit Unterricht, Ruhe mit Anstrengung, Kurzweil mit Bildung gattet [...] in dieser künstlichen Welt träumen wir die wirkliche hinweg, wir werden uns selbst wiedergegeben, unsre Empfindung erwacht, heilsame Leidenschaften erschüttern unsre schlummernde Natur und treiben das Blut in frischeren Wallungen [...] ein Triumph für die Natur! [...] wieder auferstehende Natur!

The victory ('*Triumph*') is to be understood as follows:

> When people from all circles, spheres, and classes, having left every vein of artificiality and fashion behind, being snatched away from this force of fate, are made brothers by one all-weaving sympathy, are resolved in one race, having forgotten themselves and the word, and approaching at their divine origin.[71]

> Wenn Menschen aus allen Kreisen und Zonen und Ständen, abgeworfen jede Fessel der Künstelei und der Mode, herausgerissen aus jedem Drange des Schicksals, durch eine allwebende Sympathie verbrüdert, in ein Geschlecht wieder aufgelöst, ihrer selbst und der Welt vergessen und ihrem himmlischen Ursprung sich nähernd.

To Schiller, this is the experience 'of being a *human being*'.[72] These lines would fit well in *The Birth of Tragedy*. Moreover, Nietzsche agreed with Schiller's view that the chorus should play an important part in the theatre, and in this Nietzsche was even closer to Schiller than to Wagner, who perceived the chorus a 'false' instrument by which the opera pretended to be Greek tragedy.[73]

---

69 Schiller, 'Die Schaubühne als eine moralische Anstalt betrachtet' (1784), p. 48.
70 Schiller, 'Die Schaubühne als eine moralische Anstalt betrachtet' (1784), p. 55.
71 Schiller, 'Die Schaubühne als eine moralische Anstalt betrachtet' (1784), p. 55.
72 Schiller, 'Die Schaubühne als eine moralische Anstalt betrachtet' (1784), p. 55.
73 See Borchmeyer (1982): 'The application of the chorus in opera performance was rejected by Wagner as false analogy with Greek Tragedy [...]. Wagner never gave up the idea that the orchestra was the inheritor of the antique chorus' ('Die Verwendung des Chors auf der Opernbühne hat Wagner in seinen Reformschriften als falsche Analogie zur griechischen Tragödie verworfen [...]. Die Idee, daß das Orch-

If *Tristan and Isolde* came closest to Nietzsche's ideal, then we must conclude that was the case because it offered the best reconciliation of Dionysian magic and Apollonian semblance in a musical, aesthetic play, which mirrors the composer's play with the 'figures' in his dreams.[74] Nietzsche describes the effect of Dionysian magic as follows:

A storm seizes everything that is worn out, rotten, broken, and withered, wraps it in a whirling cloud of red dust and carries it like an eagle [vulture, MP] into the sky.[75] (BT 20, p. 98)

Ein Sturm packt alles Abgelehrte, Morsche, Zerbrochne, Verkümmerte, hüllt es wirbelnd in eine rothe Staubwolke und trägt es wie ein Geier in die Lüfte. (KSA 1.132)

In *The Birth of Tragedy* 1, it is represented in a similar way, there not with a vulture this time, but with tigers and panthers and in reference to Beethoven's *Ode to Joy*:

Freely the earth offers up her gifts, and the beasts of prey from mountain and desert approach in peace. The chariot of Dionysos is laden with flowers and wreaths; beneath its yoke stride panther and tiger (BT 1, p. 18)

Freiwillig beut die Erde ihre Gaben, und friedfertig nahen die Raubthiere der Felsen und Wüste. Mit Blumen und Kränzen ist der Wagen des Dionysus überschüttet: unter seinem Joche schreiten Panther und Tiger (KSA 1.29)

One should compare this description with Wagner's portrayal of the same piece of music in 'Beethoven'. Wagner classified Beethoven's *Choral* finale as testimony to the 'most sublime naiveté' (*'erhabenste Naivität'*, DS IX, p. 78) in its representation of 'the good man', the 'primordial type of innocence' (*'Urtypus der Unschuld'*, DS IX, p. 79). It reached a joy and truthfulness that exceeded those of other forms of arts. Much earlier than the German army in the Franco-Prussian War, Beethoven thereby turned against the 'impudent fashion' and spread 'the new religion, the world-redeeming message of the most sublime innocence' ('die neue Religion, die welterlösende Verkündigung der erhabensten Unschuld,' DS IX, p. 109). Commemorating Beethoven's birthday, Wag-

---

ester der Nachfolger des antiken Chors sei, hat Wagner nie aufgegeben,' pp. 156–157). Compare 9[111], KSA 7.316.

74 I translate '*Gestalt*' as 'figure' instead of as 'form', because Nietzsche resists the 'form-play' of Italian opera and refers to figures like giants and dwarfs and gods as creations of the dreamy imagination. Nietzsche speaks of 'dreaming's prophecy' (the English does not render the beautiful coincidence of 'truth' and 'dream-illusion' in the German '*Wahrtraumdeuterei*') referring to Hans Sachs in BT 1 (p. 15/ KSA 1.26).

75 '*Geier*' is not 'eagle', but 'vulture'. Nietzsche deliberately uses '*Geier*' here instead of the – with regard to the illustration of Prometheus on the front-cover – more obvious '*Adler*' as to refer to Wagner (whose stepfather's surname was 'Geyer'). Of course, this reference is lost in every translation. In BT 10, Nietzsche speaks of Prometheus's liberation 'from his vultures' (p. 53/'von seinen Geiern', KSA 1.73). There the translator has used 'vultures' for '*Geiern*'.

ner therefore concluded, is the celebration of the birthday of 'the great pioneer in the jungle of a depraved paradise' ('den großen Bahnbrecher in der Wildnis des entarteten Paradieses', DS IX, p. 109). The first thing to notice is that, while Schiller's description of the theatrical experience would almost seamlessly fit into Nietzsche's text, Wagner's description of Beethoven's music only meets Nietzsche's Dionysian interpretation halfway. This would not be a problem if Wagner's description would not agree with the kind of joy he aimed to evoke with his music. However, Wagner's understanding of his own work of art as a combination of Beethovenian music and Shakespearean drama, hints at the contrary. Again, Wagner's 'Greekness' consisted mainly in his wish to return myth to culture. However, his *Tristan and Isolde* and *Siegfried* were not intended as 'masks of Dionysus', but as anchors of a German literary and musical canon.[76]

Let us recapitulate. In *The Birth of Tragedy*, Nietzsche calls the art that achieves this experience of 'being a human being' 'tragic' or 'Dionysian'. *Tristan and Isolde* is his paradigm of a tragic work of art in a modern age stained by the tragic experience of the insufficiency of human reason – decisively deviating from his characterization of the work as a 'tragic idyll' in the *Nachlass*. In *The Birth of Tragedy*, however, the work is portrayed as the perfect aesthetic expression of unconscious will, in which 'Dionysos speaks the language of Apollo, but finally it is Apollo who speaks the language of Dionysos' (BT 21, p. 22; 'Dionysus redet die Sprache des Apollo, Apollo aber schliesslich die Sprache des Dionysus', KSA 1.140). *Tristan and Isolde* is the harmonic marriage of Dionysus and Apollo, the two art-deities or artistic instincts Nietzsche discerned, on the lines of Schopenhauer's distinction between music – as the art that expresses the Will in itself immediately – and the plastic arts, which only copy ideas of the Will.[77]

Nietzsche presents *Tristan and Isolde* as 'of necessity, [...] a restorative draught' (BT 21, p. 98/'*nothwendige Genesungstrank*', KSA 1.132), thus proposing musical tragedy as the best healing power after war. He points to three different reactions in history towards violence, the search for '*Nichts*', that is ascetic Buddhism (in India); the '*Verweltlichung*' – hedonism and materialism (in Rome); and the transformation of pain into joy in *Tragödie*, in Greece. As a 'musical tragedy', *Tristan* distinguishes itself from 'textual drama', because its music clarifies the drama from within, thus supplying it with metaphysical meaning. Therefore, Nietzsche also called it Wagner's '*opus metaphysicum*'.[78] Moreover, because of its content (that is, the Dionysian wisdom) and the perfect, balanced manner in which this wisdom is brought to the fore (so

---

76 See BT 10 (pp. 51–52. KSA 1.71–72).

77 Cf. BT 16, where he quotes a long passage of Schopenhauer to sustain his indebtedness to Schopenhauer's philosophy of music. With this quotation Nietzsche bridges his historical analysis of the Greeks, made in chapters 1–15, and his diagnosis of and recipe for modern culture, given in chapters 16–25.

78 WB 8 (p. 232/KSA 1.479).

that its effect on the public is not only painful but also comforting, meaning that both the pain for the lost unity with Dionysus as the regained unity is being commemorated and celebrated in tragedy), *Tristan and Isolde* (ideally) elevates itself to the kernel of human identity. As said above, the theatre is the place where humanity gains self-awareness. And this forms the core of Nietzsche's hope of Wagner; he expects 'Bayreuth' to be the place where people will look into the mirror. What they would see, according to Nietzsche, is not what they ideally can be, at which Schiller aimed, but what they originally were and still, in their very core, are: mortal and powerless beings, whose only true comfort resides in the transformation of their pain into joy.

Compared with his depiction of *Tristan and Isolde* as 'tragic idyll', Nietzsche's presentation of *Tristan and Isolde* as the union of Apollo and Dionysus is highly problematic. In the remaining notes, he had uttered serious doubts about Wagner's use of the chorus and his idyllic tendencies. Nietzsche does not offer a true solution for these doubts, but rather surpasses them. Therefore, *The Birth of Tragedy* gives the impression of avoiding straightforward critique of Wagner's music drama rather than resolving the serious problem of Wagner's conflation of aesthetics and morality. Reading *The Birth of Tragedy* from the perspective of the *Nachlass*, an undercurrent of implicit Wagner-critique surfaces, as I argue in the following paragraph.

Nietsche's 'secret scepticism' about Wagner

At the onset of *The Birth of Tragedy*, poetry is explained as a matter of 'dream-analysis' (p. 15/'*Wahrtraumdeuterei*', KSA 1.26), Homer is seen as 'the naive artist', and his naive art is understood as the 'sublime' result of his 'dream-faculty' (BT 3, pp. 24– 25/'*Traumbefähigung*', KSA 1.37).[79] The naive, to Nietzsche, is 'the complete enthralment in the beauty of semblance' (BT 3, p. 24/'jenes völlige Verschlungensein in der Schönheit des Scheines', KSA 1.37), 'the complete victory of Apolline illusion' (BT 3, p. 25/'der vollkommene Sieg der apollinischen Illusion', KSA 1.37). He does not interpret the naive, 'this oneness of man with nature' as Schiller defined it, 'as a human paradise [...] at the threshold of every culture' (BT 3, p. 24/'an der Pforte jeder Cultur, als einem Paradies der Menschheit', KSA 1.37). He expressly opposes the Romanticism as personalized in Rousseau's *Émile*, arguing that

> Wherever we encounter the 'naive' in art, we have to recognize that it is the supreme effect of the Apolline culture; as such, it first had to overthrow the realm of the Titans and slay monsters, and, by employing powerful delusions and intensely pleasurable illusions, gain victory over a terrifyingly profound view of the world and the most acute sensitivity to suffering. (BT 3, p. 24)

---

79 See also BT 5 (p. 29/KSA 1.42).

> Wo uns das "Naive" in der Kunst begegnet, haben wir die höchste Wirkung der apollinischen Cultur zu erkennen: welche immer erst ein Titanenreich zu stürzen und Ungethüme zu tödten hat und durch kräftige Wahnvorspiegelungen und lustvolle Illusionen über eine schreckliche Tiefe der Weltbetrachtung und reizbarste Leidensfähigkeit Sieger geworden sein muss. (KSA 1.37)

Nietzsche poses two questions that are central to the whole account. First, 'What [...] was the enormous need that gave rise to such a luminous company of Olympic beings?' (BT 3, p. 22/'Welches war das ungeheure Bedürfniss, aus dem eine so leuchtende Gesellschaft olympischer Wesen entsprang?' KSA 1.34) and second, 'How does the world of Olympian gods relate to this piece of popular wisdom?' (BT 3, p. 23/'Wie verhält sich zu dieser Volksweisheit die olympische Götterwelt?' KSA 1.35). With 'this piece of popular wisdom' Nietzsche refers to the so-called 'Silenian myth', which story he recounts in the same chapter. He distinguishes a huge contrast between this dark, tragic, pessimistic view of life and the bright, radiant deification and celebration of every aspect of life by the Olympian gods. 'In order to be able to live, the Greeks were obliged [...] to create these Gods,' he says explicitly (BT 3, p. 23; 'Um leben zu können, mussten die Griechen diese Götter, aus tiefster Nöthigung, schaffen', KSA 1.36). And he continues:

> How else could that people have borne existence, given their extreme sensitivity, their stormy desires, their unique gift for *suffering*, if that same existence had not been shown to them in their gods, suffused with higher glory? The same drive which calls art into being to complete and perfect existence and thus to seduce us into continuing to live, also gave rise to the world of the Olympians [...] (BT 3, pp. 23–24).

> Wie anders hätte jenes so reizbare empfindende, so ungestüm begehrende, zum *Leiden* so einzig befähigte Volk das Dasein ertragen können, wenn ihm nicht dasselbe, von einer höheren Glorie umflossen, in seinen Göttern gezeigt worden wäre. Derselbe Trieb, der die Kunst in's Leben ruft, als die zum Weiterleben verführende Ergänzung und Vollendung des Daseins, liess auch die olympische Welt entstehen [...] (KSA 1.36)

In his epic use of the Olympian gods, Homer turned the Silenian wisdom around into the idea that life is worth living. Schiller called Homer a 'naive' artist because of his direct, spontaneous response to and relation with nature, but Nietzsche resists this view here, stating that 'the now generally accepted art-word "naive", is by no means such a simple, so-to-speak inevitable condition which emerges of its own accord and which we would be *bound* to encounter at the threshold of every culture, as a human paradise' (BT 3, p. 24/'das Kunstwort "naiv" [ist] [...] keinesfalls ein so einfacher, sich von selbst ergebener, gleichsam unvermeidlicher Zustand [...], dem wir an der Pforte jeder Cultur, als einem Paradies der Menschheit begegnen *müssten*', KSA 1.37). He blames the influence of Rousseau's figure *Émile* on German culture for such a misconception:

People could only believe this at a time when they were bent on thinking of Rousseau's *Emile* as an artist, and entertained the illusion that in Homer they had found just such an artist as Emile, reared at the heart of nature (BT 3, p. 24)[80]

dies konnte nur eine Zeit glauben, die den Emil Rousseau's sich auch als Künstler zu denken suchte und in Homer einen solchen am Herzen der Natur erzogenen Künstler Emil gefunden zu haben wähnte [KSA 1.37]

Homeric naiveté, he argues, differs from Schiller's definition, because it embodies the victory of Apollo over the Titans, of pleasurable illusions over a 'terrifyingly profound view of the world and the most acute sensitivity to suffering' (BT 3, p. 24). He even calls Homer's excellence in achieving this naiveté in art 'sublime', thereby reminding of, yet also inherently opposing, Wagner's description of Beethoven's sublime naiveté. Note that Wagner regarded the finale of Beethoven's *Ninth Symphony* as an expression of 'the most sublime naiveté' ('*erhabenster Naivetät*', DS IX, p. 78), because it 'fills us with the ineffable joy at having attained paradise' and the belief that 'man is good after all'. 'The good man' reflected the 'primordial type of innocence' ('*Urtypus der Unschuld*', DS IX, p. 79). Beethoven's *Ninth Symphony* turned against the French 'impudent fashion' and spread 'the new religion, the world-redeeming message of the most sublime innocence' ('die neue Religion, die welterlösende Verkündigung der erhabensten Unschuld', DS IX, p. 79).

By contrast, according to Nietzsche, 'sublime naiveté' is the evocation of joy in order to resist the tragic, horrific truth of life, a truth represented by the figures of the Titans. Furthermore, to him it is the triumph of Apollonian illusion, and not of melodic music. It has nothing to do with Rousseau's original, moral goodness and original man as, by nature, an artist – as represented as we shall see below, in the figure of the 'singing shepherd'.

---

80 Ansell-Pearson (1991) says little on Nietzsche's earliest Rousseau-critique. Nevertheless, he is right in stating: 'In his early writings we see Nietzsche's conception of Rousseau as the political philosopher of *ressentiment* in its nascent phase. Nietzsche criticizes Rousseau's paean to nature, and his belief in man's natural goodness, which have their basis in romanticism. In the *Birth of Tragedy*, for example, Nietzsche criticizes the romanticism of the modern age for conceiving of the artist in terms of Rousseau's *Émile*. Nietzsche's argument is that Rousseau's portrait of Émile's realization of his fundamental human nature and the achievement of oneness with nature, achieved by withdrawing the child and adolescent from the degenerative effects of corrupt social institutions and allowing his natural goodness to flourish, fails to recognize the dark and terrible forces of nature which must be overcome in order to arrive at a harmonious relationship to nature. In other words, there is no place in Émile's education for recognition of the dark and mysterious Dionysian forces of nature' (p. 25).

The singing shepherd contra the chorus of satyrs

Italian opera had re-introduced idyllic symbolism in the history of art with the figure of the singing shepherd, ages after Alexandrian poetry had done so, and long before German Romanticism under the influence of Rousseau's *Émile* adopted the image for its glorification of nature. The singing shepherd symbolizes the 'cheerfulness of eternal re-discovery' (BT 19, p. 92; 'Heiterkeit des ewigen Wiederfindens', KSA 1.125) against the elegiac grief for definite loss. Nietzsche calls this serenity 'Alexandrian' to express the parallel he perceives between the Italian opera and modern science; both are, in his view, humanistic and optimistic.[81] The shepherd is expression of the modern longing (BT 8, p. 41/'*Sehnsucht*', KSA 1.58) 'for what is original and natural' (BT 8, p. 41/'das Usprüngliche und Natürliche, KSA 1.57–58). According to Nietzsche, however, the satyr symbolizes humankind in its original, tragic, nature, and not the shepherd.[82] He regards the herdsman as a strongly downgraded version of the satyr, who he calls the 'emblem of the sexual omnipotence of nature' (BT 8, p. 41/'Sinnbild der geschlechtlichen Allgewalt der Natur', KSA 1.57–58).[83] While the satyr does not know fear, similar to Wagner's hero *Siegfried*, and is a kind of macho, the flute-playing herdsman has a mild, kind, and sentimental character. The satyr, a pre-Hellenistic, Greek figure, was established by the Greeks as the archetype ('*Urbild*') of humankind, Nietzsche explains. In possession of the innermost, deepest knowledge of nature, the satyr was the 'proclaimer of wisdom from the deepest heart of nature' (p. 41/'Weisheitsverkünder aus der tiefsten Brust der Natur', KSA 1.58). According to Nietzsche, the shepherd is the product of the 'cultured man' ('*Culturmensch*') and hence embodies the 'cultural lie' (p. 41/'*Culturlüge*'). The shepherd, we may say, is the product of wishful thinking, whereas the satyr (also branded as '*Naturgenie*', KSA 1.59), expressing and representing the 'genuine truth of nature' (p. 41/'*Naturwahrheit*', KSA 1.58), is the product of purely aesthetic imagination.[84] Contrary to the shepherd, the satyr is an immoral, very sexual, tough, macho, natural being that has no clue of romantic love or of the experience of pleasure in serene beauty.

Joined in the chorus, the satyrs are also the harbour of truth, 'poetic freedom', and imagination. Therefore, the chorus of satyrs is the strongest and 'main weapon'

---

81 Although Nietzsche does not mention Rousseau here, this critique of the humanistic-optimistic view of progress as 'going-back' (in history) is repeated later by example of Rousseau. See TI Skirmishes 48, pp. 221–222/KSA 6.150–151. Goethe, then, is the anti-Rousseauian figure *par excellence* for Nietzsche. Cf. Goedert (2002), pp. 127–129.

82 Nor rhapsodists like the singing and harp-strumming bard Tannhäuser, for that matter.

83 Although Nietzsche attached quite some importance to the satyr-figure, it is hardly discussed in studies on *The Birth of Tragedy*. Compare Nietzsche to Erwin Rohde, 16 July 1872 (KSB 4, pp. 23–24).

84 Note that there are both similarities and differences between the concept of satyr and child. Both are one with nature, are 'knowing' beings (and thus 'geniuses', if we assume that Nietzsche agrees with Schopenhauer in this respect), however Nietzsche's description of the child is non-sexual.

(BT 7, p. 38/'*Hauptwaffe*', KSA 1.54) against French naturalism and other degrading, non-aesthetic and non-tragic elements and aspects in music and drama. Not only is the satyr-chorus the source of the later, more sophisticated, tragedy, but there is also no tragedy without the satyr-chorus, according to Nietzsche. Schiller has understood the importance of the chorus best, he asserts, and it seems that Wagner can even learn from Schiller in this respect, albeit that this is not said with so many words. In pointing to Wagner's expression that civilization 'is absorbed, elevated, and extinguished [raised, MP] by music, just as lamplight is superseded by the day of light' (BT 7, p. 39/ 'von der Musik aufgehoben werde wie der Lampenschein vom Tageslicht', KSA 1.56),[85] Nietzsche draws the analogy that the satyr is in the same relation to the 'cultured human being' (BT 7, p. 39/'*dem Culturmenschen*', KSA 1.55) and his shepherd. Yet he also suggests that Wagner, if he indeed wants his 'Dionysian music' to bring civilization to a higher level, must follow the Greeks also in this matter, because in this poetical, idealist, aesthetic space resides a cultural power that can never be reached by politics or (economic-based) society:

> [...] state and society, indeed all divisions between one human being and another, give way to an overwhelming feeling of unity which leads men back to the heart of nature (BT 7, p. 39)

> [...] dies ist die nächste Wirkung der dionysischen Tragödie, dass der Staat und die Gesellschaft, überhaupt die Klüfte zwischen Mensch und Mensch einem übermächtigen Einheitsgefühle weichen, welches an das Herz der Natur zurückführt. KSA 1.56

The cultural power of tragic art (its main locus being the satyr-chorus) is to unite people in bringing them back to nature. Here it seems that 'nature' is equated with 'metaphysical comfort' and joy, because the satyr-chorus celebrates the fact that, despite its finitude, 'life is indestructibly mighty and pleasurable' (BT 7, p. 39/'das Leben [ist] im Grunde der Dinge [...] mächtig und lustvoll [...]', KSA 1.55).[86] Hence, here it is suggested that the source of metaphysical comfort is not the aesthetic play of the (Apollonian) drama, but the Dionysian chorus itself. This is not easy to grasp, but let us not forget that drama is the vision of the chorus projected onto the stage. And it is the sharing of this vision, of the same dream, in which the social unity of artist, actors, and the public consists.

Nietzsche describes this (Greek, aesthetic) public as a public tormented by the destruction of 'so-called world history', a public, which, aware of 'the cruelty of nature' (BT 7, p. 40/'die Grausamkeit der Natur', KSA 1.56), 'is in danger of longing to deny the will as the Buddhist does' (BT 7, p. 40/'in Gefahr ist, sich nach einer buddhaistischen Verneinung des Willens zu sehnen', KSA 1.56). At this moment in the book,

---

85 In 'Beethoven' (DS IX, p. 104).
86 In the light of Nietzsche's criticism of 'pleasure' and plea for 'joy', I would prefer to read 'joyful' for the German '*lustvoll*'.

Nietzsche is far remote from Schopenhauer and, indeed, it turns out that the satyr is a contra-figure of Schopenhauer's 'saint'.[87] Thanks to the satyrs, the Greek public does not turn to a moral and life-rejecting answer to life: 'The dithyramb's chorus of satyrs is the saving act of Greek art' (BT 7, p. 40/'Der Satyrchor des Dithyrambus ist die rettende That der griechischen Kunst', KSA 1.57): 'Art saves him, and through art life saves him – for itself' (BT 7, p. 40/'Ihn rettet die Kunst, und durch die Kunst rettet ihn sich – das Leben, KSA 1.56), and formulated in more Schopenhauerian terms, Nietzsche adds: 'Here, at this moment of supreme danger for the will, art approaches as saving sorceress with the power to heal' (BT 7, p. 40/'Hier in dieser höchsten Gefahr des Willens, naht sich, als rettende, heilkundige Zauberin, die Kunst, KSA 1.57). Art saves humankind from lethargy: 'True knowledge [...] insight into the terrible truth [...] outweighs every motive for action' (BT 7, p. 40/'die wahre Erkenntnis, der Einblick in die grauenhafte Wahrheit überwiegt jedes zum Handeln antreibende Motiv', KSA 1.57), because having attained such deep insight makes one perceive everything in life as 'terrible or absurd' (BT 7, p. 40/'das Entsetzliche oder Absurde', KSA 1.57). In re-directing (BT 7, p. 40/'umbiegen', KSA 1.57), transforming this knowledge and these extreme perspectives 'into representations with which man can live', art makes sublime (the representation of the terrible) and comical art. The sublime is defined as the moment in which 'the terrible is tamed by artistic means' (BT 7, p. 40/'die künstlerische Bändigung des Entsetzlichen', KSA 1.57) and the comical as the moment where 'disgust at absurdity is discharged by artistic means' (BT 7, p. 40/'die künstlerische Entladung vom Ekel des Absurden', KSA 1.57).

The threat of failure for Wagner

The opposition of shepherd and satyr not only confirms that Nietzsche had quite a different interpretation of Greek man and culture than Humanist philosophies, but also brings out that he and Wagner had conflicting anthropological views. While Wagner went along with the Romantic and Rousseauian idea of the naturally good man represented in the singing shepherd, Nietzsche defied this character by bringing the satyr to the fore as original man. Thus, Nietzsche's attack on the shepherd is remarkable with respect to Wagner's use of this figure in his 'Beethoven' essay, because there Wagner argued that the sublimity of Beethoven's music consisted in evoking the belief that 'man is good'. Moreover, Wagner used the figure of the shepherd to argue that a dreamlike state, necessary to create sublime, magical, music, was also attainable during daytime. By criticizing the connection of magical, sublime (Wagner) or tragic (Nietzsche) music with a moral experience and the idea that a genius (as creator of

---

87 Compare Prange (2012–3) on this opposition in *Ecce Homo*.

sublime music) is, as an original, creative, and knowing being, comparable with the shepherd, Nietzsche implicitly criticizes Wagner's moral, idyllic traits.

Whereas Wagner criticized heavily the French 'tendency' for superficiality, as expressed by the popularity of French journalism and fashion, Nietzsche extended this critique with a critique of Rousseau's 'idyllic' and moral belief in the 'good man'. This entailed a serious warning addressed to Wagner, when we take into account that Wagner contended that Beethoven's music defeats French superficiality exactly by expressing the (typically 'German') belief in the morally good man.[88] This leads to the important conclusion that, by pointing to the French roots of Beethoven's supposed 'German' belief, Nietzsche in fact warned Wagner against his own 'French tendency', his idyllic view of humanity, moral optimism, and a lack of insight into the tragic character of Greek serenity. In brief, Wagner lacked an 'eye for depth'.

However, we can raise the question whether Wagner or Nietzsche is to be blamed for having a too 'idyllic' view of things. When we concentrate on the 'idyllic', the notes of 1871 cast another light, or rather a shadow, over the hopeful, optimistic picture Nietzsche draws in *The Birth of Tragedy* of Richard Wagner as the rejuvenator of tragic art and saviour of culture. In addition, does Nietzsche's ideal representation of the return to the primordial, childlike innocence, fantasy, and playfulness, as an *'Urheimat'* in which humanity reaches its true being and finds harmony with nature and fellow people, not fulfil Schiller's definition of the idyll?

Measured against his different valuation of the idyllic in the *Nachlass* notes and *The Birth of Tragedy*, Nietzsche seems to have represented both Wagner and his own cultural ideal more tragic and less idyllic than they actually were.

Conclusion

The Birth of Tragedy is motivated by the cultural goal to save Europe from artistic and cultural decadence. In the book, Nietzsche expressed his expectation that Richard Wagner's music drama would lead Europe out of decadence due to the fact that it was a 'Greek' art-form. Wagner would conduct Europe out of 'the jungle of a depraved paradise' and spawn 'the great Renaissance'. This cultural expectation formed the directive of *The Birth of Tragedy*, just as it was the directive of Wagner's celebratory essay 'Beethoven'. That essay had indicated to the young philosopher 'what I currently want from the future', as he wrote to his best friend and fellow-Wagnerian Erwin Rohde, extolling it as 'a revelation of the spirit in which *we* – we! – shall live in the future'. Inspired by Wagner's 'Beethoven' essay, Nietzsche's view of the future of German cul-

---

88 Wagner's 'Rousseauian' nature is furthermore tenable from his egalitarianism, as Nietzsche knew well from Wagner's early essays, such as 'The Artwork of the Future' ('Das Kunstwerk der Zukunft', 1849) and 'Art and Revolution' (1849).

ture was optimistic. It had made him believe that Wagner was the person who would save Europe from artistic decadence. Rather soon though, his high hopes received a heavy undertone of scepticism due to Wagner's 'idyllic' tendency to escape into moral hope.

Wagner claimed to accomplish Goethe and Schiller's cultural war by way of the mythologicization of art. Nietzsche understood this project as a substantial part of the general 'aestheticization' of the human view of life. According to him, Wagner's genius enabled him to express the Greek insight into life in music. This 'magical' act would transform the (moral, critical) public into an 'aesthetic' public. In so doing, he would 'redeem' Germany and, in spreading his 'deep joy' 'over the mountains' alike, European culture.

Nietzsche's task in this 'aestheticization of culture' was not only to explain Wagner's cultural importance to a broader, academic, public, but also to educate the composer in the Greek way of life. Indeed, in order to accomplish the 'cultural war' successfully, Wagner had to 'Graecize'. Therefore, the analysis Nietzsche made in the first fifteen chapters of *The Birth of Tragedy* were not only meant as informing his colleagues in philology, but also to instruct Wagner. Without this instruction, Wagner would never find the firm footing the 'great Renaissance' needed, according to Nietzsche. This entails, however, that the explicit Wagner-defence in the book has an undertone of 'secret scepticism' regarding Wagner's moral and idyllic, 'sick' inclinations. This, in turn, suggests that, first, *The Birth of Tragedy* is indeed written out of Nietzsche's concern for Wagner's 'Graecization' and 'Southernization', as the philosopher had written himself in retrospect. Second, it suggests that *The Birth of Tragedy* has an ambiguous, even contradictory nature, as it both defends Wagner as the one who may rejuvenate the Greek spirit and criticizes Wagner for a lack of Greek spirit. *The Birth of Tragedy* is both a pamphlet that advertises Wagner's music dramas and a manual on Greek tragedy, addressed to Wagner in the first place.

However, Nietzsche's concern for Wagner's 'Graecization' and 'southernization' arose from his concern for Europe's 'Graecization' and 'southernization'. This concern formed the core of Nietzsche's philosophy of culture. In *The Birth of Tragedy*, Nietzsche was involved with forging a 'bond of lasting love' between pre-Socratic Greek and German culture, which would, in the end, purify Europe as a whole from its modern, 'Socratic' deviation from the truth.

Similar to Plato in the *Republic*, Nietzsche considered truth, conceived as the mirror of nature, to be the basis of social life. However, while Plato propagated the expulsion of art and artists from social power, Nietzsche resisted such abandonment by pointing to the crucial function of art for a culture to be a true culture. The truth, and thus philosophy (Plato) and art (Nietzsche) constituted, enlightened, emancipated, and enhanced a society or culture. While Plato's jettisoning of artists from the ideal society created room for modern science and technical reason to emerge, art was directed to the mere and narrow realm of aesthetics. Nietzsche's answer was to broaden the realm of aesthetics, and apply the aesthetic view to non-aesthetic disciplines. In so doing, Nietzsche followed Schiller much more than he credits him for in *The Birth of Tragedy*. Not only does his philosophy fit the idyllic, sentimental, and naive as described by Schiller – drawing upon Schiller's analysis of play – better than Nietzsche intimates, he also, like Schiller, seeks to tackle a serious, cultural problem in a time corrupted by war (the French Revolution for Schiller, the Franco-Prussian war for Nietzsche) by advocating the aesthetic realm as the defining realm of humanity, as 'the harmonizing, catalytic moment between the physical and the moral, where the individual begins the process of restoring his wholeness,' as Nicholas Martin put it,[89] as a force against destructive politics. In so doing, Nietzsche and Schiller harked back to views, which in the end form the purview of Plato's views on man and society. Although Plato dismisses artists any social and political power, he warns in *The Republic* that aesthetic education, music [inspiration and guidance by the muses, by art, MP] and philosophy are needed to harmonize and civilize the individual spirit:

> Even if he [the "feeble warrior", the one without spirit, who counts on his bodily strength in his relation to the world, MP] did have some learning in his soul, it gets no taste of learning or enquiry, and has no experience of rational argument or any artistic pursuit. As a result, since it never wakes up and has nothing to feed on, and since there is nothing to purify its senses, it becomes weak, and deaf, and blind, doesn't it? [...] Someone like this becomes an enemy of rational argument [...] and an enemy of music and literature. He abandons any attempt at persuasion using rational argument, and does everything with savage violence, like a wild animal. He lives his life in ignorance and stupidity, without grace or rhythm.[90]

According to Plato, the political should be kept under the control of the aesthetic experience in order not to lead to moral decadence. This is an example of extending the aesthetic to the non-aesthetic as Nietzsche's aestheticism advocates. Very important to Nietzsche is that it is not the other way round: that the aesthetic is under the control of political power, including the – Schillerian and Wagnerian (and Brechtian later) – idea of political theatre. The theatre should remain as remote as possible from political propaganda, especially nationalistic propaganda.

In the next part of this book, it will be argued that the different perception of the relation between aesthetics and politics, and Nietzsche's growing cosmopolitan spirit led him away from Wagner towards an eventual plea for 'good Europeanism'. The model of the good European is Goethe, who is presented as a typically anti-Wagnerian and anti-modern spirit. As I hope to show, Schiller and the idyllic spirit – despite Nietzsche's neglect of both – still form an important element of Nietzsche's new musical aesthetics, 'free-spirit' philosophy, and 'good Europeanism'.

---

89 Martin (1996), p. 100.
90 Plato (2000), pp. 103–104 [*Politeia* Book 3, 411 d-e].

Chapter 5
Nietzsche's anti-Wagnerism in the light of his increasing cosmopolitanism

Introduction

Thus, despite his doubts, Nietzsche defended Wagner in *The Birth of Tragedy* insofar as he was 'Greek', 'as a *foreign country*' (EH 'Clever' 5, p. 92/'als *Ausland,*' KSA 6.288) or a 'European event' ('europäisches Ereigniss').[1] Indeed, had Wagner not written in 'Art and Revolution' ('Kunst und Revolution,' 1849):

> Greek art spanned the mind of a beautiful nation; in like manner should the artwork of the future span the minds of a free humanity, exceeding all borders of nationalities; his national soul should not be more than a decoration, a stimulus of individual multiplicity, not a limiting narrowness.

> Umfaßte das griechische Kunstwerk den Geist einer schönen Nation, so soll das Kunstwerk der Zukunft den Geist einer freien Menschheit über alle Schranken der Nationalitäten hinaus umfassen; das nationale Wesen in ihm darf nur ein Schmuck, ein Reiz individueller Mannigfaltigkeit, nicht eine hemmende Schranke sein.[2]

And when he was only twenty-one years old, Wagner had noted in his address 'On German Opera' ('Die deutsche Oper,' 1834):

> We must grasp our time and attempt to express its new forms; and the master of this will be the one who writes neither Italian nor French – nor even German.

> Wir müssen die Zeit packen und ihre neuen Formen auszubilden suchen; und der wird der Meister sein, der weder italienisch, französisch – noch aber auch deutsch schreibt.[3]

These expressions are testimony to Wagner's early Europeanism and cosmopolitan spirit, which he traded for a dubious form of nationalism and Germanism, which Nietzsche discovered at the first Bayreuth festival, as we shall see a bit further on. The young Wagner propagated what Nietzsche designated during his 'free spirit' period as the need to 'de-Germanize' ('*entdeutschen*').[4] Indeed, Nietzsche's turn away from Wagner was, as I hope to show below, not only kindled by Wagner's 'idyllic' tendency, but

---

1 See TI Skirmishes 21, p. 202/ GD Streifzuge 21, KSA 6.125. Cf. BGE 256 (pp. 148–150/KSA 5.201–204) and Borchmeyer (1993), p. 4. Cf. BGE 254 (pp. 145–147/KSA 5.198–200). Borchmeyer writes that to Nietzsche, Wagner was 'the medium of de-provencialism and becoming European' ('das Medium der Entprovinzialisierung und Europäisierung,' 1993, p. 7) and remarks that the move to Bayreuth was interpreted by Nietzsche as a fall back into provencialism.

2 Cited after Borchmeyer's quotation (1993, p. 10).

3 Cited after Borchmeyer's quotation (1993, p. 10).

4 The desire to de-Germanize may be considered as a typically German-Romantic desire, though.

also stimulated by Nietzsche's growing cosmopolitan spirit. This expressed itself, as I shall argue, from *Human, All Too Human* (1878) onwards as the need to 'de-Germanize' and to become a 'good European' to be understood as 'the mix of cultures', i.e., northern and southern elements. This is especially tangible in his new musical aesthetics, which centres around the surprising embrace of French and Italian opera and the active attempt to 'Italianize' German music, as will be demonstrated in the next chapter.

In this chapter, I shall examine Nietzsche's growing cosmopolitan awareness by looking at, first, his interest in Ancient Greek, Goethe's, and Schiller's cosmopolitan tendencies, an interest already visible in the summer of 1872. I shall focus on the ideas of *learning* and *travelling* as the bottom-line of their cosmopolitanism. As I claim, according to Nietzsche, Greek culture was powerful due to its search for and embrace of non-Greek features, that is, due to its what I propose to call (inspired by Hoock-Demarle) 'dynamic interculturalism'. As Nietzsche had to admit, that summer, not only had Wagner not fully understood the Greeks, neither had he. In addition, this knowledge made him understand that Goethe and Schiller had indeed been the men who 'had striven most vigorously to learn from the Greeks' (BT 20, p. 95/'von den Griechen zu lernen am kräftigsten gerungen hat,' KSA 1.129), which he had already sensed in *The Birth of Tragedy*. The 'noblest struggles for self-cultivation' (*'den edelsten Bildungskampf'*)[5] had been carried out by Goethe, Schiller, and Winckelmann – not by Wagner.

Subsequently, I argue that Nietzsche's new awareness caused him to 'reform' his plea for the 'aestheticization' of modern culture. As it turned out, the aesthetic view was not something that could be developed through mere theoretical instruction (by way of a book, e.g., his own book *The Birth of Tragedy*), nor something that the theatre was likely to create, since Wagner's 'Dionysian magic' apparently was not that 'Dionysian'. Instead, it required a practice of journeying to foreign cultures, specifically Italy, and learning artistic measures, rules, and practices from the great artists (dead or alive) there. But before that, one had to learn from the Greeks how to learn and how to be a good student of other cultures.

In brief, as Nietzsche came to understand only a few months after the publication of *The Birth of Tragedy*, the key to the 'Greacization' and 'southernization' of art, culture, and humanity, was not the creation of an aesthetic public by way of Wagner's music drama, in the spirit of Greek tragedy, but the aesthetic education of northern individuals by urging them to travel to 'the south' (Italy) and learn from the people there about the aesthetic view of life, in the footsteps of Goethe. Hence, cross-cultural fertilization or 'dynamic interculturalism', is a necessary condition for 'aestheticization,' according to Nietzsche's new aesthetics.

By implication, the free-spirit books *Human all too Human I* and *II, Daybreak,* and *The Gay Science* are not only testimony to Nietzsche's 'clime of the soul' (HH II Pref-

---

5 BT 20 (p. 96/KSA 1.129).

ace 5, p. 212/'Klima der Seele,' KSA 2.375), but also 'precepts of health' (HH II Preface 2, p. 210/'eine Gesundheitslehre,' KSA 2.371),[6] books that direct the way to recovery and health rather than spout knowledge, and 'travel books' – as is shown towards the end of this chapter.

Greek cosmopolitanism in the notes of 1872–1873

As I argued in the former chapter, one important reason for Nietzsche to write *The Birth of Tragedy* was to facilitate Richard Wagner's 'Graecization,' and in so doing Europe's 'Graecization' in general. Instead of becoming 'Greek', however, Richard Wagner became more 'German' – in the political sense of *'reichsdeutsch'* (EH 'Clever' 5, p. 93/ KSA 6.289).[7]

The opposition between culture and political nationalism that Nietzsche drew in his essay on David Strauss is already visible in several texts from his notes of 1872. These show that he had discovered that the Greeks had not been 'pure' Greeks, but that their aestheticism had been the result of their cosmopolitanism.[8] This discovery, I want to argue, did not lead him to leaving the Greeks and sticking to the 'German' task of 'aestheticizing' Europe, but prompted him to adopt cosmopolitanism as the

---

6 Cf. 41[75], KSA 8.594.

7 Yovel (2002) remarks that 'there can be no doubt that Nietzsche foresaw the future career of Bayreuth as a politico musical shrine' (p. 130) and 'Nietzsche equally opposed Wagner in denouncing the politicization of culture', while 'Wagner saw culture itself as politics' (p. 131). This goes especially for Nietzsche's disavowal of Wagner's political anti-Semitism, whereas Nietzsche mainly rejects the 'resentment' of 'priestly Judaism' in the context of his fight against Christianity.

8 Morgan (2006, p. 472, footnote 22) remarks that Nietzsche dismisses cosmopolitanism and its enlightened tradition, referring to 29[109], KSA 7.681 and HL 5. Note 29[109] reads as follows: 'It is complained that cosmopolitanism is over: in history it remains as residue: however, the precondition, universal piety is gone, the desire to help everywhere' ('Man klagt, dass der Cosmopolitismus vorüber sei: in der Geschichte besteht er, als Residuum: aber die Voraussetzung, die universale Pietät ist verloren, der Wunsch überall zu helfen'). Nietzsche's rebuttal of a political or ethical cosmopolitanism born out of piety does not include the resistance of cosmopolitanism *per se*. In HL 5, Nietzsche speaks of the 'cosmopolitan Gods-, morals-, and arts carnival' ('kosmopolitischen Götter-, Sitten- und Künste-Carnevale', KSA 1.279) in virtue of which the Romans of the empire became 'un-Roman' ('unrömisch', KSA 1.279). Here, Nietzsche reflects on the problem of modern people (and art) to understand *and* imitate ancient people. He does so in discussion with Goethe's essay 'Shakespeare und kein Ende!' In this essay, Goethe contends that Shakespeare has made the Romans into English people, to which Nietzsche adds: 'as soon as we would want to decorate ancient times and people with us, we make them into ridiculous caricatures' ('sobald wir die fremden Zeiten und Menschen mit uns drapiren wollten, machen wir sie zur läppischen Carikatur,' 29[130], KSA 7.689). Rather than scorning cosmopolitanism, Nietzsche points to the difficulty and necessity of historical accuracy. He finds this accuracy in understanding the *spirit* of a people that speaks from their art. To try to reconstruct a people from 'objective' *facts*, however, leads to bad imitation and epigonism, according to Nietzsche.

way to aestheticize and 'Graecize'.[9] In other words: from the summer of 1872 onwards, he developed the tenet that, to learn and adopt the 'aesthetic' view of life, one had to travel to foreign cultures.

Had the 'Greek' lesson already not found any hearing in Wagner, the 'cosmopolitan' lesson was, if possible, even more lost on the composer. But this did not keep Nietzsche from trying to teach Wagner who the Greeks had been. For her birthday in December of 1872, Nietzsche sent Cosima *Five Prefaces to Unwritten Books* (*Fünf Vorreden zu ungeschriebenen Büchern*).[10] One of these prefaces treats the topic of slavery in the Greek state. Nietzsche must have known that this was a dicey undertaking, since it was exactly on the inhuman grounds of slavery that Wagner eventually repudiated Greek culture.[11] It was therefore not only his misunderstanding of the Greek spirit that made Wagner not Greek enough, but also the fact that he simply did not approve of the anti-humanistic, cruel features and institutions of Greek culture. Wagner's outlook was, as in his revolutionary, ultra-socialist years 1848–1849, much more 'humanistic' and 'optimistic' than Nietzsche's cultural ideal of 'health' – the term that incorporates both pain and joy and replaces 'paradise', 'Arcadia', and 'Elysium' – could ever have allowed for. Wagner did not want so much the return of the Greek spirit as the broad, European esteem of German art and culture. He mainly valued Greek culture as a source of inspiration for his own project to mythologize culture – a project that he regarded as a typical 'German' task. To Nietzsche, on the other hand, the good thing about the Germans was primarily that they could become 'Greek'. This meant not so much that Greek myths inspired them, but that they understood them and out of this deep understanding tried to revive their wisdom and aesthetics.

Nietzsche developed the idea that the Greek aesthetics had been the product of their cosmopolitanism specifically from the summer of 1872 onwards. That summer, he was writing *Philosophy in the Tragic Age of the Greeks* (*Die Philosophie im tragischen Zeitalter der Griechen*), an essay published only posthumously. In that treatise, Nietzsche concluded that the Greek style had come into being under the influence of the Orient. Notes to this essay that reflect on the cosmopolitan spirit of the

---

9 Nietzsche emphasizes that the 'Apollonian task' (AOM 219, p. 265/'apollinische Aufgabe,' KSA 2.472) for the Hellenic spirit of overcoming its natural tendency to darkness by giving its 'elementary savagery and darkness' ('elementaren Wildheit und Finsterniss') a style, was a long, historical *and* artistic process, a development from barbarism (called by Nietzsche 'Asiatic pomp, vagueness and obscurity' – as if to draw a parallel between Wagner's obscurity and his interest in Buddhism) to the clarity of Homer, the aesthetic *style* as Goethe called it. The typically Greek clarity, distinctness, lucidity (as discerned by Winckelmann), their 'lightness', is rooted in Asiatic darkness. *That* is Greek 'joy' or *'Heiterkeit'*: to strike a balance between the tragic darkness and the joyful clarity. Cf. GS Preface 4.
10 Cosima Wagner's birthday 'was actually on 24 December, but she modestly celebrated it on the 25th' (Millington 1992, p. 311).
11 Her reaction was indeed one of annoyance (see her diary-entry of 1 January 1873: Volume I, 1976, p. 623; Cosima Wagner 1994, p. 163).

Greeks, Goethe, and Schiller, evidence that Nietzsche developed the thought that a 'cosmopolitan tendency' was necessary and that the *'Reformationsarbeit'* for culture consisted precisely in this.[12] The first Untimely Meditation *David Strauss* confirms this in the sense that it is testimony to his worry about Germany's growing nationalism and philistinism, now that Germany, after the victory in the Franco-Prussian war, has developed the inclination to mix up political and military power with cultural power.

That Nietzsche did not identify with Germany's 'lack of culture' (*'Mangel an Cultur,'* 35[7], KSA 7.818), is also confirmed by a draft for this essay, stemming from 1873: 'To the German writer David Strauss. Letter by a foreigner' ('An den deutschen Schriftsteller David Strauss. Brief eines Ausländers,' 27[7], KSA 7.589). This note explicitly shows that Nietzsche refused to consider himself a German, given that someone like David Strauss was one. It anticipates Nietzsche's plea for 'de-Germanization' as well as his refusal to identify with a state that was founded on nationalism and militarism: 'to be a good German means to degermanize oneself' (AOM 323, p. 287; 'Gut deutsch sein heisst sich entdeutschen', KSA 2.511), i.e., the 'overcoming of his German qualities' (AOM 323, p. 287; 'Ueberwindung seiner deutschen Eigenschaften', KSA 2.512). It also clarifies Nietzsche's later saying that he worshipped Wagner insofar as he was not German, but 'a foreign country'. Even in *The Birth of Tragedy*, as I have argued in chapter 4, Wagner is valued for his 'Greek' qualities, not his German ones.

Philosophy in the Tragic Age of the Greeks indicates that Nietzsche's worry about the growing nationalism of Germany in general and Richard Wagner in particular coincided with a new openness on his part to the topic of cosmopolitanism and national identity in Greece. As so often, Nietzsche turned to Goethe and Schiller to probe his thoughts. His 'nationalism-cosmopolitanism' assessment marks a small yet important part of notebook P I 20, reproduced in KSA 7 under number 19. These notes not only display a growing awareness of the 'non-Greek' character of Greek identity on Nietzsche's part, but also that, according to him, learning from the Greeks amounts to becoming 'cosmopolitan'. Note 19[42] is crucial to the understanding of the major shift in thought

---

12 See 19[274], KSA 7.505. It is not entirely clear to me what exactly caused Nietzsche to consider the Greeks as cosmopolitan figures who had learned (through hard work, self-criticism, and openness to other people's ideas) rather than as 'natural geniuses' (who created out of spontaneity and a unique talent). There may have beeen a surprising influence from 'the Father of Racism', and friend of Wagner, Joseph Arthur, Comte de Gobinaeau's analysis of the Greek race in his *Essay on the Inequality of the Races* (1853–1855) on Nietzsche's interpretation of the Greeks as a 'mixed race' with mongolian and Semitic elements (5[198], KSA 8.96, cf. 18[46], KSA 8.327), even though 'Nietzsche appears to have read little, if anything, of Gobineau's work' and he 'does not share Gobineau's theory of race […] Unlike Gobineau, Nietzsche understands "race" to be the product primarily of social and environmental rather than biological factors' (Martin 2004, pp. 40–46). Nietzsche mentions Gobineau twice in his correspondence (KSB 2, p. 101 and KSB 8, p. 516). Compare also Martin's following remark: 'Nietzsche's belief that *acquired* characteristics could be passed on, and the related claim that the "purity" of a race was a late, hard-fought achievement rather than an innate quality, are central to his racial and cultural theory' (Martin 2004, p. 50).

that is taking place here: 'The Greeks as discoverers and travellers and colonizers. They know how to learn: enormous power of adoption' ('Die Griechen als Entdecker und Reisende und Kolonisatoren. Sie verstehen zu lernen: ungeheure Aneignungskraft,' KSA 7.432). This is, as far as I have been able to trace, the first explicit moment in which Nietzsche understands that the Greeks had not just been teachers for the next generation, but that they had been students of other cultures before that. Nietzsche came to understand that the aesthetic powers that they had developed and which had made them surpass the 'Titanic' age of barbarism had not (only) been a matter of natural powers, but (also) of learning from other cultures.

In *Philosophy in the Tragic Age of the Greeks*, Nietzsche indeed suggests that if we want to become 'Greek', we should first become good students of neighbouring countries:

> Nothing is more foolish than ascribing an autochthonous education to the Greeks, because they rather have soaked up all the living education of other nations. They achieved so much, because they knew how to throw the spear from the place where some other nation had left it on the ground (KSA 1.806).

> Nichts ist thörichter als den Griechen eine autochthone Bildung nachzusagen, sie haben vielmehr alle bei anderen Völkern lebende Bildung in sich eingesogen, sie kamen gerade deshalb so weit, weil sie es verstanden den Speer von dort weiter zu schleudern, wo ihn ein anderes Volk liegen ließ.

This insight not only dominated Nietzsche's newly developed view of the Greeks, but even became his new measure of culture. The talent or ability to adopt, to incorporate what is strange, and to stretch one's aesthetic and absorbing powers becomes the bottom-line of what culture is, what uplifts culture, and even of a national culture: 'In that way the Germans may achieve what the Greeks achieved with regard to the Orient – and thus to find finally that, which is "German"' ('So gelingt vielleicht den Deutschen noch, was den Griechen in Betreff des Orients gelang – und so das, was "deutsch" ist, erst zu finden,' 29[191], KSA 7.708).

Towards the end of *On the Use and Disadvantage of History for Life*, this new, learning relationship with foreign cultures, whereby one tries to 'soak up' all 'living education' is explained in more detail. One must control the foreign input in order not to be overwhelmed[13] by way of waging a 'war with oneself' ('*Kampf mit sichselbst,*' HL 10, KSA 1.333), i.e., organizing the chaos of impulses and stimuli and create 'a unity of style' out of it. Once the Greeks were successful in doing so, i.e., conquering (soaking up and organizing) the oriental influences (in a unity of style), they were 'the happiest enrichers and increasers of the inherited treasures and the firstlings and paradigms of all next cultures' ('die glücklichsten Bereicherer und Mehrer des ererbten Schatzen

---

13 Nietzsche speaks of '*Ueberschwemmung durch das Fremde*' (KSA 1.333).

und die Erstlinge und Vorbilder aller kommenden Cultur,' HL 10, KSA 1.333). The Greek 'cosmopolitan tendency' is thus a precondition to artistic excellence and cultural development. At the time, due to this active implementation and integration of various cultural characteristics in a 'mix of cultures', the 'amalgamation of nations' into one Europe, one style, found a place in Greece:

> The Greek [spirit] was the first great bond and synthesis of all Western spirits and for that very reason the beginning of the European soul. (41[7], KSA 11.682)

> das Griechische war die erste große Bindung und Synthesis alles Morgenländischen und eben damit der Anfang der europäischen Seele.

Hence, Nietzsche still advocates humanity's and culture's 'Graecization', but it now means that one should learn from the cultural highlights of the past and one's culturally successful neighbours instead of creating art works out of some natural and spontaneous bent: 'We should learn in the way the Greeks have learned from their pasts and neighbours' ('Wir sollen so lernen, wie die Griechen von ihrer Vergangenheiten und Nachbarn lernten,' 19[196], KSA 7.479). What we need to learn is: 'Not to create forms but to borrow them from abroad and transform them into the fairest appearance of beauty – that is Greek' (AOM 221, p. 266/'Die Formen aus der Fremde entlehnen, [...] zum schönsten Schein umbilden – das ist griechisch [...],' KSA 2.474). However, it is a choice for the 'surface *out of profundity!*' (GS Preface 4, p. 9/'Diese Griechen waren oberflächlich – *aus Tiefe*,' KSA 3.352) Art is not a matter of genius, but of hard work – as we shall also see in chapter 6.

The idea that the Greeks were Greek because they adopted artistic forms from strangers and created something better out of it led Nietzsche to the idea that every culture that aims to reach the height of its powers has the task of superseding the Greeks: 'To overcome Greek culture in practice would be the task' ('Das Griechenthum durch die Tat zu überwinden wäre die Aufgabe,' 5[167], KSA 8.88–89). That would only be possible by studying how the Greeks related to their pasts and neighbours, and this relation is one of rivalry and mastery. Nietzsche speaks of the 'study of COMPETITION' ('*Studium des WETTEIFERS*,' 5[167], KSA 8.88–89) Every person with artistic ambition should study the Greek way of learning, i.e., of being students, who strive to master the master. But how do we recognize our master? According to Nietzsche, it is easy to understand who one's 'master' is: 'just what provokes imitation, what is captured with love and what desires reproduction, should be studied' ('nur was zur Nachahmung reizt, was mit Liebe ergriffen wird und fortzuzeugen verlangt, soll studirt werden,' 5[171], KSA 8.89–90). Goethe had understood this: 'In that way Goethe understood ancient culture: always with a competitive soul' ('In der Art hat Goethe das Alterthum ergriffen: immer mit wetteifernder Seele,' 5[172], KSA 8.90).[14] And because he had understood this, strove to imitate and renew Greek tragedy and wandered through Italy with such a loving and competitive soul, Nietzsche takes him as his new model of the Greek way of life, his master in 'Graecization' and 'good Europeanism' – as we shall see in chapter 7.

Goethe's and Schiller's cosmopolitanism

Reflecting on the idea of learning from foreign cultures in the summer of 1872, Nietzsche also turns to Goethe and Schiller. Let us recall that in *The Birth of Tragedy* the failure of German Classicism to grasp the tragic nature of the Greeks was discussed, in the context of Nietzsche's discussion of what his modern-day people could and should learn from the Greeks, how they, in fact, could 'Graecize'. He valued the fact that German Classicism had tried to interact with the Greek past highly. The beginning of chapter 20, which I quoted in the former chapter, seems visionary. In the summer of 1872, so it appears, Nietzsche had weighed out 'through which men the German spirit had striven most vigorously to learn from the Greeks' and had come to the conclusion that Goethe, Schiller, and Winckelmann – not Wagner – had achieved the correct kind of 'self-cultivation'.

His faith that Germans share the 'impulse for the imitation of what is foreign' ('*Nachahmungstrieb des Auslandes*,' 19[261], KSA 7.501)[15] is unbroken. Yet, Nietzsche's new ideal chooses the 'cosmopolitan road to culture' ('*kosmopolitischer Weg zur Cultur*', 19[255], KSA 7.499),[16] following 'Schiller and Goethe's contest' ('*Schiller's and Goethe's Ringen*', KSA 7.499).[17] Their contest is similar to the Greeks' contest for culture in the sense that both are characterized by 'learning from foreign countries' ('*lernen vom Auslande*', KSA 7.499). The 'political fever' ('*politische Fieber*', 19[272], KSA 7.504) that emphasizes 'what is national' ('*das Nationale*', KSA 7.499) is diametrically opposed to this Greek, Schillerian, and Goethean way of learning, according to Nietzsche: 'Schiller's and Goethe's cosmopolitan tendency corresponding to the [Greek, MP] oriental tendency' ('Der kosmopolitische Tendenz Schillers und Goethes entsprechend

---

14 In TI 'What I Owe to the Ancients' 4, Nietzsche claims that Goethe did not understand the Greeks. Bishop points to the fact that this remark only applies to Goethe's exclusion of the 'orgiastic' from his image of the Greeks (Bishop 2004, p. 455). Indeed, Nietzsche still takes Goethe as the personification of the kind of sensualism he is looking for, against Christianity, Cartesianism, and Wagner's '*Halb-Kirchlichkeit*'. As he writes elsewhere in TI: 'Goethe is the last German for whom I feel any reverence: he would also have felt three things which I feel – and we also understand each other about the "cross"' (TI Skirmishes 51, p. 223/'Goethe ist der letzte Deutsche, vor dem ich Ehrfurcht habe: er hätte drei Dinge empfunden, die ich empfinde, – auch verstehen wir uns über das "Kreuz",' KSA 6.153).

15 Cf. 19[289], KSA 7.509.

16 Cf. 19[298], KSA 7.511.

17 Cf. 19[270], KSA 7.503 and Goethe to Eckermann (1984), 14 March 1830, pp. 292–293.

der orientalischen Tendenz', 19[284], KSA 7.508). The 'cosmopolitan tendency' ('*kos-mopolitische Tendenz*', 19[274], KSA 7.505) is 'necessary' ('*nothwendig*', KSA 7.499) as a continuation of the artistic 'reformation' ('*Reformationsarbeit*', KSA 7.499). Germany will not be an educated culture unless it creates an artistic style of its own, which is anti-naturalistic, mythical, musical, symbolical, and 'vivid' in the sense of 'unhistorical' or 'untimely'. This can only be achieved by turning to cultures, which have or had such art: 'education not on a national basis, however education of what is German' ('Bildung nicht auf nationaler Grundlage, sondern Bildung des Deutschen', 19[284], KSA 7.508).[18]

Nietzsche urges that a 'cosmopolitan tendency' is necessary in order to continue this cultural reformation. The purpose of the reformation is to form a national style, however, not on a national basis, for there was no such a thing as a 'German culture' yet. In order to form a national style, the Germans have to turn to other cultures, nations and style-periods in European history. This (re-) formation or '*Bildung*' is, according to Nietzsche, 'the life of a people under an artistic regime' ('Bildung ist das Leben eines Volkes unter dem Regiment der Kunst', 19[295], KSA 7.510). To come to such a formation and unification of style, people have to understand that it is absurd to talk of 'National-Germans' ('*National-Deutschen*', 19[298], KSA 7.511). A culture is only 'healthy' when formed through soaking up the 'living education' provided by other nations.

Nietzsche's plea for this 'Greek', 'Schillerian', and 'Goethean' form of cosmopolitanism is the plea for reaching out to other cultures as a means to overcome the self and grow. The active appropriation of strange, new things, the '*Aneignung des Frem-den*', is the basic element for this.[19] While Wagner was growing more and more into a 'National-German', Nietzsche became more and more cosmopolitan, developing this plea for 'Graecization' and 'southernization' as ways to 'aestheticize' into the plea to adopt the Greek and Goethean 'cosmopolitan tendency' as a way to 'de-Germanize' and become a 'good European' and 'mix of cultures'.

Adding this to Nietzsche's tragic pessimism versus Wagner's humanistic or Rousseauian optimism, and their different musical views (the central role of the orchestra in Wagner's symphonic view of music drama versus Nietzsche's preference for the chorus as the central element of tragedy or music drama), it becomes apparent that there were not only psychological reasons for the friends to grow apart, but also aesthetic and political ones. The differences in their philosophies and aesthetics, already apparent in 1871, and pre-sensed in 1870 by Nietzsche, became insurmount-

---

18 Cf. 19[285], KSA 7.508 and 19[295], KSA 7.510.
19 Cf. Stephenson (1993); Riedel (1992) speaks of 'the typical order of kinship for the Greeks is the exotic and its appropriation and vindication' ('die für das Griechentum so typische Ordnung der Verwandtschaft mit dem Fremden, dessen Aneignung und Überwindung', p. 219). Compare Orsucci (1996, pp. 116–121) for Müllenhoff's influence on Nietzsche in this matter.

able in 1874. This was not so much because of the Brahms incident, but because of Nietzsche's growing doubt regarding Wagner's Bayreuther theatre plan, in the first months of 1874, as I show below. *Parsifal*, generally viewed as the great malefactor and cause of the Nietzsche-Wagner break, was rather the last drop that triggered Nietzsche to ventilate his smouldering criticism and make his aversion a public matter. That Wagner was not a truly aesthetic, amoral, and tragic artist was something Nietzsche had been sensing for a long time.

Wagner's idyllic tendency reconsidered

Nietzsche received the *Parsifal* libretto in January of 1878.[20] A few days earlier, he had sent the *Mastersinger* score (which Richard Wagner had given to him for Christmas of 1869) to his friend Paul Widemann, dedicating it to him with the following remarkable wish:

> May this excellent friend always be aware that I shall remain faithful in my hopes of his capabilities and his art, in my belief in his great powers, his originality, and his perseverance. The day will come that all beliefs and hopes will be fulfilled.[21]

> Möge der treffliche Freund sich immer dessen bewußt sein, daß ich treu in der Hoffnung auf sein Können und seine Kunst, treu im Glauben an seine große Kraft, Erfindungsgabe und Ausdauer bleiben werde. Ja, einst kommt der Tag, wo alles Geglaubte und Gehoffte sich erfüllt hat.

The tone Nietzsche used to Paul Widemann was the same idolizing tone he had so often exercised with Wagner, as if Widemann would just easily substitute Wagner. The letter he sent to Heinrich Köselitz together with the *Tristan* score on the same day is testimony to Nietzsche's awareness that his Wagnerism has definitively ended. Although it does not have the high tone he used with Wagner and Widemann (which perhaps was so ineffective because it was seasoned with an air of defensiveness, politeness, and ineptness), it expresses hopes of Köselitz's musical talent just as well:

---

20 Nietzsche sent *Human, All Too Human* to Richard and Cosima Wagner in January 1878, around the time he received the *Parsifal* libretto (Cf. Nietzsche to Köselitz, 1 January 1878, KSB 5, pp. 297–298; Nietzsche to Richard and Cosima Wagner, begin January 1878, KSB 5, pp. 298–299. Nietzsche to Ernst Schmeitzer, 28 January 1878, KSB 5, p. 301). Nietzsche regarded this coincidence as a fate and described the event as 'the crossing of swords'. Richard Wagner reacted to *Human, All Too Human* with his article 'Public and Popularity' ('Publikum und Popularität,' *Bayreuther Blätter*, August 1878) with several very low remarks, e.g., on philosophers with bad eyesight. Nietzsche then planned to write a reaction 'Announcement to my Friends' ('Mittheilung an meine Freunde'), parodying an essay by Wagner with this title. This essay was never written, but notes for it appeared in *Assorted Opinions and Maxims*. See also Montinari (1985).
21 Benders (2000), pp. 420–421.

This score will be more fruitful in your hands, my dear friend Köselitz, than in mine. Since it has long desired a nobler owner and younger fellow of art than I am, in the event that some of the soul of the great man that gave it to me has remained stuck to it. What I wish of you will be mainly the same as what you desire from yourself; it is enough that I think of you rather often talking in a Goethe-Faustian manner:

"this earthly life/"does still allow space for great deeds./"amazing things should happen,/"I feel power to courageous diligence."[22]

Diese Partitur wird fruchtbringender in Ihren Händen sein, mein lieber Freund Köselitz, als in den meinen, sie sehnt sich gewiss längst nach einem würdigen Besitzer und Jünger der Kunst als ich es bin, im Fall etwas von der Seele des grossen Mannes, der sie mir gab, daran hängen geblieben ist. Was ich von Ihnen wünsche, wird wohl in der Hauptsache dasselbe sein, was Sie von Sich wünschen; genug dass ich Sie mir öfter Goethe-Faustisch redend denke:

"– dieser Erdenkreis/"Gewährt noch Raum zu grossen Thaten./"Erstaunenswürdiges soll gerathen,/"Ich fühle Kraft zu kühnem Fleiss."

The wish expressed to Widemann and the letter to Köselitz suggest that Nietzsche anticipated a break with Wagner, but that he had not given up his belief in 'great deeds', art that might evolve into the desired cultural uplift. He may have seriously thought, for a moment, that these two young composers were the ones that would do that. At least, as we shall see in chapter 6, this is what he strongly hoped of Köselitz's music.

By coincidence, Nietzsche received the *Parsifal* libretto at the beginning of January of 1878, just after he had sent Wagner his *Human, All Too Human*. In a draft letter to the Wagners, he wrote about this book:

This book is mine: in it, I have brought to light my deepest understanding of men and things and, for the first time, wandered the periphery of my own thinking. In times, which were filled with Paros<ismus> and ailments, this book gave me the consolation, which did not fall short, where all other means of comfort failed.[23]

Dies Buch ist von mir: ich habe meine innerste Empfind<ung> über Menschen und Dinge darin ans Licht gebracht und zum ersten Male die Peripher meines eigenen Denkens umlaufen. In Zeiten, welche voller Paros<ismus> und Qualen waren, war dies Buch mein Trostmittel, welches nicht versagte, wo alle anderen Trostm<ittel> versagten.

In addition:

Although I do not know anyone, as already said, who is still my soul mate, I do have the imagination not to have thought as an individual but as a collective – the strangest feeling of solitude and multiplicity. (KSB 5.299)

---

22 1 January 1878 (KSB 5, pp. 297–298).
23 KSB 5, pp. 298–299. '*Parosismus*', or '*paroxismus*' is a medical term for 'attack' or 'seizure'.

> Obschon ich wie gesagt niemanden kenne, der jetzt noch mein Gesinnungsgenosse ist, habe ich doch die Einbildung, nicht als Individuum sondern als Collektivum gedacht zu haben – das sonderbarste Gefühl von Einsamkeit und Vielsamkeit.

His remark that he had been in dialogue with a collective of voices is interesting with regard to Nietzsche's later idea that the self is a collective of clashing wills to power, which echoes his idea that the self must wage a war with itself in order to create a unity of style out of the chaos of foreign impulses. It also anticipates Nietzsche's later idea that solitude is a necessary precondition to come to his true philosophy.

Nietzsche had perhaps lost his soul mate in Wagner, but he kept him in his life as his principal enemy. About *Parsifal* he wrote to Reinhard von Seydlitz, also in the first week of January 1878:

> Yesterday the *Parsifal* arrived in my house, sent by Wagner. Impression of first reading: more Liszt than Wagner, spirit of Counter-reformation [...] much too much blood [...]. All these beautiful findings belong in an Epos [...]. The language sounds like a translation from a foreign language.[24]

> Gestern kam, von Wagner gesandt, der Parsifal in mein Haus. Eindruk des erstens Lesens: mehr Liszt, als Wagner, Geist der Gegenreformation [...] viel zu viel Blut [...] Alle diese schöne Erfindungen gehören in's Epos [...]. Dies Sprache klingt wie eine übersetzung aus einer fremden Zunge [...].

From then on, Nietzsche's continuing 'cultural war' implied the explicit opposition to Wagner. While he had combated French culture and Italian music with Wagner before, he openly battled German culture and Wagner's German music with the help of French philosophy and Italian music afterwards. This begs the question as to what extent Nietzsche's new preference for things French and Italian is genuine. Manfred Eger (2001) goes so far as to categorize Nietzsche as 'the Karl May amongst philosophers' ('den Karl May unter den Philosophen,') and his oeuvre 'a high-ranked counterweight to the *Reader's Digest*' ('ein hochrangiges Pendant zu *Reader's Digest*').[25] He counters Nietzsche's condemnations of Wagner as a 'stage-actor' ('*Schauspieler*') with the phrase that 'the true actor – for example – is not Wagner, but the lifelong self-exposing Nietzsche' ('Der eigentliche Schauspieler – zum Beispiel – ist nicht Wagner, sondern der lebenslängliche Selbstdarsteller Nietzsche'). Eger exaggerates and argues largely psychologically, but he has a point; the question of how genuine Nietzsche's harsh repudiation of Wagner was, is indeed justified. However, when one looks at it from a philosophical way rather than (only) a psychological one, Nietzsche's strict rejection of Wagner's music and personality are much more understandable and convincing.

What, eventually, made Nietzsche turn into the ardent anti-Wagnerian individual he openly became from the beginning of 1878 onwards? What pushed him from en-

---

24 4 January 1878, KSB 5, p. 300.
25 Eger (2001), p. 11.

thusiasm to rejection? Which philosophical reasons can be pointed out to explain the shift from 'secret scepticism' to public opposition? Wagner assumed that the break was caused by a clash between the friends over Brahms's *Victory-Song* (*Triumphlied*), in August of 1874.[26] Nietzsche had inflamed Wagner with anger by insisting on playing Brahms's music to him, escaping the room when Wagner burst out in fury because the professor dared to praise his enemy. However, this is not a sufficient explanation for Nietzsche's aggressive anti-Wagnerism. And indeed, Cosima and Richard Wagner have never really grasped the reasons for their young friend's change of heart.

An overlooked, yet decisive reason may reside in Nietzsche's growing doubt over Wagner's Bayreuth-plan in the first months of 1874. The notes in KSA 7 collected under '32' and '33', partly written for 'Richard Wagner in Bayreuth' (only written and published in 1876), bear witness to this.[27] In letters to von Meysenbug, Rohde, and von Gersdorff, Nietzsche mentions that he has been contemplating why Wagner's theatre is not getting off the ground. To Malwida von Meysenbug he remarks that 'our hopes have been too high!' ('unsere Hoffnungen waren zu groß!')[28] To Rohde, he writes:

> I started to prove the hypothesis why the enterprise would fail with greatest coldness: this taught me a lot and I believe that I understand Wagner much better now than before. And even if the 'wonder' [that the enterprise will take place, MP] is true, then this would still not overthrow the conclusion of my contemplations.[29]

> Ich begann mit der grössten Kälte der Betrachtung zu untersuchen, weshalb das Unternehmen misslungen sei: dabei habe ich viel gelernt und glaube jetzt Wagner viel besser zu verstehen als früher. Ist das 'Wunder' [that the enterprise will take place, MP] wahr, so wirft es das Resultat meiner Betrachtungen nicht um.

It is frankly suggested that, even if the festival will take place in the future, Nietzsche's changed opinion about Wagner will hold, for he understood the composer's personality much better than before, having analysed him regardless of his heartfelt friendship.[30] A letter to Carl von Gersdorff, written about a fortnight later, reveals that the

---

26 See Benders (2000), pp. 322–323.

27 The notes under '33' are revisions of the notes packed in '32', as if Nietzsche was preparing to publish a critical series of aphorisms on Wagner. These notes are generally seen as preparation for 'Richard Wagner in Bayreuth', but that essay only came out in July of 1876 and contains much more concealed criticism of Wagner. Incidentally, Nietzsche again reflected on Wagner by harking back to Goethe and Schiller, in these notes.

28 Nietzsche to Malwida von Meysenbug, 11 February 1874 (KSB 5, pp. 198–199). Cf. Nietzsche to Carl von Gersdorff, 18 January 1874 (KSB 4, pp. 192–194). In the same letter he offers Gersdorff his copy of the *Tannhäuser* text.

29 15 February 1874 (KSB 5, pp. 201–203).

30 Also to Rohde he declares, after having understood that the 'wonder' will happen after all, that he had already 'completely given up hope' ('die Hoffnung ganz aufgegeben,' Nietzsche to Rohde, 19 March 1874, KSB 5, p. 209).

plans for the first Bayreuther festival have indeed not affected the conclusion of his contemplations.[31] As part of his intended untimely meditation, *Richard Wagner in Bayreuth*, note 32[18] (KSA 7.760–761) lists the reasons why the project failed. Interestingly, external factors such as a lack of money are hardly mentioned.[32] By contrast, Nietzsche's cold contemplation is a ruthless exploration of Wagner's character and creativity, leading to positive *and* negative evaluations. Consider the following ruthless stipulations: Wagner is 'a misplaced actor' (*'ein versetzter Schauspieler,'* 32[8], KSA 7.756); 'nature' to Wagner is 'crapulence and boundlessness' (*'Unmässigkeit und Schrankenlosigkeit,'* 32[10], KSA 7.756);[33] he did not understand that music and drama do not stem from the same source and therefore blamed the public for not understanding him;[34] that he is good in the great gestures, but not in the details (32[14], KSA 7.757),[35] and, one of the most fatal expressions: 'None of our great musicians was such a bad musician as Wagner at the age of twenty-eight' ('Keiner unserer grossen Musiker war in seinem 28ten Jahr ein noch so schlechter Musiker wie Wagner'), adding that 'Wagner's youth was the youth of a many-sided dilettante' ('die Jugend Wagner's [sic] ist die eines vielseitigen Dilettanten,' 32[15], KSA 7.759).[36]

To say that Wagner was still a bad musician at twenty-eight (Wagner produced his first significant piece of work at that age, an age at which Mozart and Schubert had already written the bulk of their best works), implies that he has learned a lot between 1839 (when Wagner was twenty-eight) and 1874 (when he was sixty-one, thus in a period of thirty-five years) and that he had to learn a lot in order to come this far. Thus, Wagner is not a genius by nature. In fact, he is the least brilliant of all German composers. Nietzsche goes even further when he admits: 'I have often doubted, nonsensically, whether Wagner had musical talent' ('Ich habe oft unsinniger Weise bezweifelt, ob Wagner musikalische Begabung habe,' 32[15], KSA 7.759)[37] and repeats, 'he approaches music like an actor' ('er steht zur Musik wie ein Schauspieler,' 32[24], KSA 7.762).

The suggestion that Wagner is not a genius, but an imitator and *'Schauspieler'*, has an enormous impact on Nietzsche's further analysis of Wagner's creativity. Nietzsche concludes that his works do not originate in the inner dream visions produced by the

---

31 On 1 April 1874 (KSB 5, p. 215).

32 They are mentioned in 32[28], KSA 7.763. However, in the same note the main issue is named that Wagner's art does not suit the social and working relationships in Germany, or as he explains in 32[29], Wagner is not modest enough for the German people (KSA 7.763).

33 See also 32[15], KSA 7.758 and 33[11], KSA 7.790.

34 See 32[9], KSA 7.756 and 32[11], KSA 7.757.

35 Cf. GS 87 (pp. 87–88/KSA 3.444–445).

36 Cf. 33[13], KSA 7.791 and 33[15], KSA 7.791.

37 Cf. 32[20], KSA 7.761 and 33[15], KSA 7.791. Nietzsche compares Wagner with Goethe in this respect. Goethe was a painter at heart, but became a writer, because he did not have the 'hands' of a painter. And so Wagner is an actor, using his natural talent for acting in music. See also 33[1], KSA 7.787.

unconscious and the *'Gestaltenspiel'* that the dreamer plays with the eccentric, giant figures of his dreams. As such, he undermines the central theory that he and Wagner shared with regard to the unique creativity of Shakespeare, Beethoven, and Wagner. As a result, we must conclude that Wagner is unsuccessful in his attempt to create total artworks tapping from the same source as Shakespeare and Beethoven, to wit the inner dream visions. His works stem from a different source and therefore cannot be the perfection of the symphonic tradition set by Beethoven and continued by Liszt.

This disenchanting condemnation is underlined by his conclusion that *Tannhäuser* is idyllic. First, he wonders how one and the same person can make operas as different in style as *Tannhäuser* and *The Mastersingers*, the former being ecstatic and chaotic, the latter showing self-restraint: 'he is greater in that [in self-restraint, MP] than in ecstatically letting himself go. Restraint looks good on him' ('er ist darin [in Selbtbeherrschung, MP] grösser als in dem ekstatischen Sichgehenlassen. Die Beschränkung steht ihm wohl,' 32[15], KSA 7.759).[38] Then he states that Wagner projects his own bad habits onto Modernity, especially his idyllic belief that nature is good: 'He discharges his weaknesses by ascribing them to modernity: natural belief in the goodness of nature, as long as nature dwells freely' ('Er entladet sich seiner Schwächen, dadurch dass er sie der modernen Zeit zuschiebt: natürlicher Glaube an die Güte der Natur, wenn sie frei waltet,' 32[15], KSA 7.759).[39] In so doing, he connects Wagner's early opera *Tannhäuser* with Rousseau's 'natural man' and the 'goodness of nature,'[40] implying that Wagner's view of nature is not tragic, but idyllic. This insight is, of course, not new, because Nietzsche was already aware of this in 1871, as demonstrated in chapter 3. This time, however, his analysis of Wagner has a much more pejorative and judgmental tone than in 1871 – indeed, a tone that bears more resemblance to *The Case of Wagner*, as is also shown by Nietzsche's judgment that Wagner's art is theatrical and vulgar, and therefore uncivil.[41]

It does not end there; he denies Wagner's 'Beethoven' by stating that one cannot expect an artist to be as pure as Luther, but that, nevertheless, Bach and Beethoven are purer than Wagner, because ecstasy in the latter's art is often violent and too sharp, born from the desire to impress, to stir emotions in order to cause as much effect as possible.[42] Again, this is not a new insight, as Nietzsche had already stated this too, in 1871, as we have seen. Yet, in portraying the composer as *idyllic, artificial*, and focused on stirring *effect*, the conclusion once again must be that Wagner is not a Dionysian artist. On the contrary, he is, as the philistine people that crowd Europe and Germany

---

38 Cf. 33[14], KSA 7.791.
39 Cf. 32[33], KSA 7.765.
40 Cf. 33[14], KSA 7.791 and 33[16], KSA 7.791.
41 32[22], KSA 7.761.
42 32[25, 26], KSA 7.762.

in particular, 'powerless' or 'incompetent' in matters of art (*'kunstohnmächtige Menschen,'* 9[9], KSA 7.274).

Overall, Wagner's music does not possess the 'German talent' (*'germanische Begabung'*, 9[10], KSA 7.275) to raise the Dionysian spirit and the 'artistic view of life, myth' (*'künstlerische Weltbetrachtung, den Mythus'*, 9[10], KSA 7.274). In addition, it does not reach the depth and tragic joy that Beethoven provoked with the choral finale. It does not unite people; it does not transform the critical, morally judging public into aesthetic beholders. In brief: 'Wagner is not a reformer, since until now everything has remained the same' ('Reformator ist Wagner nicht, denn bis jetzt ist Alles beim Alten geblieben', 32[28], KSA 7.763). Nietzsche also sees that Wagner is not honest in the sense that he lacks self-criticism[43] with the result that he not only blames others (Nietzsche mentions Jews[44]) for whatever goes wrong, but reigns like a tyrant, surrounding himself with luxury goods and uncritical Yes-men.

In sum, there are multiple problems that ground Nietzsche's (in hindsight: wrongly) anticipated failure of Bayreuth: his dominant, at times despotic character; his idyllic view of nature; his focus on dramatic effect, for which reason the drama rules the music instead of the other way round.[45] These were not new insights, but Nietzsche formulates them in a much stronger and pejorative fashion, leaning to the rethoric of *The Case of Wagner*. What is new, and a turning point in his musical aesthetics, is Nietzsche's view that the history of German music owed its fame and strength to the adoption of foreign forms, more precisely *Italian forms*. Where part of *Tristan and Isolde* and even *The Mastersingers* fail due to a lack of 'measure' and 'unstylized nature', Beethoven and Mozart have overcome the 'rural-petty boorishness' (*'bäuerlich-bürgerlichen Rüpelei,'* 32[43], KSA 7.767) thanks to the richness and refinement of the Italian forms they incorporated in their works. In light of the above, we may explain their successes as the result of their 'cosmopolitan tendency'. Wagner, on the other hand, had remained 'German', and Germans are not able to understand opera, unless they 'de-Germanize':

> There is no doubt that Wagner would have achieved his goal if he had been Italian. The German person does not respect opera and considers opera as imported and non-German. (32[61], KSA 7.775)

> Es ist wohl kein Zweifel, dass Wagner als Italiäner sein Ziel erreicht haben würde. Der Deutsche hat keine Achtung vor der Oper und betrachtet sie immer als importirt und als undeutsch.

Soon after writing these anti-Wagnerian notes, Nietzsche explains to Emma Guerrieri-Gonzaga: 'I do not know a higher goal than to become a "teacher" in a truly great man-

---

43 32[33], KSA 7.765.
44 32[32], KSA 7.765.
45 32[52], KSA 7.770. Cf. 32[42, 43], KSA 7.767.

ner, someday; just that I am very far from this goal now' ('Ich kenne auch für mich kein höheres Ziel, als irgend wie einmal "Erzieher" in einem grossen Sinne zu werden: nur dass ich sehr weit von diesem Ziele bin').[46] To this, he adds that becoming free requires 'self-education' and the liberation of unproductive negativity. It is no coincidence that he mentions his great example in this, Goethe, only a few lines later. Could it be that Nietzsche, expressing that he is far from being the teacher he aspired to be, is thinking of his failure to educate Wagner? And is this one reason more for him to conclude that one can only educate oneself?

Nietzsche's shock about Wagner's Germanization: the first Bayreuth festival

As I suggested in the former chapter, Nietzsche's Wagner-enthusiasm in *The Birth of Tragedy* was partly based on Nietzsche's trust in his own teaching abilities. The Bayreuth festival of 1876 must have shown Nietzsche that he had failed in his task of teaching Wagner how to '*Graecize*' and 'southernize'. In lobbying for sponsors and associating with the VIPs, Wagner must have appeared as commercial and superficial as the artists he was supposed to compete, and thus as a philistine rather than the Dionysian artist desribed in *The Birth of Tragedy*. If so, then Nietzsche must have understood that his lessons on Ancient Greek culture had failed, as his essays were never only written out of historical interest, but also in order to instruct practically on what was needed to develop culture for the future.[47]

Let me sum up. First, his ears did not appreciate the music; second, Wagner was mainly busy pleasing would-be sponsors instead of leading the Dionysian *komos* consisting of Nietzsche, Rohde, and Gersdorff;[48] third, the Wagnerian public present at the event was there with the purpose to be seen, to parade, and to network rather than to experience a modern form of the Dionysian celebration of life; fourth, Wagner revealed his *Parsifal* plans to Nietzsche; five: Wagner had become more and more 'German' in the philistine sense of 'political nationalist'; the composer had switched from cosmopolitanism to nationalism. In addition, Wagner was quite openly practising his love-affair with Judith Gaultier, placing her on the seat next to his. This may have been disturbing to Nietzsche, given his high estimation of Cosima. Hence, the whole atmosphere at the festival expressed seamlessly the philistinism Nietzsche detested:

> The beginnings of this book [*Human, All Too Human*, MP] belong in the middle of the first Bayreuth festival; it presupposes a deep sense of alienation from everything around me there [...]. *What had*

---

46 10 May 1874 (KSB 5, p. 224).
47 Cf. Winteler (2011), p. 266.
48 See 13[2], KSA 7.372, where Nietzsche describes his hopes of Bayreuth as the place where tragic human beings will celebrate their feast of consecration as a sign that a new culture begins.

happened? – Wagner had been translated into German! [...] We who are different, we know all too well the sort of refined artists, the sort of cosmopolitanism Wagner's taste is aimed at, we were beside ourselves when we found Wagner decked out in German 'virtues'. (EH HH 2, pp. 116–117)

Die Anfänge dieses Buchs [*Menschliches, Allzumenschliches*, MP] gehören mitten in die Wochen der ersten Bayreuther Festspiele hinein; eine tiefe Fremdheit gegen Alles, was mich dort um- gab, ist eine seiner Voraussetzungen. [...] *Was war geschehn?* – Man hatte Wagner ins Deutsche übersetzt! [...] Wir Andern, die nur zu gut wissen, zu was für raffinirten Artisten, zu welchem Cosmopolitismus des Geschmacks Wagners Kunst allein redet, waren ausser uns, Wagner mit deutschen 'Tugenden' behängt wiederzufinden. (KSA 6. 323–324)

Nietzsche summarizes the shock he experienced at the first Bayreuth festival as caused by the sudden Germanization of Wagner's art, which had been, until then, always cos- mopolitan in taste – as he knew only too well. Indeed, as we saw at the beginning of this chapter, Nietzsche had always venerated Wagner as a foreign country and a Euro- pean event. It was exactly this *foreignness*, this cosmopolitan spirit of Wagner, which he admired most about him:

I do not have any reasons, just a contemptuous scowl, for Wagnerians *et hoc genus omne* who think that they are honouring Wagner by saying how similar he is to *themselves*... Being what I am, with my deepest instincts foreign to anything German [...] my first contact with Wagner was also the first time in my life I was really able to breathe freely: I saw him, I worshipped him as a *foreign country*, as the opposite of – a living protest against – all "German virtues" [...]; the *délicatesse* that Wagner's art presupposes, the finger for nuances, the psychological morbidity, you only find these in Paris (EH 'Clever' 5, p. 92)

ich habe keine Gründe, ich habe bloss einen verachtenden Mundwinkel gegen Wagnerianer et hoc genus omne übrig, welche Wagner damit zu ehren glauben, dass sie ihn *sich* ähnlich find- en... So wie ich bin, in meinen tiefsten Instinkten Allem, was deutsch ist, fremd [...] war die erste Berührung mit Wagner auch das erste Aufathmen in meinem Leben: ich empfand, ich verehrte ihn als *Ausland*, als Gegensatz, als leibhaften Protest gegen alle "deutschen Tugenden" [...] die délicatesse in allen fünf Kunstsinnen, die Wagner's Kunst voraussetzt, die Finger für nuances, die psychologische Morbidität, findet sich nur in Paris, (KSA 6.388)

At the festival, however, the great composer appeared as one of the provincial 'stupid brothers in Wagnero'. On top of his provincialism, he turned out to be 'pious' (EH HH 5, p. 119/'*fromm*', KSA 6.327) too – as the *Parsifal* plans, unfolded to Nietzsche at the fes- tival, showed. To Nietzsche, the true aestheticist and tragic artist is not only a sen- sualist ('immoral', ' beyond good and evil'), but also a cosmopolitan. Henceforth, it was confirmed to Nietzsche once and for all that Wagner was no longer the (possi- ble) 'physician', but one of the 'symptoms' of modern, sick, and decadent culture. All things considered, 'Bayreuth' was the visible, dramatic expression of what Nietzsche had been suspecting for a long time. It was not the birthplace of a new German and European cultural highlight that would 'deprave the jungle of paradise lost'. Instead, it was the culmination of philistinism, of the anti-aesthetic.

After repudiating Wagner, Nietzsche felt as if on top of a mountain, in 'high air' ('*Höhenluft*'),[49] from where he looked down upon his old beliefs and the people of his past, who still believed in those things, while he could finally develop his own thoughts: 'how myself I am at the moment, living in the pursuit of knowledge in the smallest things, while before I only adored and idolized the wise men' ('wie ich jetzt selber bin in's Kleinste, nach Weisheit strebend lebe, während ich früher nur die Weisen verehrte und anschwärmte').[50] By this he means: 'now I dare to pursue wisdom myself, and be a philosopher myself; before I worshipped the philosophers' ('jetzt wage ich es, der Weisheit selber nachzugehen und selber Philosoph zu sein; früher verehrte ich die Philosophen').[51] It seems that Nietzsche after and through his break with Wagner, was finally ready to give birth to the centaurs as an independent philosopher, as he had predicted to Erwin Rohde in February 1870, – in the same letter in which he had expressed his first doubt about the composer. To Mathilde Maier, Nietzsche confessed why and when he had come to the view that he had to develop his own philosophy:

> During the summer in Bayreuth, I became fully aware of this: I escaped into the mountains after the first rehearsals I attended, and there, in a small village in the woods, I made the first drafts, around a third of my book [*Human, All Too Human I*], then under the title "the ploughshare".[52]

> Im Bayreuther Sommer wurde ich mir dessen völlig bewußt: ich flüchtete nach den ersten Aufführungen denen ich beiwohnte, fort in's Gebirge, und dort in einem kleinen Walddorfe, entstand die erste Skizze, ungefähr ein Drittel meines Buches [*Menschliches Allzumenschliches I*], damals unter dem Titel "die Pflugschar".

The Ploughshare became the book now known as *Human, All Too Human*. It meant a radical break with Nietzsche's early philosophy and aesthetics. In the following chapter, I delineate Nietzsche's new musical aesthetics, and in chapter 7, the last chapter of this book, its relation to his new, 'healthy' philosophy of culture and ideal of Europe. According to this new philosophy, the free spirit transforms itself into a cosmopolitan 'good European'. For this, he must travel to other, European countries. With this in mind, Nietzsche designed his free spirit books *Human, All Too Human I* and *II*, *Daybreak*, and *The Gay Science* as travel books.

---

49 See 13[2], KSA 7.372. Cf. Nietzsche to Carl Fuchs, June 1878 (KSB 5, p. 335).
50 See 13[2], KSA 7.372
51 Nietzsche to Carl Fuchs, End of June 1878 (KSB 5, p. 335).
52 To Mathilde Maier, 15 July 1878 (KSB 5, p. 338). Nietzsche later claimed that Wagner saw him as 'an enemy' since 1876, i.e., since the first Bayreuther festival (Nietzsche to Ferdinand Avenarius, 10 December 1888, KSB 8, p. 517).

'De-Germanization': Free spirit books as travel books and 'precepts of health'

The free spirit books can be characterized as anti-German, anti-philistine, and cosmopolitan books, given their propagation of a Europe consisting of cosmopolitan and sensualist 'free spirits':

> That free spirits of this kind *could* one day exist, that our Europe *will* have such active and audacious fellows among its sons of tomorrow and the next day, physically present and palpable [...] *I* should wish to be the last to doubt it (HH I Preface 2, p. 6)

> Dass es dergleichen freie Geister einmal geben *könnte*, dass unser Europa unter seinen Söhnen von Morgen und Uebermorgen solche muntere und verwegene Gesellen haben wird, leibhaft und handgreiflich [...] daran möchte *ich* am wenigsten zweifeln, (KSA 2.15)

The 'free spirit' is a 'type' (HH I Preface 3, p. 6/'*Typus*', KSA 2.15), onto which one is challenged to mould one's character by following a certain way of education, namely the road of 'de-Germanization'. 'De-Germanization' requires 'estrangements' (HH I Preface 3, p. 7/'*Entfremdung*', KSA 2.16), 'self-alienation' (HH I Preface 5, p. 8/'*Selbstentfremdung*', KSA 2.19), and the embrace of what is strange and forbidden by traditional *morality*:

> Philosophy as I have understood it and lived it so far is [...] visiting all the strange and questionable aspects of existence, everything banned by morality so far. (EH Preface 3, p. 72)

> Philosophie, wie ich sie bisher verstanden und gelebt habe, ist [...] das Aufsuchen alles Fremden und Fragwürdigen im Dasein [...] eine [...] *Wanderung im Verbotenen*. (KSA 6.258)

The 'self-education' as 'self-alienation' Nietzsche propagates, develops into a matter of literally travelling to foreign regions and of exploring intellectually the unknown *as unknown*, in its strangeness, i.e., without reducing it to what is known – as *différence*.[53]

This exploration of foreign things must ultimately lead to the creation of the 'Good European' as a 'mix of cultures', stylized in a unity. 'Self-stylization' is needed to reach 'self-satisfaction' (GS 290), and this helps the 'beautification' of life, because one makes oneself 'tolerable' to others, in this way. This completes the process of recovery, which further includes the 'satisfaction with the world' (WS 350; GS 276) – also to 'beautify' the world – and the creation of 'immortal' art (GS 370) out of '*Selbstsucht*' (GS 291) and the experience of the 'abundance of life' (GS 370).

Nietzsche's new aesthetics culminates in a what I want to call 'threefold aesthetics', primarily detectable in *Sanctus Januarius*. There, he develops an aesthetics of art, an aesthetics of seeing, and an aesthetics of the self. As I shall show in chapter 7, in

---

53 Cf. GS 355 (p. 214–215/KSA 3.593–594).

all three aesthetic modes, the south, as embodied in the *'überdeutsche'* and 'Italian-ized' Goethe, as well as the city of Genoa, plays a central part. This is in line with his new musical aesthetics, which demands of music that it is 'southern', i.e., based on the Italian opera style. That Nietzsche demands the 'southernization' of free spirits to liberate oneself from Romanticism and Modernism, i.e., 'sickness', in his wake becomes abundantly clear in the prefaces Nietzsche wrote in 1886 for the new editions of his free spirit books.[54] There, Nietzsche reveals in more detail the process he went through, however, not only to *inform* his readers, but also to *instruct* them.

The 1886 prefaces

When Nietzsche changed publishing-houses, in 1886, he agreed with his new publisher E.W. Fritzsch to re-publish the free spirit books. For this occasion, Nietzsche wrote new prefaces, in which he looked back on the years in which he had been writing these books, the years between the summer of 1876, when the first Bayreuth Festival took place, and the summer of 1882, when *The Gay Science* came out and he lived a new pinnacle of joy because of his friendship with Lou Andreas-Salomé. Some scholars think that the prefaces of 1886 together in fact form a separate essay.[55] Such a view is certainly justified, because the prefaces have only one subject: Nietzsche's 'recovery' (p. 3/*'Genesung'*, KSA 3.345).

Nietzsche recalls his Wagner discipleship, musical taste, hopes of German culture, and metaphysical beliefs, describing those years as a time of 'sickness'. Additionally, Nietzsche's cosmopolitanism had during these years expanded from the idea of learning from neighbouring countries to the conviction that travelling abroad was necessary to overcome this 'sickness'. As he clarifies in the 1886 prefaces, it took him six years to go through this difficult process, and regain his health and himself. The process of recovery started by 'forbidding myself, totally and on principle, all romantic music' (HH II Preface 3, p. 211/'Ich begann damit, dass ich mir gründlich und grundsätzlich alle romantische Musik verbot', KSA 2.373). Nietzsche's shocking experience of the first Bayreuther Festival kindled what he calls 'anti-romantic self-treatment' (HH II Preface 2, 210/'antiromantische Selbstbehandlung', KSA 2.371), which he aptly designates as 'changing his skin' (HH II Preface 2, p. 210/*'die Haut* [...] *wechseln'*, KSA 2.372). He had to rid himself of the skin of the 'Romantic pessimist' to reveal the skin of the 'courageous pessimist'. His farewell to Wagner, he recounts, requested a U-turn of his 'clime of the soul' (HH II Preface 5, p. 212/*'Klima der Seele,'* KSA 2.375) and in order to accomplish this, he needed to go to new, foreign regions:

---

54 See GS 317 (pp. 178–179/KSA 3.549). Cf. Montinari (1982), p. 64.
55 Van Tongeren (1994), p. 95 and IJsseling (1997). Nietzsche indeed devised the plan to publish the prefaces together with the *Songs of Prince Vogelfrei* separately (cf. 6[3], KSA 12.231).

Just as a physician places his patient in a wholly strange environment so that he may be removed from his entire 'hitherto', from his cares, friends, letters, duties, stupidities and torments of memory and learns to reach out his hands and senses to new nourishment, a new sun, a new future, so I, as physician and patient in one, compelled myself to an opposite and unexplored *clime of the soul*, and especially to a curative journey into strange parts, into *strangeness* itself, to an inquisitiveness regarding every kind of strange thing... (HH II Preface 5, p. 212)

Gleich wie ein Arzt seinen Kranken in eine völlig fremde Umgebung stellt, damit er seinem ganzen "Bisher", seinen Sorgen, Freunden, Briefen, Pflichten, Dummheiten und Gedächtnissmartern ertrückt wird und Hände und Sinne nach neuer Nahrung, neuer Sonne, neuer Zukunft ausstrecken lernt, so zwang ich mich, als Arzt und Kranker in Einer Person, zu einem umgekehrten unerprobten *Klima der Seele*, und namentlich zu einer abziehenden Wanderung in die Fremde, in *das Fremde*, zu einer Neugierde nach aller Art von Fremden... (KSA 2.375)

However, this recovery, Nietzsche believed, was not only for him to conquer:

– Shall my experience – the history of an illness and recovery, for a recovery was what eventuated – have been my personal experience alone? And only *my* 'human, all-too-human'? Today I would like to believe the reverse, again and again I feel sure that my travel books were not written solely for myself [...] (HH II Preface 6, p. 213)

– Sollte mein Erlebnis – die Geschichte einer Krankheit und Genesung, denn es lief auf eine Genesung hinaus – nur mein persönliches Erlebniss gewesen sein? Und gerade nur *mein* 'Menschliches-Allzumenschliches'? Ich möchte heute das Umgekehrte glauben; das Zutrauen kommt mir wieder und wieder dafür, dass meine Wanderbücher doch nicht nur für mich aufgezeichnet waren [...] (KSA 2.376)

And: 'What has happened to me [...] must happen to everyone in whom a *task* wants to become incarnate and "come into the world"' (HH I Preface 7, p. 10/'Wie es mir ergieng [...] muss es Jedem ergehn, in dem eine *Aufgabe* leibhaft werden und "zur Welt kommen" will,' KSA 2.21). His free spirit books therefore contain, as he says, 'precepts of health' (HH II Preface 2, p. 210/'eine *Gesundheitslehre*,' KSA 2.371), a doctrine or recipe exlaining how to regain health and become a 'free spirit'. Indeed, by 1886, Nietzsche was convinced that his task of recovery is not only his, but 'ours', a task of 'the healthy ones', the 'good Europeans'. They are the 'homeless' persons, who resist nationalism, Romanticism, and (German) idealism. The 'homeless' persons do not feel at home 'in this today' (GS 377, p. 241/'in diesem Heute,' KSA 3.628), because they consider themselves 'children of the future' (GS 377, p. 241/'Kinder der Zukunft,' KSA 3.628). This future is one of a post-Christian and cosmopolitan Europe.

To become a free-spirited, good European, Nietzsche teaches us here, involves 'self-mastery' (HH I Preface 4, p. 8/'Selbstbeherrschung,' KSA 2.17) and the permission to 'access [...] many and contradictory modes of thought' (HH I Preface 4, p. 8/'die Wege zu vielen und entgegengesetzten Denkweisen,' KSA 2.17):

You shall become master over yourself, master also over your virtues [...]. You shall get control over your For and Against [...]. You shall learn to grasp the sense of perspective in every value

judgement – the displacement, distortion and merely apparent teleology of horizons and whatever else pertains to perspectivism [...]. You shall learn to grasp the *necessary* injustice in every
For and Against, injustice as inseparable from life, life itself as *conditioned* by the sense of perspective and its injustice [...] (HH I, Preface 6, p. 9)

Du solltest Herr über dich werden, Herr auch über die eigenen Tugenden [...]. Du solltest Gewalt
über sein für und Wider bekommen [...]. Du sollest das Perspektivische in jeder Werthschätzung
begreifen lernen – die Verschiebung, Verzerrung und scheinbare Theologie der Horizonte und
was Alles zum Perspektivischen gehört [...]. Du solltest die *nothwendige* Ungerechtigkeit in jedem
Für und Wider begreifen lernen, die Ungerechtigkeit als unablösbar vom Leben, das Leben selbst
als *bedingt* durch das Perspektivische und seine Ungerechtigkeit [...] (KSA 2.20)

Hence, one of the reasons to live in other cultures is to acquire access to other modes of
thought and to assay non-Christian, more cosmopolitan, and more sensualist perspectives of life. In so doing, the free spirit develops a more sensualist and aesthetic view
of life, as opposed to his former metaphysical one, and learns to take 'pleasure in fore-
grounds, surfaces, things close and closest, in everything possessing colour, skin and
apparitionality' (HH I Preface 1, p. 5/'Genuss an Vordergründen, Oberflächen, Nahem,
Nächstem, an Allem, was Farbe, Haut und Scheinbarkeit hat,' KSA 2.14). This ability
to stay at the surface '*out of profundity*', he now calls 'Greek'.[56] Nietzsche labels this
experience of '*great liberation*' (HH I Preface 3, p. 6/'*grossen Loslösung,*' KSA 2.15) –
alluding to the figure of Prometheus, which illustrated the cover of his first book, *The
Birth of Tragedy* – the liberation of a 'fettered spirit' (HH I Preface 3, p. 6/'*gebundener
Geist*', KSA 2.16), who was 'chained [...] to its pillar and corner' (HH I Preface 3, p. 6/
'an seine Ecke und Säule gefesselt,' KSA 2.16).[57] From his early youth onwards, he had
been constricted by the chains of duty and morality. But he suddenly cast doubt on
morality, asking: 'Can all values not be turned round?' (HH I Preface 3, p. 7/'Kann man
nicht alle Werthe umdrehn?' KSA 2.17). With this question, Nietzsche continues, his
recovery from Christianity had begun.[58]

In the 1886 preface to *Daybreak*, morality is blamed for rhetorically seducing him
and philosophers in general: 'Morality has shown itself to be the greatest of all mis-
tresses of seduction – and, so far as we philosophers are concerned, the actual *Circe of
the philosophers*'.[59] Nietzsche explains that morality seduced philosophers into pro-

---

56 See GS Preface 4 (pp. 8–9/KSA 3.351–352).
57 Cf. Willemsen (1996) for a description of Nietzsche's intellectual development with regard to the
figure of Prometheus in his works.
58 This provokes the question whether 'free-spiritedness' is the *result* or the *condition* of the revaluation of values. See for an exploration of this question: Prange [2012–3].
59 D Preface 3, p. 2 ('Die Moral hat sich eben von jeher [...] als die grösste Meisterin der Verführung
bewiesen – und, was uns Philosophen angeht, als die eigentliche *Circe der Philosophen*,' KSA 3.13).
Nietzsche also uses the image of the seductive Circe in criticizing Wagner in *The Case of Wagner*. Compare CW 4 (p. 240/KSA 6.21).

viding morality with a rational foundation. In his view, our trust in rationality itself is already a moral phenomenon. German pessimism, therefore, has not been accomplished yet: 'Perhaps German pessimism still has one last step to take? Perhaps it has once again to set beside one another in fearful fashion its *credo* and *absurdum*?' (D Preface 4, p. 4/'Vielleicht hat der deutsche Pessimismus seinen letzten Schritt noch zu thun? Vielleicht muss er noch Ein Mal auf eine furchtbare Weise sein Credo und sein Absurdum neben einander stellen?' KSA 3.15).[60] According to Nietzsche, Schopenhauer was the first true atheist and German pessimist.[61] However, his pessimism resulted in a poor answer, namely the 'Buddhist' rejection of life. Nietzsche's 'courageous', 'Dionysian' pessimism seeks to find an answer that affirms life.[62] As such, it will be the 'last step' of German pessimism.

Goethe as educator

Nietzsche's growing suspicion of Wagner went hand-in-hand with a turn to Goethe. Not only did he turn to his (and Schiller's) cosmopolitanism, but he also venerated, and sought to imitate, his ability to learn. Goethe understood life as a 'school of education' (WS 140, p. 343/'Erziehungs-schule,' KSA 2.612),[63] according to Nietzsche, where he could learn from history, neighbouring countries, foreign people, and friends. Nietzsche comes to propagate this Goethean way of learning (which, as we saw earlier in this chapter, was a 'Greek' way of learning), characterized by a loving yet competitive attitude. One has to adopt the conventions and standards of neighbouring styles, he says, and at the same time set oneself the goal to set a new norm, a new standard, which will live on in the future as conventions ('chains,' WS 140, p. 343/'Fessel,' KSA 2.612).[64] One must then strive to be imitated, loved, and challenged by others in the future. In Germany, this attitude was not common but unique to figures like Goethe; however much they loved and opposed him, according to Nietzsche, the Germans have never been able to adopt and learn from this attitude.

Yet in order to create a culture and to set a new, European, artistic standard, it is necessary, he insists, to learn from Goethe how to learn from other cultures, to adopt

---

60 Here, Nietzsche alludes to a saying of Tertullianus: 'credo, quia absurdum est'. In Nietzsche's view, Tertullian's humble way of thinking represents the deliberate sacrifice of one's intellect. The person that reasons like that says, as it were, '*credo quia absurdus sum*' (D 417, p. 176/KSA 3.256).

61 Compare GS 357 (pp. 217–221/KSA 3.597–602). There, Nietzsche regards Schopenhauer's pessimism as the pessimism of a 'good European' and expressly non-German.

62 Cf. GS 99 (pp. 94–98/KSA 3.453–457) and GS 370 (pp. 234–236/KSA 3.619–622).

63 Hollingdale translates '*Erziehungs-Schule*' as 'the school in which [...] were raised'. Cf. Nietzsche's reference to the 'south' as 'an immense school for convalescence' (BGE 255, p. 147/'eine grosse Schule der Genesung,' KSA 5.200).

64 Cf. WS 159 (p. 347/KSA 2.618).

his aesthetics, and subsequently to supersede them. 'Constraint and its conquest' (WS 140, p. 343/'Zwang und Sieg,' KSA 2.612) are necessary in the process of creating culture, rules and the overcoming of rules, norms and the creation of new norms. In music, Chopin, surprisingly, was most successful in applying the rules: 'These [...] he admits without dispute, but does so playing and dancing in these fetters like the freest and most graceful of spirits' (WS 159, p. 347/'Diese ['Fesseln', MP] liess er gelten [...] aber wie der freieste und anmuthigste Geist in diesen Fesseln spielend und tanzend', KSA 2.618). As long as the rules are artistic rules to 'bind' ('*bändigen*') inner chaos and create a 'wholeness' ('*Ganzheit*') – both of oneself and of an artwork – they must be followed, adopted, incorporated, and overcome. Chopin, Homer, Raphael (in *The Birth of Tragedy* still called 'naive'), and Goethe (formerly too 'idyllic') had the insight and sensibility to do so:

> Already in Homer we can perceive an abundance of inherited formulae and epic narrative rules *within* which he had to dance: and he himself created additional new conventions for those who came after him. This was the school in which the Greek poets were raised: firstly to allow a multiplicity of constraints to be imposed upon one [by the older poets, MP]; then to devise an additional new constraint, impose it upon oneself and conquer it with charm and grace: so that both the constraint and its conquest are noticed and admired. (WS 140, p. 343)

> Schon bei Homer ist eine Fülle von vererbten Formeln und epischen Erzählungsgesetzen wahrzunehmen, *innerhalb* deren er tanzen musste: und er selber schuf neue Conventionen für die Kommenden hinzu. Dies war die Erziehungs-Schule der griechischen Dichter: zuerst also einen vielfältigen Zwang sich auferlegen lassen, durch die früheren Dichter; sodann einen neuen Zwang hinzuerfinden, ihn sich auferlegen und ihn anmuthig besiegen: sodass Zwang und Sieg bemerkt und bewundert werden. (KSA 2.612)

'Convention' instead of 'originality' as the standard of art is the distinction between 'classic' and 'Romantic' art and Nietzsche opted for convention, in his later, post-Wagnerian aesthetics.[65] But one should play with and within these conventions, and in playing within these borders strive for the 'enduring immortality' (WS 144, p. 344/'*eine unsterbliche Dauer,*' KSA 2.613) of one's work. 'Imitation of [foreign] models' (WS 91, p. 333/'*Nachahmung von Mustern,*' KSA 2.594) to create *style* was the aesthetic task Nietzsche now set. The only model in their own past that Germans have, is Goethe, according to Nietzsche, but the Germans never knew how to relate to him, except by using him as 'decoration of national vanity' ('*Dekoration der nationalen Eitelkeit*').[66] No German person has ever grasped how to adopt Goethe as his 'educator' (WS 107, p. 336/'*Erzieher,*' KSA 2.599). This implies for Nietzsche that German culture is not yet ready for Greece or Goethe.[67] However, Nietzsche did take Goethe as his 'educator'. Via

---

65 Cf. WS 122 (p. 339/KSA 2.604–605).
66 See draft to WS 107 in KSA 14.191.
67 See HH I 203 (pp. 95–96/KSA 2.169) and its draft-version as given in KSA 14.136. See also: 'Goethe stood above the Germans in every respect and still stands above them: he will never belong to them'

Goethe, he adopted the 'Greek', competitive, agonal, and imitating way of relating to history and other people. And by letting German culture begin with Goethe, he 'fixed' German culture in the Greek way of life, which is a cosmopolitan *and* aesthetic way of living, and founded a German 'classic.'[68]

We saw at the beginning of this chapter that Wagner had striven to 'span the minds of a free humanity, exceeding all borders of nationalities' and to write 'neither Italian nor French – nor even German'. Likewise, Nietzsche says that the 'great European music' overcomes nationalities, because 'the good European' wants to make him- or herself understood 'out over the nations' (WS 87, p. 332/'*über die Volker hinweg*', KSA 2.592) and therefore writes in a way which makes his or her work more easily 'translatable into the language of one's neighbour' (WS 87, p. 332/'übersetzbar werden für die Sprachen der Nachbarn,' KSA 2.592) in order that the good Europeans make themselves 'accessible to the understanding of those foreigners who learn our language' (WS 87, p. 332/'zugänglich sich dem Verständnisse jener Ausländer machen, welche unsere Sprache lernen,' KSA 2.592). To read and write well form the foundation of a European culture of 'good Europeans', if they want to perform their task of directing and supervising 'the total culture of the earth' well. The ones who do not promote an education directed at communicating with others, neighbours, and other countries are the 'nationalists', who enclose themselves in their own country, excluding other people and cultures, hence cutting themselves off from the rest of the world. These people augment 'the sickness of this century [nationalism, MP]' (WS 87, p. 332/'*die Krankheit dieses Jahrhunderts*,' KSA 2.593) and are 'an enemy of all good Europeans, an enemy of all free spirits' (WS 87, p. 332/'ein Feind der guten Europäer, ein Feind der freien Geister', KSA 2.592).

Nietzsche's model of this good European, an anti-Wagnerian and anti-German figure *par excellence*, was Goethe. The 'good European' is a mix of German, French, and Italian features, a 'mixed race' that exceeds national borders, a 'supra-national' ('*übernational*') individual characterized by multiplicity. The 'good European' was what Nietzsche himself set to become, hoping that others would follow his, and Goethe's, example. Therefore, he wrote in the preface to *Human, All Too Human II* that his 'travelbooks' were 'not written solely for me'. A note of 1877 explains further what is meant by this:

(AOM 170, p. 252/'Goethe stand über den Deutschen in jeder Beziehung und steht es auch jetzt noch: er wird ihnen nie angehören', KSA 2.448–449).

68 'The church' ('*Kirche*') and 'national characteristics' ('*Nationalitäten*') must be overcome. WS 149, p. 345/KSA 2.615.

Travel-book

To read on the way.

> [...] We modern people must all travel much because of our mental health: and the more people will work, the more they will travel. Hence, the ones who work on altering public opinions should turn to the travellers. From this point of view, a certain form of announcement is required: because the stretched systems of thought conflict with the hasty and turbulent soul of travelling [...]. [For them] books should not be books that one reads, but books to which one often turns: one clings to some sentence today, and to another tomorrow and one thinks finally again with the heart: back and forth, up and down, for the mind drives one in such a way that one finds pleasure and well-being every time again. Gradually, a certain general reconsideration of opinions emerges out of such excited – genuine, because unforced – reflection: and with it that general feeling of spiritual recovery, as if the bow has been stringed with a new tendon and stronger than ever before. One has travelled with benefit. (23[169], KSA 8.473–474)

Reisebuch

Unterwegs zu lesen.

> [...] Wir modernen Menschen müssen alle viel unserer geistigen Gesundheit wegen reisen: und man wird immer mehr reisen, je mehr gearbeitet wird. An den Reisenden haben sich also die zu wenden, welche an der Veränderung der allgemeinen Ansichten arbeiten. Aus dieser bestimmten Rücksicht ergiebt sich aber eine bestimmte Form der Mittheilung: denn dem beflügelten und un-ruhigen Wesen der Reise widerstreben jene lang gesponnenen Gedankensysteme [...] Es müssen Bücher sein, welche man nicht durchliest, aber häufig aufschlägt: an irgend einem Satze bleibt man heute, an einem anderen morgen hängen und denkt einmal wieder aus Herzensgrunde nach: für und wider, hinein und drüber hinaus, wie einen der Geist treibt, so dass es einem dabei jedes-mal heiter und wohl im Kopfe wird. Allmählich entsteht aus dem solchermaassen angerergten – Nachdenken eine gewisse allgemeine Umstimmung der Ansichten: und mit ihr jenes allgemeine Gefühl der geistigen Erholung, als ob der Bogen wieder mit neuer Sehne bespannt und stärker als je angezogen sei. Man hat mit Nutzen gereist.

The 'reconsideration of opinions' ('*Umstimmung der Ansichten*') is a 'revaluation of values' ('*Umwerthung aller Werte*'). This revaluation occurs during travelling and is corroborated by the aphoristic style of books and the spontaneous, intervallic way of reading. A traveller in the Nietzschean sense does not merely go out sightseeing, but goes out to change his way of seeing.[69] The term 'travel' thus has to be taken in both a literal and metaphorical sense. Nietzsche's 'travel books' are the reports of his 'inner journey' from sickness to health, of his 'recovery' (GS Preface 1, p. 3/'*Genesung*,' KSA 3.345). They contain the story of his physical and mental journey from Germany to the south.[70] Three ingredients were crucial for Nietzsche's recovery; first, music (his recov-

---

69 Cf. Heller in the introduction to the translation of HH MA (1986), p. xvii.
70 It must be noted that Nietzsche was mainly fond of the Mediterranean seasides and not of big cities. His feelings about Rome, which he visited briefly in 1882, were mixed, despite the fact that he met Lou

ery started with ceasing to listen to German music); second, travelling to 'the south', i.e., southern France, Italy, the Mediterranean areas; third, Goethe (as his model of 'de-Germanization' and 'good Europeanism'). The recovery was a matter of emerging in southern natural and cultural environments ('dynamic interculturalism') in order to learn and create the self as a 'mix of cultures' or 'good European', as the final stage of free-spiritedness.

Conclusion

From *Human, All Too Human* onwards, the attempt to 'de-Germanize' forms the heart of Nietzsche's philosophy as the result of his growing cosmopolitan spirit. His turn away from Wagner was, therefore, not only a matter of a divergent aesthetics and personalities, but also of differing political preferences – Nietzsche's becoming a 'cultural cosmopolitanism', Wagner's a political nationalism. This was the result of Nietzsche's new understanding of the Greeks, developed only six months after the publication of *The Birth of Tragedy*; the Greeks, he found out, had not been '*autochthones*', but they had formed themselves by way of an '*allochtonous education*', i.e., interacting with foreigners. They thus owed their uniqueness and greatness to their 'cosmopolitan tendency', and not to their natural giftedness and to become 'Greek' apparently required the embrace of the non-Greek. This urged Nietzsche to promote cosmopolitanism or – as I prefer call it in this case – 'dynamic interculturalism', the active interaction and cultural exchange between people from different cultures, in order to 'aestheticize', i.e., intensify one's artistic powers and aesthetic view of life.[71]

The 'mix of cultures', the 'abolition' ('*Vernichtung*') or 'amalgamation' ('*Verschmelzung*') of the European nations into one, united Europe, which would be inhabited by a 'mixed race' of 'good Europeans', as he had already formulated in *The Wanderer and his Shadow* (1880),[72] would instigate the 'new Renaissance'. This is a

---

Andreas-Salomé there. From 1883 onwards, he regularly spent the winters in Nice. As a young professor, he had nourished the fantasy of moving to Paris. However, he would never even visit Paris, although it was undoubtedly the European capital of art in Nietzsche's days. See for an excellent account on Nietzsche's relation to France: Groot (2003), pp. 73–108.

71 Hence, there were philosophical reasons for Nietzsche to turn away from Wagner in addition to the latter's 'genufluxion for the cross'. Cf. Winteler (2011). Winteler is right in ascribing Nietzsche's exclamation that he was 'deadly insulted' to Wagner's turn to Christianity and not (as Young 2010, p. 240; Babich 2008, p. 333; Eger 2001, p. 221; and Niemeyer 1998, p. 211ff claim) to his insinuations with regard to Nietzsche's sexuality. Cf. Nietzsche to Malwida von Meyenbug, 21 February 1883 (KSB 6, p. 335) and to Franz Overbeck, 22 February 1883 (KSB 6, p. 337).

72 HH I 475 (pp. 174–175/KSA 2.309). Cf. also 7[67] (KSA 12.321) and 1[153], KSA 12.45, in which Nietzsche holds that the 'source' of great culture is 'mixed races' (and not genius).

Europe for 'free spirits,'[73] who keep remote from politics[74] and dedicate themselves to the former German task of making European culture the 'continuation of the Greek' (HH I 475, pp. 174–175/'*Fortsetzung der griechischen,*' KSA 2.311).[75] In this will to create the 'lasting bond of love' (BT 20, p. 96/'*dauernden Liebesbund,*' KSA 1.129) with the Greeks, in this process of 'Graecization,' Nietzsche declared in a *Nachlass* note from 1885, 'resided (and always resided) my hope for the German soul!' ('liegt [und lag von jeher] meine Hoffnung für das deutsche Wesen!' 41[4], KSA 11.679). Although at that time he considered his former Wagnerism a matter of youthful 'self-blinding' (BGE 31, pp. 31–32/'*Selbst*-Verblendung,' KSA 5.49),[76] because – in a typically German way – he had mistaken Wagner's 'obscurity' ('*Unklarheit*') for 'depth' ('*Tiefe,*' 41[2], KSA 11.674),[77] he still assigned a special role to the Germans in the achievement of this renaissance, as 'people of the middle' ('*Volk der Mitte,*' 43[3], KSA 11.703). He still hoped that the Germans would be the pioneers of a new European Renaissance. However, this time they would be pathfinders not because of Germany's unique 'metaphysical', 'aesthetic', and 'tragic talent', but rather due to their talent for 'de-Germanization' ('*Entdeutschung,*' 43[3], KSA 11.702) and lust for travelling, that is, for their dynamic interculturalism, despite the fact that so far only Goethe (and Mozart) had succeeded in this and the Germans had been unable so far to learn from him how to be cosmopolitan and a 'good European'.

The Renaissance, as Nietzsche then understood the matter, had to be generated not so much by closing off from French taste and Italian formalism, as Wagner had propagated in 'Beethoven', as with the help of 'our good will, our patience, our fairmindedness and gentleness with what is strange' (GS 334, p. 186/'unsere guten Willen, unsere Geduld, Billigkeit, Sanftmüthigkeit gegen das Fremde,' KSA 3.560). The cultural redemption had to be established by 'borrowing' ('*entlehnen*') 'forms [...] from abroad' ('die Formen aus der Fremde') in order to 'transform them into the fairest appearance of beauty' ('zum schönsten Scheine umbilden'), yet still for the reason that 'that [my emphasis, MP] is Greek' (AOM 221, p. 266/'das [my emphasis, MP] ist griechisch,' KSA 2.474). For this reason, Nietzsche, 'opening up' to other forms, turned to Italian opera most of all, as we shall see in the next chapter.

---

73 HH I Preface 6 (p. 9/KSA 2.15).

74 19[77], KSA 8.348.

75 In D 272, Nietzsche calls this process a 'process of purification' (p. 274/'der Process der Reinigung,' KSA 3.214): 'The Greeks offer us the model of a race and culture that has become pure: and hopefully we shall one day also achieve a pure European race and culture,' (p. 274/'Die Griechen geben uns das Muster einer reingewordenen Rasse und Culture: und hoffentlich gelingt einmal auch eine reine europäische Rasse und Culture,' KSA 3.214) Cf. Duschinsky (2011) for a more extensive account of Nietzsche's ideal of the 'mix of races' versus/as racial purity.

76 See also 42[2], KSA 11.670.

77 At that time, Nietzsche underlines that Wagner *used to be* a 'free spirit', an atheist and amoralist. Of course, Nietzsche hints at the pre-Parsifalian Wagner. Cf. 37[15], KSA 11.592.

A last question remains to be posed before coming to Nietzsche's turn to Italian opera. Nietzsche thus still saw a special role for the Germans in the formation of Europe. Given Nietzsche's awareness that being 'Greek' meant the embrace of the 'non-Greek', the question is justified whether his plea for 'de-Germanization' must be understood in any way as an attempt to 'Germanize' after all. Consider, for example, the following note from 1885:

> One would be inclined to believe that, if there should be something like a *'German spirit'* after all, such a spirit has only become possible by way of de-Germanization, I mean the mix with foreign blood (43[3], KSA 11.702).[78]

> Man möchte fast glauben, daß, wenn es endlich doch so etwas geben sollte, wie *'deutschen Geist'*, er erst durch Entdeutschung, ich meine die Mischung mit ausländischem Blut ermöglicht worden ist.

Following this line, the question is how 'Wagnerian' Nietzsche's anti-Wagnerism was. Can his opposition to Wagner still be seen as the attempt to teach Wagner (who died in 1883) how to become the pioneer in the European 'jungle of paradise lost'? And does this imply that Nietzsche's 'immoralism' is a 'moralism' after all?

---

78 In that sense, I agree with Morgan, who claimed: 'Nietzsche's analysis of national identity was far more complex, nuanced, and ambivalent than is generally recognized. It does not suffice to present Nietzsche merely as a "good European" who espoused the adoption of the "supranational" and nomadic "homelessness"', arguing that 'rather than simply jettisoning the concept of national identity in favour of that which supersedes its boundaries, he instead combined his interrogation of the relevance of the nation-state in a changing context with an appreciative analysis of cultural specificity and nascent independent movements' (2006, p. 455). Morgan uses Nietzsche to analyze the emergence of new nation-states within the context of an expanding European Union and ever-increasing globalization, focusing on eastern Europe as a way of sidestepping the traditional, 'straightforward' reading of Nietzsche on national identity 'as something negative and unproductive that has to be overcome, either in favour of a European identity and culture, or in favour of the trans-national and global' (2006, p. 456). I join the more straightforward reading, yet with the specific emphasis that Nietzsche's understanding is more hybrid than generally recognized. He perceives the national and trans-national in a binary synthesis: to become German means to become Greek and later he holds, in a nutshell, that 'Greek' means to be European. Thus, his analysis of national identity is indeed 'more complex, nuanced, and ambivalent', yet – according to me – in another way than Morgan reveals, for the reason that her – very stimulating – reading of Nietzsche in this matter is more politically informed than mine.

Chapter 6
'La Gaya Scienza' in music: Nietzsche's new musical aesthetics

Introduction

In 1886, when Nietzsche wrote new prefaces to his books for a second edition, he also wrote a new foreword to *The Birth of Tragedy*. In that foreword, entitled 'Attempt at Self-Criticism', he famously noted:

> I regret [...] that I had *ruined* the grandiose *Greek problem* in general, as I had come to understand it, by mixing it up with the most modern things. Also, the fact that I had attached hopes to things where there was nothing to hope for, where everything pointed all too clearly to an end. And that I should have begun to invent stories about the 'German character', on the basis of the latest German music, as if it were about to discover or re-discover itself – and this at a time when the German spirit, which had recently shown the will to rule Europe and the strength to lead Europe, had *abdicated*, finally and definitively [...]. Since then I have indeed learned to think hopelessly and unsparingly enough about this 'German character', and the same applies to current *German music*, which is Romanticism through and through and the most un-Greek of all possible forms of art [...]. Setting aside all the premature hopes and the erroneous morals applied to the most contemporary things with which I ruined my first book, however, the great Dionysiac question it poses remains (with regard to music, too) as valid as ever: what would music be like if it were no longer Romantic in its origins, as German music is, but *Dionysiac*? [...] (ASC 6, pp. 10–11)

> ich [...] bedauere [...] dass ich mir [...] überhaupt das grandiose *griechische Problem* [...] durch Einmischung der modernsten Dinge *verdarb*! Dass ich Hoffnungen anknüpfte, wo Nichts zu hoffen war, wo Alles allzudeutlich auf ein Ende hinwies! Dass ich, auf Grund der deutschen letzten Musik, vom "deutschen Wesen" zu fabeln begann [...] und das zu einer Zeit, wo der deutsche Geist, der nicht vor Langem noch den Willen zur Herrschaft über Europa, die Kraft zur Führung Europa's gehabt hatte, eben letztwillig und endgültig *abdankte* [...] In der That, inzwischen lernte ich hoffnungslos und schonungslos genug von diesem "deutschen Wesen" denken, insgleichen von der jetzigen *deutschen Musik*, als welche Romantik durch und durch ist und die ungriechischeste aller möglichen Kunstformen [...] – Abseits freilich von allen übereilten Hoffnungen und fehlerhaften Nutzanwendungen auf Gegenwärtigstes, mit denen ich damals mein erstes Buch verdarb, bleibt das grosse dionysische Fragezeichen, wie es darin gesetzt ist, auch in Betreff der Musik, fort und fort bestehen: wie müsste eine Musik beschaffen sein, welche nicht mehr romantischen Ursprungs wäre, gleich der deutschen, – sondern *dionysischen*?... (KSA 1.20)

While Nietzsche formerly spoke of a *German* problem, he now speaks of a *Greek* problem, admitting that his hope for German 'character', 'spirit', and 'music' had 'ruined' the true problem, which he now defines as concerning the nature and future of Dionysian music. Although Nietzsche had presented Wagner in *The Birth of Tragedy* as the creator of Dionysian music, he now condemns 'the latest German music' as 'Romanticism through and through' and 'the most un-Greek of all possible forms of art'.

In the course of this chapter, I try to delineate Nietzsche's new, anti-Wagnerian, musical aesthetics in the light of this reassessment. I argue that the 'southernization' Nietzsche continues to propagate not only requires the abandonment of Romantic music, but also the embrace of Italian opera – to the extent that Nietzsche tries to compose Italian operas with the help of Peter Gast. This triggers the question I hope to answer below: 'How does Nietzsche's continuous search for 'Dionysian' music relate to his turn to Italian opera?'

As we recall, in *The Birth of Tragedy*, Nietzsche burnt down Italian opera as 'the opposite of the Dionysian' on account of its 'idyllic tendency'. Nevertheless, from 1881 onwards, the 'Dionysian' seems to serve increasingly as the idyllic; how else must we understand Nietzsche's declaration that Bizet's comical opera *Carmen*, his favourite piece of music in the anti-Wagnerian period, was an 'idyll' to him, and that he needed the 'idyll' for his 'health'? This suggests that the 'Dionysian' and the 'idyllic' are two different terms for the same experience, to wit the experience of 'recovery', which forms the axis of Nietzsche's free-spirited 'travel books', specifically *The Gay Science*.[1]

To answer this question, I first reconstruct Nietzsche's new musical aesthetics, referring to reflections on music expressed in *Human, All Too Human I* and *II, Daybreak, The Gay Science, Beyond Good and Evil, Ecce Homo* and *The Case of Wagner*. All these books have at least one thing in common, which is that they are significantly marked by Nietzsche's anti-Wagnerism, aestheticism, and cosmopolitanism. I further discuss his friendship with the young composer Peter Gast. In Peter Gast, Nietzsche came to see the musician who would fulfil his wish for 'southern' music and a form of music that could function as the 'best-toning spokeswoman' (*'wohltönendste Fürsprecherin'*) of his philosophy.[2] In this context, I pay particular attention to the 'Prelude in German Rhymes' ('Vorspiel in deutschen Rheimen') *Joke, Cunning, and Revenge* (*Scherz, List und Rache*), asking how it relates to Peter Gast's opera *Joke, Cunning, and Revenge*, and Goethe's *Singspiel* of the same name. With this prelude, Nietzsche introduced his 'most personal', healthy, and 'truly Genoese' book, *The Gay Science*.[3]

Next, I return to the problem of the idyll and the Dionysian by discussing Nietzsche's veneration of landscape painting and the motto of the free spirit to live 'for the sake of joy and for no further goal' (WS 350, p. 393/'um der Freudigkeit willen [...] und um keines weiteren Zieles willen', KSA 2.702). My conclusion suggests that Nietzsche's new musical aesthetics demands that music 'becomes mediterranean',

---

1 Stegmaier points to the fact that, in these years 'music' for Nietzsche receives the meaning of 'music of life', exceeding the common concept of music. He also remarks correctly that Nietzsche then sought to connect 'Dionysian' music and 'gay science' (Stegmaier 2011, p. 498ff.) One important criterion for true Dionysian music now becomes the physiological criterion: can one dance to music? How do ears and *feet* respond to music? Wagner's music obviously fails to meet this criterion. See GS 368 (pp. 232–233/KSA 3.616–618).

2 To Franz Overbeck, 18 May 1881 (KSB 6, p. 89).

3 Nietzsche to Karl Knortz, 21 June 1888 (KSB 8, p. 340). This will be discussed further in chapter 7.

which comes down to the 'southernization' and 'Italianization' of German music. Nietzsche's main example of 'southern' music is Bizet's *Carmen*, the perfect expression of 'la gaya scienza' in music. His primary models of the successful 'Italianization' of German music are Mozart and Goethe.

Finally, I conclude that Nietzsche's new embrace of Italian opera marries the Dionysian and idyllic in a heroic idyllicism, which finds its philosophical expression, as we shall see in the next chapter, in doctrine of the *amor fati* and 'good Europeanism'. This philosophy is, as we shall see, embodied by Goethe.

Let us first delineate Nietzsche's new aesthetic principles, and concomittant culture, as outlined by *Human, All Too Human I* chapter 4 and 5, before we turn to the identification of his new musical aesthetics.

New aesthetic principles and a new conception of 'Greekness'

The fact that Nietzsche did not attend musical concerts anymore for more than five years after the greatly disappointing Bayreuth festival of 1876 did not stop him from reflecting upon music, as *Human, All Too Human I* (1878) reveals. In fact, in those years, he even changes his musical aesthetics entirely, as becomes clear when reading chapter 4 of *Human, All Too Human I*, 'From the Souls of Artists and Writers' ('Aus der Seele der Künstler und Schriftsteller'). Part of this book is very resentful in character, for example when Nietzsche addresses his former 'superstition' in the genius (however not in such an uncivilized, unseemly, and unrestrained way as Wagner fulminated against Nietzsche in his paper 'Public and Popularity' ['Publikum und Popularität']).[4]

Crucial to the new aesthetics formulated here are two new insights and the launch of a new exemplary artist: Goethe. Both attest to Nietzsche's new, anti-Romantic and anti-Wagnerian position. The first new principle claims that perfection is a matter of hard work: 'All the great artists have been great workers' (HH I 155, p. 83/'Alle Grossen

---

4 See 'Public and Popularity' ('*Publikum und Popularität*') III in *Bayreuther Blätter* VIII, August 1878, pp. 213–222. Wagner does not explicitly name Nietzsche, but expressions such as 'perpetrator of German "scholarship"' ('*Pfleger der deutschen "Wissenschaft"*') allude to him. Wagner's essay not only lacks manners, but also esprit and power of discernment. In any case, whether the following phrase is meant as attacking Nietzsche in particular or not, it is illustrative of Wagner's pettiness: 'Glasses seem to be invented for this university system [the gymnasium and university system in Sachsen, MP] in particular, and the reason that people in ancient times clearly had brighter heads, was definitively because they viewed more clearly with their eyes and did not need glasses' ('Die Brillen scheinen für dieses Unterrichtssystem [the gymnasium and university system in Sachsen, MP] besonders erfunden zu sein, und warum die Leute in früheren Zeiten offenbar hellere Köpfe hatten, kam gewiss daher, dass sie mit ihren Augen auch heller sahen und der Brillen nicht bedurften', August 1878, p. 215). Incidentally, this expression strikes me as contradicting Wagner's idea that deaf and/or blind people such as Beethoven and Tiresias are 'seers', because knowledge is a matter of the power of *inner* vision, as advanced in 'Beethoven'.

waren grosse Arbeiter', KSA 2.147).[5] The 'seriousness of the efficient workman' (HH I 163, p. 86/'*Handwerker-Ernst*', KSA 2.153) substitutes the former 'Dicnysian talent' ('*Dionysische Begabung*'). The second principle says that art should be about 'artistic moderation' (HH 221, p. 103/'*künstlerische Maass*', KSA 2.182).[6]

Nietzsche still opposes naturalism (HH I 221, pp. 103–104/KSA 2.181) and the modern spirit in art, which he again equates with 'the constraints of logic' (HH I 221, p. 103/ '*die Zügel der Logik*', KSA 2.182), but now also with 'restlessness' (HH I 221, p. 103/'*Unruhe*', KSA 2.182), 'hatred for bounds and moderation' (HH I 221, p. 103/'*Hass gegen Maass und Schranke*', KSA 2.182), and 'the fever of revolution' (HH I 221, p. 103/'das Fieber der Revolution', KSA 2.182). In addition, [aesthetic, MP] 'appearance' (HH I 221, p. 102/'*Schein*,' KSA 2.181) is 'the supreme outcome of a necessary evolution in art' (HH I 221, p. 102/'das höchste Ergebniss einer nothwendigen Entwickelung in der Kunst', KSA 2.181), which reminds one of the redemption of Dionysian pain offered by Apollonian semblance. The new exemplary artist that comes to replace Wagner is Goethe. He is the key-figure in Nietzsche's new aesthetics and 'free spirit' philosophy. Remembering the former expression that a culture in which strangers are no longer strangers, and which is able to understand Wagner, Beethoven, and Shakespeare, the new challenge for culture consists in finding a culture, which matches Goethe (something the Germans had failed to do, so far, as chapter 5 illustrated).[7]

Goethe is regarded as the only German artist who understood 'moderation' and keeping 'measure'. He was 'Greek' in the sense that he 'attempted to rescue himself from this situation [leaping into naturalism through unfettering, MP] through his ability again and again to impose different kinds of constraint upon himself' (HH I 121, pp. 102–103/KSA 2.184) and 'he felt the profoundest desire to regain the traditional ways of art and to bestow upon the ruins and colonnades of the temple that still remained their ancient wholeness and perfection at any rate with the eye cf imagination' (HH I 121, p. 104/'er [empfand] das tiefste Verlangen [...] die Tradition der Kunst wieder zu gewinnen und den stehen gebliebenen Trümmern und Säulengängen des Tempels mit der Phantasie des Auges wenigstens die alte Vollkommenheit und Ganzheit an zu

---

5 Typically, Nietzsche puts Beethoven in the spotlight as a hard worker in this aphorism against Wagner's defence of Beethoven as a true genius in his 1870 essay.

6 Compare Nietzsche to Mathilde Maier: 'That metaphysical obfuscation of all that is true and simple [...] in addition to a very appealing but overstraining Baroque-art and the idolized lack of measure – I am referring to the art of Wagner – these are the two things that made me finally sick and even sicker [...].' ('Jene metaphysische Vernebelung alles Wahren und Einfachen [...] dazu eine ganz entsprechende Barockkunst der Überspannung und der verherrlichten Maßlosigkeit – ich meine die Kunst Wagner's – dies Beides ware es, was mich endlich krank und kränker machte [...]', 15 July 1878, KSB 5, p. 338).

7 See draft version to HH I 203, KSA 14.136. Compare also the rhetorical question: 'Goethe has not yet produced any effect at all and that his time is still to come?' (HH I 221, p. 104/'Goethe habe noch gar nicht gewirkt und seine Zeit werde erst kommen?', KSA 2.184).

dichten', KSA 2.184). For this reason, Nietzsche understood Goethe's art as a means to 'recollect' true art.

Thus, Goethe's classicist writings [that is, after *Werther's Sorrows* and Goethe's dissociation from the *Storm and Stress* movement, MP] are testimony to his change from a revolutionary to a 'traditional' mind, from an interest in cultural change of modern Germany to a concern for cultural memory, to enliven the great legacy of ancient Greek culture and Italian Renaissance. To Nietzsche, the cultural change resides in the living, cultural memory of the Greeks and, in part, Italian Renaissance. This memory is enlivened by the competition artists engage in, in the attempt to master their models eventually. In so doing, they hope to leave their own mark and create lasting artworks. Thus artists have the best chance of gaining lasting names and fame by renewing artistic history. Note that this renewal is not the mere attempt to imitate, to copy as faithfully as possible, but to create works united by *style*. However, the focus changes from the theatre, composer, and poet to the 'free spirit' and 'good European', who adopt the Greek, aesthetic 'lifestyle', the Greek 'art of living'.

Nietzsche's use of the term 'Greek' underwent serious alteration. While it formerly represented the Dionysian spirit, the artistic reconciliation of the Dionysian and Apollonian, and the aesthetic perception of life, it came to symbolize 'the highest freedom of spirit' (HH I 121, p. 103/'die höchste Freiheit des Geistes', KSA 2.182), 'an altogether unrevolutionary disposition' (HH I 121, p.103/'eine schlechterdings unrevolutionäre Gesinnung', KSA 2.182), and 'artistic moderation' (HH I 121, p. 103/'künstlerische Maass', KSA 2.182). Thus, while Nietzsche's early aesthetics was dominated by the idea of the 'unchaining of symbolic powers' ('*Entfesselung symbolischer Kräfte*'), which included a vehement opposition to the 'beat' because of its mathemathical nature, his new, 'Greek' aesthetics is ruled by 'constraint by artistic measure' ('*Bändigung durch künstlerisches Maass*'), as if the emphasis shifts from the Dionysian to the Apollonian.

'Measure' or 'constraint' becomes the main aesthetic principle the free spirit lives by. In addition, while music was indispensable to reach the symbolic level and stimulate cultural progress before, the question now is, whether 'Dionysian' music is equally necessary now that the 'Apollonian' principle of 'measure' has become a central feature of Nietzsche's aesthetics? Does Nietzsche still believe that the 'innocence of melody' will ennoble culture? And how does this new aesthetics relate to his philosophy of culture and his cosmopolitan spirit? Let us have a closer look at Nietzsche's new musical reflections and then, in chapter 7, the philosophy of culture that goes with it.

Nietzsche's new musical aesthetics

Describing Nietzsche's turn away from 'northern', Romantic music, the 1886 prefaces also reveal what kind of music Nietzsche would still allow for: 'if I continued to harbour any hope at all for music it lay in the expectation that a musician might come who was sufficiently bold, subtle, malicious, southerly, superhealthy to confront that music and in an immortal fashion *take revenge* on it' (HH II Preface 3, p. 211 'wenn ich überhaupt noch etwas von der Musik hoffte, so war es in der Erwartung, es möchte ein Musiker kommen, kühn, fein, boshaft, südlich, übergesund genug, um an jener Musik auf eine unsterbliche Weise *Rache zu nehmen*', KSA 2.373). Below, I shall further analyse the 'southern' music Nietzsche embraces, from 1881 onwards.

While developing his new aesthetics, Nietzsche reconsiders his old ideas about music, both in relation to the metaphysical wisdom it was supposed to purvey and in relation to the technical construction of music. As we have seen, Nietzsche's earliest taste concerned the Old German School, then he developed an aesthetics, which met the avant-garde ideas of the New German School in *The Birth of Tragedy*, and afterwards, beginning with *Human, All Too Human*, Nietzsche propagated a musical aesthetics that was all about 'southern' music.[8]

Most important for Nietzsche's new musical aesthetics is the influence of Peter Gast. Together with this young musician (his real name was Heinrich Köselitz; Nietzsche invented the stage name Peter Gast), Nietzsche buried himself in opera music, especially from May 1881 onwards, when they holidayed together in Recoaro, not far from Venice. In his new musical aesthetics, Nietzsche continues to reflect on music within the context of 'German' and 'Italian' music, now supporting Italian music and opposing German music. As noted, and this is generally overlooked, the interesting and problematic aspect of this is how 'Italian' connects to 'Dionysian' music, which is still Nietzsche's ideal music according to the 'Attempt at Self-Criticism'. Below, I claim that Nietzsche's new musical aesthetics hangs on three pillars: his notion of the South, his notion of health, and his revaluation of the idyll.

In the preface to *Human, All Too Human II*, Nietzsche states that Wagner had made him sick and that was the reason that he forbade himself to listen to German, Romantic music any longer, in order to heal. This embargo on Romantic music implied a revaluation of Italian opera and the Old German School, the tonal system, and of rhythm as an important musical element. Moreover, it implied attention and a positive estimation for musical formality in general. While rejecting 'northern' music, though, Nietzsche reveals something about what 'southern' music is: 'superhealthy', 'bold,' and 'subtle', but also malicious enough to take revenge. The latter aim is curious and not comforting, given Nietzsche's rejection of the feeling of revenge or 'resentment' as a typically Christian characteristic. I do not know what the motivation was to use the term 'revenge' ('*Rache*') here, but it suggests that Nietzsche's attraction to 'southern' music is, at least partly, kindled by the fact that it may finish with Wagner's 'German'

---

8 According to Dufour (1999, p. 215), Nietzsche's musical aesthetics developed from a musical metaphysics in *The Birth of Tragedy* to a Hanslickian 'musical formalism' in *Human, All Too Human* and a 'physiology of music' by the time of *Ecce Homo, Twilight of the Idols*, and *The Case of Wagner*. See also on 'Nietzsche's southern music': Gruber (1997), pp. 115–128.

music. Let me remark immediately, though, that this 'revenge' remark is a one-time only event and that there are many passages that testify to other motives for Nietzsche to embrace Italian and French opera, such as pleasure in listening, the experience of relief, innocence, and style, and honesty in depiction. Revenge, in any case, does not seem to agree with the 'aesthetic conscience' (AOM 133, p. 244/'*ästhetisches Gewissen*', KSA 2.434) out of which Nietzsche turned his back on Wagner. His 'aesthetic conscience' makes him, in terms of musical techniques, prefer rhythm and dance-music over the 'endless melody', by which means Wagner attempted to move people's moods or 'soul'. In *Human, All Too Human II* (when he has not discovered Italian opera yet, but sought to contradict his early musical aesthetics), Nietzsche makes a turn from the metaphysical and symbolical to the bodily experience of music and musical form. According to Nietzsche, music to which one can dance is music that is created according to the law of 'measure' (AOM 134, p. 244/'*Maass*', KSA 2.434). Because of the endless melody, Wagner's music is 'without measure' (AOM 154, p. 248/'*Maasslosigkeit*', KSA 2.442).[9]

At the time of *Human, All Too Human*, Nietzsche had already befriended Peter Gast, but it is only from November 1881 onwards that Nietzsche starts gaining interest in Italian opera *buffa* and French comical opera, after having seen *Carmen* in Genoa.[10] This experience kindles his hopes of a 'Greek' future again. This is confirmed by his poem of 1884 for Peter Gast, in which the hope is expressed that the young composer as a 'German Orpheus' ('*Deutscher Orpheus*') – in the tradition of Mozart, Rossini, and Chopin (this self-made tradition is not further explained) – will create 'a pure, new Greece' ('*ein reines, neues Griechenland*,' 28[10], KSA 11.302–303)[11] and accomplish Nietzsche's former hope in Wagner ('now falls to me still/what my eagle had shown me'; 'nun wird mir alles noch zu Theil/Was je mein Adler mir erschaute- [...],' 28[10], KSA 11.303). 'Greek' is now defined as the will to art in order to encounter in it personal perfection ('*Vollkommenheit*'), hence, the will to art is in fact the will for 'self-enjoyment' (AOM 169, p. 251/'*Selbstgenuss*', KSA 2.447). If we may equate 'Greek' with 'Dionysian', it would mean that Nietzsche longs for a music, 'outflowing and overflowing of their [the Greeks, MP] own healthiness and wellbeing' (AOM 169, p. 251/'das Aus- und Ueberströmen ihres eigenen Wohl- und Gesundseins', KSA 2.447). This abundance of self-love, love of life, enjoyment, and health is indeed what Nietzsche associates with his new musical loves, Bizet's *Carmen*, and Peter Gast's compositions, especially his *Joke, Cunning, and Revenge*, composed after a libretto written by Goethe. The self-love is

---

9 The English translation by Hollingdale gives 'extravagance', which is correct, but I prefer 'without measure', because that renders more precisely the 'lack of measure', including the lack of '*Takt*' (beat, bar, rhythm) of the mathematical in Wagner's music.
10 See for more on this: Prange 2005.
11 Cf. 28[7] (KSA 11.300), where it is made clear that Nietzsche had expected Wagner to redeem the Germans by leading them to Greece.

what Nietzsche will also venerate in the people of Genoa, and will demand from art – calling it indeed 'Dionysian'.

Hence, 'Dionysian' and 'Greek' still represent the abundance and celebration of life. However, they are no longer names for the metaphysical and tragic truth of life, and the concomitant aesthetic and symbolic answer,[12] but rather for the individual joy one experiences in one's own life. This true joy then is still the aim of art for Nietzsche, just as it had always been. As we have seen, this was the influence of Goethe and Schiller on his aesthetics. Although before the expression of metaphysical unity was the source of true joy, 'Romantic' is now understood as 'self-disgust' (AOM 169, p. 251/'*Selbstverdruss*'), the experience of displeasure. As a highlight of this wallowing *Weltschmerz* Romanticism, Wagner offers exactly what his public expects, Nietzsche contends. He scares away 'their discontent, boredom[,] and uneasy conscience for moments or hours at a time and if possible magnify the errors of their life and character into errors of world-destiny' (AOM 169, p. 251/'für Stunden und Augenblicke das Unbehagen, die Langeweile, das halbschlechte Gewissen [...] und womöglich [soll sie] den Fehler ihres Lebens und Characters als Fehler des Welten-Schicksals in's Grosse umdeuten', KSA 2.447). Wagner's music is sentimental music for 'last men', not the powerful music for an 'aesthetic public' Nietzsche had held it to be.[13] 'Dionysian' or 'Greek', we may conclude, takes on the new meaning of living according to the aesthetic or artistic measure or law, to constrain oneself (one's passions) by subsuming them to that law, and in so doing, shape the self into a dynamic whole of striving and fighting passions and fantasy, fed by strange, foreign influences. It is, in fact, the Apollonian constraining or 'stabilising' power and the Dionysian abundance of life. This, of course, prompts the question where 'play' abides.

As mentioned above, Nietzsche's 'de-Germanization' as the process to regain health was not only a matter of ceasing to listen to German music, but also of starting to listen to Italian and French comic music and even, as we shall see further on in this chapter, meddling in the composition of an Italian *buffa* style *Singspiel*.

Carmen: health and the south

Thus, Nietzsche saw *Carmen* for the first time in November 1881 in Genoa, at the time that he was also working on *The Gay Science*. Nietzsche enjoyed the 'cloudless' sky of Genoa, because it made his thoughts cloudless as well. He loved Genoa for its vitality,

---

12 Music was no longer considered to be 'so significant for our inner world, nor so profoundly exciting, that it can be said to count as the *immediate* language of feeling' (HH I 215, p. 99/'so bedeutungsvoll für unser Inneres, so tief erregend, dass sie als *unmittelbare* Sprache des Gefühls gelten dürfte', KSA 2.175).
13 Cf. WS 168 (p. 349/KSA 2.621–622).

sun, and relaxed, un-modern ambience. Soon Genoa became a symbol of Nietzsche's longing for health, courage, adventure, and solitude, topics *The Gay Science* abounds in and that he associates with *Carmen*.[14]

Indeed, Nietzsche described his new musical taste or aesthetics in the same terms as his free-spirited philosophy and Genoa. Despite the fact that he later said that he had used Bizet's comical opera *Carmen* (1875) mainly as an 'ironical antithesis' to Wagner, he formulated his new aesthetics with the help of this opera. The statement that he went to see it twenty times[15] (even though it is probably an overstatement) denies the depiction as merely ironical antithesis; it was at least more than just that. Not only did he grasp his free-spirit philosophy in terms similar to Bizet's music, but he also analyzed the score to show Köselitz the characteristics of music made 'beyond the Alps' ('*jenseits der Alpen*') in order to stimulate him to adopt these characteristics.[16] In fact, Nietzsche had been instantly impressed by the opera: 'Has *Carmen* not put a greater spell on me than any other opera, in which this beloved world [Genoa, MP] resonates to me?' ('Hat mich nicht Carmen mehr bezaubert als irgend eine Oper, in der mir diese geliebte Welt [Genoa, MP] [...] wiederklingt?' 15[67], KSA 9.657), he exclaimed.

Nietzsche sets up an opposition between *Carmen*'s charm and the captivation of Wagner's music. In comparison to the innocent, musical attraction of *Carmen*, Wagner's music hypnotises like the witch Circe, Nietzsche says. Whereas Bizet makes music, Wagner harangues, whereas Bizet shows delicacies in emotions, Wagner exaggerates them, and whereas the former presents love in an honest, natural way, that is as innocent, fatal, and destructive, the latter turns love into a romantic sentiment, equipped with redemptive power. Wagner places the dramatic effect above musicality, whereas Bizet prefers music to the dramatic effect, Nietzsche concludes. Wagner satisfies his public in a typically Germany way, namely by offering it an idea, and his writings contribute to his attempts to convince his German public of the heavy weight and importance of these ideas. For Wagner's music is not just music, but a splendid source of ideas, so at least Wagner wants us to believe. Music, however, not in itself as an art form, but as a vehicle of ideas, is abhorrent to Nietzsche's new halcyonism.[17] Music should predominate, determine the composition, and consolidate the work's unity.[18] Wagner, by contrast, treats his public not to music, but to heavy clouds formed by dramatic effects, which leads, by lack of a structuring melody, to a hubbub of sounds.

---

14 See also Nietzsche to Overbeck of 14 October 1881 (KSB 6, p. 134), 21 October 1881 (KSB 6, p. 135), and 28 October 1881 (KSB 6, p. 137), to Köselitz (27 October 1881, KSB 6, p. 136; 6 November 1881, KSB 6, p. 138), and to Rée (6 November 1881, KSB 6, p. 139). Compare also Prange (2005), esp. pp. 15–26, pp. 79–81, pp. 86–89, and pp. 117–119.
15 CW 1 (p. 234/KSA 6.13).
16 EH 'Clever' 7 (p. 94 /KSA 6.291).
17 See WA 6 and WA 10. Cf. EH Preface 4, EH Z 4, and EH Z 6.
18 Nietzsche writes to Köselitz: 'This is One Point: to compose the text *after* the music' ('Dies ist Ein Punkt: den Text *nach* der Musik zu dichten,' 10 January 1883, KSB 6, p. 317). Cf. Curt-Paul Janz (1988).

To become 'healthy' was what Nietzsche saw as his 'greatest experience'. He underwent his 'recovery' overtly when he, attending a *Carmen* performance, noticed that he was able to 'take pleasure in anything ever again'. The southern spirit of *Carmen* opened his senses and made him return to the world and nature, in a Goethean way, as an 'immoral', 'pagan' understanding of nature, 'a coming-towards' (TI Skirmishes 48, p. 221/'ein Hinaufkommen', KSA 6.150) nature, against Rousseau's moral 'return to nature' (TI Skirmishes 48, p. 221/'*Rückkehr zur Natur*', KSA 6.150). As I already mentioned in chapter 4, it is for his aestheticism, naturalism, and sensualism that Nietzsche regarded Goethe in his later anti-Wagnerian years as the philosopher-poet who came closest to the Greeks, and, therefore, was 'not a German event but a European one,'[19] a true free spirit and philosopher of *amor fati*, because 'he does not negate any more...'.[20]

Carmen turned out to be the medicine he had been craving for to heal him from his (German) narrow-mindedness and Wagnerism. It made him feel healthier and 'a better philosopher' (CW 1, p. 234/'*ein besserer Philosoph*,' KSA 6.13). 'Health' meant 'unmodern' and 'anti-Wagnerian', because 'modernity speaks its most *intimate* language in Wagner (CW Preface, p. 234/'durch Wagner redet die Modernität ihre *intimste* Sprache,' KSA 6.12). His *Parsifal* plans were a 'deadly insult' to Nietzsche, because they were the definite proof that Wagner's 'idyllic tendency', his moral inclination, had overtaken the spirit of his music. Bringing the church to the theatre was the definite end of Nietzsche's hope that Wagner would liberate Europe from its artistic decadence, which existed exactly in looking at art and life from the *moral* concepts of good and evil. As Nietzsche saw it, Wagner had given up his artistic freedom. From a 'free spirit' he had turned himself into a moral 'judge and hangman' (D 56, p. 57/'*Richter und Henker*,' KSA 3.58).

Carmen showed to Nietzsche that he had been wrong about Italian and French opera; rather than being 'idyllic' in the sense of 'non-Greek' and non-tragic, Nietzsche saw in it the musical and psychological honesty that he had always associated with Wagner. Hence, *Carmen* gave Nietzsche the hope that music could still overcome modern decadance. Therefore, as the same preface explains, 'it is not just malice when I praise Bizet at Wagner's expense in this essay' (CW Preface, p. 233/'Es ist nicht nur die reine Bosheit, wenn ich in dieser Schrift Bizet auf Kosten Wagner's lobe,' KSA 6.11).[21]

---

19 TI Skirmishes 49 (p. 222/'kein deutsches Ereigniss, sondern ein europäisches', KSA 6.151). Cf. WS 125, where Goethe is praised as 'not only a good and great human being but a culture' (p. 340/'nicht nur ein guter und grosser Mensch, sondern eine Cultur', KSA 2.607) for the fact that he had always tried to learn with the intention to overcome himself and create new norms.

20 TI Skirmishes 49 (p. 223/'*er verneint nicht mehr...*', KSA 6.152). Cf. BGE 256 (pp. 148–150/KSA 5.201–204).

21 Most bizar is Scheib's (2008) suggestion that Nietzsche used *Carmen*, rather than another opera, as ironical anti-thesis to Wagner not because of its musical qualities but because the triangular relationship portrayed in the drama resembles the one Richard (Escamillo), Cosima (Carmen), and Nietzsche (Don Jose) had. There is no evidence for such an interpretation in Nietzsche's works whatsoever.

Indeed, *Carmen* can be viewed as the musical counterpart or 'spokeswoman' (*'Für-sprecherin'*) of *The Gay Science*, which propagates the aesthetic, naturalist, and sensualist lifestyle. That book emerged from the same experience of recovery, as it testifies to Nietzsche's joy about the 'typically Greek' ability of taking pleasure again 'in the things nearby'.

This sensualist turn to the world manifests itself as 'lightness' and 'lightness' is 'the first principle of my aesthetics,' Nietzsche claims (CW 1, p. 234/KSA 6.13). He needs the lightness in music as a sign and expression of the philosophical truth that there is nothing more than the appearance of things. 'Lightness' can be found in 'the south', a term that indicates both geographically the area 'south of the Alps' and points to a mental state of lightness, joy, and health. Wagner's music does not match the principle of lightness at all and, mainly for this reason, is rejected: 'no beauty, nothing of the south, none of the fine, southern, brilliant skies [...]' (BGE 240, p. 131/'keine Schönheit, kein Süden, Nichts von südlicher feiner Helligkeit des Himmels [...]', KSA 5.179). Lightness is, in Nietzsche's view, typical for 'southern' music and 'beauty'. Hence, 'the southernness of music' (BGE 254, p. 147/*'Süden der Musik'*, KSA 5.200) becomes the measure of the quality of a work, and the (adaptation of the) southern spirit becomes the standard for the qualify of life and philosophy.

Italy (specifically Genoa, the Cinque Terre area down to Portofino, and Venice) and the south of France (Nice) are the places where the 'southern' or 'Mediterranean' spirit can be found. Hence, in order to 'de-Germanize' and become a 'very free spirit' and 'good European' one must go over the Alps and submerge oneself in the southern lightness. Nietzsche understands Italy as 'an immense school for convalescence' (BGE 255, p. 147/'eine grosse Schule der Genesung', KSA 5.200), where both senses and the spirit are 'liberated' from German-ness. Nietzsche calls himself 'southern not by descent but by belief' (BGE 255, p. 147/'Südlander, nicht der Abkunft, sondern dem Glauben nach', KSA 5.200), who is dreaming of the redemption of northern music by a deeper, sensuous, 'supra-German' kind of music, a music that 'no longer knowing anything of good and evil' (BGE 255, p. 148/'von Gut und Böse nichts mehr wüsste,' KSA 5.201), enriched by the voluptuous blue colour of the sea and a clear sky. Music beyond good and evil dances, plays, and glides above morality, because it is directed by – and treats the – human passions. Against the dominance of Christian morality and mythology, pivotal factors in Wagner's *Parsifal*, Nietzsche demands of music a natural, serene, and stylish representation of inner human passions. Bizet composed honest music and such music, says Nietzsche, is characteristic of 'good Europeans' and *'Mittelländer'* (BGE 254, KSA 5.200) people, who love the South in the North and the North in the South, people who have integrated the best of both worlds and succeeded in creating a synthesis of it.

Carmen expresses exactly this spirit. Bizet's southern streak says goodbye to 'the damp North, to all the steam of the Wagnerian ideal' (CW 2, p. 235/'vom feuchten Norden, von allem Wasserdampf des Wagnerischen Ideals,' KSA 6.15). The 'South' and *Carmen* are both understood as signs of 'health'. The north and Wagner's music, on the other hand, are 'decadent'. 'Wagner's art is sick', Nietzsche declares (CW 5, p. 241/ 'Wagner's Kunst ist krank,' KSA 6.22).[22] He misses in Wagner 'la gaya scienza [...] the shiver of southern light; smooth seas – perfection...' (CW 10, p. 253/'la gaya scienza [...] die Lichtschauder des Südens; das glatte Meer – Vollkommenheit...,' KSA 6.37). In Wagner's music, Nietzsche finds a typical German coarseness and chaos, while he is looking for a southern, light subtlety and refinement of form.[23]

Whereas German people are hollow and tired, and do not know any high moment in their life, except for the intoxicated moments provided by Wagnerian music, Nietzsche recognizes the lust for life and the longing for the extension of life in the Italians. Italians do not need moments of intoxication in which they can forget their apathy and lethargy through the excitement aroused by sensational music drama. They do not desire 'redemption' ('Erlösung'). What they seek is 'alleviation' ('Erleichterung') of their inner passions by giving them a style: 'Through the artist the Germans want to achieve a kind of imagined passion; the Italians want to rest from their real passions' (D 217, p. 135/'Die Deutschen wollen durch den Künstler in eine Art erträumter Passion kommen; die Italiäner wollen durch ihn von ihren wirklichen Passionen ausruhen' KSA 3.193). Nietzsche is looking for the same alleviation, as shown in GS 368: '[...] what does my whole body actually *want* from music? Its own *relief*, I believe [...]' (p. 232/. Was *will* eigentlich mein ganzer Leib von der Musik überhaupt? Ich glaube seine *Erleichterung*', KSA 3.617).

In this light form of music, mythology has disappeared, in virtue of psychological *Verism*, the honest, sensualist representation of human emotions and suffering. Against Wagner's 'genuflexion for the cross', that is his turn away from his former sensualist approach to the world, Nietzsche would agree with Ludwig Feuerbach's programme for the 'emancipation of the flesh': 'the denial of the senses is the source of all insanity and malice and sickness in human life; the affirmation of the senses is the source of physical, moral, and theoretical health'.[24]

Seen from this 'sensualist' perspective, the question advanced in the 'Attempt at Self-Criticism': 'what would music be like if it were no longer Romantic in its origins, as German music is, but Dionysiac?', begins to retain the shape of an answer. The matter is, however, complicated by the fact that Nietzsche not only associates *Carmen* with the sensualism, clarity of form, and health he is looking for, but also with the idyll.

---

22 It has a healthy colour, though, because Wagner is a master of illusion (D 255).

23 BGE 240 (pp. 131–132/KSA 5.179–180).

24 Translation by Paul Bishop (2006–1, p. 226) from Ludwig Feuerbach, 'Wider den Dualismus von Leib und Seele, Fleisch und Geist' [1846] in his *Sämtliche Werke*. Eds. Wilhelm Bolin and Friedrich Jodl, 10 vols. Stuttgart: Fromann, 1966 [2nd ed.], vol. 2, pp. 326–357, p. 350.

Nietzsche's revaluation of the idyll: *Carmen*, Claude, Poussin

Seen in the light of his initial musical taste for the Old German School, Nietzsche's veneration of *Carmen* is less surprising than when compared only to his Wagner-estimation. More surprising is that he designates *Carmen* as an 'idyll'. Did he, in *The Birth of Tragedy*, not vehemently condemn the idyllic in music and art as a 'moral tendency'? And does his free-spiritedness, revaluation of values, and aestheticism not include opposition to the moral perspective of life? How could it happen that Nietzsche came to a positive revaluation of the idyll? And how should we understand that with regard to the desired 'Dionysian' nature of music? It becomes even more surprising when Nietzsche equates the idyll *Carmen* with the experience of health:

> Bizet was a great joy, I wished some 'spirit of Bizet' around me in all kinds of forms. I need the idyll – for my health.[25]

> Bizet war ein großer Genuß, ich wünschte um mich herum etwas Bizetismus in allerlei Gestalt. Ich habe die Idylle nöthig – zur Gesundheit.

To Nietzsche, *Carmen* represents Genoa, Genoa represents health, and health is connected with idyllic surroundings and atmospheres. 'Health', according to Nietzsche, requires the idyll. As far as I know, this is the only place where Nietzsche links the idyll, music, health, and 'joy' so intimately and expressly. Nietzsche says that he needs the idyll for his health; that he wished he had more 'spirit of Bizet' around him, and that Bizet was a 'great joy'. In associating the idyll with health and joy, he dissociates the former intimacy between *Gestaltenspiel* and joy, implying instead that the *Formenspiel* of idyllic opera styles is the source of joy.

Furthermore, the joy he experienced hearing *Carmen* again is a joy that reminds us of the joy expressed in WS 295 and a note stemming from the summer of 1879, in which the idyllic experience is re-introduced. A sudden shift in Nietzsche's estimation of the idyllic has meanwhile taken place. Excited and emotionally moved, he notes:

> The day before yesterday, towards the evening, I was submerged totally in Claude Lorrainian raptures and in the end I burst into long, fierce crying. That I was still to experience this! I had not known that the world could be like this and it appeared to me that the good painters had invented this. The heroic-idyllic is the discovery of my soul at the moment: and everything bucolic of the Ancient has become unveiled and public to me at once – until now I did not understand anything of it! (43[3], KSA 8.610)

> Vorgestern gegen Abend war ich ganz in Claude Lorrain'sche Entzückungen untergetaucht und brach endlich in langes, heftiges Weinen aus. Daß ich dies noch erleben durfte! Ich hatte nicht gewußt, daß die Erde dies zeige und meinte, die guten Maler hätten es erfunden. Das Heroisch-

25 Nietzsche to Franz Overbeck, around 20 December 1882 (KSB 6, p. 306).

Idyllische ist jetzt die Entdeckung meiner Seele: und alles Bukolische der Alten ist mit einem Schlage jetzt vor mit entschleiert und offenbar geworden – bis jetzt begriff ich nichts davon!

In his excitement about the beauty of nature in St. Moritz, Nietzsche discovered the idyllic, or rather 'heroic-idyllic' side of his personality.[26] Looking at nature and enjoying its beauty guides Nietzsche's philosophy strongly from this point onwards.[27] Note 43[3] is elaborated on in *The Wanderer and His Shadow* 295.[28] This aphorism is entitled '*Et in Arcadia Ego*'. This famous motto was used by, amongst many others, Goethe for his *Italian Journey*, but also by Nicolas Poussin, who together with Claude Lorrain is known as a painter of heroic and idyllic landscapes.[29] The fact that Nietzsche turns to pictorial art is, in light of his desire for a form of music that can serve as the *spokeswoman* of his philosophy, a quite remarkable turn. As I shall argue in the next chapter, Nietzsche indeed seems to replace his former musical 'eye for depth' with a new plastic 'eye for the surface', inspired by, above all, Goethe.

In Claude Lorrain and Nicholas Poussin, Goethe famously recognized exactly that high, plastic understanding ('*anschauenden Begriff*') of nature and art, that he himself hoped to incorporate in Italy, or as he wrote in his *Italian Journey*: 'I shall not rest until everything that is still merely words and tradition for me becomes a living concept' ('Ich will auch nicht mehr ruhen, bis mir nichts mehr Wort und Tradition, sondern lebendiger Begriff ist').[30] According to note 43[3], Nietzsche arrived at exactly such a plastic understanding – an understanding which is not 'intuitive' but empirical – which moved him so much that he burst into tears.[31]

---

26 In the summer of 1882, a time marked by his friendship with Lou Andreas-Salomé, Nietzsche claims that everything that crosses his path at that time is 'heroic-idyllic' (Nietzsche to Heinrich Köselitz, 4 August 1882, KSB 6, p. 236). About the nature of St. Moritz, Nietzsche wrote in WS 338 that it was a 'Doppelgänger', describing it as the place where the north and the south come together in a bond: 'here, where Italy and Finland have entered into a union' (p. 392/'hier, wo Italien und Finnland zum Bunde zusammengekommen sind', KSA 2.699).

27 According to Schulze (1998), Nietzsche might have visited the Galleria Doria Pamphili in Rome not later than 1883 (p. 221). Here, one can find several paintings of Claude Lorrain. Shapiro (2003) suggests that Nietzsche had seen (two) paintings of Claude in the Dresden Gallery (p. 42). Bertram (1929) points to the influence exercised by Goethe's *Conversations with Eckermann*, – one of Nietzsche's favourite books – , in which Goethe speaks positively about Claude on several occasions (p. 277f).

28 WS 295, p. 385/KSA 2.686–687. See also Meyer-Sickendiek (2001), pp. 316–321.

29 Its origin is not certain, but likely to be the painting *Il Guercino* (1621) by Giovanni Francesco Barbieri (1594–1666). It became famous through two paintings by Nicolas Poussin (1594–1665). Arcadia, part of the Greek Peloponnesus, had been cherished as a paradise by Greek, Bucolic poetry and Virgil. Herder and Goethe equated Arcadia with Italy.

30 Rome, 27-06-1787 (p. 279/MA 15, p. 427).

31 He must have agreed with Goethe, who said to his secretary Eckermann of Claude Lorrain that his paintings contained the highest truth without representing reality, meaning that the illusionary effect was so strong, that what we see in his paintings makes us truly believe that we are looking at the world itself (10 April 1829, MA 19, pp. 321–322).

The *Wanderer and his Shadow* 295 gives a longer account of this crucial moment in Nietzsche's life. Here, he even imagines Greek heroes walking around in the land-scape, in terms that are reminiscent of Nietzsche's reference to the *'Wahrträume'*, in BT 1, in which the artists walks with the giant figures of his dreams, the gods. Hence, it is suggested that not music but painting is the highest form of art, the best voice of dreams. Nietzsche also refers to the heroic-idyllic landscapes of Nicolas Poussin and to the heroic-idyllic philosophy of Epicurus.[32] He describes that he actually felt how they experienced life, and went on to integrating this experience into his philosophy from then on. This is shown, for example, by *Daybreak* 530, in which a mild and flexible philosophy is described as follows:

> They are rivers with many meanderings and secluded hermitages; there are places in their course where the river plays hide-and-seek with itself and creates for itself a brief idyll, with islands, trees, grottos and waterfalls: and then it goes on again, past rocky cliffs and breaking its way through the hardest stone (p. 533).

> Ströme mit vielen Krümmungen und abgeschiedenen Einsiedeleien; es giebt Stellen in ihrem Laufe, wo der Strom mit sich selber Verstecken spielt und sich eine kurze Idylle macht, mit In-seln, Bäumen, Grotten und Wasserfällen; und dann zieht er wieder weiter, am Felsen vorüber und sich durch das harteste Gestein zwingend [...] (KSA 3.303)

'Heroism' is viewed as a token of freedom, to which 'the most affectionate contribution to small, idyllic things' ('der herzliche Antheil am Kleinen, Idyllischen,' 7[28], KSA 10.255) belongs as well. Nietzsche was still looking for the union of humankind and nature, but at that time seemed to find it in the heroic-idyllic tendencies of Goethe, Poussin, Lorrain, and even Schiller. Does *The Wanderer and His Shadow* 350 not re-mind us of Schiller's definition of the idyll, when Nietzsche explains what the motto of the free spirit is, namely *'Peace all around me and goodwill to all things closest to me'* (p. 393; *'Frieden um mich und ein Wohlgefallen an allen nächsten Dingen,'* KSA 2.702)? On top of this, he found it in the lightness of Bizet, Bellini, Rossini, Mozart, and his 'Venetian maestro Pietro Gasti'. Of Wagner, he then only tolerated the pastoral and intimate *Siegfried-Idyll*, the piece written for Cosima's birthday in 1870 and during which rehearsals in Mannheim Nietzsche felt very close to Wagner.[33] Otherwise, French and Italian operas were the order of the day, not least, it seems, because of their idyllic tendencies. Writing the *Idylls from Messina*, in which he explicitly commemo-

---

32 In connection with Epicurus, Nietzsche usually points to his moderate and quiet soul. In WS 192 (p. 358/KSA 2.638), he points to the moderate sensual pleasures of Epicurus.

33 Nietzsche was in Tribschen when the *Siegfried-Idyll* famously premiered on the stairs by an orches-tra in celebration of Cosima's birthday (25 December 1870) and attended the rehearsals in Mannheim one year later for the first public performance. Compare Nietzsche's letter to mother and sister, 23 De-cember 1871 (KSB 3, pp. 259–260).

rates the Alexandrian poet and Epicurean Theocritus[34] and cherishes the idyllic South, Nietzsche even transformed himself into an idyllic poet.

This all implies that Nietzsche's convalescence was not only a matter of ceasing to listen to German music, but also a matter of listening to Italian opera and emerging in the heroic idyllic spirit. As I argue below, it also became a matter of *creating* Italian opera as a way of making the northern mind more 'southern'. In his friendship with the young composer Peter Gast, Nietzsche tried to accomplish both his own and Peter Gast's 'southernization'.

Nietzsche's revaluation of the idyll: *Carmen*, Claude, Poussin

Nietzsche established a rather rigid opposition between Wagner's music and his new favourite *Carmen* (which, rather than typically French, recasts the nature of Italian *buffa* music and is additionally interpreted as 'Genoese' by Nietzsche and not as 'French') in which Wagner's music was called 'sick' and *Carmen* put forward as the best example of 'healthy' music. In order for 'sick' music to become 'healthy', Nietzsche argued that music had to *'become Mediterranean'* (CW 3, p. 236/'il faut méditerraniser la musique,' KSA 6.16).[35] This meant, however, that northern music had to insert the 'southern' manners rather than that northern music had to be replaced with southern music. This turns out to be 'European' or even 'supra-European' (BGE 255, p. 147/'*übereuropäisch*', KSA 5.201) music, i.e., music made by and for 'good Europeans' or 'Mediterranean [people]' (BGE 254, p. 147/'*Mittelländer*', KSA 5.200).

Such music is not only made by Bizet, but also by Heinrich Köselitz, alias *Peter Gast*, according to Nietzsche. In *Beyond Good and Evil* 255, Nietzsche advocates the redemption of northern music by a deeper, sensuous, 'supra-German' ('*überdeutsche*'), and 'supra-European' ('*übereuropäische*') kind of music, a music 'whose rarest magic consisted in no longer knowing anything of good and evil' (p. 148/'deren seltenster Zauber darin bestünde, dass sie von Gut und Böse nichts mehr wüsste', KSA 5.201), enriched by the voluptuous blue colour of the sea and a clear sky. 'Lightness' here must be taken in all its meanings as bodily weight, melodic effects, the spiritual effect on the listener et cetera. 'Lightness' as the parameter of the music that expresses Nietzsche's free-spirit philosophy stands for everything that can be described as 'southern', 'supra-German', 'free-spirited', and 'amoral'. Nietzsche transfers the key term of his new musical aesthetics completely with all its associations to his philosophy: 'lightness' of soul, being, and life becomes the axis of Nietzsche's free-spirit philosophy and of the free spirit itself, and, eventually, of 'the good European'. 'Light'

---

34 Theocritus's (3th century B.C.) poems were the first to appear under the name of 'idylls', literally 'short forms'.

35 See also Prange (2005).

music is music beyond good and evil, and music beyond good and evil is music that makes one dance and play with moral views. It is music directed by and treating the human passions. Against the dominance of Christian morality and northern mythology, pivotal factors in Wagner's *Parsifal*, Nietzsche demanded of music a natural, serene, and stylish representation of inner human passions. Bizet composed honest music and such music, Nietzsche argued, is characteristic of 'good Europeans', people who love the south in the north and the north in the south, people who have integrated the best of both worlds and created a synthesis out of it.

Such music was what Peter Gast also had in mind. Peter Gast, Nietzsche hoped, would be the first musician from the North to connect the North and the South in 'perfect' and 'supra-German' music. Nietzsche's aim was, with Peter Gast's music as the 'spokeswoman' of his philosophy, to drag the curative power of the natural, truthful, happy, frivolous, and self-conscious south up to the cold, sick North in order to liberate the north from the dominance of morality and religion. Peter Gast, similar to Nietzsche, was a former lover of Wagner's music, and, similar to Nietzsche, in search of new musical authorities. Under their mutual influence, Nietzsche and Peter Gast started gaining sympathy for the cheerful Italian opera, especially for Rossini, Bellini, and Bizet.

Their stay together in the Italian countryside of Recoaro in May 1881 was crucial for their friendship.[36] Here, Peter Gast introduced Nietzsche to his opera *Joke, Cunning, and Revenge (Scherz, List und Rache)*, composed after Goethe's libretto. It made Nietzsche prefer 'Venice' to 'Bayreuth', or the innocent, light, and cheerful music of Peter Gast to Wagner's heavy compositions. In Gast's music, he recognized the same innocence, lightness, frivolity, and technical superiority as in *Carmen*. Nietzsche praised Gast as a 'musician of the first order' ('*Musiker ersten Ranges*') and *Joke, Cunning, and Revenge* for its gaiety, technical superiority, and southern innocence. He even marked the composition the 'best-toning spokeswoman' ('*wohltönendste Fürsprecherin*') of his philosophy.[37] As the 'spokes-woman' ('*Fürsprecherin*') of *The Gay Science*, it contains the message that we are holding a truly southern-spirited book in our hands. Later, he regarded *Joke, Cunning, and Revenge* as an omen of the thought of the eternal return of the same, the doctrine that 'came' to him three months after their stay in Recoaro.[38] Nietzsche would also extol Gast's re-composition of Cimarosa's *Il matrimonio segreto*, which after Nietzsche's suggestion, was re-baptized as *The Lion from Venice (Die Löwe*

---

36 Ross (1999) regards Köselitz 'as the only insignificant one of Nietzsche's friends' ('als einziger unter Nietzsches Freunden unbedeutend', p. 569). Love is more correct when he calls this friendship 'on the edge of despair' (1981, p. VII).

37 To Franz Overbeck, 18 May 1881 (KSB 6, p. 89).

38 See Nietzsche to his mother and sister 18 May 1881 (KSB 6, p. 88) and to Franz Overbeck on the same day (KSB 6, p. 89).

von Venedig), for its southern atmosphere.[39] In Nietzsche's view, no other northern composer before Gast succeeded so well in conveying the spirit of the south. In a letter to Franz Overbeck, Nietzsche even praised Gast as 'a new Mozart' ('a new Mozart').[40]

Whereas Nietzsche, in the early seventies, regarded Wagner as a new Aeschylus, who would introduce the Greek, tragic view of life into modern German culture, he, in the eighties, hoped that Gast's Mozart-like music would drag the warmth of the south into the northern spirit. Although Wagner's return to Christian morality in *Parsifal* was a great disappointment to him, he never really gave up his hope for a transformation of the German soul by means of music.[41] Over the years, Nietzsche remained invariably enthusiastic about Gast's music. However, Nietzsche's high hopes for the success of Gast's music proved in vain. Although Nietzsche wrote to all the opera houses that might be interested in organizing performances of Gast's operas, no one other than Nietzsche saw in him a great composer. Hence, Nietzsche had to alter the northern, German mind on his own, by the power of his books and without the help of music. Gast's intercultural music did not gain much recognition, not even when it was based on texts by Goethe, as was the case with *Joke, Cunning, and Revenge*.

Joke, Cunning, and Revenge

Below, I argue that Nietzsche's insertion of the 'prelude' *Joke, Cunning, and Revenge* in *The Gay Science* is testimony to his attempt to 'de-Germanize' and become a 'good European'. I claim that these rhymes were not so much mere rhymes as a libretto for an opera *buffa*, with which Nietzsche follows Goethe's objective to 'bring home the Italian way to a German composer'. That, at least, was Goethe's aim with his libretto *Joke, Cunning, and Revenge* (*Scherz, List und Rache*). Seen in this light, the 'prelude' Nietzsche wrote may be understood as an expression of 'dynamic interculturalism' *and*, intrinsically connected to this, 'aestheticization'. Below, I therefore look at Nietzsche's prelude from Goethe's libretto *Joke, Cunning, and Revenge*.

Obviously, Goethe is chiefly known for his poetical and not for his musical achievements.[42] However, both Goethe and Schiller contemplated the relation between music and text and the possibilities of musical theatre in particular. This even led Goethe to produce several librettos and *Singspiele*. Other than many a writer today, who for variety's sake occasionally writes a screenplay, Goethe had a clear aesthetic and cul-

39 Cf. Nietzsche to Heinrich Köselitz, 4 October 1881 (KSB 6, p. 133), and Nietzsche to Franz Overbeck, 14 November 1881 (KSB 6, p. 141).
40 Letter of 10 November 1882 (KSB 6, p. 276).
41 Cf. Love (1977), pp. 155–156.
42 In the dedication to his tragedy *Sardanapalus*, Lord Byron called Goethe 'the acknowledged Monarch of European letters' (1821). Cf. Goethe, *Briefe*, HA 4, p. 537.

tural goal in mind with his musical interest. To put it differently, he expected to reach an artistic and cultural effect with opera, which he was unable to achieve with poetry alone.[43] With this view, I go against the dominant view that Goethe turned to opera mainly for practical, and trivial, indeed philistine, reasons, a view based on Goethe's expression that 'opera remains the most secure and appropriate means to attract and amuse the public' ('die Oper immer ein Publikum anzuziehen und zu ergötzen das sicherste und bequemste Mittel bleibt').[44] I believe that Goethe's practical considerations served his aesthetic and cultural aims in general; to take his expression at face value would contradict seriously his quest for style, for example. Moreover, it is worthwhile to see what a less philistine perception of his musical activities would deliver. Goethe endeavoured to participate actively in the creation of a supra-provincial, national theatre, which would be inspired by and be strong enough to compete with the best of Greek, French, English, and Italian artistic history: Homer, Racine, Shakespeare, and Italian opera. In other words, dynamic interculturalism at its best.

Goethe's turn to Italian opera was motivated by the fact that German music, specifically the popular lyrical dramas ('*Singspiele*'), was not able to fulfil his theatrical ends. Thanks to Mozart, who had popularized the Italian opera for the German-speaking world and to whom Goethe turned firstly and chiefly to learn about Italian music, German music had made a giant step towards establising opera in Europe. It seems to me that Goethe aspired to play a role in this too. At least numerous fragments of his *Conversations with Eckermann, Italian Journey*, and *Wilhelm Meisters Lehrjahre* seem to hint at such an intention. The fact that Goethe had the strong desire to be a painter, and considered himself an '*Augenmensch*' (which Wagner held against Goethe as 'lack of musicality'), did not hold him back from designing a theory of sound, with which he had been preoccupied for about sixteen years, between 1810 and 1826.[45] Goethe famously wrote: 'The eye was the most important organ with which I grasped the world' ('Das Auge war vor allem das Organ, womit ich die Welt faßte')[46] and indeed he may have used his eyes to perceive and apprehend the world (as we shall also see in chapter 7). Yet, he applied all the senses to create art and develop culture. This is, I assume, also how Nietzsche understood Goethe when he described him as a person of

---

43 Therefore, I do not agree with Lubkoll, who writes: 'Surely, he was not so much interested in the potency of the immediate expression of music – which had been put in front by the musical aesthetics of feeling of the late 18th century – as in music's structural characteristics, the complexity of composition' ('Allerdings faszinierte ihn weniger das – seit der empfindsamen Musikästhetik des späten 18. Jahrhunderts hervorgehobene – unmittelbare Ausdruckspotential der Musik als vielmehr ihre strukturellen Eigenheiten, die Komplexität der Komposition', Lubkoll, 2002, p. 399). This is the same as asserting that Goethe, because he developed a theory of colour, was more interested in the structure of paint and the lines in drawings than in the effect of the artwork on the beholder.
44 *Annalen* 1791.
45 See for a discussion of Goethe's theory of sound: Walwei-Wiegelmann (1985), pp. 211–225.
46 Dichtung und Wahrheit II/6, p. 354.

'totality'.[47] Not only did Goethe set out to harmonize art and knowledge, as is generally known, but also to integrate body and mind – and all senses for that matter.

From 1791 until 1817, Goethe was the general manager and director of Weimar's courtly theatre, which he had founded, after he was ordered so by Duke Charles August. As general manager, he was not only in charge of the repertoire, but also of the setting and dressing of the stage. He translated, rewrote, and directed plays from all over the world, amongst which were plays of Caldéron, Corneille and Racine, Shakespeare and many young German writers such as Heinrich von Kleist, Friedrich Schiller, the Schlegel-brothers, his favourite Iffland, and his own plays. On top of this, he acted in many of those plays. For example, he played Franz Moor in Schiller's *Robbers (Die Räuber)* and Wallenstein in the latter's *Wallenstein*. He also worked closely together with Anna Amalia, who composed music for two lyrical dramas written by Goethe, *Erwin and Elmire (Erwin und Elmire,* 1776) and the burlesque *Annual festival of Plundersweilern (Jahrmarktsfest zu Plundersweilern,* 1778).[48]

Apart from writing lyrical dramas already at such an early stage of his career (Goethe just came out of his *Storm and Stress* period, highlighted by the publication of his début, *Werther's Sorrows* in 1775),[49] Goethe continued his interest in musical drama by programming, translating, and directing various Italian operas for the Weimar theatre, amongst which were operas by Pasquale Anfossi (1729–1797) and Domenico Cimarosa (1749–1801). In fact, more than thirty percent of all performances under the direction of Goethe comprised operas and *Singspiele*.[50] We often think of him as the 'last Olympian' and the mature, wise creator of the gigantic *Faust*, but Goethe was young and up-to-date in spirit at all times, and perhaps ageless rather than '*unzeit-gemäss*' in the Nietzschean sense of 'unmodern'.

Erwin and Elmire and *Claudine von Villa Bella* (which Franz Schubert put to music in 1815) drew upon French comedy, yet later on he rewrote them in Italian opera *buffa* style, which also impregnated his *Joke, Cunning, and Revenge (Scherz, List und Rache)*.[51] All these lyrical dramas were written before Goethe even went to Italy in 1786.

---

47 TI Skirmishes 49 (pp. 222–223/KSA 6.151–152).

48 Goethe maintained a close intellectual and artistic friendship with Anna Amalia. At her request, he founded the Duchess Anna Amalia library in Weimar. They also spent some time together in Rome in 1788.

49 At the age of seventeen, Goethe wrote his first Italian libretto, '*La sposa rapita*' ('the abducted bride'), perhaps inspired by his mother, who loved to sing arias from Italian operas. Unfortunately, Goethe burned the libretto.

50 To be even more exact: 104 operas and 31 *Singspiele* (Fischer-Dieskau 2000, p. 45).

51 Goethe made his first *Singspiel* (*Erwin and Elmire*) in 1775 and published another *Play with Song (Schauspiel mit Gesang)* in *Iris*, a journal edited by Jacobi, in the same year. *Erwin and Elmire* had great success in the musical version of Reichhardt (it was performed in Frankfurt am Main, Munich, Vienna, and Berlin; it premiered in 1777 in Weimar with music by Anna Amalia). Schubert's *Claudine von Villa* is known as D 239. Unfortunately, only the first act survived (act II and III were admittedly

Nevertheless, they were based on a quite thorough and up-to-date knowledge of Italian *buffa* music, which he had not only acquired through his work as programme director of the Court-Theatre but also through his intensive contact with musicians and conductors such as Philipp Kayser, Carl Friedrich Zelter, Eberwein, and Friedrich Reichhardt. Goethe himself was very open about his admiration for Mozart, which had been instantly instilled in him when he attended a live piano concert performed by Mozart, then only seven years old. Goethe directed *The Magic Flute (Die Zauberflöte)* in his theatre in 1794,[52] and five other lyrical dramas and operas by Mozart – which puts Mozart on top of the ranking of operas performed in Goethe's theatre.[53] On the other hand, he felt intimidated by Mozart's talent and this seems to have prevented further attempts on his part to follow Mozart's example after *The Magic Flute II*, which Goethe had started to write in 1795 yet had never completed.[54]

Of all Goethe's lyrical dramas, *Joke, Cunning, and Revenge* most distinctly roots in the opera *buffa* model.[55] It was directly inspired by Rousseau's writings on music, Pergolesi, Piccini, and Salieri. It was intended for Goethe's old friend Kayser to set it to music, yet Kayser was as unsuccessful as Peter Gast about ninety years later. Just as Nietzsche overrated Gast's qualities, Goethe allegedly overestimated Kayser's. He also invited Kayser to come to Rome in order to learn more about Italian music. The libretto was accompanied by a clear musical aesthetics, which sought to stir the outer senses so as to penetrate the inner feelings or mood by appealing to the imagination, or 'the mind's eye'. The aim was to provoke images in the beholder's imagination and the meaning of music, for Goethe, resided precisely in this stirring of the imagination.[56] This is, clearly, in perfect accordance with Schiller's dramaturgy (as discussed in chapter 3) and similar to Wagner's appreciation of the musical genius and his 'inner eye' or 'inner vision' – however, without the Schopenhauerian, Romantic, and metaphysical components.

It appears that Wagner fairly misunderstood Goethe's and Schiller's creativity: theirs was more 'musical' and 'lyrical', and also more complex, than Wagner's dichotomist rigidity allowed for. Moreover, Goethe's turn to opera was largely motivated by his and Schiller's 'war' against naturalism in art.[57] Music, Schiller had argued, was

---

destroyed in a fire during the 1848 revolution). Goethe's *Singspiele* in Italian style for Anna Amalia's amateur theatre were *Lila, Der Triumph der Empfindsamkeit, Jery und Bätely*, and *Die Fischerin*.

52 Adapted by Christiane Vulpius, Goethe's lover and later wife. The performance was on 16 January 1794. Cf. Abert (1990-Vol. 2), p. 689.

53 *The Magic Flute* was performed 82 times, *Don Juan* 68 times, *Abduction from the Serial* 49 times, *Cosi fan tutte* 33 times, *Titus* 28 times, and *Figaro* 19 times (Fischer-Dieskau, 2000).

54 *The Magic Flute II* was published as unfinished fragment in 1802.

55 Love calls it 'Goethe's Italianate' (1981, p. 53).

56 Borchmeyer (2002), p. 429ff.

57 See Goethe's essay 'On Truth and Probability in Art' ('Über Wahrheit und Wahrscheinlichkeit der Kunstwerke' [1797], in which Goethe takes opera as the basis of his distinction between '*Kunstwahren*'

able to make mankind's inner mood more 'indifferent' to the outer world and thus freed mankind's imagination from its attachment to empirical reality or 'servile imitation' ('*servile Naturnachahmung*'). Schiller regarded this detachment as the beginning of dramatic reformation, in which the symbolic replaces imitation. The similar idea, I think, is behind all Goethe's decisions to dedicate part of his creativity to composing. However, this does not answer the question why he chose to adopt the Italian opera style. What did Italian opera have that German *Singspiele* lacked?

Goethe started writing *Joke, Cunning, and Revenge* in the spring of 1784 and finished it by the end of the year. The libretto was expressly conceived as an Italian opera *buffa*, a comic opera in the Italian style (as, for example, Mozart's *Così fan tutte*) and not as a *Singspiel*, a lyrical drama in German style. The extensive correspondence with Philipp Kayser (who was supposed to set the libretto to music) and letters to Charlotte von Stein, reveal how eager Goethe was to fulfil this project and have his opera performed not only in Weimar but on different stages throughout the German states.[58] Goethe hoped to kill two birds with one stone, namely explore new domains for his own creativity, and offer Kayser the possibility of an artistic break-through by 'making a German composer familiar with the Italian style' ('einen deutschen Componisten der italiänischen Manier näher zu bringen').[59] Yet, Goethe's personal objectives were formed by the cultural dimension of the project: to serve and help German culture to progress. Cultural progress to Goethe and Schiller was a matter of intercultural relations rather than of the so-called independent creation of a national style, to which Wagner aspired. Their cultural war against naturalism, therefore, must be seen in a more cosmopolitan dimension than Wagner's, who, by strongly opposing France and Italy, hoped for the domination of German art in Europe. In fact, Goethe and Schiller's method matched Nietzsche's interpretation of artistic and cultural relations in the sense that they were open to other styles and cultures and tried to adopt what was good about them. In brief, Goethe and Schiller were focused on art itself rather than on German art. Their aesthetics and artistic enterprises were all about symbolization, reaching the level of style, and, in so doing cultural progress. The hybrid form of music drama was not reserved for Germans alone; neither was the artistic genius.

When Goethe started focusing on the Italian style, the German *Singspiel* was a relatively young genre. However, the particular involvement in it by Wieland may have been more of a reason for him to turn his focus from *Singspiel* to opera *buffa*. Wieland had been presenting the *Singspiel* as Germany's national form and 'opera' as distinctively Italian and French, for the past ten years then.[60] With *Alceste*, Wieland

---

and '*Naturwahren*'). Cf. Schiller's so-called 'opera letter' of 29 December 1797, to which I also referred earlier.

58 Cf. Goethe to Kayser and Goethe to Charlotte von Stein, 14 June 1784 (HA I, pp. 442–444).

59 See Bötcher (1911), p. 31 (Goethe's letter Kayser is undated, but probably from the end of 1784).

60 See Colvin (2005), pp. 204–205.

had sought to create a national, German, form of opera. It was precisely because of Wieland's nationalism that Goethe persiflaged *Alceste* in the essay 'Gods, Heroes, and Wieland' ('Götter, Helden, und Wieland', 1774).[61]

Thus, Goethe conceived *Joke, Cunning, and Revenge* as completely Italian in style. Seen from this perspective, what can be said about Nietzsche's prelude in German rhymes of the same name?

Kathleen Marie Higgins, in her book-chapter on Nietzsche's *Joke, Cunning, and Revenge*, justifiably remarks that 'Nietzsche's own remarks scarcely enlighten us'.[62] In a letter to Erwin Rohde, Nietzsche hints that the verses have been written in the troubadour-spirit of the whole book.[63] Higgins first understands *The Gay Science* as a plea for 'a broadly based but light-hearted scholarship', and the prelude, in light of this, as a 'call for a rebirth of the troubadour spirit'.[64] Second, she perceives the verses as a parody of Goethe's work.[65] By way of a comparative study of Goethe's and Nietzsche's text, she concludes that Nietzsche presented himself as a 'physician' with *Joke, Cunning, and Revenge*, who advises to live 'light-heartedly' and in a childlike way, thus pre- or amoral – which is a doctor's advice that will not suit every reader, she remarks. Third, she interprets the prelude as a parody of childhood nursery rhymes, claiming that normally such rhymes have a moralistic character, but in Nietzsche's case they defend amoralism. Although I agree with the fact that the verses, in the light of the rest of *The Gay Science*, seem to call for 'immoralism', there is, I want to argue below, more to it. Therefore, I first have to say something about the English translation of the verses by Kaufmann, Higgins, and Del Caro.

I shall give an example of the poem 'invitation', because it indicates not only how difficult it is to make an accurate translation, but also how a false translation can lead to a confused interpretation. Adrian del Caro made the Cambridge-translation of the poems.[66] This is his translation of the last lines of 'Invitation': 'I'll make it,/from past inspiration take it,/turning food for thought to food'. Kaufmann translates: 'All the

---

61 Wieland's *Singspiel Alceste* was inspired by Gluck's opera, while it in fact criticized the heroism of Euripides's play of the same name. Wieland wrote it together with the musician Anton Sweitzer. It was premiered in Weimar in 1773. As a reaction to Goethe's essay, Wieland published an essay in his magazine *Teutsche Merkur*, in which he argued that the *Singspiel* resembled closely Greek ancient drama, and more so than opera. Here we see the basis of Wagner's later claim. Despite Goethe's criticism of Wieland's rejection of Euripides, the two men became good friends, after Goethe had moved to Weimar in 1775, where Wieland had been living since 1773.

62 Higgins (2000), p. 14.

63 Letter of begin December 1882 (KSB 6, p. 292).

64 Higgins (2000), p. 15. The title 'gay science' refers to the '*gai saber*' of the Provençal troubadours of the 11th-13th-century, who, in short, tried to combine art and wisdom according to the principles '*joi*', '*cortesia*', and '*mesura*'. See Prange (2005), pp. 127–133.

65 See also Gilman (1975) and (1976).

66 On p. 11 of the 2001 Cambridge translation, Del Caro refers to *Scherz, List und Rache* as *Joke, Cunning, and Revenge*. *The Gay Science* is further translated by Josefine Nauckhoff.

things I've done before/Will inspire things quite new'.[67] Higgins renders the lines as: 'I'll take cues from my old stuff/to make something new'.[68] Higgins's translation is no better than Kaufmann's in the sense that the words 'something new' are too neutral to give an indication of what Nietzsche said (while Del Caro makes a too interpretative translation). Rather than just 'something new' or 'things quite new', Nietzsche says 'more stuff', more 'bits-and-pieces', more 'titbits' or 'scraps'. The whole poem goes as follows:

> *Einladung.*/Wagt's mit meiner Kost, ihr Esser!/Morgen schmeckt sie euch schon besser/Und schon übermorgen gut!/Wollt ihr dann noch mehr, – so machen/Meine alten sieben Sachen/Mir zu sieben neuen Muth (KSA 3.353)

An alternative translation could be:

> *Invitation.*/Take a dare with my fare, you guests! /Tomorrow you will like the fare already better/ And the day after very much indeed!/And if you then feel like more/– my old stuff will/hearten me to new scraps.[69]

What Nietzsche says here is that his courage to write more verses depends on our liking. If we like his 'stuff' (his *'sieben Sachen'*), he will cook us some more. So, first we try them, then we shall not reject them, then we will even like them, and then, in the fourth instance, only then, if we feel like more, then he will have the heart to freshly cook us some more of the like.[70] Higgins, inspired by Koelb, interprets this 'wordplay' as having 'a deeper significance', namely 'the transformation of trifles into insights'.

According to her, the lines are about 'the transformation of banalities into something else', because it is 'the philosopher's task' to make 'the familiar problematic'.[71] Despite Higgins's stimulating interpretation, I do not think that the first little verse goes this far. Nietzsche just asks his readers to go along with him, to listen to what he has to say, and then, the moment we are doing that, he orders us to follow our own ideas (in poem 7 *'vademecum, vadetecum'*), well in the spirit of the free-spirit philosophy of *The Gay Science*: 'think for yourself, but: think!' Poem 7, it seems to me, points to poem 23 ('wer nur steigt auf seiner eignen Bahn,/Trägt auch mein Bild zu hellerm Licht hinan', KSA 3.357) and GS 99, where Nietzsche's cites Goethe's motto preceding the second edition of *Werther's Sufferings*: 'Be a man and do not follow me – but

---

67 *The Gay Science*, translated by Kaufmann 1974, p. 41.
68 Higgins (2000), p. 25.
69 In *Faust*, there is also a sexual connection, when Mephisto uses the term to indicate the seven places of a female body, which could be touched (*Faust I* 2031, HA III, p. 66).
70 Langer (2011) interprets the food metaphor as to suggest that Nietzsche's philosophy 'is not meant for detached contemplation,' but for incorporation, 'becoming part of the eaters' flesh and blood (p. 15).
71 Higgins (2000), p. 26.

yourself! Yourself!' (p. 98/'Sei ein Mann und folge mir nicht nach, – sondern dir! Sondern dir!' KSA 3.457). Nietzsche explains: *'everyone who wants to be free must become
so through himself'* (p. 98/'*Jeder, der frei werden will, [muss] es durch sich selber werden [...]*', KSA 3.457). 'Freedom', then, is understood as 'the innocence of the utmost
selfishness; the faith in great passion as the good in itself' (p. 96/'die Unschuld der
höchsten Selbstsucht, der Glaube an die grosse Leidenschaft als an das Gute an sich',
KSA 3.455).

The fact that Wagner initially appeared to him as a true '*K. Freigedank*', a free
spirit, who followed his own ideas and passions, had attracted Nietzsche, because
his free spirit promised the purely and highly artistic mode of being, the innocent
and aesthetic way of life, unpolluted and unconstrained by moral conventions. This is
what the important aphorism GS 99 suggests. However, in order to find this freedom,
Nietzsche suggests that we *do* follow him in his process of 'de-Germanization', in his
travel to the idyllic and 'innocent' South.[72] He invites us to change our musical taste
from German music to Italian music. In the first poem, he therefore asks his readers to
follow his lead, which results eventually in this plea for aesthetic freedom. In addition,
connecting it to Peter Gast, he may even be indirectly asking his audience to listen to
Peter Gast's opera *Joke, Cunning, and Revenge*, one, two, three, four times. And we will
be given more, if we wish so.

Perceiving the plea for immorality is not enough, though, for grasping the whole of
Nietzsche's free-spirit philosophy. If one fails to connect the amoral nature of the prelude (and the book in general) to the south or Italy, one misses much of Nietzsche's
recipe. The main reason for Nietzsche to follow Goethe at all is Goethe's ability to look
purely aesthetically at life, a look he developed particularly in Italy. Rather than being
a recipe on its own, Nietzsche's amoralism is the result of another recipe, which says
that one should 'become Mediterranean': travel to the South to rid oneself of one's
northern, moral spirit. *Joke, Cunning, and Revenge* must be viewed within Nietzsche's
call to become Mediterranean, a call he addresses to (northern) music in the first place,
but also, in *The Gay Science* specifically, to (northern) philosophers and artists in general. Nietzsche's insertion of the 'prelude' *Joke, Cunning, and Revenge* within *The Gay
Science* is testimony to his attempt to become 'Mediterranean', to mix the north and
the south and shape himself into a 'good European'. This is what his 'de-Germanizing'
path eventually aims at. Moreover, with his poetry, he also offers Peter Gast an example as how to 'de-Germanize' and make 'Mediterranean' music, namely by inserting
the Italian way. Thus, whereas I argued that *The Birth of Tragedy* was meant, amongst
other things, to help Wagner on the path of his *'Graecization'* and 'southernization',

---

72 As 'In the South' (p. 251–252/KSA 3.641–642) makes explicit. This poem is part of the *Songs of Prince
Vogelfrei* (Prince Free-as-a-bird) and an adaptation of the poem 'Prince Vogelfrei' ('Prinz Vogelfrei').
See for an interpretation of these poems and their connection Prange (2005), pp. 120–126, Prange
[2006-2], and Prange [2011-2].

Joke, Cunning, and Revenge supports Gast's attempt to synthesize the north and the south in his music. The prelude introduces the aim Nietzsche had with *The Gay Science* as a whole, namely to urge German philosophers and artists alike to travel to 'the South' in order to transform themselves into 'good Europeans'. Cast in this light, *Joke, Cunning, and Revenge* offers a 'European' form of art, as it mixes the Italian *buffa* style into the German Singspiel. *Joke, Cunning, and Revenge* comprises, just as *The Gay Science* (including 'The Songs of Prince Vogelfrei'), a plea for (and result of) 'de-Germanization' or 'dynamic interculturalism'.

Next, rather than as a comical parody, I regard Nietzsche's verses in German rhymes as a confirmation of Goethe's creativity and musicality. Nietzsche was very pleased with his *Joke, Cunning, and Revenge*, and hinted at the troubadour spirit of the rhymes, as Higgins justifiably remarks.[73] She also admits that 'other bases for interpretation also have merit' and she therefore turns to what she calls the 'farcical *Singspiel* by Goethe'.[74] She thus understands that there is a the musical aspect in Nietzsche's rhymes, however she does not see the cultural impact of it, that is, to see it as a part of Nietzsche's 'dynamic interculturalism', his attempt to 'Italianize' or make German music and culture more Mediterranean.

Joke, Cunning, and Revenge as 'prelude' to *The Gay Science* is more than a random bunch of funny nursery rhymes with which the gay scientist makes his or her gay entrée, and the public meets the frivolity and scepticism as cornerstones of the gay scientist's world. Seen in relation to Goethe's libretto, much can be said for the musicality of this gay scientist and his or her Italian character, or also his or her 'health'. Nietzsche's *Joke, Cunning, and Revenge* is not the attempt to create German verses or to create Italian music for its own sake. Rather, it is a libretto created to infuse the German Singspiel with the Italian style. By connecting different artistic forms, Nietzsche seeks to carry out his and German culture's 'de-Germanization' and 'Mediterranization'. Goethe did so with the explicit intention to mix up cultures too, both in his *Westöstlicher Divan* (1826), with which he tried to bring together Persia and Europe by bringing the Eastern soul to life in the Oriental poetical tradition of '*Divan*' ('compilation') through a Western, European language.

Subsequently, when we relate the above to Wagner's musical and cultural objectives, it makes even more sense. Whereas Wagner primarily regarded himself as the heir of Beethoven's symphonic legacy, Nietzsche put more emphasis on Wagner as the successor to Goethe's and Schiller's legacy to reform the German theatre. When Nietzsche attended the Bayreuth festival in the summer of 1876, it not only became

---

73 Higgins (2000), pp. 14–15. See for Nietzsche on GSJ: Nietzsche to Ernst Schmeitzner, 8 May 1882 (KSB 6, p. 191). Cf. Nietzsche to Jacob Burckhardt, August 1882 (KSB 6, pp. 234–235), Nietzsche to Lou Andreas-Salomé, 15 June 1882 (KSB 6, p. 205) and 16 September 1882 (KSB 6, p. 260), and Nietzsche to Peter Gast, 25 July 1882 (KSB 6, p. 232).
74 Higgins (2000), p. 15.

clear to him that Wagner was not truly 'Greek', but also that Wagner would not accomplish the artistic reformation ushered in by Goethe and Schiller. Goethe and Schiller can justifiably be regarded as the forerunners of Wagner's, not only because of their project to create a national theatre, but also because of the way they had chosen to achieve this, namely by creating operas, which could compete with Italian and French opera in artistry and cultural value. This legacy was still there to be taken up by someone else, and Nietzsche, so it seems, took up this legacy himself with the help of Peter Gast.

In the early seventies, Nietzsche did not really care for Goethe's interest in music. This is understandable given his critique of Italian opera at that time and his plea for 'Graecization' rather than 'Italianization'. Ten years later, however, Nietzsche understood Goethe as the only German before him who had understood the importance of aesthetics and the mix of cultures. Only Goethe had not mixed up aesthetics and morality, Nietzsche asserts. It is under the umbrella of the 'aestheticization' of the perception of life and of culture that Goethe and Nietzsche practised 'dynamic interculturalism'; their interest in Italian music was one means to do so.

Aphorism GS 103 is perhaps the pinnacle of Nietzsche's musical turn from Wagnerism to anti-Wagnerism, from 'German' to 'southern' music, and from Wagner's 'Beethoven' essay as containing '*the* philosophy of music' to the creation of his own standards.[75] There he asserts that German music is the product of a revolutionary spirit, and that it misses the 'esprit' and 'elegance' of a courtly society (like the ones of the troubadours), and attests to a 'contempt for melody'. He summarizes this in opposing Beethoven, who to him now symbolizes Germany's 'semi-barbarism' (p. 100/'*Halbbarbarei*', GS 103, KSA 3.460) and is called 'the untamed human being' (p. 101/'*der ungebändigte Mensch*', GS 103, KSA 3.460) against Goethe, the symbol of 'culture' (p. 101/ '*Cultur*', GS 103, KSA 3.460) and 'exception among Germans' (p. 101/'*der Ausnahme-Deutsche*', GS 103, KSA 3.460).[76] This opposition can be understood as confirmation and representation of the antagonism between Wagner, whose great example was Beethoven, and Nietzsche, who had replaced his model of the ideal artist and cultural saviour Wagner with Goethe. By means of opposing Goethe and Beethoven, Nietzsche then confirms his veneration of Goethe as a searcher for and guardian of 'totality', in making musical drama, thereby criticizing Wagner's narrow perception of Goethe's creativity, and his failed, moral music dramas.

---

75 GS 103 (pp. 100–101/KSA 3.459–460).
76 Cf. BGE 46, where he opposes the 'nothern barbarian of the spirit' to the 'skeptical, southern, free-spirited world' (p. 44/KSA 5.66). Cf. GS 350 (p. 208/KSA 3.586).

Conclusion

As chapter 5 revealed, Nietzsche regarded his 'free-spirit' books as travel books. They were testimony to his departure from Germany and, even more so, of his new life in (the surroundings of) Genoa, the Italian city at the Ligurian coast. *Daybreak* (1881) and *The Gay Science* (1882) were especially 'Genoese' books, in reporting his 'convalescence' or 'de-Germanization'. In this chapter, I argued that Nietzsche developed a new musical aesthetics in line with his 'anti-Romantic therapy', which he came to formulate from the winter of 1881 onwards, when he heard *Carmen* for the first time in Genoa.

In addition, Italian music even stimulated him to write a libretto as a means to mix the north (German) and south (Italy) and carry out the 'cultural war' ushered in by Goethe and Schiller. His old ideal of 'musicalizing' art and culture thus found a new impetus in the 'idyllic' music he formerly rejected so harshly. Together with his discovery of the beauty and pleasure of Italian opera, the 'idyll' made a spectacular comeback in Nietzsche's life, namely as a tool to describe his perception of landscapes, music, landscape painting and painters (Claude Lorrain, Nicholas Poussin) as well as Epicurean philosophy – to which he felt particularly drawn after his farewell to Schopenhauerian metaphysics. This return of the idyll implies that the notion of the idyll has affected both Nietzsche's position as a 'tragic' and as a 'heroic' philosopher, yet transfering the ability to generate 'joy' from the *Gestaltenspiel* that the genius played in his dreams to the *Formenspiel* of idyllic, Italian opera.

Despite his turn to what he used to call 'idyllic', and thus 'moral' music, Nietzsche claimed that his new taste for the 'light' music was a sign of health. 'Lightness' also turned out to be the key to his new musical aesthetics, which was still focused at expressing the 'Dionysian'. Given his pre-Wagnerian preference for the Old German School, his return to the tonal system made sense, yet the question why he did not return to that music, but to Italian opera instead, had to be answered. Rather than as an 'ironical antithesis' to Wagner, I claim that Nietzsche's turn to Italian comical opera, including *Carmen*, must be understood as an expression of his 'dynamic interculturalism' and his continuous belief in the powers of combining music and drama. Strikingly, though, he seemed to have had fully abstained from the chorus in those days, seeking connection rather to the troubadours and individual singers of Italian opera, and the constraint of passions by way of technical superiority – a superiority which was again revealed in the 'innocence of melody'. Apparently, 'melody' was no longer regarded as hostile to rhythm and based upon breaking rhythm open by way of 'Zeitfolge', but included the – old-fashioned – 'Periodenbau'. Moreover, the fact that the musician excels by way of technical superiority and not by the special talent for dreaming and inner visions, intimates that the levels of the symbol, style, 'health,' and culture were reached by the technical perfection of music within the classical tonal system, in Nietzsche's new musical aesthetics. The (cultural) meaning of music came to reside in the tones, i.e., its *formal beauty*, not so much in a Hanslickian way, but in the way of 'light' music, in which the representation of the tragic experience (of love and life and death) went hand-in-hand with a lightness of tone and joyfulnes in dramatic representation.

His new musical aesthetics, thus, was almost the complete opposite of his former musical aesthetics. Germany and Wagner had been replaced by Italy and Goethe, while the relation between the 'Dionysian' and the 'idyllic' had turned from an exclusive opposition (in *The Birth of Tragedy*) into an intimate, harmonious bond, in which the abundance of passion and life found aesthetic style. This bond celebrates, we may say, the successful marriage of the 'north' and 'south' in 'good Europeanism', and the victory of the aesthetic view of life over the moral view, and therefore the perfection of the 'free spirit' as a healthy 'good European', as we shall see in the next chapter.

Chapter 7
Goethe as model of the 'Good European'

Introduction[1]

What, exactly, is the free-spirited philosophy, of which *Joke, Cunning, and Revenge* is the '*wohltonendste Fürsprecherin*'? While this is open to many interpretations, it certainly expresses an aestheticist, naturalist, sensualist, and cosmopolitan life-style, which Nietzsche calls 'good Europeanism' and of which Goethe is the model. The aim of this chapter is straightforward: to reconstruct the identity of the free spirit as 'good European', by analysing further Nietzsche's understanding of Goethe as a model of the good European. I argue that the 'free spirit' coincides with the figure of the 'good European'. This is particularly indicated by *The Wanderer and His Shadow* 87 (the first aphorism to mention the 'good European') and the preface of *Beyond Good and Evil*, which introduces the good Europeans as 'very free spirits' and the 'new philosophers of the future', who will set the values for the post-Christian and post-modern era. In *The Wanderer and His Shadow* 87, Nietzsche claims that nationalism augments 'the sickness of this century and is an enemy of all good Europeans, and enemy of all free spirits' (*The Wanderer and His Shadow* 87/'die Krankheit dieses Jahrhunderts und ist ein Feind der guten Europäer, ein Feind der freien Geister', KSA 2.593). In addition, the aphorism states that the Good Europeans have the great task of assuming 'the direction and supervision of the total culture of the earth' (p. 332/'die Leitung und Ueberwachung der gesammten Erdcultur', KSA 2.592). Good Europeans promote the 'mix of cultures' and the 'amalgamation of nations'.

I further claim that the figure of the 'good European' is drafted upon the example of Goethe; the 'good European' has adopted Goethe's cosmopolitanism as 'dynamic interculturalism' and has adopted his aesthetic, sensualist take on life. As we recall from chapter 4, Goethe had taught Nietzsche that the Greeks had an aesthetic answer even to the most tragic events in life. This insight became central to the aesthetics developed in *The Birth of Tragedy*. In *The Gay Science*, Nietzsche once again investigates humanity's aesthetic powers, pleading for an aesthetic approach to life. The book claims that this is especially urgent since religion's powers are fading and alternative approaches (Socratic, scientific ones or Christian, moral ones) are life-denying, i.e., nihilistic. In line with this, I claim that *The Gay Science* can, similar to *The Birth of Tragedy*, also be regarded as a manual, this time addressed to 'good Europeans'. While Nietzsche had written *The Birth of Tragedy* as, amongst other things, an instruction to Wagner on how to become 'more Greek', *The Gay Science* offers its readers the report of

---

1 This chapter draws on and uses substantial parts of Prange (2005), Prange (2006-2), and Prange (2011-2).

Nietzsche's personal recovery, so that persons suffering from the same sickness (and we can congregate them as 'all Europeans living under the "shadow of God"'[2]) can learn from it the last lessons of the 'anti-Romantic therapy'.

The last lessons consist of, first, a 'threefold aesthetics', consisting of an aesthetics of seeing, an aesthetics of the self, and an aesthetics of art. As I hope to show, in all three aesthetic modes, the south, as embodied in the 'supra-German', 'Italianized' Goethe and the city of Genoa, plays a central part. In addition, I make a comparative analysis of the poems 'Prince Vogelfrei' and 'In the South', which was published as part of *The Songs of Prince Vogelfrei* and added to the 1887 edition of *The Gay Science*. This will suggest the conclusion that, according to Nietzsche, philosophers and artists alike should travel to the south in order to become 'truly free spirits' and healthy 'good Europeans', who live 'for the sake of joy and for no further goal'.

Goethe is the central figure in the following discussion. Although Nietzsche's indebtedness to him is acknowledged by many commentators,[3] neither 'Goethe' nor 'the south' has ever been taken as the key figure and term respectively with which his Good Europeanism and *The Gay Science* can be understood.

The Gay Science's 'threefold aesthetics'

Amor fati: finding health

The 'Graecization' or 'southernization' that Nietzsche pleaded for in *The Birth of Tragedy*, is also the essence of Nietzsche's later, anti-Wagnerian aesthetics, which comes to completion in *The Gay Science*, specifically book IV, *Sanctus Januarius*.

Sanctus Januarius sets off with the first public announcement of Nietzsche's new philosophy of *amor fati*, in aphorism GS 276.[4] The famous text has the form of a New Year's greeting.[5] Nietzsche declares that he has decided to do things differently in the new year of 1882.[6] He wanted to mend his ways forever. The lesson he had to learn

---

2 Compare GS 108 (p. 109/KSA 3.467) and GS 125 (p. 119–120/KSA 3.480–482).

3 See for example: Bertram (1929), Heller (1988), pp. 18–38, Montinari (1982), pp. 56–63 and Meyer (2001). Especially Bishop and Stephenson (2005), Venturelli (1989), and Vivarelli (1991 and 1994) seem to recognize the fundamental impact of Goethe's influence on Nietzsche.

4 *Sanctus Januarius* is the result of three weeks of continuous, high spirit in January 1882. Cf.: 'Basically, "the gay science" is just an exuberant way to rejoice over the fact that one has had a clear sky above one's head for one month' ('Im Grunde ist "die fröhliche Wissenschaft" nur eine überschwängliche Art sich zu freuen, daß man einen Monat *reinen Himmel über sich* gehabt hat.' Nietzsche to Franz Overbeck, 20 January 1883, KSB 6, pp. 318–319).

5 GS 276 (p. 157/KSA 3.521).

6 One could argue whether one should not separate Nietzsche from the author here, but given that Nietzsche regarded *The Gay Science* as his most personal book, and the clear and abundant testimonies

was to consider the necessity of life as beauty, to say with total conviction 'yes' to life, however ugly or repulsive life sometimes could be. Moreover, *amor fati* contains the – often overlooked but important – task of making everything more beautiful. This 'yes' and beautification of life, was supposed to be the last step of Nietzsche's return to himself, the world, and his health.

In the epilogue to *Nietzsche contra Wagner*, Nietzsche states: 'Amor fati: that is my innermost nature' (NW Epilogue, p. 280/'Amor fati: das ist meine innerste Natur', KSA 6.436), expressing the awareness that every moment, happy or sad, is necessary for the fulfilment of one's personal destiny and happiness.[7] Nietzsche recognized this form of happiness in Epicurus:

> I see his [Epicurus's, MP] eyes gaze at a wide whitish sea, across shoreline rocks bathed in the sun, as large and small creatures play in its light, secure and calm like the light and his eye itself. Only someone who is continually suffering could invent such happiness – the happiness of an eye before which the sea of existence has grown still and which now cannot get enough of seeing the surface and this colourful, tender, quivering skin of the sea: never before has voluptuousness been so modest. (GS 45, p. 59)

> ich sehe sein [Epicurus's, MP] Auge auf ein weites weissliches Meer blicken, über Uferfelsen hin, auf denen die Sonne liegt, während grosses und kleines Gethier in ihrem Lichte spielt, sicher und ruhig wie diess Licht und jenes Auge selber. Solch ein Glück hat nur ein fortwährend Leidender erfinden können, das Glück eines Auges, vor dem das Meer des Daseins stille geworden ist, und das nun an seiner Oberfläche und an dieser bunten, zarten, schaudernden Meeres-Haut sich nicht mehr satt sehen kann; es gab nie zuvor eine solche Bescheidenheit der Wollust. (KSA 3.411)

He calls Epicurus's 'garden-happiness' ('*Garten-Glück*'[8]), because it has a fundament of pain, typically Greek 'cheerfulness' ('*Heiterkeit*'). He models the free spirit, next to Goethe, on Epicurus. This spirit chooses to remain at the surface, near the skin of things, out of tragic depth. Nietzsche labels this as typically *Greek*: 'Those Greeks were superficial – *out of profundity!*' (GS Preface 4, p. 9/'Diese Griechen waren oberflächlich – *aus Tiefe*/KSA 3, 352)'.[9] Such spirits 'no longer believe that truth remains truth when one pulls off the veil; we have lived too much to believe this' (GS Preface 4, p. 8/ 'glauben nicht mehr daran, dass Wahrheit noch Wahrheit bleibt, wenn man ihr die

---

he gave to the fact that the free-spirit books are products of his personal recovery, it is safe to put the author and Nietzsche on a par. Moreover, rather than reducing his philosophy to psychology here, it was the philosopher, who created the free-spirit philosophy and *amor fati* doctrine in line with his psychological and physiological analyses and experiments.

7 Cf. GS 338, where Nietzsche speaks of 'a personal necessity of misfortune' (p. 191/'persönliche Nothwendigkeit des Unglücks', KSA 3.566).

8 See 30[31], KSA 8.527. Duncan Large calls this Epicurus 'distinctly Genoese' (1995, p. 168) and I fully agree with this epithet.

9 In GS 107 (pp. 104–105/KSA 3.464–465), it is made clear that 'we' still need art in order to not kill ourselves, i.e., to be able to deal with the tragic.

Schleier abzieht [...]', KSA 3.352). Here, the idyllic and tragic come together in the affirmation of the world as an aesthetic appearance 'out of profundity'.

Hence, to become a truly free spirit, one has to adopt an 'Epicurean' lifestyle. *Sanctus Januarius* distinguishes the Epicurean lifestyle from the Stoic one. Whereas the Stoic develops a hard, insensitive skin, the Epicurean has a 'subtle sensitivity' (GS 306, p. 174/*'feine Reizbarkeit,'* KSA 3.544), according to Nietzsche. Instead of trying to get rid of this, as the Stoics, the Epicureans attempt to retain this sensitivity. To the Stoic, however, even the slightest sense of lust or distress spells danger to his peace of mind. Arming himself so firmly, the Stoic, Nietzsche writes, cuts himself off from 'the most beautiful fortuities of his soul' (GS 305, p. 174/'von den schönsten Zufälligkeiten der Seele', KSA 3.543) and 'from all further instruction' (GS 305, p. 174/'von aller weiteren Belehrung', KSA 3.543). It is the more open, Epicurean approach to life, the more sensitive, 'porous' skin that Nietzsche takes as exemplary to his alternative, selfish, southern morality, against the 'Stoic' fear of the unknown as a northern hallmark.[10] However, in addition to an 'Epicurean' lifestyle, one should adopt a Goethean view of the world: As a *'Ketten-Kranke'* living in the North, Nietzsche looked upon things 'with a terrible coldness' (D 114, p. 69/'[...] mit einer entsetzlichen Kälte', KSA 3.105). Being in Genoa and developing his warm, loving eye for the world under supervision of Johann Wolfgang von Goethe, Nietzsche defrosted and learned, as a true cosmopolitan individual, how to incorporate foreign forms and elements.[11]

Learning to love the world: Nietzsche's aesthetics of seeing

In his *Italian Journey* (*Italienische Reise*, 1816/1829), which Nietzsche re-read in Genoa,[12] Goethe wrote: 'At present I am only concerned with sense impressions, which no book, no picture, can give. The fact is that I am taking an interest in the world again' ('Mir ist es jetzt nur um die sinnlichen Eindrücke zu thun, die kein Buch, kein Bild gibt. Die Sache ist, daß ich wieder Interesse an die Welt nehme').[13] In Italy, where he stayed between 1786 and 1788, Goethe trained his 'powers of observation' (*'Beobachtungsgeist'*)[14] to ascertain that his 'eye [is] clear, pure, and bright' ('Auge licht, rein und hell ist'),[15] and that he was able to express his visual impressions

---

10 'Selfish' can be negative and positive. Here, it is used in its positive sense, as a characteristic of healthy people.
11 *The Gay Science* is the result of the *'triumph* over winter' (GS Preface 1, p. 3/'*Sieg* über den Winter', KSA 3.345), and its language is the 'language of the wind that brings a thaw' (GS Preface 1, p. 3/'Sprache des Thauwinds', KSA 3.345).
12 Vivetta Vivarelli, (1991), p. 134.
13 *Italian Journey*, 11 September 1786, p. 25/HA XI, p. 25.
14 *Italian Journey*, 11 September 1786, p. 25/HA XI, p. 25.
15 *Italian Journey*, 11 September 1786, p. 25/HA XI, p. 25.

creatively. In Italy, he looked at art and nature with the eye of an Italian painter. In his reports, Goethe holds the view that one's natural environment shapes the brightness of one's perception of life. During his stay in Venice, for that reason he wrote:

> Obviously the eye is formed by the objects it beholds from childhood on, and so the Venetian painter must see everything more clearly and brightly than other people. We who live on ground that is either dirty and muddy or dusty, that is colourless and dims reflections, and who perhaps even live in narrow rooms, cannot independently develop such a cheerful eye.[16]

> Es ist offenbar, daß sich das Auge nach den Gegenständen bildet, die es von Jugend auf erblickt, und so muß der venezianische Maler alles klarer und heiterer sehn als andere Menschen. Wir, die wir auf einem bald schmutzkotigen, bald staubigen, farblosen, die Widerscheine verdüsternden Boden und vielleicht gar in engen Gemächern leben, können einen solchen Frohblick aus uns selbst nicht entwickeln.

The opposition of north and south or Germany and Italy formed the main frame of Goethe's experience of Italy. In this, the north stands out in darkness to the bright south. In Italy, Goethe experienced a 'rebirth' ('*Wiedergeburt*').[17] This rebirth consisted in a return to the world and gaining sensuous knowledge.[18] The artist Goethe did not want to work from theory alone any longer, but add to it sensual observation, in which he tried to catch the vitality of things and reach the highest plastic grasp of art and nature.[19] He aspired to master the Italian 'cheerful eye' ('*Frohblick*').

Following Goethe's example, Nietzsche wanted to find the way back to the appearance of things, to the reflection and colours which things catapult into the world. Against the modern scientists, he sought the same clear, bright, and warm eye as Goethe. Modern scientists assume that they see better by looking at the world with a so-called objective eye, Nietzsche articulates, but their attitude is 'frozen and dry like a bright morning in winter' (D 539, p. 213/'gefroren und trocken wie ein heller Morgen im Winter', KSA 3.308). Contrary to science's claim to objectivity, Nietzsche advocates that 'intellectual honesty' and 'justice to the world' require a warm, engaged attitude towards the unknown, which he in The Gay Science describes as learning to love 'what is strange' (GS 334, p. 186/'das Fremde', KSA 3.560).[20]

This is a process in which one first discriminates one's immediate surroundings, then learns to tolerate this strange environment with patience, good will, exertion,

---

16 *Italian Journey*, 08 October 1786, p. 73/HA XI, pp. 86–87.
17 *Italian Journey*, 20 December 1786 (p. 123/HA XI, p. 150).
18 Cf. 27 June 1787: 'I shall not rest until everything that is still merely words and tradition for me becomes a living concept' (p. 279/'Ich will auch nicht mehr ruhen, bis mir nichts mehr Wort und Tradition, sondern lebendiger Begriff ist', HA XI, p. 352).
19 Cf. 28 August 1787: 'I must advance in art to the point where everything becomes intuitive knowledge, where nothing remains tradition and name' (p. 310/'In der Kunst muß ich es so weit bringen, daß alles anschauende Kenntnis werde, nichts Tradition und Name bleibe', HA XI, pp. 388–389).
20 Cf. 6[67], KSA 9.211.

and sympathy, and in the end appreciates its beauty and becomes a 'lover' of 'what is strange', experiencing 'goodwill to all things closest to me' (WS 350, p. 393/'ein Wohlgefallen an allen nächsten Dingen', KSA 2.702). Emphasizing once again the competitive nature of the engagement with people from other cultures, Nietzsche calls this learning attitude one of 'calm hostility': 'you let foreign things, new things of every type come towards you while assuming an initial air of calm hostility' (TI *What the Germans Lack* 6, p. 191/'Man wird Fremdes, Neues jeder Art zunächst mit feindseliger Ruhe herankommen lassen', KSA 6.109). By this, Nietzsche means 'getting your eyes used to calm, to patience, to letting things come to you; postponing judgment, learning to encompass and take stock of an individual case from all sides' (TI *What the Germans Lack* 6, p. 190/'dem Auge die Ruhe, die Geduld, das An-sich-herankommen-lassen angewöhnen; das Urtheil hinaus-schieben, den Einzelfall von allen Seiten umgehn und umfassen lernen', KSA 6.108).

Learning to love oneself: Nietzsche's aesthetics of the self

In order to become a truly free spirit (and 'gay scientist', for that matter), however, one needs not only to learn to love the world, but also to learn to love oneself. According to aphorism 107 of *The Gay Science*, life can be justified only aesthetically. This, of course, is the great constant in Nietzsche's thought, as it already dominated *The Birth of Tragedy*. Art, Nietzsche supposes, enables us to make a work of art out of our character. Aphorism 290 of *Sanctus Januarius* reveals how a free spirit might turn his personality into a paragon of 'art and reason' ('Kunst und Vernunft') in order to reach complete satisfaction with him- or herself. According to the last sentence of aphorism 107, this process of loving oneself can only begin by shedding one's shame. Shamelessness is *'the seal of having become free'* (p. 153/*'das Siegel der erreichten Freiheit'*, KSA 3.519), as Nietzsche declares in aphorism 275. To no longer feel ashamed of oneself means that one no longer views one's passions as stains of nature,[21] as the northern type of man had learned from the Stoics and Christians.

Noble and 'Greek' individuals such as Epicurus and Goethe are not ashamed of what they feel. They rather live on their passions and trust these as 'the good in itself' (GS 99, p. 96/'das Gute an sich', KSA 3.433). Nietzsche calls this attitude 'the innocence of the utmost selfishness' ('die Unschuld der höchsten Selbstsucht', KSA 3.433) and he finds this absence of shame, which forms the foundation of the natural, noble, and free person, in Italy. He even calls it 'the peculiarity of Southern humanity' (GS 77, p. 78/ 'die Eigenheit der südländischen Humanität', KSA 3.433).

Shamelessness is the first step to developing an anti-Christian, selfish morality, and a free, creative, heroic philosophy that opposes personal wisdom to general opin-

---

21 See 6[382], KSA 9.296.

ion. A heroic philosophy implies the absence of fear of pain and the ability to be alone. Pain should ground his particularity. Western society understands 'happiness' as the absence of pain.[22] However, a true heroic philosopher celebrates his suffering, because he accepts it as a natural effect of his decision to embrace life and he knows that misery may result in wisdom.[23] His experiences form the source of his wisdom. He seeks harmony between life and philosophy. Life, to him, is a practice in accordance with his view of life, which, on the other hand, is the consequence of his life-experiments: 'we want to be our own experiments and guinea-pigs' (GS 319, p. 180/'Wir selber wollen unsere Experimente und Versuchs-Thiere sein', KSA 3.551).[24] The free spirit 'experiments' with thought to liberate his or her mind from old habits and to awaken society to boot, anticipating the task assigned in *Beyond Good and Evil* to the 'new philosophers', 'very free spirits', and 'good Europeans' of keeping humanity awake.[25]

Goethe as Nietzsche's model of the 'good European'

Nietzsche's heroic philosopher is an engaged, practical thinker, for whom every thought is expressed in an action and every action functions as a touchstone for his ideas. His daily life is an experiment, and conducting experiments supplies him

---

22 GS 326 (p. 181–182/KSA 3.553–554).

23 GS 318 (p. 179/KSA 3.550).

24 The free spirit does not share the 'habitual and undiscussable principles' (HH I 224, p. 107/'gewohnten und undiscutirbaren Grundsätze', KSA 2.187) of a community. On the contrary, it discusses exactly these principles. In so doing, Nietzsche argues, they guarantee the 'spiritual progress' ('geistige Fortschreiten') of humanity. Without free spirits a society would become gradually dumber. Cf. HH I 225, p. 108/2. 189 and HH I 229 (p. 110/KSA 2.193) and HH I 235 (pp. 112–113/KSA 2.196–197);

25 Nietzsche also calls them 'the guardians of Europe' (BGE Preface). They are the inventors of new values and they break with the old values, set by Plato and Kant (but also Cartesian rationalism and British empiricism, and forms of what Nietzsche calls "weak" skepticism). What these different approaches to reality and knowledge have in common is their (according to Nietzsche, moral) belief in something real and the belief in the possibility of attaining knowledge of that reality. For an analysis of Nietzsche's scepticism in *Beyond Good and Evil*, see van Tongeren (1999). Plato and Kant lie at the root of the long history of humankind's metaphysical, idealist, rationalist, universalist, and moral view of life; namely, the belief in the human soul and the universally applicable concept of "the good" (that is, life under "the shadow of God"). Plato and Kant have been 'standing truth on its head' by neglecting life's 'perspectivism', ignoring that the appearance of things is all there is, and discounting that body and reason cannot be divided. Hence, the very free spirits or 'guardians of Europe' have the task of protecting Europe from Christiany, Platonism, Kantianism, etc. The 'good Europeans' are viewed as the creators of a new world-view revolving around the view that perspectivism [...] is the fundamental condition of all life' (BGE Preface, p. 4/'das Perspektivische, die Grundbedingung alles Lebens,' KSA 5.12). Cf. Prange [2012–1].

with delight.[26] He calls the idea that he could regard life as a means to knowledge 'the great liberator' (GS 324, p. 181/'der grosse Befreier', KSA 3.552), which gave him great joy. With 'joy' Nietzsche does not mean 'relaxation' in the spare-time after work with health as its object, but true joy, emanating from life as *'otium'* and *'vita contemplativa'*, where the status of work is lower than the status of the *'vita contemplativa'*.[27] Similar to the Greeks, Nietzsche tries to insert *'otium'* and *'bellum'* in his life and thinking. He wants to join those Greek philosophers who said, '"we thinkers are, as thinkers, the happiest"' (GS 328, p.183/'wir Denker sind als Denker die Glücklichsten', KSA 3.555). Similar to Socrates and Diogenes of Sinope, Nietzsche dares to be alone and set himself apart from the mass. Socrates *cum suis* went against the current. They found true happiness in being selfish. *Sanctus Januarius* instils new life into this Greek morality of selfishness.

Instead of being ashamed of our passions, desires, and ideas, we should explore them to form ourselves under the motto 'we [...] want to become who we are' (GS 335, p. 189/'wir [...] wollen Die werden, die wir sind', KSA 3.563), that is those 'who are new, unique, incomparable, who give themselves laws, who create themselves' (GS 335, p. 189/'die Neuen, die Einmaligen, die Unvergleichbaren, die Sich-selber-Gesetzgebenden, die Sich-selber-Schaffenden', KSA 3.563). The perfect harmony of art and reason implies that the law of a single taste binds all these to create a strong and self-sufficient individual. It is typical for modern times that people lack such a strong, disciplining, and forming taste, Nietzsche analyses. In the 'most unmodern city' Genoa, however, he did find this self-sufficient, loving, and autocratic character:

> The whole region is overgrown with this magnificent, insatiable lust for possessions and spoils [...]. In the North one is impressed by the law and by the general delight in lawfulness and obedience [...] But here [in Genoa, MP] you find, upon turning every corner, a separate human being who knows the sea, adventure, and the Orient; a human being averse to the law and to the neighbour as to a kind of boredom [...]. (GS 291, p. 165)

> Diese ganze Gegend [Genoa, MP] ist mit dieser prachtvollen unersättlichen Selbstsucht [...] überwachsen [...]. Im Norden imponirt das Gesetz und die allgemeine Lust an Gesetzlichkeit [...]. Hier aber findest du, um jede Ecke biegend, einen Menschen für sich [...], welcher dem Gesetze und dem Nachbar wie einer Art von Langerweile abhold ist [...]. (KSA 3.531–532).[28]

---

26 Cf. GS 51: '[...] I want to hear nothing more about all the things and questions that don't admit of experiment' (p. 62/'[...] ich mag von allen Dingen und allen Fragen, welche das Experiment nicht zulassen, Nichts mehr hören. Diess ist die Grenze meines "Wahrheitssinnes" [...]', KSA 3.416).

27 See GS 329 (pp. 183–184/KSA 3.556–557). Cf. GS 283 (p. 160/KSA 3.526–527).

28 Cf.: 'I go through the new streets of our [German] cities and consider how of all these greyish houses, built by the opining species, nothing will be left standing one century from now and how then also the opinions of these house-builders will have toppled down' ('Ich gehe durch die neuen Strassen unserer [deutschen] Städte und denke wie von allen diesen greulichen Häusern, welche das Geschlecht der öffentlich Meinenden erbaut hat, in einem Jahrhundert nichts mehr steht und wie dann auch wohl die Meinungen dieser Häuserbauer umgefallen sein werden', SE 1, KSA 1.339).

In Genoa, Nietzsche found the courage and self-glorification he desired in human beings. He contrasted this southern self-sufficiency to the northern craving to be similar to one's neighbour and obey the law. There are gaps between people in Genoa. Freedom, to Nietzsche, means the courage to maintain these spaces, to keep distance, to take the responsibility not to become like anyone but oneself.[29]

The only German person in whom Nietzsche recognized this ideal was Goethe, not in the least because of his aesthetic perception of life and his self-conception as a student of life, which manifested itself in the will to incorporate strange elements (character traits, ideas, habits, affects) to attribute to his style in personality and art. In his art, Goethe manifested himself as a 'tamer of the will' (AOM 172, p. 254/'Willens-Bändiger', KSA 2.452), of the heap of desires, habits, ideas, values, and affections that form a person. The modern poet, on the other hand, is an 'unchainer of the will' (AOM 172, p. 254/'*Entfesseler des Willens*,' KSA 2.452). Modern – Romantic – poetry is barbarian, says Nietzsche, because it is created by uncontrolled, chaotic souls, whereas classical poetry demonstrates an abundance of wisdom and harmony.[30] Poets such as Goethe are 'Greek', says Nietzsche, because they know how to unite the manifold in one style, to manage the chaos of foreign impulses, and achieve such a controlled adoption of the foreign way (by way of a serious 'war' within themselves), that they even become 'the happiest enrichers and increasers of the inherited treasures and the firstlings and paradigm of all next cultures'. As we saw in chapter 5, cosmopolitanism, understood as travelling to foreign cultures to immerse oneself in strangeness and start this dynamic, inter-cultural process of enlarging the self through the incorporation of foreign elements, is according to Nietzsche a precondition to cultural development and excellence. In *The Gay Science* particularly, this is taken up again; in raising one's daily life to the level of 'style' (in the Goethean sense), one takes up Europe's mission of making human history one that is a continuation of Greek culture.[31] In so doing, the free spirit is a 'good European'.[32]

The classical, 'Greek' and European poet has a 'complete' ('*vollkommen*') character and lives his life perfectly, because he himself is a 'fine poem' (AOM 172, p. 254/ 'ein gutes Gedicht', KSA 2.452).[33] He knows that art has to be spread out over life. By

---

29 Cf. TI Skirmishes 38 (pp. 213–214/KSA 6.139–140). Nietzsche calls this distance 'pathos of distance' (TI Skirmishes 37, p. 212/'*Pathos der Distanz*', KSA 6.138). He declares this to be 'the will to be yourself, to stand out' (TI Skirmishes 37, p. 212/'der Wille, selbst zu sein, sich abzuheben', KSA 6.138). The 'pathos of distance' is a precondition for the creation of higher human beings and culture.
30 AOM 173 (pp. 254–255 /KSA 2.453).
31 Compare HH I 475 (pp. 174–175/KSA 2.310–311).
32 Cf. Venturelli (2010), p. 180ff. Venturelli focuses on GS 377 as a key source for understanding the 'good European', stating that it clarifies that Nietzsche addresses his 'gaya scienza' first and foremost to the 'good Europeans', who he regards as the 'caretakers' of the gay science (pp. 181–182).
33 Cf. 6[204], KSA 9.251.

applying artistic skills to his daily life, he ennobles his life.[34] *The Gay Science* shows that Nietzsche projected the idea of applying artistic skills to the moulding of the individual character and that he transfers this idea to daily life, stating that we should be the 'poets of our lives, starting with the smallest and most commonplace details' (GS 299, p. 170/'Dichter unseres Lebens [...] und im Kleinsten und Alltäglichsten zuerst', KSA 3.538).[35] As poets of our lives, we voice every particular thing we experience, small or big. Now again, as in his early aesthetics, this means to rise from the particular to the general: art is the act of symbolization, of supplying the daily with a wider and cultural meaning. Culture then is the event of transforming the ordinary into the extra-ordinary, not by levelling the extra-ordinary down to the ordinary (that would be an act of resentment rather than of artistic creativity) or by equating the extra-ordinary with the ordinary and triviality (as in pop art and its epigones). Art, Dionysian art or 'art of apotheosis' ('Apotheosenkunst'), as he calls it in GS 370, develops culture out of what seems trivial at first. It is produced out of the artist's longing for the eternity of life, as he loves life and feels thankful for it. This art is 'dithyrambic [...], blissfully mocking [...], bright and fracious [...], spreading a Homeric light and splendour over all things' (GS 370, p. 235/'dithyrambisch [...], selig-spöttisch [...], hell und gütig [...], und einen homerischen Licht- und Glorienschein über alle Dinge breitend,' KSA 3.622). Exemplary are the painter Rubens, the poet Hafiz, and Goethe. Art's meaning is not in the metaphysical depth, but in the act of transformation itself, the artistic transformation of the ephemeral world of sense-perception into 'something solid' (WS 106, p. 336/ '*zu Gute*,' KSA 2.598), out of a desire for eternity for 'immortalization'.[36] As such, it contributes to the 'festival roads of humanity':

> Formerly, all artworks were displayed on the great festival road of humanity, as commemorations and memorials of high and happy moments. Now one uses artworks to lure poor, exhausted, and sick human beings to the side of humanity's road of suffering for a short lascivious moment; one offers them a little intoxication and madness. (GS 89, p. 89)

> Ehemals waren alle Kunstwerke an der grossen Feststrasse der Menschheit aufgestellt, als Erinnerungszeichen und Denkmäler hoher und seliger Momente. Jetzt will man mit den Kunstwerken die armen Erschöpften und Kranken von der grossen Leidensstrasse der Menschheit bei Seite locken, für ein lüsternes Augenblickchen; man bietet ihnen einen kleinen Rausch und Wahnsinn an. (FW 89, KSA 3.446)

Nietzsche wants human history to be a 'festival road of humanity'.

In addition, there is cultural meaning in the artwork itself, in the sense that it sets a new norm for others in the future to take as an ideal ready to be imitated and competed. Such an artwork has come into being as the product of 'the constraint and

---

34 AOM 174 (p. 255/KSA 2.453–454).
35 Compare GS 290 (pp. 163–164/KSA 3.530–531).
36 GS 370 (p. 234–236/KSA 3.619–622).

its conquest' (WS 140, p. 343/'*Zwang und Sieg*', KSA 2.612), 'violence and conquest' (GS 291, p. 165/'*Gewalt und Eroberung*', KSA 3.531). The artwork is the expression of the will to triumph, a 'victory', and a 'triumph' over time, over Modernity, over finitude, and over sentimentality. And this, to Nietzsche, is typical for Genoese people and for Greek artists.[37] The 'enduring immortality' (WS 144, p. 344/'*unsterbliche Dauer*', KSA 2.613) of the artwork, then, resides in the fact that it poses a new norm, a new convention, a new 'constraint' or '*Gewalt*' to others to adopt and conquer. However, this does not go only for the artwork, but for the person, too: 'art is above and above all supposed to beautify life, thus make us ourselves endurable, if possible pleasing to others' (ACM 174, p. 255/ 'Die Kunst soll vor Allem und zuerst das Leben verschönern, also uns selber den Andern erträglich, womöglich angenehm machen', KSA 2.453–454). Art honours life, it helps us to become yes-sayers to life, and helps us to become bearable for others. The latter issue is an important, yet highly neglected, element of Nietzsche's philosophy of *amor fati*. Because in this moment, individual freedom meets social interaction and tolerance. Within the social sphere, the individual bears the responsibility to behave in such ways, that he makes himself tolerable for others. In other words, Nietzsche's cosmopolitanism does not call for tolerance, but includes the ethical demand to *make oneself* tolerable. And one does so with the help of one's aesthetic powers: by making one's life more beautiful and poetic.

Amor fati is not only or not just about learning to say 'yes' to life, but includes making life and the self beautiful: 'I want to learn more and more how to see what is necessary in things as what is beautiful in them – thus I will be one of those who make things beautiful' (GS 276, p. 157/'Ich will immer mehr lernen, das Nothwendige an den Dingen als das Schöne sehen: – so werde ich Einer von Denen sein, welche die Dinge schön machen', KSA 3.521). What is ugly is not so much accepted as ugliness as transformed into beauty with the help of aesthetic semblance.[38] At this point, Nietzsche seems to return to the old idea that art is not confined to artworks (which should then have some moral effect on us), but a natural force in human beings. Just as he ascribes a certain artistically organizing and conquering power to the gaze of Genoese people (they did not travel or colonize, but still want to conquer their environment and impose their 'plan' upon it), he localizes art in the human psyche and body as 'beautifying, concealing, and reinterpreting powers' (GS 276, p. 157/'verschönernden, verbergenden und umdeutenden Kräften', KSA 3.521). In other words, a person – as free spirit – must create him- or herself into a work of art. While, in fact, all people have certain interpreting forces, 'passions and their raptures' (AOM 172, p. 254/'Leidenschaften und deren Krämpfe', KSA 2.452), not every single person makes art out of these by subsuming or

---

37 WS 122 (p. 339/KSA 2.604).
38 '[...] art is supposed to *conceal* or *reinterpret* everything ugly, those painful, dreadful, disgusting things' (AOM 174, p. 255/'sodann soll die Kunst alles Hässliche *verbergen* oder *umdeuten*, jenes Peinliche, Schreckliche, Ekelhafte', KSA 2.454).

organizing them under one law. Therefore, people need to be 'sculptors and remod-ellers of life' (AOM 172, p. 254/'Bildner, Um- und Fortbildner des Lebens', KSA 2.452). And one can only become such a 'sculptor and remodeller of life' under the guidance of a ('Greek-spirited') artist, who is already perfected into 'a fine poem, a fair statue' (AOM 172, p. 254/'ein gutes Gedicht, ein schönes Gebilde', KSA 2.452).

Thus, in order to reach the level at which one is able to beautify life, one has to edu-cate oneself, and this education implies the goal of making oneself bearable for others. Therefore, it is necessary to give oneself style; not by decoratively dressing up, but by imposing an artistic rule upon oneself to create a 'bold and autocratic human being' (GS 290, p. 164/'*kühnen und selbstherrlichen Menschen,*' KSA 3.531), who embraces life and strives to impose himself upon life, and in so doing elevate it to the level of dura-bility. One must '"give style" to one's character' (GS 290, p. 163/'seinem Charakter "Stil geben"', KSA 3.530) by 'binding' and 'perfecting' oneself 'into an artistic plan' (GS 290, p. 163/'einen künstlerischen Plan', KSA 3.530), into a 'stylized nature' (GS 290, p. 163/ 'stilisirte Natur', KSA 3.350), a oneness by way of 'the constraint of style' (GS 290, p. 163/'die Gebundenheit des Stils', KSA 3.531), or the 'unity of style'. This person with style is someone who has triumphed over himself. This educational self-relation brings the 'most exquisite pleasure' (GS 290, p. 163/'*feinste Freude*', KSA 3.530), and that is what one must strive for, 'that a human being should attain satisfaction with himself' (GS 290, p. 163/'dass der Mensch seine Zufriedenheit mit sich erreiche', KSA 3.531), for the reason that 'only then is a human being at all tolerable to behold' (GS 290, p. 163/ 'dann erst ist der Mensch überhaupt erträglich anzusehen', KSA 3.531). This is the mo-ment that he is 'ennobled' ('*veredelt*'), cured of his 'chain-illness' ('*Ketten-Krankheit*'), has reached the 'peace all around me' and lives 'for the sake of joy'.[39]

This is, according to Nietzsche, a 'Greek' way of relating to the self and the world, although in *The Gay Science* it is more associated with Epicurus. 'Style' and 'joy' are then still the measurements of the relation between self and world, and the self and self. The major difference is that at the time of *The Birth of Tragedy* this 'self' sub-merged in the world in the experience of the sublime was prompted by the 'Dionysian magic'. This experience made the self forget 'himself' and brought him back to the ex-perience of childlike innocence, that is, unity with himself, his fellow-humans, and nature. At the time of *The Gay Science*, the 'self' is overcome in another way. The self does not 'vanish' in the (temporary) experience of Dionysian sublimity, but is continu-ously put at stake by the perspectivist act of multiplication. The self knows that it is not one, neither a fragment from the original wholeness of life – as Nietzsche understood the self metaphysically at the time of *The Birth of Tragedy*. The free spirit comprehends

---

39 In this artistic process of transformation, stylistic, artistic, and technical form and emotional, epis-temological, or dramatic content play an equally important role; if emotions, for example, would dom-inate, only sentimental poetry would result. See AOM 172 (p. 254/KSA 2.452–453) and AOM 173 (pp. 254–255/KSA 2.453).

itself as a multitude. The oneness is only created by the act of stylization. This aesthetic stylization is, indeed as in *The Birth of Tragedy*, still a matter of responding to the deep psychological and bodily pain about the absurdity and meaninglessness of life. Hence, in a way, the individual free spirit creates himself as a tragicomic character – not as a shallow caricature, but as a Dionysian symbol of the healthy life.[40]

Convalescence: changing the north for the south

Goethe as Nietzsche's bridge between the north and the south

In order to recuperate from Wagnerian music and German idealistic and pessimistic philosophy, Nietzsche believed he had to leave the North and, following Goethe's lead, head for the South. The return to health implies 'the rediscovery of the *south* in oneself [...] to reconquer the southern health and hidden power of the soul' ('den *Süden* in sich wieder entdecken [...] die südliche Gesundheit und verborgene Mächtigkeit der Seele sich wieder erobern,' 41[7], KSA 11.682). Travelling to the south, the German returns to health, as Winckelmann, Goethe, and Mozart had demonstrated.[41] They went to Italy, where they shaped themselves into 'more than Germans' and 'good Europeans', students of the South, lovers of life, and producers of art created out of the desire for eternal life to set a new norm for future artists and writers at the same time.

In the early 90s, as a supra-German and good European Goethe becomes Nietzsche's anti-Wagnerian exemplar. The name 'Goethe' stands for the South, paganism, naturalism, and sensualism. 'Wagner', then, stands for the North, for religious tendency, morality, and Romanticism. Goethe is the noble character against Wagner's coarseness. He stands for playfulness and gentleness against Wagner's far-fetched seriousness, for perfection ('*Vollkommenheit*') against 'imperfection' ('*Unvollkommenheit*'), for self-constraint against the loss of control, for honesty against Wagner's playing the gallery, for pride as opposed to vanity, natural passion to forced emotion, innocence to shame, harmony to chaos. Goethe versus Wagner, shortly, means health against sickness, the classical poet against the archetype of modernism, the gay scientist against the Romantic artist.

Goethe versus Wagner also means Nietzsche's scientific ideal against Wagner's abhorrence of science.[42] We recall Nietzsche's ideal of the scientist, who mixes artistic powers and practical wisdom.[43] Goethe was indeed such a scientist:

---

40 In *Ecce Homo*, this is represented as an act of 'satyrization'. See Prange (forthcoming 2).
41 See 25[162], KSA 11.56.
42 Cf. 4[213], KSA 9.153.
43 GS 113, pp. 113–114 /KSA 3.464.

He did not remove himself from life, he put himself squarely in the middle of it; he did not despair, and he took as much as he could on himself, to himself, in himself. What he wanted was *totality*; he fought against the separation of reason, sensibility, feeling, will [...], he disciplined himself to wholeness, he *created* himself, (TI Skirmishes 49, p. 222)

Goethe löste sich nicht vom Leben ab, er stellte sich hinein; er war nicht verzagt und nahm so viel als möglich auf sich, über sich, in sich. Was er wollte, das war *Totalität*; er bekämpfte das Auseinander von Vernunft, Sinnlichkeit, Gefühl, Wille [...], er disciplinirte sich zur Ganzheit, er *schuf* sich (KSA 6.151)

As the ideal scientist-poet, Goethe is the best example of Nietzsche's ideal of the philosopher-artist with a truly liberated, healthy, and affirmative mind:

A spirit like this who has *become free* stands in the middle of the world with a cheerful and trusting fatalism in the *belief* that only the individual is reprehensible, that everything is redeemed and affirmed in the whole – *he does not negate any more*...But a belief like this is the highest of all possible beliefs: I have christened it with the name *Dionysus* (TI Skirmishes, pp. 222–223)

Ein solcher freigewordner Geist steht mit einem freudigen und vertrauenden Fatalismus mitten im All, im Glauben, dass nur das Einzelne verwerflich ist, dass im Ganzen sich Alles erlöst und bejaht – er *verneint nicht mehr* ... Aber ein solcher Glaube ist der höchste aller möglichen Glauben: ich habe ihn auf den Namen des *Dionysos* getauft (KSA 6.152).

It is this man, this exceptional mind that Nietzsche strives to be, when he, at the beginning of *Sanctus Januarius*, expresses the wish of *amor fati*, the wish to become a lover of life, to affirm his destiny and to deny no longer.

'Prince Vogelfrei' and 'In the South'

Nietzsche celebrates the Italian, southern lifestyle he advocates in *The Gay Science* in several poems. After receiving the long-expected typewriter from his sister in February 1882, Nietzsche started to write a series of verses and poems, during his overwintering in the 'electric-free' and 'cloudless' city of Genoa.[44] Eight of these were published as *Idylls from Messina* (*Idyllen aus Messina*) the same year. Some time later, in 1884, he decided to rewrite six of these eight poems as the *Songs of Prince Vogelfrei* (*Lieder des Prinzen Vogelfrei*) and add them to the re-issue of *The Gay Science* (1887). The poem

---

44 Compare, for example, Nietzsche to Carl von Gersdorff, end of August 1882 (KSB 6, p. 248). The typewriter was a Malling-Hansen writing ball from Denmark, and broke quite immediately. Nietzsche expected the typewriter to help him write blindly, which would be a solution for his eye problems. The first things that Nietzsche wrote on the machine are the verses published as *Joke, Cunning, and Revenge* nr. 13 ('Für Tanzer. Glattes Eis/Ein Paradeis/ Für Den, der gut zu tanzen weiss') – which therefore should be understood as: 'the typewriter is heaven for the one who knows how to use it' (Cf. KSA 9.673–674) and Nietzsche to Peter Gast, 17 February 1882 (KSB 6, pp. 171–172).

'Prince Vogelfrei' opens the *Idylls* and returns, substantially modified, in the *Songs of Prince Vogelfrei* under the name 'In the South' ('*Im Süden*'). In the 1886 preface to *Human, All Too Human I*, written in Nice, Nietzsche describes a 'midway condition' in between convalescence and health, 'characterized by a pale, subtle happiness of light and sunshine, a feeling of bird-like freedom, bird-like altitude, bird-like exuberance' (HH I Preface 4, p. 8/'Es giebt einen mittleren Zustand darin, dessen ein Mensch solchen Schicksals spatter nicht ohne Rührung eingedenk ist: ein blasses feines Licht und Sonneglück ist ihm zu eigen, ein Gefühl von Vogel-Freiheit, Vogel-Umblick, Vogel-Uebermuth,' KSA 2.18). This bird-like condition in between convalescence and health (often already disguised as health) speaks from the poems 'Prince Vogelfrei' and 'In the South'. These poems reveal the explicit influence that his stays along the Mediterranean Sea, in Genoa and, later, Nice, exercised upon his thought. While 'Prince Vogelfrei' confines itself to the point that the free spirit must learn how to sing (as a sign that the old Christian morality is conquered), 'In the South' straightforwardly shows that this singing can only be mastered in the south.

Hence, the recovery and health that Nietzsche is looking for by placing himself under the restraint of an '*anti-romantic* self-treatment' includes the journey to the south. This suggests that the 'revaluation of values' that Nietzsche expects from the 'new', 'good European' philosophers, can only be carried out successfully on the condition that these (northern, German) philosophers have transformed themselves into a 'mix of cultures', i.e. 'supra-national' '*Mittelländler*', that are (like Goethe) '*more* than German'. In other words, the revaluation of values seems to require the kind of 'southernization' or '*méditerranisation*' that Nietzsche requested from music.[45]

Let us take a closer look at the two poems.

'Prince Vogelfrei'

'Prince Vogelfrei' tells the story of prince Vogelfrei, who was taught by birds how to fly and sing. Flying enabled the prince's liberation from conceptual thought, while it supplied him with the power to interchange his former rigidity with the enjoyment of momentum, for a certain lightness of being. The main character Prince Vogelfrei recounts in 'Prince Vogelfrei,' which consists of five stanzas of five verses each, that he learned how to fly from the birds. The poem elucidates the meaning of flying to Prince Vogelfrei. In the first stanza, the technique of flying is central. Prince Vogelfrei learns the technique of sitting in tall trees and beating his wings by imitating the birds. The second stanza shows that flying has a wider meaning to Prince Vogelfrei than just learning a new technique. It offers him the possibility of forgetting his origin, terminus, and morals. Consequently, Prince Vogelfrei goes where the winds take

---

45 '*Il faut méditerraniser la musique*,' Nietzsche writes in WA 3 (p. 236/KSA 6, p. 16).

him instead of taking one step at a time towards a set goal, as the third stanza demonstrates. The limited, one-sided perspective of taking one's ambition as guidance on life is interchanged for the experience of the multi-perspectivism of life, for an openness to and enjoyment of the spontaneity and lightness of being: 'Nur Schritt für Schritt—das ist kein Leben!/Stäts Bein vor Bein macht müd und schwer!/Ich lass mich von den Winden heben,/Ich liebe es, mit Flügeln schweben/Und hinter jedem Vogel her'.

In the fourth stanza, human reason is defined as the source of all human errors – an important Nietzschean insight. By contrast, flying does not cost much power and effort, but it provides new energy and, surprisingly, also teaches one (or, the prince) how to sing. Singing takes the position of morality and the traditional expectations of the future. As it turns out, by learning to fly, Prince Vogelfrei also learnt how to romp around and sing. This is more worthwhile to him than his old ideas, which is presented in the antithesis drawn in stanza four between reason as 'bad business' and flying, which 'taught me better things,/to sing, joy, and songplay' (IM, KSA 3.333). The birds teach Prince Vogelfrei to fly and to turn his purposeful life into enjoyment of the moment: 'Reason? – that is bad business:/Reason and tongues often stumble!/Flying gave me new energies/and taught me better things,/to sing, joy, and songplay' (IM [*my translation*]/Vernunft? – das ist ein bös Geschäfte:/Vernunft und Zunge stolpern viel!/Das Fliegen gab mir neue Kräfte/Und lehrt' mich schönere Geschäfte,/Gesang und Scherz und Liederspiel, KSA 3.333).

In the final stanza, Prince Vogelfrei encourages communal singing and calls the birds to join in: 'To think in solitude – that is wise./To sing in solitude – that is silly!/So, hear me therefore in my way/and sit down still around me in a circle,/You, beautiful birds!' ('Einsam zu denken—das ist weise./Einsam zu singen—das ist dumm!/So horcht mir denn auf meine Weise/Und setzt euch still um mich im Kreise,/Ihr schönen Vögelchen, herum!') The singing indicates that Prince Vogelfrei has abandoned morality and the concomitant organization of life. The 'bird perspective' has freed him from his rational way of living. He understands that reason is not sanctifying but, contrarily, a source of errors, an approach and morality that are hostile and unnecessarily strict towards life. Nietzsche indicates the dominant, linear view of time with the phrase '*Ziel und Hafen*', in the first stanza. '*Ziel*' or 'purpose,' points to the future and the 'Hafen,' 'harbour,' to the traditional morality of the past. The words '*Furcht und Lob und Strafen*' intimate morality. The misleading and erroneaous character of reason is revealed by the first two verses of the fourth stanza, while the hostility towards life is expressed by the first verse of stanza three, 'Just step by step – that is not living!'

The birds have taught Prince Vogelfrei how to fly. In stanza one, flying appears as a technique; in stanza two as a source of forgetfulness; in the third stanza, as source of lightness and purposelessness, in contrast to verses three and four of stanza two. In stanza four, flying functions as a breeding ground of new powers and beauty, in the form of taking pleasure in singing. In the fifth stanza, singing substitutes for thought. Here, it is clarified that the poem must be interpreted within this opposition of singing and thinking: flying, it turns out, has realized the transition of thinking to singing. In the end, Prince Vogelfrei wants to learn how to sing. But in order to sing, he must first learn to fly.

'In the South'

In the reworked poem 'In the South' ('*Im Süden*') – which consists of five stanzas of five verses and a sixth stanza of six verses – the bird metaphor returns, now accompanied by the north-sourth perspective. The purposeful and strict, straight thought above that Prince Vogelfrei flies, is now explicitly tied to Germany, at the beginning of the third stanza:

> Just step by step – that is not living,/the German's stride's too dull for me./I asked the wind to lift me heaving,/with birds I soared without misgiving, –/and south I flew across the sea.

> Nur Schritt für Schritt – das ist kein Leben,/Stets Bein vor Bein macht deutsch und schwer./Ich hiess den Wind mich aufwärts heben,/Ich lernte mit den Vögeln schweben, –/Nach Süden flog ich über's Meer.

'*Müde*' has become 'German' ('deutsch'). In addition, the north is unambiguously connected with the 'bad business' of reason, which causes a lot of distress, and the truth, in which the poet does not believe any longer. This is how 'In the South' ends: 'In the north – I admit hesitantly – I loved an old woman to shudder:/Her name was "the truth"...' ('Im Norden – ich gesteh's mit Zaudern – /Liebt' ich ein Weibchen, alt zum Schaudern:/"Die Wahrheit" hiess dies alte Weib...').

The hesitation and shudder in this confession seem to be occasioned by a certain feeling of shame for an old love, of which one recognizes its absurdity.[46] The hesitation, shudder, and shame that this 'I' is said to feel opposes his supplication, addressed to the 'innocence of the south', in the second stanza to accomodate him. The southern innocence comes in the stead of the love of truth. But what does this innocence consist of? If it is difficult to say exactly, at the very least we can say, it consists of a constellation of things that, put together, form an idyllic environment:

---

[46] This is more understandable when the reach of this metaphor is taken into account. The truth which 'old woman' indicates is that the philosopher has given up the battle of thinking out of weariness and is no longer 'heroic.' He is ashamed of this, but he just can no longer afford the solitude that this attitude requires (see D 487, p. 486/KSA 3.288). He is now looking for 'party followers' (D 542, p. 216/ '*Parteigänger*,' 3, p. 312) rather than enemies. The weariness has come in the place of the passion of knowledge and instinct for truthfulness. The philosopher does not experience any 'Not' and therefore he has achieved the opposite of life.

> The sleeping sea, its colour fleeting,/a purple sail, pure indolence./Rocks, fig trees, spires and harbour meeting,/around me idylls, sheep are bleating –/absorb me, southern innocence![47]

> Das weisse Meer liegt eingeschlafen,/Und purpurn steht ein Segel drauf./Fels, Feigenbäume, Thurm und Hafen,/Idylle rings, Geblök von Schafen, –/Unschuld des Südens, nimm mich auf!

This time, he writes that he does not learn to fly with the birds, wherever they go. On the contrary, he has a clear destination, because he flies from the north to the south, in stanza three. Flying around in and of itself did not cure him, but very specifically flying to the south:

> I hoisted the wind to lift me up,/I learned to levitate with the birds –/Over the sea I flew to the South.

> Ich hiess den Wind mich aufwärts heben,/Ich lernte mit den Vögeln schweben, –/Nach Süden flog ich über's Meer.

In this resides the poem's main re-working; in the new version, it is not so much flying that liberates (in preparing the transition from thinking to singing, from rigidity to freedom), but the voyage to the south. Indeed, here too the soaring and flying oppose the 'step by step', but the 'I' is not lifted by the winds to go wherever his wings take him. This time, he is taken up by the wind that guides him and other birds to the south. There, he finds the opportunity to discuss his passion for his 'old love' the truth and open up new ways for philosophical reflection. The south supplies him with the courage, blood, and energy for a new life, a new kind of play, as we can read in the fourth stanza, where he admits that he feels new courage for life and play.

Because this poem does not mention 'Gesang und Scherz und Liederspiel,' the singing of stanza five comes as a surprise. On top of that, the 'I' suddenly speaks to the birds, which he continues to do in stanza six, in which he talks of love to them. He tells them that he thinks they are made for love and confesses that he, when he was still living in the north, loved the 'old woman', truth.

Even though 'In the South' is unbalanced, it becomes clear what the speaker wants to convey.[48] Due to his stay in the south, he was able to take a distance from the convictions he was raised in and in which he still believed when he lived in Germany and

---

[47] The 'white' sea may be an allusion to GS 45, in which Epicurus's eye 'gazes at a wide, whitish sea' (p. 59). This is a happy eye, according to Nietzsche, which has witnessed the sea become calm. Here something similar is meant.

[48] The poem is unbalanced for the following reasons: 1. The fifth and sixth stanza do not add to the content of the poem; 2. The functioning of the singing, in stanza five, remains unclear, in contrast to 'Prince Vogelfrei'; 3. The rhythm of the second verse of the sixth stanza deviates from all other second verses, which breaks the rhythm of the poem as a whole; 4. With his confession to the birds towards the end of the poem, a new topic is introduced, which remains unclear, without being mysterious in the good sense of the word; 5. This is reinforced by the forced rhythm of the sixth stanza: the question

Switzerland. In fact, he does not need the bird metaphor any longer. The new title also indicates this. Because Nietzsche did not want to abandon this metaphor, for some reason, the components have become a bit too much for him. But what is the point? The point is not that the poem is a success as a poem. The important thing is that Nietzsche wanted to present himself as a philosopher-poet (or composer of songs). His poems 'Prince Vogelfrei' and 'In the South' voice the change of perspective that took place when Nietzsche learned to love the south and adopt a foreign culture.[49] He manifests himself as a troubadour, who sings about his own life experiences and passions, as a 'poet of his own life,' '*Mittellander*' and 'good European.' He shows that the kind of 'light' and 'joyful' philosophy he proclaims is the result of his 'recovery'. He made the transition from northern morality and mentality, revolving around 'self-lessness' (GS 21, pp. 43–45/'Selbstlosigkeit', KSA 3.391–393) to the 'innocence of the utmost selfishness' (GS 99, p. 96/'Unschuld der höchsten Selbstsucht, ' KSA 3.455). In other words, to the 'faith in great passion as the good in itself' (GS 99, p. 96/'Glaube an die grosse Leidenschaft als an das Gute an sich,' KSA 3.454) what Nietzsche used to appreciate in Wagner's *Siegfried*. This means so much as the liberation from imprisonment in the common herd with its traditional morality as well as gaining personal freedom by adopting a sensualist, aesthetic attitude to life.[50]

As birds migrate to the south in winter, Nietzsche also migrated to the south every winter, only to return to the north towards the end of springtime.[51] From 'Prince Vogelfrei', it transpires that Nietzsche develops himself by imitating successful examples, including not only Goethe but birds that master the technique of flying. 'In the South' teaches us that the goal of self-development requires more than just flying; in addition, one needs to visit pagan, sensual, and vital environments. This poem attests to Nietzsche's thankfulness for Italian culture, without which he would have remained imprisoned in the northern coldness and morality instead of developing a new view of things, undergoing a strange and unique experience of life. Nietzsche understands and is thankful that due to his stay in Italy, he gained the necessary distance to himself so as to regard his 'Romantic' disease – German culture – and life in general as a comedy, or at least as a short and tragic moment in the 'eternal comedy of existence' (GS 1, p. 29/'die ewige Komödie des Daseins,' KSA 3.370). Without his visits to the south, Nietzsche would never have been able to act out his resistance to the power of numbers, the lack of form and one-dimensional mass at the expense of quality, nuance, and multi-perspectivism with the help of laughter, jokes, and mockery. Without the

---

mark after '*Zeitvertreib*' breaks the rhythm, as does the mystifying or shameful silence to which the ellipses point.

49 Prince Vogelfrei is between two forms of 'seriousness' (cf. KSA 14.712). We must probably think here of the '*Priesterernst*' and the intellectual seriousness that comes in its place.

50 See for a discussion of Nietzsche's sensualism and idealism in GS 372: Stegmaier 2004.

51 Initially, Nietzsche considered as a title for *Songs of Prince Vogelfrei* : 'Prince Vogelfrei. Or: the good European' ('Prinz Vogelfrei. Oder: der gute Europäer', KSA 14.712).

south, he would never have found the weapon of cheerfulness as partner of wisdom. In that case, he would never have experienced the 'recovery', which founds *The Gay Science*, as a pinnacle of free-spiritedness and good Europeanism.

Goethe envied Walter Scott's 'super-European' or 'non-European' view of Europe, and tried to look at himself, Germany, and Europe with non-German eyes.[52] He did so by reflecting within the three different models, which Nietzsche engages too, and which are characteristic of German reflection on Europe in the nineteenth century. In the first model, the West is a chaotic 'reality' put in contrast to the ideal of the peaceful 'East'. The East functions as a counterweight and ideal paradise. In this context, the West is formed by ignorant people, who wander through a 'paradise in decay' or 'paradise lost'.[53] The second model consists of Europe as the 'old world', ruled by what is actual reality, and the United States of America as the 'promised land', the land where everything is possible, potentiality.[54] The third opposition is drawn between contemporary Europe and Ancient Greece. Ancient Greece functions as the criterion of what is 'truly' European. This model assumes that Europe is off track and must return to its Greek roots in order to recover and find itself again. Goethe and Nietzsche turn to Winckelmann and Mozart to reflect on good European citizenship. This consists indeed in participating in the dynamic process of interculturalism, i.e., to bring together two different worlds actively, to connect their different customs, views, and styles.

By heading for the south, Nietzsche hoped to become 'supra-national' (*'übernational'*), 'supra-German' (*'überdeutsch'*), and 'European' (*'Europäisch'*).[55] However, in the later eighties, Nietzsche starts longing to overcome his Europeanism too. The dynamics of Nietzsche's 'intercultural' project made him overcome his 'Europeanism' and strive for supra-Europeanism, eventually. Below, I want to suggest however, that this 'supra-Europeanism' is an integral part of being a good European citizen.

---

52 Goethe to Zelter, 4 December 1827 (MA 20/1, pp. 1086–1088). Cf. Marie-Claire Hoock-Demarle (2002), p. 477.
53 Goethe to Cotta, 16 May 1815: 'It is my intention herewith [with the *West östlicher Divan*, MP] to connect the West and the East in a joyful manner, the past and the present, Persia and Germany and to have both their moral traditions and way of thinking penetrate each other' ('Meine Absicht ist dabei [bei *Westöstlicher Divan*, MP] auf heitere Weise den Westen und Osten, das Vergangene und Gegenwärtige, das Persische und Deutsche zu verknüpfen und beiderseitige Sitten und Denkarten übereinandergreifen zu lassen', *Briefe*, HA III, p. 306). That is what Nietzsche tries to do in *Thus Spoke Zarathustra*.
54 In the *Wilhelm Meister* books. See for example HA 7, p. 431 and HA 8, p. 430. See for further discussion Marie-Claire Hoock-Demarle (2002), p. 478–479 and Walter Hinderer (2002).
55 Compare also the following statement: 'Thus, even if I would be a bad German, I am, in any case, *a very good European*' ('Denn, wenn ich auch ein schlechter Deutscher sein sollte, – jedenfalls bin ich *ein sehr guter Europäer*,' Nietzsche to his mother, 17 August 1886, KSB 7, p. 233).

From Europeanism to supra-Europeanism

In the later eighties, Nietzsche's cosmopolitanism or 'dynamic interculturalism' got ever-widening proportions. The prefix 'supra'- ('*über-*') started oftentimes appearing with the substantive 'European' ('*Europäer*') and the adjective 'European' ('*europäisch*'). Nietzsche desired to travel overseas to Mexico and Africa and to live in a 'stern Muslim country' for a while.[56] He longed for a country 'with palms' to be able to look at Europe 'with far eyes'. It seems that the free-spirited philosopher did not feel so free anymore and had to liberate himself again. But from what did he have to liberate himself? From Christian morality or his 'will to truth'? Why did he want to leave Europe? Were the southern medicines of Genoa and Nice not efficacious in the long term? In brief, how does the idea of 'supra-Europeanism' relate to the idea of being a 'good European'?

Whereas Nietzsche used to advocate the integration of the southern, Greek, Italian spirit into the northern, German, spirit, he turned his southern perspective to the East, from *Thus Spoke Zarathustra* (1883–1885) onwards. Although the term 'Europe' does not appear much in that book, notes from 1884 largely testify to Nietzsche's continuing preoccupation with Europe.[57] Several ideas for titles of new books contain the formula 'good European' and the chapter 'The Shadow' was first labelled 'The good European'. And indeed, as it turns out, Zarathustra wants to get rid of his own shadow, precisely because it is so European.[58] He longs for an oasis with palms and good air, in fact, the best air possible, that is the 'air of Paradise' ('*Paradieses-Luft*').[59] *Thus Spoke Zarathustra* depicts the time of transition between a 'sick' and a 'healthy' Europe. It is clearly suggested to remain 'healthy', to find the 'air of paradise' again, one needs to go outside European borders, in the long run.

Nietzsche had suggested before that one needs to be 'outside' the country to be able to gain a clear view and make justifiable criticism of a nation.[60] One has to 'de-Germanize' to gain a clear view of what '*Germanentum*' comprises. He headed for the

---

56 'I want to live amongst Muslims for a longer period, and even there, where their religion is at its most severe: in that way, my judgment and eye for everything European will be sharpened' ('Ich will unter Musselmänners eine gute Zeit leben, und zwar dort, wo ihr Glaube jetzt am strengsten ist: so wird sich wohl mein Urtheil und mein Auge für alles Europäische schärfen'. Nietzsche to Peter Gast, 13 March 1881, KSB 6, p. 86).

57 See 25[524], KSA 11.150, 26[297], KSA 11.229, 26[320], KSA 11.234.

58 Cf. Marco Brusotti (2004), pp. 32–33 and pp. 35–37. Brusotti remarks: 'The fact that "Europe" hardly appears in *Zarathustra*, is, one can say with good reason, a not very important terminological detail' ('Daß im *Zarathustra* "Europa" kaum vorkommt, ist, so wird man mit gutem Grund sagen, ein nicht sehr bedeutendes terminologisches Detail', p. 32).

59 Z IV 'Amongst the Daughters of the Desert' (p. 317/'Unter Töchtern der Wüste', KSA 4.382). Cf. for example 26[293], KSA 11.228, 26[298], KSA 11.229–230, 26[308], KSA 11.232 and 26[309], KSA 11.232.

60 GM Preface 7, pp. 8–9/KSA 5.254–255.

south to de-Germanize and, in *Thus Spoke Zarathustra*, for the East to gain an 'eastern view of Europe' ('morgenländischer Überblick über Europa') and to learn to think in a more 'oriental' manner. Was he thinking of Persia (which *Zarathustra* suggests), Saudi Arabia, or another Muslim country southeast of Europe? It is interesting that Nietzsche uses the connection of 'south and East' (*'Süden und Morgenland'*) – especially with regard to music, though.[61] As if he, again, expected music to be able to mix different styles and cultures in the first place, that is: to bring together different cultures in a 'unity of style'.

Brusotti remarks that 'the south and East are two vague concepts, or rather visions rather than concepts and they are not only deliberately vague'.[62] I propose that we understand these terms not only in the literal, geographical sense but also as metaphors for a 'mental space', the space, where one can liberate oneself from one's old beliefs. 'South' and 'East' signify a 'symbolic' rather than an actual geographical space. It is a space, where one questions oneself again and transgresses oneself. It is the space in which self-criticism is exercised and culture created. 'South' and 'north' are loaded with traditional, old, and moral meaning and therefore represent a *'Sinnordnung'* rather than a definite place.[63] This implies that southern people should go to the north, that 'Italians' should de-Italianize and that after having seen more of Europe, one should travel outside Europe to 'de-Europeanize'. Nietzsche's 'Orientalism' then amounts to a plea for 'supra-Europeanism' or even 'globalization'. However, this does not mean that he makes a post-modern plea for cultural relativism. His supra-Europeanism must be regarded in light of the perspectivistic task he continually sets of actively overcoming the self, of incessantly educating the self by incorporating new ideas and norms, and subsequently putting them at stake. This is another way of saying that one has to become 'Greek'. Yet, despite his stubborn holding to Greek culture, Nietzsche is also sceptical about the return of old times, given the current situation:

> What from now on will never again be built, *can* never again be built, is – a society in the old sense of the term; to build that, everything is lacking, mainly the material. *We are no longer material for a society*; this is a timely truth! (GS 356, p. 216)

> Was von nun an nicht mehr gebaut wird, nicht mehr gebaut werden *kann*, das ist – eine Gesellschaft im alten Verstande des Wortes; um diesen Bau zu bauen, fehlt Alles, voran das Material. *Wir Alle sind kein Material mehr für eine Gesellschaft*: das ist eine Wahrheit, die an der Zeit ist! (KSA 3.597)

---

61 While *Beyond Good and Evil* contains relatively many terms deriving from 'Europe' and 'European', the term 'supra-European' ('über-Europäisch') is only employed with reference to music in aphorism 255 (discussed in chapter 6 in relation to *Carmen*).

62 'Süden und Morgenland sind zwei vage Begriffe, oder eher noch Visionen als Begriffe und sie sind nicht nur absichtlich vage' (Brusotti, 2004), p. 39.

63 Cf. Cassirer (1931), pp. 411–432.

This situation is caused by the current 'short-sightedness', the lack of courage to make far-reaching plans, and the *diktat* 'to make a living', 'to adopt a particular *role* – their [all European men] so-called profession' (GS 356, p. 215/'eine bestimmte *Rolle* [...] ihren sogenannten Beruf,' KSA 3.595). This leads to the situation in which 'almost all Europeans, at an advanced age, confuse themselves with their role' (GS 356, p. 215/'fast alle Europäer verwechseln sich in einem vorgerückten Alter mit ihrer Rolle,' KSA 3.595). This, however, is not the 'artistic' (GS 356, p. 215/'künstlerisch', KSA 3.595) Europe Nietzsche would like to see. His former high hopes of cultural change (by way of activating cultural memory) seem to have diminished due to his renewed perception of the actual situation. Europe, Germany in particular, as it then was, is plagued by political nationalism more than ever, and thus a culture in which the 'good European' is a stranger, not at home, a *'Heimatlose'*. Yet, Nietzsche keeps on focusing on a future in which things may be different, and grasping Europe in terms of 'transition'.[64] This is specifically articulated by *Thus Spoke Zarathustra*. The *Mensch-Uebermensch* relation there is described as a transition humankind has to make. Nietzsche speaks of a cord, which is tied between humanity and supra-humanity.[65] This transition should not only be understood on an anthropological and individual level, but also culturally as the transition of the 'last-men' Europeans to a new, artistic Europe, a continent controlled by 'free spirits', or 'the spirit of freedom'. This freedom is, as we have seen, not achieved by way of political means but through art. While Nietzsche's hopes of European culture seem to lose ground, he turns to the individual stylization as a 'good European', seeking for *'Heimatlosen'* that might become 'good Europeans' more than ever. Which Europeans are 'good Europeans' who are not at home in their culture and time, and seek to overcome the self by crossing (state-) borders? It seems that since Goethe no one has achieved a lifestyle that was so focused on becoming and overcoming the self by way of an incessant *'Aneingnung des Fremden'*.[66] In taking recourse to stylizing himself, Goethe was both 'Greek' and a 'good European'. In viewing himself as a cosmopolitan artist (contributing to 'world literature'[67] rather than to national literature only), he was also 'supra-European', thereby reinforcing the kind of 'free' spirit Nietzsche ascribed to truly good Europeans.

---

64 Compare Krell and Bates (1997), p. 2.

65 'Man is a rope, fastened between animal and Superman – a rope over an abyss' (Z Preface 4, p. 43/ 'Der Mensch ist ein Seil, geknüpft zwischen Thier und Übermensch, – ein Seil über einem Abgrunde' KSA 4.16).

66 In dialogue with the great musician and conductor Daniel Barenboim, Edward Said praised Goethe's cosmopolitan artistry, because it is 'all about a voyage to the "other"' (Barenboim and Said, 2002, p. 11). To this I would like to add that Goethe's cosmopolitanism was never a mere 'voyage to the other', but rather a 'voyage to the other so as to educate the self'.

67 Admittedly, this term was invented by Goethe.

In book V of *The Gay Science*, published only in 1887, Nietzsche's cosmopolitanism has reached a breath that can only be captured by the desire for, or experience of, 'homelessness' (*'Heimatlosigkeit'*) and 'namelessness'.[68] At the same time, Europe and 'the good Europeans' form the central topic of the thoughts assembled in this book.[69] Some aphorisms attest to Nietzsche's open-minded cosmopolitanism, because they encourage the good European to keep distance from his (or her) own views of life by leaving and heading for the 'beyond' (*'jenseits'*), that which takes the traveller beyond his morality and thus, eventually, away from 'everything European' ('"Europa"' says the German original) too, that is from Europe understood 'as the sum of commanding value judgments that have become part of our flesh and blood' (p. 244/'als eine Summe von kommandirenden Werturtheilen [...], welche uns in Fleisch und Blut übergangen sind', KSA 3.633).[70] His or her scepticism and 'will to knowledge' drive the good European over borders. This is saliently formulated in aphorism 380 of book V, which accords with Nietzsche's preference for the 'supra-European', light music of *Carmen*:

> In order to see our European morality for once as it looks from a distance, and to measure it up against other past or future moralities, one has to proceed like a wanderer who wants to know how high the towers in a town are: he *leaves* the town. "Thoughts about moral prejudices", if they are not to be prejudices about prejudices, presuppose a position *outside* morality, some point beyond good and evil to which one has to rise, climb, or fly – and in the present case, at least a point beyond *our* good and evil, a freedom from everything "European", by which I mean the sum of commanding value judgments that have become part of our flesh and blood. That one *wants* to go precisely out there, up there, may be a slight rashness, a peculiar and unreasonable "you must" – for we seekers of knowledge also have our idiosyncrasies [sic] of unfree will: – the question is whether one *really can* get up there. This may depend on manifold conditions. Mainly,

---

68 Cf. GS 377 (pp. 241–243/KSA 3.628–631) and GS 382 (pp. 246–247/KSA 3.635–637). In GS 377, Nietzsche also expresses serious critique of German nationalism, regarding it as making a 'wasteland' of the German spirit.

69 Nietzsche remarked that he had always wanted to write book V as a part of *The Gay Science*, nevertheless he also considered publishing it as part of *Beyond Good and Evil*, which contained his 'thoughts on the dear Europeans of today and – tomorrow' ('meine Gedanken über die lieben Europäer von heute und – Morgen,' KSB 7, p. 59; cf. Prange 2012–1). Although the ground for this pondering must be sought in typography – the letter in which *The Gay Science* was set, was no longer available –, it also hints at the spiritual kinship between *The Gay Science* and *Beyond Good and Evil*. Both are written with the free spirit as 'good European' in mind. Compare Görner: 'In *Die fröhliche Wissenschaft*, the good European is identical with the perpetual migrant who has been made homeless by narrow-minded nationalists. According to Nietzsche in 1882, these migrating true Europeans live in opposition to those who idolise their own races and nations and succumb to self-adulation [...] he represents a type of person beyond nations and races' (2006, p. 256). It must be noted, though, that Görner bases this thought on GS 380, which is part of GS book V (entitled *'Wir Furchtlosen'*), and thus does not stem from the 1882 edition, but from the 1887 edition of GS. See for a detailed account of GS book V in context: Stegmaier 2012.

70 Such as GS 380 (pp. 245–246/KSA 3.632–633). Other aphorisms, especially GS 362, may cause readers to be disillusioned due to their sexism, or praise of Napoleon, whose ideal of 'one Europe' Nietzsche shared.

the question is how light or heavy we are – the problem of our "specific gravity". One has to be *very light* to drive one's will to knowledge into such a distance and, as it were, beyond one's time; to create for oneself eyes to survey millennia and, moreover, clear skies in these eyes. One must have liberated oneself from many things that oppress, inhibit, hold down, and make heavy precisely us Europeans today. The human being of such a beyond who wants to catch a glimpse of the highest measures of value of his time must first of all "overcome" this time in himself – this is the test of his strength – and consequently not only his time but also his aversion and opposition to this time, his suffering from this time, his untimeliness, his *romanticism* … (GS 380, pp. 244–245).

Um unsrer europäischen Moralität einmal aus der Ferne ansichtig zu werden, und sie an anderen, früheren oder kommenden, Moralitäten zu messen, dazu muss man es machen, wie es ein Wanderer macht, der wissen will, wie hoch die Thürme einer Stadt sind: dazu *verlässt* er die Stadt. "Gedanken über moralische Vorurtheile", falls sie nicht Vorurtheile über Vorurtheile sein sollen, setzen eine Stellung *ausserhalb* der Moral voraus, irgend ein Jenseits von Gut und Böse, zu dem man steigen, klettern, fliegen muss, – und, im gegebenen Falle, jedenfalls ein Jenseits von *unsrem Gut* und Böse, eine Freiheit von allem "Europa", letzteres als eine Summe von kommandirenden Werturtheilen verstanden, welche uns in Fleisch und Blut übergangen sind. Dass man gerade dorthinaus, dorthinauf *will*, ist vielleicht eine reine Tollheit, ein absonderliches unvernünftiges "du musst" – denn auch wir Erkennenden haben unsre Idiosynkrasien des "unfreien Willens" –: die Frage ist, ob man wirklich dorthinauf *kann*. Dies mag an vielfachen Bedingungen hängen, in der Hauptsache ist es die Frage darnach, wie leicht oder wie schwer wir sind, das Problem unsrer "spezifischen Schwere". Man muss *sehr leicht* sein, um seinen Willen zur Erkenntniss bis in eine solche Ferne und gleichsam über seine Zeit hinaus zu treiben, um sich zum Ueberblick über Jahrtausende Augen zu schaffen und noch dazu reinen Himmel in diesen Augen! Man muss sich von Vielem losgebunden haben, was gerade uns Europäer von Heute drückt, hemmt, niederhält, schwer macht. Der Mensch eines solchen Jenseits, der die obersten Werthmaasse seiner Zeit selbst in Sicht bekommen will, hat dazu vorerst nöthig, diese Zeit in sich selbst zu "überwinden" – es ist die Probe seiner Kraft – und folglich nicht nur seine Zeit, sondern auch seinen bisherigen Widerwillen und Widerspruch *gegen* diese Zeit, sein Leiden an dieser Zeit, seine Zeit-Ungemässheit, seine *Romantik* … (KSA 3.632–633)

Here we have a programme for the good European or the programme to learn how to become a good European.[71] One has to overcome (one's own) 'Europeanism', understood as a moral unity. One has to overcome one's old, incarnated 'good and evil', as well as one's 'time', one's '*Gegenwart*'.[72] However, the good European is not only ahistorical, but also 'supra-national', and even 'supra-European' and deliberately '*heimatlos*'. The

---

71 Marco Brusotti (2004) and Giuliani Campioni (1987) claim that we should not take this literally. Brusotti writes: 'When Nietzsche says here that one should leave the 'city', he not only thinks of travelling, but he thinks especially of historical knowledge of far-away cultures […]. Thus he does not take this leaving as literally as when he says that he does not want to live in Germany' ('Wenn Nietzsche hier sagt, daß man die "Stadt" verlassen muß, denkt er nicht nur an Reisen, sondern vor allem an eine historische Kenntnis ferner Kulturen […]. Er versteht dieses Verlassen also nicht so wörtlich, wie wenn er sagt, er wolle nicht in Deutschland leben', p. 35). This may be the case regarding GS 380, but in general Nietzsche advocates '*Heimatlosigkeit*', and that one should leave Germany in order to 'de-Germanize'.
72 See WS 307 (p. 387/KSA 2.689f) and HH I 616 (p. 195/KSA 2.349).

'good European' seems to desire to become a '*Weltbürger*', a true cosmopolitan, and this is only reachable by becoming 'light'.[73]

Conclusion

This chapter investigated Goethe as Nietzsche's model of 'the good European'. The 'good European' is a successful 'cosmopolitan' person, who pleads for a Dionysian affirmation of all of life's lust and pain, as well as of its sensualist and aesthetic character. We also learned about the necessity of becoming 'supra-European' in order to be a 'good European' and the 'programme' for the 'good European' established in *The Gay Science*.

While the young Nietzsche measured cultural development according to the place of the artistic genius in society (in the centre or in the margin), he later measured 'good Europeans' according to their nomadic power to estrange and dissociate themselves from their culture of origin, and their physiological powers of adaptation to strange environments and thoughts. The individual rather than the Wagnerian theatre Bayreuth, became the place where culture happens, and the measure of culture was no longer the unity experienced in Dionysian intoxication, but the unity of 'style'.

Learning by incorporating foreign elements and, hence, creating a unity out of variety, which will uplift culture, is a constant in Nietzsche's thought and the heart of his aesthetics and cultural ideal. This leads, eventually, to the idea that a 'good European' develops a 'supra-European' or 'global' view of things. According to Nietzsche, Europe will become healthier by developing 'global eyes', not because of a growing moral sense of cultural pluralism, but because of a growing aesthetic sense for cultural plurality as the foundation of cultural unity. By developing the view of the foreign person, of the 'outsider' on our (Christian) morality, we may be able to overcome ourselves. Hence, Europe should exactly not persist in its Christian roots, and so should Arabic countries and people not persist in their beliefs. The Christian European should travel to Islamic and Arabic countries in order to gain another view of himself, and the Islamist, when coming to Europe, should be willing to put all his beliefs at stake and adopt new, Western eyes by which means he is able to generate a different view of himself. In order to become 'someone else than the one you were before', one must be 'light' ('leicht'). Nietzsche underlines the importance of being 'light' in order to re-

---

73 In *Beyond Good and Evil*, Nietzsche describes himself as one of the 'Europeans of the day after tomorrow' (BGE 214, p. 109/'Europäer von Übermorgen,' KSA 5.151), explaining that '*good Europeans*' are '*very* free spirits' (BGE Preface, p. 4/KSA 5.13) as opposed to the present-day Europeans he criticizes elsewhere. These future Europeans are not the inhabitants of the European federation of the nation-states of today, but the ones that are 'awake' in contrast to the 'dogmatic' philosophers. The 'dogmatists' are Plato and Kant, and all philosophers that operate in the wake of their idealism. See also Prange (2012-1).

lease oneself from the heavy moral burdens and, in general, the spiritless spirit of the modern age. One must 'fly' above morality, as the poem 'In the South' ('Im Süden') revealed.

The Gay Science is Nietzsche's report of his personal process of convalescence. However, Nietzsche wrote this book not only out of personal interest: ' "What has happened to me", he says to himself, must happen to everyone in whom a task wants to become incarnate and "come into the world"' (HH I, Preface 7, p. 10/' "Wie es mir ergieng [...]", sagt er sich, [...] muss es Jedem ergehn, in dem eine Aufgabe leibhaft werden und "zur Welt kommen" will [...],' KSA 2.21). The free spirit- or travel-books, set a task for every 'good European'. Regarded from this perspective, The Gay Science is not just a report of Nietzsche's convalescence, but also offers a recipe to others, like The Birth of Tragedy delivered a manual for Wagner and others on how to become Greek. The personal history of sickness and health contains guidelines for all future 'good Europeans', and, in that sense, is (a-chronically) the personal history of the convalescence of all good Europeans, and even of the convalescence and regained health of Europe.

The Gay Science is a hand-book, travel-book, and history-book for Good Europeans. The Gay Science is Nietzsche's report of his personal journey from sickness to convalescence. However, the task he had set himself should inspire other 'good Europeans' to follow Nietzsche's example, what had happened to him 'must happen to everyone' (HH I Preface 7, p. 10/'muss es Jedem ergehn', KSA 2.21). The journey from sickness to health, the process of recovery is the subject of Nietzsche's 'travel'- or 'free spirit' books. The free spirit is a traveller, someone who lingers in unknown areas for a while as a real 'homeless' wanderer ('Heimatlose'). Nietzsche's free spirit has emancipated himself from German culture, Christianity (asking 'Can all values not be turned round?' HH I Preface 3, p. 7/'Kann man nicht alle Werthe umdrehn?' KSA 2.17), and analysing his morality with his ratio instead of founding moral convictions in reason. Moreover, the free spirit has freed himself from German music and philosophy, and, recovering slowly, developed his own (im-) moral, aesthetic rules, and a positive, aesthetic conception of freedom. In that idea of freedom, Nietzsche assigned an important role to the following leads, to sum up: self-restraint; self-ishness; self-love; self-experiment; self-observation; self-stylization; a loving eye for 'all nearby things'; and the ability not to reduce the unknown to something known, but to merit the unknown in its strangeness and otherness. Furthermore, the free spirit was 'total' in the sense that he attached as much importance to the body as to the mind (affirmed in his slogan 'sum, ergo cogito; cogito, ergo sum'). He appreciated the indefinite character of the truth and tried to 'beautify' or 'ennoble' the world by giving it colour. To be a free spirit includes shaping oneself in a daily practice. The 'highest freedom' of the free spirit consists in this continuous, aesthetic, heroic, and ethical practice.

Although Nietzsche is generally seen as a founding father of postmodernism and of anti-humanism, I would like to point to the 'binary synthetic' character of Nietzsche's anti-humanism: Nietzsche was an anti-humanist out of true humanism. Whenever one reads a line of Nietzsche, the focus of his attention is always humanity, the current state it is in and how it can be improved. One of the reasons he turned his back on Schopenhauer and metaphysics, was because he was always seeking humanity: 'to me, everything rested upon Man' ('mir lag alles am Menschen').[74] The fact that Nietzsche wanted the best for humankind made him warn against too much optimism, a too bright and idyllic view of life's and humanity's alleged original goodness, and morality as an, in its unmasked nakedness, anti-humanizing power. Nietzsche's anti-Christendom and anti-humanism is born out of genuine concern for humanity. His focus on aesthetics as the locus of true humanity, true human freedom, and culture, is to safeguard humanity from de-humanizing powers such as nationalism.

Similar to Diogenes, thus, Nietzsche has always been looking for a 'genuine human being'. A real human being is defined as follows:

> But to stand in the midst of this *rerum concordia discors* and the whole marvellous uncertainty and ambiguity of existence *without questioning*, without trembling with the craving and rapture of questioning, without at least hating the person who questions, perhaps even being faintly amused by him – that is what I feel to be *contemptible*, and this is the feeling I look for first in anyone (GS 2, p. 30)[75]

> Aber inmitten dieser rerum concordia discors und der ganzen wundervollen Ungewissheit und Vieldeutigkeit des Daseins stehen *und nicht fragen*, nicht zittern vor Begierde und Lust des Fragens [...] das ist es, was ich als *verächtlich* empfinde [...] diese Empfindung ist es, nach der ich zuerst bei Jedermann suche: – irgend eine Narrheit überredet mich immer wieder, jeder Mensch habe diese Empfindung, als Mensch (KSA 3.373)

The genuine human being does not just wonder about life, life amazes, bewilders him. At that moment, the development of European culture starts, i.e., when this question triggers the individual to cross national borders, beliefs, and norms and shape himself into a 'good European'.

Nietzsche's constant ideal is the rebirth of the classical spirit in Europe for the benefit of human culture. *The Gay Science* revolves around this ideal too. For this, he is in search of a new, higher history, one without God, one set by artists and free spirits, Wagner, at first, Goethe, later.[76] These artists are supposed to be so influential that they set the new standards, the 'new weights', the new perspectives, the new sun and

---

74 Nietzsche to Cosima Wagner, 19 December 1876 (KSB 5, p. 210).

75 Is Nietzsche referring to Horace's *Epistles* (1.12.19) here, or to Schopenhauer, who writes: 'it is *rerum concordia discors* [the discordant concord of the world], a true and complete picture of the nature of the world' while discussing Beethoven's symphonic work? See Schopenhauer W II, p. 450.

76 The people that ask questions incessantly are the people the fool in GS 125 is looking for. Looking amongst atheists, he hopes to find genuine human beings on the market square, people that ask, that confront their own moral convictions with their 'intellectual consciousness', as the title of aphorism 2 runs. See GS 124 (p. 119/KSA 3.480) and GS 125 (pp. 119–120/KSA 3.480–482). Compare GS 343 (p. 199/KSA 3.573–574) and See GS 320 (p. 180/KSA 3.551).

horizon.[77] 'Apotheosis' artists, Nietzsche calls them in GS 370. For such a new future, 'health' is needed, a 'southern' health, by which artists elevate themselves above their national origin. By 'Graecization' and 'southernization', he becomes a 'supranational' European.[78]

Nietzsche found the 'dancing', 'floating', and 'playing' above morality in the Genoese people[79] and in the troubadours of the *'gai saber'* in Provence. Hence, the title *'la gaya scienza'*. 'Provencalism' stands for the combination of amoralism and naturalism, for the natural experience of life as the basis of existence, and of all art and knowledge.[80] This natural experience goes beyond the dominance of good and evil, pity (or compassion or sympathy) and selflessness in our perception of things. It also signifies sensualism, southern paganism, and courtly love. Therefore, against Christian and Parsifilian chastity, Nietzsche calls to the aid of the troubadours to advocate the combination of sensuality and wisdom. This advocacy must be viewed as part of his call for an artistic and aesthetic Europe, a Europe that, according to Herder and Nietzsche, owes its first 'Reformation' to the Provencal poets. In the spirit of the troubadours, Nietzsche promotes in his *Gay Science* the virtues chivalrous bravery, measure, and joy (*'joi, mesura, cortesia'*). The troubadours attempted to wrest themselves free from the yoke of the church, Latin, and, with their free verses, from scholarly discipline. Similar to them, Nietzsche wants to free himself from the dominance of the Christian church over life and from the one-sided scholarly mind. Moreover, he hoped to provide Europe with a new 'weight', to push Europe into the direction of a 'higher history' via his philosophy of *amor fati*.

'Gay science' thus signifies heroism and joy in knowledge, the farewell to the search for one metaphysical truth, affirmation of the semblance, the unity of thought, life, and art, and the combination of sensualism and amoralism. As such, *The Gay Science* propagates an ideal of Europe that places itself in the tradition of Ancient Greece, the Provencal troubadours, the Italian Renaissance, and Weimar Classicism. These were all cultures or artistic streams, whose main aim consisted in the affirmation of

---

77 However, when one wants to become such a 'binding institution for future humanity' (D 542, p. 216/ 'eine bindende Institution für die zukünftige Menschheit', KSA 3.313), one wastes so much power, that one dies from it. However, better thus than 'in sand'.

78 Nietzsche uses different names for this supranational human being: Goethe, good European, free spirit, supra-human, Zarathustra. In any case, he is the counterweight to the 'teacher in the goal of existence' (GS 1, pp. 27–29/KSA 3.369–372), and, hence, counter picture of a sick culture. The 'teachers in the goal of existence' represent sick and decadent Europe, Zarathustra and the like represent a healthy and reborn Europe. The thought of the eternal return, at least as it comes forward in aphorism 341 of *The Gay Science* (pp. 194–195/KSA 3.570) examines one's health. Does he act because his instinct presses him? His 'yes' to the demonic question amounts to the fact that he lives out of a deep necessity and honest intellectual consciousness. This 'yes' is the benchmark of one's health. See also Prange (2005), pp. 90–119.

79 See GS 291 (pp. 164–165/KSA 3.531–532).

80 For a precise account of Nietzsche's provencalism, see Stegmaier (2012), pp. 35–41.

all human aspects alike, that is of man as conscious and unconscious, as rational and irrational being, and therefore sought the unity of art and knowledge. Yet, Nietzsche's 'supra-Europeanism' is as restricted as his conception of Europe is: Nietzsche not only turned his back on northern Europe and East Asia (because of its Buddhism), but also to the United States of America.[81] Only the south of Europe, and perhaps this includes the north of Africa and South America, at least parts of the world where artistic cultures lived, that created art as tributes to life, to honour life, and that view life, however painful, aesthetically, preferably as an aesthetic play, can be Nietzsche's model of an ideal culture.

As mentioned above, *The Gay Science* is the report of Nietzsche's experience of convalescence. However, viewed from the demand that this 'task' should be undertaken by all 'good Europeans', *The Gay Science* is also a recipe or a guidebook for good Europeans. Nietzsche's personal history of sickness and health is achronically the history of all good Europeans. That is the reason why the 'travel-books' are also the (future) history books of Europe's recovery and regained health. *The Gay Science* tells the story of the rebirth of Europe. *The Gay Science* is meant as a book, which tells other 'homeless' people how to travel through Europe, whereto, and what one can expect on the other side.

---

81 See GS 329 (pp. 183–184/KSA 3.183–184).

Epilogue

Nietzsche's ideal Europe in respect of Europe today

The first part of this book made clear that the young Nietzsche promoted the 'Graeci-zation' and 'southernization' of art and culture. He stated that Richard Wagner had to '*Graecize*' and 'southernize' first, if he wanted to liberate European culture from the commercial and superficial spirit that ruled German and European art and culture of their day. While Wagner, in 'Beethoven', chiefly blamed the damaging influence of French journalism and Italian opera on Germany's artistic taste and Europe's pub-lic life in general, Nietzsche regarded the Germans' inclination to equate military and cultural victory as a symptom of philistinism, as the perversion of the aesthetic. Never-theless, he defended Wagner's 'German' music as a remedy against this philistinism, despite his awareness of Wagner's 'idyllic' tendency to view art, life, and humanity from a moral and optimistic perspective in the Rousseauian tradition.

The second part showed that Nietzsche continued to advocate the 'southerniza-tion' and '*Graecization*' of music and culture during his 'free spirited', anti-Wagnerian period and later years. However, the plea for '*Graecization*' and 'southernization' then included the task of 'de-Germanizing' and becoming a 'good European', following Goethe's example. To become more 'Greek' became a cosmopolitan matter of 'dynamic interculturalism', the deliberate, active search for contact with foreign cultures in or-der to learn from them in matters of art, life, and wisdom. Rather than 'Graecizing' 'German music and culture by infusing it with 'metaphysical depth' and the Dionysian spirit, 'Italianizing' the German *Singspiel* became the new task of German music, in correspondence with the cosmopolitan task of 'de-Germanizing' and '*to become medit-teranean*'. Hence, despite the dramatic change of his musical aesthetics, Nietzsche al-ways beseeched the 'southernization' of art as a precondition for man and culture to 'aestheticize', i.e., gain the purely aesthetic response to life's tragedy that Goethe had admired so much in the Greeks. Germans had to become Greek and northern people had to integrate the 'southern' lifestyle in order to liberate themselves from what ob-structed them from embracing and affirming life as it is: tragic, discordant, and a will to power.

Having delineated Nietzsche's ideal of Europe as mixing northern and southern spirits, one question remain to be answered: what value does his ideal have for today's Europe?[1]

---

1 Nietzsche's repeatedly proposes a drastic separation of culture and politics (in the sense of 'small politics', parliamentarism), and, consequently, the separation of aesthetics and art from politics. The question is whether or not this is at all possible and desirable. Politics can also play a positive role in the promotion of art and culture in human life, and, to the extent that its task consists in the promotion of 'the good life', it can and should reinforce art for the sake of human growth. In addition, Nietzsche's

Nevertheless, Nietzsche's pleas for aestheticization, dynamic interculturalism, supra-nationalism, perspectivism, self-criticism, and broad-mindedness form the kind of plea we need today in Europe. Especially with the global economic crisis since 2008, the focus has re-shifted to the EU as a political and economic unity rather than a cultural one. Exactly now, Europe needs to rethink its 'wider cultural meaning' and justify its existence on the basis of cultural, and not merely economic, arguments. Behind the economic crisis, there is a cultural crisis, and to such an extent that politicians all over Europe have refused to think of Europe's union in other than political, economic, and legal terms. Europe is in a crisis precisely because it primarily conceives itself as an economic and political union. Since the Messina declaration, the search for European prosperity and prestige has concentrated on trans-national economic development, put on the right track by a communal politics. By stating that Europe's prosperity depends on its commercial successes, as in the quotations cited at the beginning of this book, European politics officially institutionalized the reign of consumerism in Europe. Since 1955, European politicians have been stimulating and protecting the predominant consumerist spirit in Europe, turning the scientific and artistic spirit into its servants. As a result, today, 'art', 'history', and 'scholarship', which are the protectors and creators of culture and cultural change, and economy, politics, and law move on separate grounds, incapable or unwilling to intersect. Unfortunately, we have today adjusted to the fact that the emphasis is laid on the latter sectors, while the former disciplines are indispensable for Europe's identity and the prestige European declarations claim to desire. How can the Union be justified without concern for its cultural identity?

My thesis is that an artistic-cultural view, to which Nietzsche gives a rich and stimulating boost, may substantially enrich contemporary views of Europe and significantly contribute to discussions about Europe's current identity. Adducing such an artistic view may in this way even serve the practical end of reinvigorating and justifying the existence of the European Union, which is in our time increasingly questioned.

In the general introduction, I referred to Anthony Pagden, who summarized the current problem in the following manner:

> "Europe" now exists as an economic, and increasingly political, entity. But this has no wider cultural or affective meaning.[2]

In the same book, discussing the 'idea' of Europe, J.G.A. Pocock explains:

---

claim that the Jews will play an important role in the unification of Europe, and his support for that, can hardly be explained as a non- or anti-political statement of 'the last anti-political German', even if this unification is supposed to be a matter of art in the first place. Cf. D 205, pp. 205–206/KSA 3.180–183; Stegmaier (2000) and Simon (1997).

2 Pagden (2002), p. 33.

> Whereas the Enlightened theorists invented "Europe" as a system of states in which the partner-
> ship of civil sovereignty and civil society was necessary to commerce and the spread of manners,
> we, apparently, are committed to the submergence of the state and its sovereignty, not in some
> pan-European or universal confederation, but in a postmodern era in which the global market
> demands the subjugation of the political community and perhaps of the ethnic and cultural com-
> munity also; we are to give up being citizens and behave exclusively as consumers. This is why
> the European Union is ineffective as an empire.[3]

With Pagden and Pocock, I share the diagnosis of present Europe as a culture controlled by the mercantile spirit, which turns its citizens into consumers and slackens
any possible wider cultural or affective meaning. To Pocock, politics capitulates to the
consumerist spirit. Thinking along Pocock's line, the question arises whether the role
of politics today is not virtually limited to the legitimization of the economic and technocratic unification of the twenty-seven European states in treaties and laws. Politics
erodes its own possible moral and cultural role in Europe by confining to administer-
ing and facilitating the consumerist spirit. The following rhetorical question of Terry
Eagleton may elucidate this: 'how can any political order flourish which does not address itself to this most tangible area [of the aesthetic, MP], of the "lived", of everything that belongs to a society's somatic, sensational life?'[4] Even Plato, despite his
suspicion of art with regard to the representation of the truth, advocates 'music' (in its
broad sense of 'the musical spirit', the spirit as guided by the muses') as a necessary
complement to politics.[5]

Thomas Docherty (2006) claims something similar to Pocock when he states that
politics in Western democracies have become the victim of their own politics. He holds
that in furthering the consumerist spirit, politics has given up its defining moment,
that which makes politics 'political' in the first place. In order to counterbalance the
consummation of politics in mercantilism, he proposes a new definition of 'democracy', which includes a moment of aesthetics. Docherty thus pleads for an understanding of democracy as inherently aesthetic. A democracy is always an 'aesthetic democracy', he argues, because democracy by definition includes the operation of a moment
of openness provided by the aesthetic within the political, public realm: 'it is the aesthetic determinants of a given social formation that enables us to be political beings
at all'.[6]

A more antagonistic view as maintained by Nietzsche may, at face value, appear
hostile and the product of political scepticism. However, in my view it opens up possibilities for politics too. Because of its aim to exceed the level of 'petty politics' – and
thus the political praxis of forming a society by way of identifying and solving social

---

3 Pocock (2002), p. 70.
4 Eagleton (1990), p. 13.
5 Cf. *Republic* 411 d-e.
6 Docherty (2006), p. IX.

problems by bordering off social and moral actions in laws – Nietzsche's aesthetic approach to European culture gives the message that the debate on Europe should expand its range from the political and economic unification, and its legal institutionalization beyond this 'pettiness' and insert cultural debate and self-reflection. The merit of Nietzsche's philosophy for current questions is that he contributes to the 'idea' of Europe and European identity from the standpoint that there cannot be a justification of the European Union without giving serious attention to the aesthetic and (inter-) cultural dimension of this question. His input further lies in the ways he opens up present thought to new perspectives, by stressing the centrality of the cultural dimension to questions of identity and internationalism. This dimension, admittedly, tends to be weak, if not almost absent, in contemporary European politics.

Nietzsche's aesthetic-cultural philosophy illustrates that in engaging in the process of aestheticization, politics could obtain a meaning as the praxis that engages in the formation of a society in which human beings can pursue the good life and develop their human potency at full scale.[7] Taking Aristotle's definition of politics into account, one could argue that European politics in its constricted focus on economic welfare and the interpretation of 'freedom' as 'freedom of choice' contravenes justice and democracy. If politicians want to bridge the gap between the political-economic establishment of the European Union and its inhabitants, they should address people as 'total' human beings, thus as affective, sensual and rational, sensible human begins. This requires the fulfilment of the political and economic formation of Europe with a concern for aesthetics and culture.

While Plato's exclusion of artists from the ideal society created room for modern science and technical reason to emerge, art was directed to the 'mere' realm of aesthetics. Nietzsche's answer was to broaden the realm of aesthetics by pushing the aesthetic to its limits, holding to the Goethean purpose of finding an aesthetic answer to even the most tragic event in life – as the Greeks had – and the Schillerian position that art has an answer when morality or logic both fail to provide one. Against the current technocratic task of politics, politics must assign itself with a more cultural task, out of the awareness of humanity's need for art to express and understand itself in style. If Europe strives to be a union with cultural and affective meaning, European politics should, in Nietzschean terms, develop a sense for 'tragic' culture in which art and truth, imagination and reason, work together for humanity in order for it to explore both its 'Dionysian' and 'Apollonian' powers and find a place in the heart of Europe as human beings.

Against the current reduction of humanity to 'consumers' and human freedom to 'freedom of choice', Goethe's and Nietzsche's aesthetic view of humanity serves as a critical and positive theory with the help of which we can redefine humanity in Europe today. Goethe and Nietzsche may help us in a time of widespread Euro-scepticism

---

7 Aristotle, *Nicomachean Ethics* (1990), I-2, 1–2; X-9, 269–276.

and political scepticism, because they point to the source of the gap between 'Europe' and Europeans. The gap is rooted in the way in which Europe and Europeans are defined and addressed by European politicians. Current debates about Europe lack precise views of human beings as 'total' beings, as beings that are reasonable, bodily, emotional, and sensual beings, and also of culture as a matter of art and aesthetics. By consulting Goethe and Nietzsche, we may create a counterbalance to the economic interpretation of the European Union. Interweaving current economic-political debates with aesthetic discourses will enrich the debate, put the economic-political domination into perspective, and may in the long-term succeed in bridging the gap between the European administration and the inhabitants of Europe. Such would certainly strengthen the European Union. Continuing to focus on the European market will lead to 'the creation of a large, anonymous, potentially disaffected market society'[8] inhabited by what Baudrillard termed the '*ego consumans*'.[9] 'Anonymous' should be understood as 'de-humanized'. The *ego consumans*, or '*hominus economicus*', however, understands this anonymous, de-humanized market as his or her home country and 'Golden Age', because he or she define his or her existences according to objects – as Baudrillard holds – in line with the motto 'I consume, therefore I am', rather than according to his or her human possibilities.

To summarize, for a successful and lasting unification of European countries, economic bonding and political association do not suffice. In order for the current union to survive at all, European identity must be considered anew from a perspective, which addresses Europeans as whole human beings instead of as fragmented consumers or citizens only. Moreover, the union should be regarded from a perspective, which transcends economic and political powers. This perspective is provided by aesthetics, as a domain in which reason, imagination, and the senses come together, as well as by art, as the domain where human beings experience aesthetic, thus non-political and non-consumerist, but true, human freedom. In practice, this would mean that politics opens up to culture and its aesthetic foundation.

According to Derrida, an understanding of 'culture' and the human self as transformative and pluralistic is by itself typically European.[10] Notably, this is a typically Nietzschean understanding of European man and culture, seen in the light of his 'perspectivalism'. Europe, in this Nietzschean and Derridaian view, is a land upon which continuous movement takes place, of human beings and goods. The perpetual travelling of human beings should be encouraged if we want to promote the cosmopolitan spirit of 'globalism'. Therefore, borders should be opened and crossed all over Europe and outside Europe. True cosmopolitanism seemingly implies an anarchic tendency.

---

8 Fontana (2002), p. 127.
9 Baudrillard (1988), p. 54. Baudrillard took this term from Alfred Whitehead, who in 1944 already spoke of the '*homo economicus*'.
10 See Derrida (1991), pp. 16–17; Cf. Pagden (2002), p. 12.

'This process of the European in a state of becoming' is, in Nietzsche's view, indeed not so much a political and economic process as a physiological process of 'adaptation', that is, 'the slow approach of an essentially supra-national and nomadic type of person'.[11] Becoming one Europe thus needs the process of 'becoming Europeans', according to Nietzsche. The 'good European' or *'homo Europeanus'*[12] must indeed form the basis of a society with 'wider cultural or affective meaning' in order to achieve Europe's true unification at all.

---

11 BGE 242, p. 133/KSA 5.182. Democracy in itself does not ensure this process of 'becoming Europe', it even leads to slavery and, thus, tyranny, according to Nietzsche. Although his formulation may appear harsh ('What I'm trying to say is: the democratization of Europe is at the same time an involuntary exercise in the breeding of *tyrants*,' BGE 242, p. 134/'Ich wollte sagen: die Demokratisierung Europas ist zugleich eine unfreiwillige Veranstaltung zur Züchtung von *Tyrannen*'), his argumentation is sound when we keep in mind that 'democracy' in Nietzsche's view leads to 'levelling and mediocritization' (BGE 242, p. 134/'Ausgleichung und Vermittelmässigung,' KSA 5.183) and thus to 'garrulous, impotent and eminently employable workers' (BGE 242, p. 134/'geschwätzigen willensarmen and äusserst anstellbaren Arbeitern,' KSA 5.183), who need a chef who tells them what to do, also and above all on the spiritual level. Note also that 'imitation' understood as the 'adoption of foreign forms, styles, and ways of doing' triggered by travelling and the agonal, competitive learning attitude, grounds the 'adaptation'.

12 I take this term from D'Appollonia (2002), p. 190.

Bibliography

Works of Nietzsche in German

Briefwechsel. Kritische Gesamtausgabe [KGB]. Ed. Giorgio Colli and Mazzino Montinari. Berlin/ New York: Walter de Gruyter, 1975ff.

Frühe Schriften. In 5 vols. [BAW]. Ed. Hans Joachim Mette. Munich: Beck, 1994.

Sämtliche Werke. Kritische Studienausgabe [KSA.] Ed. Giorgio Colli and Mazzino Montinari. Munich: Deutscher Taschenbuch Verlag, Berlin/New York: Walter de Gruyter, 1988 (2nd rev. ed.).

Sämtliche Briefe. Kritische Studienausgabe in 8 Bänden [KSB]. Ed. Giorgio Colli and Mazzino Montinari. Munich: Deutscher Taschenbuch Verlag; Berlin/New York: Walter de Gruyter, 1986.

Werke. Kritische Gesamtausgabe [KGW]. Ed. Giorgio Colli and Mazzino Montinari. Berlin/New York: Walter de Gruyter, 1967ff.

Works of Nietzsche in English

Thus Spoke Zarathustra. A Book for Everyone and Noone. Transl. R. J. Hollingdale. Baltimore/ Maryland: Penguin Books, 1961.

Daybreak Thoughts on the Prejudices of Morality. Transl. R.J. Hollingdale. Cambridge/New York/ Melbourne: Cambridge University Press, 1982.

Human, All Too Human. A Book for Free Spirits. Transl. R. J. Hollingdale. Cambridge/New York/ Melbourne: Cambridge University Press, 1986.

On the Genealogy of Morality. Ed. Keith Ansell-Pearson. Transl. Carol Diethe. Cambridge/New York/Melbourne: Cambridge University Press, 1994.

The Birth of Tragedy and Other Writings. Eds. Raymond Geuss and Ronald Spiers, transl. Ronald Spiers. Cambridge/New York/Oakleigh: Cambridge University Press 1999.

The Gay Science. With a Prelude in German Rhymes and an Appendix of Songs. Ed. Bernard Williams. Transl. Josefine Nauckhoff/Adrian del Caro. Cambridge, New York, Melbourne: Cambridge University Press, 2001.

Beyond Good and Evil. Eds. Rolf-Peter Horstmann and Judith Norman. Transl. Judith Norman. Cambridge/New York/Melbourne: Cambridge University Press, 2002.

The Anti-Christ, Ecce Homo, Twilight of the Idols and Other Writings. Eds. Aaron Ridley and Judith Norman. Transl. Judith Norman. Cambridge, New York, Melbourne: Cambridge University Press, 2005.

Works of Wagner in German

Das Braune Buch, Tagebuchaufzeichnungen 1865–1882. Ed. Joachim Bergfeld. Zürich und Freiburg im Breigau: Atlantis, 1975.

Bayreuther Blätter, Monatsschrifte 1878–1882. Bayreuth: Patronats-Vereines, 1878–1882

Dichtungen und Schriften in ten vols. Ed. Dieter Borchmeyer. Frankfurt am Main: Insel, 1983.
'Beethoven' in: Vol. IX, p. 9ff [DS IX], pp. 38–101.

Works of Schopenhauer in German

Sämtliche Werke. Ed. Hans-Wolfgang von Löhneysen. Stuttgart: Cotta, 1960–1965 (Bd. 1+2: *Die* Welt als Wille *und* Vorstellung).

Works of Schopenhauer in English

The World as Will and Representation I. Transl. E.F.J. Payne, Mineola: Dover, 1969.[WWR I].
The World as Will and Representation II. Transl. E.F.J. Payne. New York: Dover, 1958 [WWR II].

Works of Schiller in German

Werke. Nationalausgabe. Weimar: Böhlaus Nachfolger, 1958ff. Vols: NA 10, *Die Braut von Messina e.a.* Ed. Siegfried Siegel, 1980; NA 20: *Philosophische Schriften I.* Ed. Benno von Wiese. 1962; NA 21: *Philosophische Schriften II.* Ed. Benno von Wiese, 1963; NA 22: *Vermischte Schriften.* Ed. Herbert Meyer, 1958; NA 30: *Schillers Briefe.* Ed. Lieselotte Blumenthal, 1961..
'Die Schaubühne als moralische Anstalt betrachtet' in: Friedrich Schiller, *Über Kunst und Wirklichkeit. Schriften und Briefe zur Ästhetik.* Leipzig: Reclam, 1985.

Works of Schiller in English

On the Naive and Sentimental in Literature. Transl. Helen Watanabe-O'Kelly. Manchester: Carcanet New Press, 1981.
On the Aesthetic Education of Man. In a Series of Letters. Ed., transl., and intr. Wilkinson & Willoughby, Oxford: Clarendon Press, 1982 [1967].

Works of Goethe in German

Werke. Hamburger Ausgabe [HA] in 14 vols. Ed. Erich Trunz. Munich: Beck, 1994 (12. rev. ed.).
Sämtliche Werke nach Epochen seines Schaffens. Münchner Ausgabe. Ed. Karl Richter. Hanser: Munich [MA]. Vol. 8/1 + 8/2: Briefwechsel zwischen Schiller und Goethe in den Jahren 1794 bis 1805. Ed. Manfred Beetz, Munich, 1990 [MA 8]; Vol 15: Italienische Reise. Eds. Andreas Beyer und Norbert Miller, 1992 [MA 15]; Vol. 19: *Johann Peter Eckermann,* Gespräche mit Goethe in den letzten Jahren seines Lebens. Ed. Heinz Schlaffer, 1986 [MA 19]. MA 20/1: Briefwechsel zwischen Goethe und Zelter in den Jahren 1799 bis 1832. Eds. Hans-Günter Ottenberg and Edith Zehm, 1991.
Goethes Briefe. 4 Vols., Hamburger Ausgabe [HA], Hamburg. Ed. Christian Wegner. 1967.
Goethes Gedanken über Musik. Eine Sammlung aus seinen Werken, Briefen, Gesprächen und Tagebüchern. Ed. Hedwig Walwei-Wiegelmann. Frankfurt am Main: Insel, 1985.

Works of Goethe in English

Johann Peter Eckermann, *Conversations with Goethe (1823–1832)*. Transl. John Oxenford. San Francisco: North Point, 1984.

The Collected Works. Ed. John Geary. Princeton: Princeton University Press, 1994; Vol. 3: *Essays on Art and Literature*. 1994; Vol. 6: *Italian Journey*. 1989.

Other literature

Ruth Abbey, *Nietzsche's Middle Period*. Oxford: Oxford University Press, 2000.

Hermann Abert, *W.A. Mozart* (reworked and enlarged edition of Otto Jahn's *Mozart*), Vol. I and II. Leizig: Breitkopf & Härtel, 1989–1990.

Theodor W. Adorno, *Philosophie der neuen Musik*. Frankfurt am Main: Suhrkamp, 2003.

Gérard Alvoët, Nietzsche et l'Europe: "nous autres, bons Européens". Paris: l'Harmattan, 2006.

Detlef Altenburg, 'Die Neudeutsche Schule – eine Fiktion der Musikgeschichtsschreibung?' in: Detlef Altenburg (ed.), *Liszt und die Neudeutsche Schule*. Weimarer Liszt-Studien 3. Laaber: Laaber Verlag, 2006, pp. 9–22..

Warren D. Anderson, Ethos and Education in Greek Music. The Evidence of Poetry and Philosophy. Cambridge (MU): Harvard University Press, 1966.

David B. Allison, 'Musical Psychodramatics: Ecstasis in Nietzsche', in: Alan D. Schrift (ed.), *Why Nietzsche Still? Reflections on Drama, Culture, and Politics*. Berkeley/Los Angeles/London: University of California Press, 2000, pp. 66–78.

Keith Ansell-Pearson, *Nietzsche* contra *Rousseau*. *A Study of Nietzsche's Moral and Political Thought*. Cambridge, New York, Melbourne: Cambridge University Press, 1991.

Kwame Anthony Appiah, *Cosmopolitanism*. *Ethics in a World of Strangers*. New York/London: W.W. Norton & Company, 2006.

Aristotle, *Poetics*. Transl. George Whalley. Montreal: Mc Gill-Queen's University Press, 1997.

Aristotle, *The Nichomachean Ethics*. Transl. David Ross. Oxford/New York: Oxford University Press, 1990.

Steven E. Aschheim, *The Nietzsche Legacy in Germany 1890–1990*. Berkeley/Los Angeles/London: University of California Press, 1992.

M. S. Asquith, 'Francis Hueffer and the Early Reception of Richard Wagner's Aesthetics in England,' in: J. Rademacher (ed.), *Modernism and the Individual Talent: re-canonizing Ford Madox Ford (Hueffer)*. Berlin/Hamburg/Münster: LIT Verlag, 2002, pp. 135–147.

Stuart Atkins, '*Italienische Reise* and Goethean Classicism', in: Stanley A. Corngold, Michael Curschmann, Theodore J. Ziolkowski (eds.), *Aspekte der Goethezeit*, Göttingen: Vandenhoeck & Ruprecht, 1977, pp. 81–96.

Achim Aurnhammer, 'Goethes "Italienische Reise" im Kontext der deutschen Italienreisen', in: Werner Frick, Jochen Golz and Edith Zehm (eds.), *Goethe-Jahrbuch 120* (2003). Weimar: Böhlaus Nachfolger, pp. 72–86.

Babette Babich, 'Musik und Wort in der Antiken Tragödie und *La Gaya Scienza*: Nietzsches "Fröhliche" Wissenschaft', in: *Nietzsche-Studien* 36 (2008). Berlin/New York: De Gruyter, pp. 243–270.

Babette Babich, 'Sexualität', in: Stefan Lorenz Sorgner, H. James Brix, Nikolaus Knoepffler (eds.), *Wagner und Nietzsche. Kultur – Werk – Wirkung. Ein Handbuch*. Reinbek: Rowohlt, 2008.

Rebecca Bamford, 'Nietzsche's Aestheticism and the Value of Suffering', in: Paul Bishop and R. H. Stephenson (eds.), *Cultural Studies and the Symbolic 1*. Leeds: Northern University Press, 2003, pp. 66–81.

Barenboim, Daniel & Said, Edward, *Parallels and Paradoxes. Explorations in Music and Society*. London: Bloomsbury, 2002.

Jean Baudrillard, *Selected Writings*. Ed. Mark Foster. Stanford: Stanford University Press, 1988.

Dave Beech and John Roberts (eds.), *The Philistine Controversy*. London: Verso, 2002.

Ernst Behler, 'Die Auffassung des Dionysischen durch die Brüder Schlegel und Friedrich Nietzsche', in: *Nietzsche-Studien* 12 (1983). Berlin/New York: Walter de Gruyter, pp. 335–354.

Walter Benjamin, 'The Storyteller. Reflections on the Works of Nikolai Leskov', in: *Illuminations*. London: Pimlico, 1999, pp. 83–107.

Raymond J. Benders and Stephan Oettermann, *Friedrich Nietzsche. Chronik in Bildern und Texten*. Munich/Vienna: Carl Hanser Verlag; Munich: Deutscher Taschenbuch Verlag, 2000.

J. M. Bernstein, *The Fate of Art. Aesthetic Alienation from Kant to Derrida and Adorno*. Cambridge: Polity Press, 1992.

J. M. Bernstein, 'Against Voluptuous Bodies of Satiation without Happiness', in: D. Beech and J. Roberts (eds.), *The Philistine Controverse*. London: Verso, 2002, pp. 103–124.

Jessica N. Berry, 'The Pyrrhonian Revival in Montaigne and Nietzsche', in: Journal of the History of Ideas 65/3 2004, pp. 497–514.

Jessica N. Berry, 'Nietzsche and Democritus: The Origins of Ethical Eudaimonism' in: Paul Bishop (ed.), *Nietzsche and Antiquity. His Reaction and Response to the Classical Tradition*. Rochester/Suffolk: Camden House, 2004, pp. 98–113.

Ernst Bertram, *Nietzsche. Versuch einer Mythologie*. Berlin: Georg Bondi, 1929.

Benjamin Biebuyk, 'Een nieuwe Mozart. Nietzsches muzikale brieven aan Heinrich Köselitz', in: Feit & Fictie 2001-3. Groningen: Historische Uitgeverij, pp. 96–111.

Paul Bishop, 'Nietzsche's "New" Morality: Gay Science, Materialist Ethics', in: History of European Ideas 32-2, 2006, pp. 223–236 [2006–1].

Paul Bishop, 'Nationalism and Europeanism in German Romantic Literature', in: Mary-Anne Perkins and Martin Liebscher (eds.), *Nationalism* versus *Cosmopolitanism in German Thought and Culture, 1789–1914. Essays on the Emergence of Europe*. Lewiston/Queenston: The Edwin Mellen Press, 2006, pp. 93–130 [2006–2].

Paul Bishop and R. H. Stephenson, *Nietzsche and Weimar Classicism*. New York: Camden House, 2005.

Paul Bishop, 'Nietzsche's Anti-Christianity as a Return to (German) Classicism', in: Paul Bishop (ed.), *Nietzsche and Antiquity. His Reaction and Response to the Classical Tradition*. Rochester/Suffolk: Camden House, 2004, pp. 441–457.

Alfred Bock, *Deutsche Dichter in ihren Beziehungen zur Musik*. Gießen: J. Ricker, 1900.

Pim den Boer, *Europa. De geschiedenis van een idee*. Amsterdam: Ooievaar, 1999.

Dieter Borchmeyer, *Nietzsche, Cosima, Wagner. Porträt einer Freundschaft*. Frankfurt am Main/Leipzig 2008.

Dieter Borchmeyer, *Das Theater Richard Wagners. Idee-Dichtung-Wirkung*. Stuttgart: Reclam, 1982.

Dieter Borchmeyer, '"… dem Naturalismus in der Kunst offen und ehrlich den Krieg zu erklären…". Goethes und Schiller Bühnenreform', in: Wilfried Barner, Eberhard Lämmert (eds.), *Unser Commercium. Goethes und Schillers Literaturpolitik*. Stuttgart 1984, pp. 351–370.

Dieter Borchmeyer, '"Ein Dreigestirn ewig verbundener Geister" Wagner, Nietzsche, Thomas Mann und das Konzept einer übernationalen Kultur', in: Heinz Gockel (ed.), *Wagner-Nietzsche-Thomas Mann*. Frankfurt am Main: Klostermann, 1993, pp. 1–15.

Dieter Borchmeyer, *Weimarer Klassik. Portrait einer Epoche*. Weinheim: Beltz Athenäum, 1994.

Dieter Borchmeyer, '"Dichtung der Zukunft"? Goethe, der Überdeutsche, im Bilde Nietzsches', in: Alessandro Di Chiara (ed.): *Friedrich Nietzsche 1900–2000*. Genoa, 2000, pp. 196–215.

Dieter Borchmeyer, Jörg Salaquarda, *Nietzsche und Wagner. Stationen einer epochalen Begeg-nung* in two vols. Frankfurt am Main/Leipzig: Insel, 1994.

Dieter Borchmeyer, '"Eine Art Symbolik fürs Ohr". Goethes Musikästhetik', in: Walter Hinderer (ed.), *Goethe und das Zeitalter der Romantik*. Würzburg, 2002, pp. 413–446.

Fritz Bornmann, 'Nietzsches Metrische Studien', in: *Nietzsche-Studien* 18 (1989). Berlin/New York: Walter de Gruyter, pp. 472–489.

Karl Borinski, *Die Antike in Poetik und Kunsttheorie. Von Ausgang des Klassischen Altertums bis auf Goethe und Wilhelm von Humboldt*. Vol. II. Darmstadt: Wissenschaftliche Buchge-sellschaft, 1965.

Tilman Borsche, 'Fröhliche Wissenschaft freier Geister – eine Philosophie der Zukunft?' in: Mi-hailo Djuric (ed.), *Nietzsches Begriff der Philosophie*. Würzburg: Königshausen & Neumann, 1990, pp. 53–72.

Elmar Bötcher, Goethes Singspiele "Erwin und Elmire" und "Claudine von Villa Bella" und die "opera buffa". Marburg: Frantzen, 1911.

Andrew Bowie, *From Romanticism to Critical Theory*. London/New York: Routledge, 1997.

Andrew Bowie, 'Confessions of a "New Aesthete": A Response to the "New Philistines", in: D. Beech and J. Roberts (eds.), *The Philistine Controverse*. London: Verso, 2002, pp. 73–102 [2002–1].

Andrew Bowie, 'Another Third Way?' in: in: D. Beech and J. Roberts (eds.), *The Philistine Contro-verse*. London: Verso, 2002, pp. 161–174 [2002–2].

Andrew Bowie, *Music, Philosophy, and Modernity*. Cambridge/New York/Melbourne: Cambridge University Press, 2007.

R. Bracht Branham, 'Nietzsche's Cynicism: Uppercase or lowercase?' in: Paul Bishop (ed.), *Nietzsche and Antiquity. His Reaction and Response to the Classical Tradition*. Rochester/Suffolk: Camden House, 2004, pp. 170–181.

Dieter Bremer, 'Vom Mythos zum Musikdrama. Wagner, Nietzsche und die griechische Tragödie', in: Dieter Borchmeyer (ed.), *Wege des Mythos in der Moderne*. Munich: Deutscher Taschen-buch Verlag, 1987, pp. 41–63.

Menahem Brinker, 'Nietzsche and the Jews', in: *Nietzsche, Godfather of Fascism? On the Uses and Abuses of a Philosophy*. Ed. Jacob Golomb and Robert S. Wistrich. Princeton/Oxford: Princeton University Press, 2002, pp. 107–125.

Thomas Brobjer, 'Nietzsche as German Philosopher: His Reading of the Classical German Philosophers', in: *Nietzsche and the German Tradition*. Ed. Nicholas Martin. Oxford/Bern/Berlin: Peter Lang, 2003, pp. 39–82.

Thomas Brobjer, 'Sources and Influences on Nietzsche's Birth of Tragedy', in: *Nietzsche-Studien* 34 (2005). Berlin/New York: Walter de Gruyter, pp. 278–296.

Klaus-Detlef Bruse, 'Die Geburt der Tragödie als "Gesamtkunstwerk" – Anmerkungen zu den musikästhetischen Reflexionen des frühen Nietzsche', in; *Nietzsche-Studien* 13 (1984). Berlin/New York: Walter de Gruyter, pp. 156–176.

Marco Brusotti, *Die Leidenschaft der Erkenntnis. Philosophie und ästhetische Lebensgestaltung bei Nietzsche von Morgenröthe bis Also sprach Zarathustra*. Berlin/New York: Walter de Gruyter, 1997.

Marco Brusotti, '"Europäisch und über-Europäisch", Nietzsches Blick aus der Ferne', in: *Tijd-schrift voor Filosofie* 66. Leuven: Hoger Instituut voor Wijsbegeerte, 2004, pp. 31–48.

Marco Brusotti, 'Européen et supra-européen', in: Paulo D'Iorio and Gilbert Merlio, *Nietzsche et l'Europe*. Paris: Éditions de la maison des sciences de l'homme, 2006, pp. 193–211.

Marco Brusotti, 'Verkehrte Welt und Redlichkeit gegen sich. Rückblicke Nietzsches auf seine frühere Wagneranhängerschaft in den Aufzeichnungen 1880–1881', in: Tilman Borsche,

Federico Gerratana, Aldo Venturelli (eds.), *Centauren-Geburten, Wissenschaft, Kunst und Philosophie beim jungen Nietzsche*. Berlin/New York: Walter de Gruyter, 1994, pp. 435–460.

Malcolm Bull, 'The Ecstacy of Philistinism' in: Dave Beech and John Roberts (eds.), *The Philistine Controversy*. London: Verso, 2002, pp. 48–72.

J.W. Burrow, *The Crisis of Reason. European Thought, 1848–1914*. New Haven and London: Yale University Press, 2000.

James Buzard, *The Beaten Track: European Tourism, Literature, and the Ways to "Culture"*. Oxford: Clarendon Press, 1993.

Daniel Came, 'Nietzsche's Attempt at a Self-Criticism: Art and Morality in *The Birth of Tragedy*', in: *Nietzsche-Studien* 33 (2004). Berlin/New York: Walter de Gruyter, pp. 37–67.

Daniel Came, 'The Aesthetic Justification of Existence', in: Keith Ansell-Pearson (ed.), *The Nietzsche Companion*. Malden/Oxford/Carlton: Blackwell, 2006, pp. 41–57.

Giuliano Campioni, Paulo D'Iorio, Maria Christina Fornari e.a. (eds.), *Nietzsches persönliche Bibliothek*. Berlin/New York, Walter de Gruyter, 2003.

Claus Canisius, *Goethe und die Musik*. Münich/Zürich: Piper, 1998.

David E. Cartwright, 'Reversing Silenus' Wisdom', in: *Nietzsche-Studien* 20 (1991). Berlin/New York: Walter de Gruyter, pp. 309–313.

Ernst Cassirer, *Essay on Man*. New Haven: Yale University Press, 1944.

Ernst Cassirer, *Freiheit und Form. Studien zur Deutschen Geistesgeschichte*. Darmstadt: Wissenschaftliche Buchgesellschaft, 1961[3].

Ernst Cassirer, *Idee und Gestalt. Goethe, Schiller, Hölderlin, Kleist*. Darmstadt: Wissenschaftliche Buchgesellschaft, 1973.

Ernst Cassirer, 'Mythischer, ästhetischer und theoretischer Raum', in: Ernst Cassirer, *Gesammelte Werke*, Band 17. Hamburg: Meiner, 2004, pp. 411–432.

Rodolfo Celletti, *A History of Bel Canto*. Oxford: Clarendon Press, 1991.

Sarah Colvin, 'Musical Culture and Thought', in: Barbara Becker-Cantarino (ed.), *German Literature of the Eighteenth Century. The Enlightenment and Sensibility*. New York: Camden House, 2005, pp. 185–220.

Nicholas Cook, 'Beethoven', *Symphony No. 9*. Cambridge/New York/Melbourne: Cambridge University Press, 1993.

Daniel W. Conway, 'Nietzsche's Germano-Mania', in: Nicholas Martin (ed.), *Nietzsche and the German Tradition*. Oxford/Bern/Berlin: Peter Lang, 2003, pp. 1–37.

Maurice Cranston, *The Romantic Movement*. Oxford UK/Cambridge USA: Blackwell, 1994.

Luca Crescenzi, 'Nietzsches Idyllen aus Messina. Das Volkslied als Form des Philosophierens', in: Andreas Schirmer and Rüdiger Schmidt (eds.), *Entdecken und Verraten. Zu Leben und Werk Friedrich Nietzsches*. Weimar: Böhlaus Nachfolger, 1999, pp. 191–201.

Hugo Daffner, *Nietzsches Randglossen zu Bizets Carmen*. Regensburg: Bosse, 1938[2].

Carl Dahlhaus, *Between Romanticism and Modernism. Four Studies in the Music of the Later Nineteenth Century*. Transl. Mary Whittall. Incl. the Nietzsche fragment "On Music and Words" (transl. Walter Kaufmann). Berkeley/Los Angeles/London: University of California Press, 1980.

Carl Dahlhaus, *Wagners Konzeption des musikalischen Dramas*. Munich/Kassel: Deutscher Taschenbuch Verlag, 1990.

Carl Dahlhaus, *Die Musiktheorie im 18. und 19. Jahrhundert. Geschichte der Musiktheorie*. Ed. Frieder Zaminer. Vol. II: *Deutschland*. Ed. Ruth E. Müller. Darmstadt: Wissenschaftliche Buchgesllschaft, 1989.

Ariane Chebel D'Appollonia, 'European Nationalism and European Union', in: Anthony Pagden (ed.), *The Idea of Europe. From Antiquitiy to the European Union*. Washington: Woodrow Wilson Center Press/Cambridge (UK): Cambridge University Press, 2002, pp. 171–190.

Adrian Del Caro, 'Nietzschean Self-Transformation and the Transformation of the Dionysian', in: Salim Kemal, Ivan Gaskell (eds.), *Nietzsche, Philosophy, and the Arts*. Cambridge/New York/ Melbourne: Cambridge University Press, 2002, pp. 70–91.

Gilles Deleuze, *Nietzsche and Philosophy*. Transl. Hugh Tomlinson. New York: Columbia University Press, 1983.

Gilles Deleuze, 'Nomad Thought', in: D. B. Allison (ed.), *The New Nietzsche*. Cambridge (Mass.): MIT Press, 1994, pp. 142–150.

Jacques Derrida, *L'autre cap*. Paris: Minuit, 1991.

Jacques Derrida, *Le droit à la philosophie du point de vue cosmopolitique*. Vendôme: Verdier, 1997.

Carol Diethe, *Nietzsches Schwester und* Der Wille zur Macht. Hamburg/Vienna: Europa Verlag, 2001.

Thomas Docherty, *Aesthetic Democracy*. Stanford: Stanford University Press, 2006.

James H. Donelan, *Poetry and the Romantic Musical Aesthetic*. Cambridge, New York, Melbourne: Cambridge University Press, 2008.

Maarten Doorman, *De romantische orde*. Amsterdam: Bert Bakker, 2004.

Éric Dufour, 'L'esthétique musicale formaliste de *Humain trop humain*', in: *Nietzsche-Studien* 28 (1999). Berlin/New York: Walter de Gruyter, pp. 215–233.

Éric Dufour, 'L'année 1872 de Nietzsche. La naissance de la tragédie et Manfred Meditation', in: Éditions de l'Herne, Paris, 2000, pp. 245–259.

Éric Dufour, 'La physiologie de la musique de Nietzsche', in: *Nietzsche-Studien* 30 (2001). Berlin/ New York: Walter de Gruyter, pp. 222–245.

Éric Dufour, 'Métaphysique de la musique dans *Le monde comme volonté et comme representation* et dans *La naissance de la tragédie*', in: Les études philosophiques 4 (1997). Paris: Presses Universitaires de France, pp. 471–492.

C. N. Dugan and Tracy B. Strong, 'Music, Politics, Theater, and Representation in Rousseau', in: Patrick Riley (ed.), *The Cambridge Companion to Rousseau*. Cambridge/New York/ Melbourne: Cambridge University Press, 2001, pp. 329–364.

Robbie Duschinksky, 'Nietzsche: Through the Lens of Purity', in: Journal of Nietzsche Studies 41 (2011), pp. 50–64.

Terry Eagleton, *The Ideology of the Aesthetic*. Malden/Oxford/Carlton: Blackwell Publishing, 1990.

P. E. Easterling (ed.), *The Cambridge Companion to Greek Tragedy*. Cambridge/New York/ Melbourne: Cambridge University Press, 2003.

Manfred Eger, *Nietzsches Bayreuther Passion*. Freiburg im Bresgau: Rombach, 2001.

Manfred Eger, 'Zum Fall Wagner/Nietzsche/Hanslick', in: Andreas Schirmer und Rüdiger Schmidt (eds.), *Entdecken und Verraten. Zu Leben und Werk Friedrich Nietzsches*. Weimar: Böhlaus Nachfolger, 1999, pp. 111–131.

Louis Ehlert, *Briefe über Musik an eine Freundin*. Berlin: J. Guttenberg, 1859.

Louis Ehlert, *Letters on Music, to a Lady*. Transl. Fanny Raymond Ritter. London, 1877.

Stefan Elbe *Europe. A Nietzschean Perspective*. London/New York: Routledge, 2003.

Amos Elon, *The Pity of it All. A Portrait of the German-Jewish Epoch, 1743–1933*. New York: Picador, 2002.

David Farrel Krell and Donald L. Bates, *The Good European: Nietzsche's Work Sites in Word and Image*. Chicago: University of Chicago Press, 1997.

Frank Ferudi, *Where Have All the Intellectuals Gone? Confronting 21st Century Philistinism*. London/New York: Continuum, 2004.

Dieter Fischer-Dieskau, 'Die Musik und Goethe', in: Dieter Borchmeyer (ed.), *Goethe im Gegen-licht: Kunst, Musik, Religion, Philosophie, Natur, Politik.* Heidelberg: Palatina, 2000, pp. 35–58.

Margot Fleischer, 'Dionysos als Ding an sich. Der Anfang von Nietzsches Philosophie in der äs-thetischen Metaphysik der "Geburt der Tragödie"', in: *Nietzsche-Studien* 17 (1988). Berlin/New York: Walter de Gruyter, pp. 74–90.

Biancamaria Fontana, 'The Napoleonic Empire and the Europe of Nations', in: Anthony Pagden (ed.), *The Idea of Europe. From Antiquitiy to the European Union.* Washington: Woodrow Wilson Center Press/Cambridge (UK): Cambridge University Press, 2002, pp. 116–128.

Elizabeth Förster-Nietzsche, *The Nietzsche-Wagner Correspondence.* New York: Liveright, 1949.

Michel Foucault, *Le souci de soi.* Paris: Gallimard, 1984.

Michel Foucault, 'What is Enlightenment', in: Paul Rabinow (ed.), *The Foucault Reader.* New York: Pantheon Books, 1984, pp. 32–51.

Michel Foucault, 'Nietzsche, Genealogy, History', in: Paul Rabinow (ed.), *The Foucault Reader.* New York: Pantheon Books, 1984, pp. 76–100.

Manfred Frank, *Der kommende Gott. Vorlesungen über die neue Mythologie.* Frankfurt am Main: Suhrkamp, 1982.

Lilian R. Furst, 'Goethe's *Italienische Reise* in its European Context' in: Gerhart Hoffmeister (ed.), *Goethe in Italy, 1786–1986.* Amsterdam: Rodopi 1988, pp. 115–132.

Thrasybulos Georgiades, *Musik und Rhythmus bei den Griechen. Zum Ursprung der abendländis-chen Musik.* Hamburg: Rowohlt, 1958.

Sander L. Gilman, *Nietzschean Parody. An Introduction to Reading Nietzsche.* Bonn: Bouvier, 1976.

Sander L. Gilman, '"Incipit Parodia": The Function of Parody in the Lyrical Poetry of Friedrich Nietzsche', in: Nietzsche-Studien 4 (1975), pp. 52–74..

Georges Goedert, 'Egalitarismus und Kultur – Zu Nietzsches Kritik der demokratischen Gleich-heitsnorm', in: Georges Goedert, Uschi Nussbaumer-Benz (eds.), *Nietzsche und die Kultur – ein Beitrag zu Europa?* Hildesheim/Zürich/New York: Georg Olms Verlag, 2002, pp. 124–139.

Peter Gommers, Europe. *What's in a Name? Geography, Mythos, Arts.* Leuven University Press, 2001.

Rüdiger Görner, *Nietzsches Kunst. Annäherung an einen Denkartisten.* Frankfurt am Main: Insel, 2000.

Rüdiger Görner, 'Nietzsche, the "good European"? Or: The Praise of Prejudice in *Beyond Good and Evil* and the Will to Power', in: Mary-Anne Perkins and Martin Liebscher (eds.), *Nation-alism* versus *Cosmopolitanism in German Thought and Culture, 1789–1914. Essays on the Emergence of Europe.* Lewiston/Queenston: The Edwin Mellen Press, 2006, pp. 243–256.

David Gramit, *Cultivating Music. The Aspirations, Interests, and Limits of German Musical Cul-ture, 1770–1848.* Berkeley/Los Angeles/London: University of California Press, 2002.

Martin Gregor-Dellin, *Richard Wagner, Sein Leben, Sein Werk, Sein Jahrhundert.* Munich: Gold-mann/Schott, 1983.

Reinhold Grimm, 'Antiquity as Echo and Disguise: Nietzsches "Lied eines theokritischen Ziegen-hirten," Heinrich Heine, and the Crucified Dionysus', in: *Nietzsche-Studien* 14 (1985). Berlin/New York: Walter de Gruyter, pp. 201–249.

Ger Groot, *Vier ongemakkelijke filosofen: Nietzsche, Cioran, Bataille, Derrida.* Amsterdam: Sun, 2003.

Gernot Gruber, 'Nietzsches Begriff des "Südländischen" in der Musik', in: Günther Pöltner and Helmut Vetter (eds.), *Nietzsche und die Musik.* Frankfurt am Main: Peter Lang, 1997, pp. 115–128.

Karl Gründer (ed.), *Der Streit um Nietzsches 'Geburt der Tragödie'. Die Schriften von E. Rohde, R. Wagner, U. v. Wilamowitz-Möllendorff*. Olms: Hildesheim, 1969.

Philip Grundlehner, *The Poetry of Friedrich Nietzsche*. New York/Oxford: Oxford University Press, 1996.

Eduard Hanslick, *Vom Musikalisch-Schönen. Ein Beitrag zur Revision der Ästhetik der Tonkunst*. Leipzig: Johann Ambrosius Barth, 1891.

Eduard Hanslick, *The Beautiful in Music*. New York: The Library of Liberal Arts, 1957.

Thomas Harrison (ed.), *Nietzsche in Italy*. Standford: Stanford University Press, 1988.

Peter Heckman, 'The Role of Music in Nietzsche's *Birth of Tragedy*', in: British Journal of Aesthetics 30–4, 1990. Oxford: Oxford University Press, pp. 351–360.

Erich Heftrich, 'Nietzsches "Tristan". Richard Wagner als semiotische Figur', in: *Nietzsche-Studien* 14 (1985). Berlin/New York: Walter de Gruyter, pp. 22–34.

Erich Heftrich, 'Nietzsche's Goethe: Eine Annäherung', in: *Nietzsche-Studien* 16 (1987). Berlin/New York: Walter de Gruyter, pp. 1–20.

Martin Heidegger, *Sein und Zeit*. Tübingen: Max Niemeyer Verlag, 1993⁶ [1927].

Martin Heidegger, *Being and Time*. Transl. John Macquarrie and Edward Robinson. Oxford: Basil Blackwell, 1980 [1962].

Martin Heidegger, *Nietzsche*. Vol I. Pfullingen: Neske, 1961.

Annette Hein, *'Es ist viel "Hitler" in Wagner'. Rassismus und antisemitische Deutschtumsideologie in den 'Bayreuther Blättern' (1878–1938)*. Tübingen: Max Niemeyer, 1996.

Erich Heller, *The Importance of Nietzsche. Ten Essays*. Chicago/London: The University of Chicago Press, 1988.

Niels Helsloot, *Vrolijke wetenschap: Nietzsche als vriend*. Baarn: Kok Agora, 1999.

Johann Gottfried Herder, *Ideen zur Philosophie der Geschichte der Menschheit*. Darmstadt: Melzer, 1966.

Kathleen Marie Higgins, *Comic Relief. Nietzsche's Gay Science*. New York/Oxford: Oxford University Press, 2000.

Dieter Hildebrandt, *Die Neunte. Schiller, Beethoven und die Geschichte eines musikalischen Erfolgs*. Munich, Vienna: Hanser, 2005.

Kurt Hildebrandt, *Wagner und Nietzsche, Ihr Kampf gegen das Neunzehnte Jahrhundert*. Breslau: Ferdinand Hirt, 1924.

Hans Gerald Hödl, 'Italienische Städte: Orte in Nietzsches metaphorischer Landschaft. Eine Annäherung', in: Volker Gerhardt and Renate Reschke (eds.), *Nietzscheforschung* 10. Berlin: Akademie Verlag, 2003, pp. 299–315.

E.T.A. Hoffmann, *Review of Symphony No. 5, by Ludwig von Beethoven*. Transl. F. John Adams Jr., in Elliot Forbes (ed.): *Symphony No. 5 in C Minor*, by Ludwig von Beethoven. New York: Norton, 1971.

E.T.A. Hoffmann, *Ludwig von Beethoven, 5. Symphonie* in: E.T.A. Hoffmann, *Schriften zur Musik. Singspiele*. Berlin/Weimar: Aufbau 1988, pp. 22–42.

R. J. Hollingdale, *Nietzsche. The Man and His Philosophy*. Cambridge/New York/Melbourne: Cambridge University Press, 1999 (rev. ed.).

Roger Hollinrake, *Nietzsche, Wagner, and the Philosophy of Pessimism*. London, Boston, Sydeny: George Allen and Unwin, 1982.

Angela Holzer, 'Neuerscheinungen zur Konstellation Nietzsche-Wagner', in: Nietzsche-Studien 39 (2010). Berlin/New York: De Gruyter, pp. 420–435.

Homer, *The Iliad*. Transl. Robert Fagles. New York/London/Camberwell: Penguin, 1990.

Horace, *The Complete Odes and Epodes*. Transl. David West. Oxford/New York: Oxford University Press, 1997.

Marie-Claire Hoock-Demarle, 'Europa, die Frühromantik und der "europäische" Goethe', in: Walter Hinderer (ed.), *Goethe und das Zeitalter der Romantik*. Würzburg: Königshausen & Neumann, pp. 475–488.

Max Horkheimer and Theodor W. Adorno, *Dialektik der Aufklärung. Philosophische Fragmente*. Franfurt am Main: Fischer, 1969.

Paolo D'Iorio and Gilbert Merlio, 'Avant-propos: Un bon Européen à Cosmopolis', in: Paolo D'Iorio and Gilbert Merlio (eds.), *Nietzsche et l'Europe*. Paris: Éditions de la maison des sciences de l'homme, 2006, pp. 7–11.

John Claiborne Isbell, *The Birth of European Romanticism. Truth and Propaganda in Staël's De l'Allemagne 1810–1813*. Cambridge/New York/Melbourne: Cambridge University Press, 1994.

Otto Jahn, *Gesammelte Aufsätze über Musik*. Leipzig, 1867 [2nd ed.].

Christopher Janaway, 'Nietzsche, the Self, and Schopenhauer', in: Keith Ansell-Pearson (ed.), *Nietzsche and Modern German Thought*. London/New York: Routledge, 1991, pp. 119–142.

Christopher Janaway, 'Schopenhauer as Nietzsche's Educator,' in: Nicholas Martin (ed.), *Nietzsche and the German Tradition*. Oxford/Bern/Berlin: Peter Lang, 2003, pp. 155–185.

Curt Paul Janz, 'Das "Räthsel" Peter Gast', in: Curt Paul Janz, *Die Briefe Friedrich Nietzsches. Textprobleme und ihre Bedeutung für Biographie und Doxographie*, pp. 33–41. Zürich: Theologischer Verlag, 1972.

Curt Paul Janz, *Nietzsche Biographie* in three vols. Munich/Vienna: Carl Hanser, 1978 [1978a].

Curt Paul Janz, 'Nietzsches Verhältnis zur Musik seiner Zeit', in: *Nietzsche-Studien* 7 (1978). Berlin/New York: Walter de Gruyter, pp. 308–338 [1978b].

Curt Paul Janz, 'The Form-Content Problem in Friedrich Nietzsche's Conception of Music', in: Michael Allen Gillespie and Tracy B. Strong (eds.), *Nietzsche's New Seas. Explorations in Philosophy, Aesthetics, and Politics*. Chicago/London: The University of Chicago Press, 1988, pp. 97–116.

Curt Paul Janz, 'Die Musik im Leben Nietzsches', in: *Nietzsche-Studien* 26 (1997). Berlin/New York: Walter de Gruyter, pp. 72–86.

Karl Jaspers, *Nietzsche. An Introduction to the Understanding of his Philosophical Activity*. Transl. Charles F. Wallraff, Frederick J. Schmitz. Baltimore/London: The John Hopkins University Press, 1997 (1936).

David Wyn Jones, 'Beethoven', *Pastoral Symphony*. Cambridge, New York, Melbourne: Cambridge University Press, 1995.

John Joughin and Simon Malpas (eds.), *The New Aestheticism*. Manchester/New York: Manchester University Press, 2003.

Gerhard Kaiser, *Von Arkadien nach Elysium: Schiller-Studien*. Göttingen: Vandenhoeck & Ruprecht, 1978.

Gerhard Kaiser, *Wandrer und Idylle: Goethe und die Phänomenologie der Natur in der deutschen Dichtung von Gessner bis Gottfried Keller*. Göttingen: Vandenhoeck & Ruprecht, 1977.

Immanuel Kant, *Critique of Judgment*. Transl. J.H. Bernard. New York: Hafner Press/London: Collier Macmillan, 1951.

Kai Kaufmann, '"Gondeln, Lichter, Musik"', in: *Nietzsche-Studien* 17 (1988). Berlin/New York: Walter de Gruyter, pp. 158–178.

Walter Kaufmann, *Nietzsche. Philosopher, Psychologist, Anti-Christ*. Princeton: Princeton University Press, 1974[4].

Salim Kemal, 'Nietzsche's Politics of Aesthetic Genius', in: Salim Kemal, Ivan Gaskell, Daniel W. Conway (eds.), *Nietzsche, Philosophy, and the Arts*. Cambridge/New York/Melbourne: Cambridge University Press, 1998, pp. 257–286.

Hans Keller, 'Goethe and the *Lied*', in: Elizabeth Wilkinson (ed.), *Goethe Revisited. A Collection of Essays*. London: John Calder/New York: Riverrun, 1984, pp. 73–84.

David Kimbell, *Italian Opera*. Cambridge, New York, Melbourne: Cambridge University Press, 1991.

Lawrence Kramer, *Music as Cultural Practice, 1800–1900*. Berkeley, Los Angeles, Oxford: University of California Press, 1990.

Fritz Krökel, *Europas Selbstbesinnung durch Nietzsche, Ihre Vorbereitung bei den französischen Moralisten*. München: Verlag der Nietzsche-Gesellschaft, 1929.

Klaus Kropfinger, *Wagner und Beethoven. Untersuchungen zur Beethoven Rezeption Richard Wagners*. Regensburg: Gustav Bosse Verlag, 1975.

Klaus Kropfinger, *Wagner and Beethoven. Richard Wagner's Reception of Beethoven*. Transl. Peter Palmer. Cambridge/New York/Melbourne: Cambridge University Press, 1991.

Klaus Kropfinger, 'Wagners Musikbegriff und Nietzsches "Geist der Musik"', in: *Nietzsche-Studien* 14 (1985). Berlin/New York: Walter de Gruyter, pp. 1–12.

Elisabeth Kuhn, *Friedrich Nietzsches Philosophie des europäischen Nihilismus*. Berlin/New York: Walter de Gruyter, 1992.

Elisabeth Kuhn, 'Die Gefährten Zarathustras in Nietzsches gutem Europa', in: Georges Goedert, Uschi Nussbaumer-Benz (eds.), *Nietzsche und die Kultur – ein Beitrag zu Europa?* Hildesheim, Zürich, New York: Georg Olms, 2002, pp. 56–66.

Bernd Kulawik, '"…ich nehme, aus drei Gründen, Wagner's Siegfried-Idyll aus"', in: Hans-Martin Gerlach, Renate Reschke (eds.), *Nietzscheforschung* 2. Berlin: Akademie Verlag, 1995, pp. 205–219.

Lukas Labhart, *"Meine Art Natur". Individualität-Landschaft-Stil bei Friedrich Nietzsche*. Basel: Schwabe, 2006.

Christoph Landerer and Marc-Oliver Schuster, 'Nietzsches Vorstudien zur *Geburt der Tragödie* in ihrer Beziehung zur Musikästhetik Eduard Hanslicks', in: *Nietzsche-Studien* 31 (2002). Berlin/New York: Walter de Gruyter, pp. 114–133.

Christoph Landerer and Marc-Oliver Schuster, '"Begehrlich schrie der Geyer in das Thal". Zu einem Motiv früher Wagner-Entfremdung in Nietzsches *Nachlass*', in: *Nietzsche-Studien* 34 (2005). Berlin/New York: Walter de Gruyter, pp. 246–255.

Manfred Landfester (ed.), *Friedrich Nietzsche, Die Geburt der Tragödie. Schriften zu Literatur und Philosophie der Griechen*. Frankfurt am Main: Insel, 1994.

Victor Lange, 'Goethe's Journey in Italy: The School of Seeing', in: Gerhart Hoffmeister (ed.), *Goethe in Italy, 1786–1986*. Amsterdam: Rodopi, 1988, pp. 147–158.

Monika M. Langer, *Nietzsche's Gay Science. Dancing Coherence*. New York: Palgrave Macmillan, 2010.

Duncan Large, 'Nietzsche and the Figure of Columbus', in: *Nietzsche-Studien* 24 (1995). Berlin/New York: Walter de Gruyter, pp. 162–183.

Duncan Large, '"Our greatest Teacher": Nietzsche, Burckhard, and the Concept of Culture', in: *International Studies in Philosophy*, Augusto Guzzo (ed.). Vol. 32, 2000. Torino, pp. 3–23.

Duncan Large, '"Der Bauernaufstand des Geistes": Nietzsche, Luther and the Reformation', in: Nicholas Martin (ed.), *Nietzsche and the German Tradition*. Oxford, Bern, Berlin: Peter Lang, 2003, pp. 111–137.

Albert Lesky, *A History of Greek Literature*. London: Duckworth/Indianapolis: Hackett, 1996.

Gotthold Ephraim Lessing, *Laocoon; or, On the Limits of Painting and Poetry*. Transl. Edward Allen McCormick. Indianapolis: Bobbs-Merrill, 1962.

Christian Lipperheide, *Die Ästhetik des Erhabenen bei Friedrich Nietzsche*. Würzburg: Königshausen & Neumann, 1999.

Héctor Julio Pérez López, 'Die doppelte Wahrheit von Nietzsches Tätigkeit 1870–1872: zur Beziehung griechischer Rhythmik und moderner Musikästhetik im Umkreis der "Geburt der

Tragödie"', in: Volker Gerhardt and Renate Reschke (eds.), *Nietzscheforschung* 2. Berlin: Akademie Verlag, 1995, pp. 219–233.

Héctor Julio Pérez López, 'Gesellschaftspolitische Argumente einer Artistenmetaphysik im Vorfeld der *Geburt der Tragödie aus dem Geiste der Musik*', in: Volker Gerhardt and Renate Reschke (eds.), *Nietzscheforschung* 4. Berlin: Akademie Verlag, 1998, pp. 101–117 [1998–1].

Héctor Julio Pérez López, 'Shakespeare jenseits des dramas. Zur frühen Shakespeare-Rezeption Nietzsches (1869–1872)', in: *Nietzsche-Studien* 27 (1998), pp. 238–267 [1998–2].

Martin Lorenz, *Die Metaphysik-Kritik in Nietzsches Carmen-Rezeption*. Würzburg: Königshausen & Neumann, 2005.

Frederick R. Love, *Young Nietzsche and the Wagnerian Experience*. New York: Ams Press, 1966.

Frederick R. Love, *Nietzsche's Saint Peter. Genesis and Cultivation of an Illusion*. Berlin/New York: Walter de Gruyter, 1981.

Karl Löwith, *Nietzsches Philosophie der Ewigen Wiederkehr des Gleichen*. Stuttgart: Kohlhammer, 1956.

Karl Löwith, 'Nietzsches Vollendung des Atheismus', in: Hans Steffen (ed.), *Nietzsche, Werk und Wirkungen*. Göttingen: Vandenhoeck & Ruprecht, 1974, pp. 7–18.

Georg Lukács, 'The Correspondence between Schiller and Goethe', in: Georg Lukács, *Goethe and his Age*. London: Merlin Press, 1968, pp. 68–100.

Jean-François Lyotard, *The Postmodern Condition: A Report on Knowledge*. Manchester: Manchester University Press, 2004.

Bernhard Lypp, 'Der symbolische Prozess des Tragischen', in: *Nietzsche-Studien* 18 (1989). Berlin/New York: Walter de Gruyter, pp. 127–140.

Bryan Magee, *Wagner and Philosophy*. London/New York: Penguin Books, 2000.

Bryan Magee, *The Philosophy of Schopenhauer*. Oxford: Clarendon Press/New York: Oxford University Press, 1997.

Thomas Mann, *Deutschland und die Deutschen. Essays 1938–1945*. Frankfurt am Main: Fischer, 1996.

Thomas Mann, *Nietzsche's Philosophy in the Light of Contemporary Events*. Washington DC, 1947.

Oswald Marbach, *Dramaturgische Blätter. Beitrag zur Wiedererhebung dramatischer Kunst in Deutschland*. Leipzig: G. Kreysing [pr.], 1870.

Urs Marti, '"The Good, the bad and the ugly European": Les trois faces de l'européisme de Nietzsche', in: Paolo D'Iorio and Gilbert Merlio, *Nietzsche et l'Europe*. Paris: Éditions de la maison des sciences de l'homme, 2006, pp. 179–192.

Nicholas Martin, '"Aufklärung und kein Ende": The Place of Enlightenment in Friedrich Nietzsche's Thought', in: German Life and Letters 61, 2008, pp. 79–97.

Nicholas Martin, '"Ewig verbundene Geister": Thomas Mann's Re-Engagement with Nietzsche, 1943–1947', in: Oxford German Studies 14–2, 2005, pp. 197–203.

Nicholas Martin, 'Breeding Greeks: Nietzsche, Gobinau, and Classical Theories of Race', in: Paul Bishop (ed.), *Nietzsche and Antiquity. His Reaction and Response to the Classical Tradition*. Rochester/Suffolk: Camden House, 2004, pp. 40–53.

Nicholas Martin, *Nietzsche and Schiller: Untimely Aesthetics*. Oxford: Clarendon Press, 1996..

Nicholas Martin, 'We Good Europeans: Nietzsche's New Europe in "Beyond Good and Evil"', in: History of European Ideas 20 (1–3), 1995, pp. 141–144.

Alan Megill, Prophets of Extremity: Nietzsche, Heidegger, Foucault, Derrida. Berkeley: University of California Press, 1985.

Theo Meyer, *Nietzsche. Kunstauffassung und Lebensbegriff*. Tübingen: Francke, 1991.

Theo Meyer, 'Nietzsche und Goethe. Goethes Wirkung auf Nietzsches Lebens, -Kunst- und Kulturbegriff', in: Wiebke Schrader, Georges Goedert, Martina Scheibel (eds.), *Perspektiven der Philosophie* 27 (2001). Amsterdam/New York: Rodopi, pp. 223–268.

Theo Meyer, 'Nietzsche und Europa – Kritik und Utopie', in: Georges Goedert and Uschi
  Nussbaumer-Benz (eds.), *Nietzsche und die Kultur – ein Beitrag zu Europa?* Hildesheim,
  Zürich, New York: Georg Olms, 2002, pp. 11–34.
Burkhard Meyer-Sickendiek, *Die Aesthetik der Epigonalität*. Tübingen/Basel: Francke, 2001.
Prosper Mérimée, *Carmen*. Transl. Paul de Bruin. Amsterdam/Antwerpen: Veen, 1994.
Barry Millington (ed.), *The Wagner Compendium: A Guide to Wagner's Life and Music*. New York/
  Oxford/Singapore: Schirmer Books, Maxwell Macmillan, 1992.
Thomas Mittmann, *Friedrich Nietzsche, Judengegner und Antisemitenfeind*. Erfurt: Alan Sutton,
  2002.
Mazzino Montinari, *Nietzsche lesen*. Berlin/New York: Walter de Gruyter, 1982.
Mazzino Montinari, 'Nietzsche-Wagner im Sommer 1878', in: *Nietzsche-Studien* 14 (1985) Berlin/
  New York: Walter de Gruyter, pp. 13–21.
Mazzino Montinari, 'Nietzsche mit Goethe in Italien', on: www.hypernietzsche.org (12-03-2002).
J.J.A. Mooij, *Het Europa van de Filosofen*. Kampen: Klement/Kapellen: Pelckmans, 2006.
Diane Morgan, 'Nietzsche and National Identity', in: Keith Ansell Pearson (ed.), *A Companion to
  Nietzsche*. Malden/Oxford/Carlton: Blackwell, 2006, pp. 455–474.
Renate G. Müller, 'Anmerkungen zu Nietzsches Tragödienproblem. Von der Schulzeit bis zu den
  Vorarbeiten zur "Geburt der Tragödie" unter Berücksichtigung des Verhältnisses zu Wagner',
  in: Hans-Martin Gerlach and Renate Reschke (eds.), *Nietzscheforschung 2*. Berlin: Akademie
  Verlag, 1995, pp. 237–253.
Ulrich Müller and Peter Wapnewski, *Richard Wagner Handbuch*. Stuttgart: Kröner, 1986.
Joachim Müller-Warden, 'Die aktuelle Entwicklung Europas, erörtert im Lichte der Philosophie
  Friedrich Nietzsches', in: Volker Gerhardt, Renate Reschke (ed.), *Neitzscheforschung 4*.
  Berlin: Akademie Verlag, 1998, pp. 119–146.
Christian Niemeyer, *Nietzsches andere Vernunft. Psychologische Aspekte in Biographie und Werk*.
  Darmstadt: Wissenschaftliche Buchgesellschaft, 1998.
Novalis (Friedrich von Hardenberg), *Die Christenheit oder Europa, ein Fragment*. Stuttgart:
  Reclam, 1973.
Martha Nussbaum, 'The Transfigurations of Intoxication: Nietzsche, Schopenhauer, and Diony-
  sus', in: Salim Kemal and Ivan Gaskell (eds.), *Nietzsche, Philosophy, and the Arts*. Cam-
  bridge/New York/Melbourne: Cambridge University Press, 2002, pp. 36–69.
Martha Nussbaum, *Frontiers of Justice. Disability, Nationality, Species Membership*. Cambridge
  MA/London: Belknap Press of Harvard University Press, 2006.
Horst Oppel, *Studien zur Auffassung des Nordischen in der Goethezeit*. Halle: Max Niemeyer,
  1944.
Andrea Orsucci, *Orient-Okzident, Nietzsches Versuch einer Loslösung vom europäischen Weltbild*.
  Berlin/New York: Walter de Gruyter, 1996.
Henning Ottmann (ed.), *Nietzsche Handbuch, Leben-Werk-Wirkung*. Stuttgart: Metzler, 2000.
M. Owen Lee, *Athena Sings. Wagner and the Greeks*. Toronto, Buffalo, London: University of
  Toronto Press, 2003.
Anthony Pagden, 'Introduction', in: Anthony Pagden (ed.), *The Idea of Europe. From Antiquitiy
  to the European Union*. Washington: Woodrow Wilson Center Press/Cambridge (UK): Cam-
  bridge University Press, 2002, pp. 1–32.
Anthony Pagden, 'Europe: Conceptualizing a Continent,' in: Anthony Pagden (ed.), *The Idea of
  Europe. From Antiquitiy to the European Union*. Washington: Woodrow Wilson Center Press/
  Cambridge (UK): Cambridge University Press, 2002, pp. 33–54.
Detlev Pätzold, 'Ernst Cassirers Philosophiebegriff', in: H.J. Sandkühler, D. Pätzold (eds.), *Kultur
  und Symbol. Ein Handbuch zur Philosophie Ernst Cassirers*. Stuttgart: Metzler, 2003, pp.
  45–69.

Detlev Pätzold, 'Concepts of Space in Mythical and Scientific Thought. A Challenge to Cassirer's Apriorism?' in: Paul Bishop and R.H. Stephenson (eds.), *Cultural Studies and the Symbolic Form* 3. Leeds: Northern University Press, 2007 (forthcoming).

Terry Pinkard, *German Philosophy 1760–1860. The Legacy of Idealism.* Cambridge/New York/ Melbourne: Cambridge University Press, 2002.

Plato, *The Republic.* Ed. G.R.F. Ferrari, transl. Tom Griffith. Cambridge/New York/Melbourne: Cambridge University Press, 2000.

J.G.A. Pocock, 'Some Europes in their History' in: Anthony Pagden (ed.), *The Idea of Europe. From Antiquitiy to the European Union.* Washington: Woodrow Wilson Center Press/Cambridge (UK): Cambridge University Press, 2002, pp. 55–71.

Sebastian Posth, 'The Meteorological Aesthetics of the Late Nietzsche' [unpublished paper for the 13th annual FNS Conference. Warwick, 2003].

Martine Prange, 'Two Cosmopolitan Paradoxes: Productive Conflict in Kant and Nietzsche's Cosmopolitan Philosophy', in: Publications of the XI. International Kant Congress (Pisa May 2010). Berlin/New York: De Gruyter. (forthcoming 1).

Martine Prange, 'From Saint to Satyr: Nietzsche's Ethics of Self-Transformation in Ecce Homo', in: Duncan Large, Nicholas Martin (Eds.), *Nietzsche's Ecce Homo.* (forthcoming 2).

Martine Prange, 'Beyond Good and Evil: On the Future of Europe', in: Paul Bishop (ed.), *A Companion to the Life and Works of Friedrich Nietzsche.* Rochester, NY: Boydell & Brewer [Camden House], 2012, pp. 232–250 [2012–1].

Martine Prange, 'The Influence of Schopenhauer's and Wagner's Theories of Dreams, Clairvoyance, and Ghost-Seeing on Nietzsche's Aesthetics of the Creative Genius', in: Jutta Georg, Claus Zittel (eds.), *Nietzsches Philosophie des Unbewussten.* Berlin: De Gruyter, 2012, pp. 127–136 [2012–2].

Martine Prange, 'Was Nietzsche Ever a True Wagnerian?' in: Nietzschestudien 40 (2011). Berlin/ New York: De Gruyter, pp. 43–71 [2011–1].

Martine Prange, '"Méditerraniser": The Flight from North to South. A Reading of Nietzsche's Poems "Prince Vogelfrei" and "In the South"', in: The Agonist IV-I, spring 2011, pp. 57–63 [2011–2].

Martine Prange, 'Why Do We Need Myth? Homer, Nietzsche, and Helen's Weaving-loom', in: Paul Bishop and R.H. Stephenson (eds.), *The Persistence of Myth as Symbolic Form* [Cultural Studies and the Symbolic 3]. Leeds: Maney Press, 2008, pp. 18–34.

Martine Prange, '"Cosmopolitan Roads to Culture" and the "Festival Road of Humanity": The Cosmopolitan Praxis of Nietzsche's Good European in the Light of Kantian Cosmopolitanism,' in: Ethical Perspectives 2007–3, 269–286 [2007–1].

Martine Prange, 'Nietzsches Artistic Ideal of Europe: *The Birth of Tragedy* in the Spirit of Wagner's centenary 'Beethoven' essay', in: Volker Gerhardt and Renate Reschke (eds.), *Nietzsche und Europa – Nietzsche in Europa* [Nietzscheforschung 14]. Berlin: Akademie Verlag, 2007, pp. 91–117 [2007–2].

Martine Prange, 'The Symbolization of Culture: Nietzsche in the Footsteps of Goethe, Schiller, Schopenhauer, and Wagner', in: Paul Bishop and R. H. Stephenson (eds.), *The Path to Symbolic Knowledge.* [Cultural Studies and the Symbolic 2]. Leeds: Maney Press, 2006, pp. 70–91 [2006–1].

Martine Prange, '"Im Süden": Nietzsche, Goethe, and Italy', in: Interculture 3 (2006), pp. 1–27 [2006–2].

Martine Prange, 'Valuation and Revaluation of the Idyll, Schillerian Traces in Nietzsche's Early Musical Aesthetics', in: Volker Gerhardt and Renate Reschke (eds.), *Friedrich Nietzsche – Zwischen Musik, Philosophie und Ressentiment* [Nietzscheforschung 13]. Berlin: Akademie Verlag, 2006, pp. 269–278 [2006–3].

Martine Prange, *Lof der Méditerranée. Nietzsches vrolijke wetenschap tussen noord en zuid*. Kampen: Klement, 2005.

J. Rademacher, 'Münster in Westphalia', in: J. Rademacher (ed.), *Modernism and the Individual Talent: re-canonizing Ford Madox Ford (Hueffer)*. Berlin/Hamburg/Münster: LIT Verlag, 2002, pp. 120–134.

Birgit Recki, '"Artisten-Metaphysik" und ästhetisches Ethos, Friedrich Nietzsche über Ästhetik und Ethik', in: Andrea Kern and Ruth Sonderegger (eds.), *Falsche Gegensätze. Zeitgenössische Perspektiven zur philosophischen Ästhetik*. Frankfurt am Main: Suhrkamp, 2002, pp. 262–285.

Renate Reschke, *Denkumbrüche mit Nietzsche, Zur anspornenden Verachtung der Zeit*. Berlin: Akademie Verlag, 2000.

Alexander Rehding, 'Wagner, Liszt, Berlioz and the "New German School"', in: Mary-Anne Perkins and Martin Liebscher (eds.), *Nationalism* versus *Cosmopolitanism in German Thought and Culture, 1789–1914. Essays on the Emergence of Europe*. Lewiston/Queenston: The Edwin Mellen Press, 2006, pp. 159–188.

Joachim Reiber, '"Auch das Gegenteil kann wahr sein". Johannes Brahms, Josef Viktor Widmann und Friedrich Nietzsche', in: Günther Pöltner and Helmut Vetter (eds.), *Nietzsche und die Musik*. Frankfurt am Main: Peter Lang, 1997, pp. 57–79.

Barbara von Reibnitz, *Ein Kommentar zu Friedrich Nietzsche. 'Die Geburt der Tragödie aus dem Geiste der Musik' (Kapitel 1–12)*. Stuttgart: Metzler, 1992.

Simon Richter, *Laocoon's Body and the Aesthetics of Pain. Winckelmann-Lessing-Herder-Moritz-Goethe*. Detroit: Wayne State UP, 1992.

Manfred Riedel, "Die Perspektive Europas, Nietzsche in unserer Zeit", in: Gerhardt Volker and Herold Norbert (eds.), *Perspektiven des Perspektivismus*. Würzburg: Königshausen & Neumann, 1992, pp. 219–233.

Manfred Riedel, 'Ein Seitenstück zur "Geburt der Tragödie"', in: *Nietzsche-Studien* 24 (1995). Berlin/New York: Walter de Gruyter, pp. 45–61.

Vasti Roodt, 'The Loss of the Human: Nietzsche and Arendt on the Predicament of Modernity', in: *Ethical Perspectives* 9–1, 2002. Leuven: Peeters, 31–47.

Paul Lawrence Rose, *Wagner: Race and Revolution*. New York, London: Yale, University Press, 1992.

Thomas G. Rosenmeyer, *The Greek Cabinet. Theocritus and the European Pastoral Lyric*. Berkeley/Los Angeles/London: 1969.

Werner Ross, *Der ängstliche Adler. Friedrich Nietzsches Leben*. Munich: Deutscher Taschenbuch Verlag, 1984.

Jean-Jacques Rousseau and Johann Gottfried Herder, *On the Origin of Language*. Transl. John H. Moran and Alexander Gode. Chicago/London: The University of Chicago Press, 1966.

Jean-Jacques Rousseau, *Discours sur les sciences et les arts* (1750). Ed. George Remington Havens. New York: Modern Language Assoc. of America/London: Oxford University Press, 1946.

Jean-Jacques Rousseau, *Dictionnaire de musique*. In: *Oeuvres complètes*, vols. 12 and 13. Paris: Garnery, 1828.

Jean-Jacques Rousseau, *Écrits sur la musique*. In: *Oeuvres complètes* vol. 11. Paris: Garnery, 1828, pp. 249–312.

Martin A. Ruehl, '*Politeia* 1871: Young Nietzsche on the Greek State', in: Paul Bishop (ed.), *Nietzsche and Antiquity. His Reaction and Response to the Classical Tradition*. Rochester/Suffolk: Camden House, 2004, pp. 79–97.

Ted Sadler, 'The postmodernist politicization of Nietzsche', in: Paul Patton (ed.), *Nietzsche, feminism and political theory*. London/New York: Routledge, 1993, pp. 225–243.

Jörg Salaquarda, 'Mythos bei Nietzsche', in: Hans Poser (ed.), *Philosophie und Mythos*. Berlin/
New York: Walter de Gruyter, 1979, pp. 174–198.
Jörg Salaquarda, 'Die fröhliche Wissenschaft zwischen Freigeisterei und neuer Lehre', in:
Nietzsche-Studien 26 (1997). Berlin/New York: Walter de Gruyter, pp. 165–182.
Lou Andreas-Salomé, *Friedrich Nietzsche*. Amsterdam: Arbeiderspers, 1987.
William H. Schaberg, *The Nietzsche Canon. A Publication History and Bibliography*.
Chicago/London: Chicago University Press, 1995.
Andreas Scheib, 'Nietzsches Carmen. Anmerkungen zu einer Verirrung', in: Nietzsche-Studien
2008. Berlin/New York: De Gruyter, pp. 249–254.
Karl Schlechta, 'The German "Classicist" Goethe as Reflected in Nietzsche's Works', in: James
C. O'Flaherty, Timothy F. Sellner, and Robert M. Helm (eds.), *Studies in Nietzsche and the
Classical Tradition*. Chapel Hill: University of North Carolina Press, 1976, pp. 144–155.
Bertram Schmidt, *Der ethische Aspekt der Musik. Nietzsches 'Geburt der Tragödie' und die
Wiener klassische Musik*. Würzburg: Königshausen & Neumann, 1991.
Jochen Schmidt, *Die Geschichte des Genie-Gedankens in der deutschen Literatur, Philosophie
und Politik 1750–1945*. Vols. I & II. Darmstadt: Wissenschaftliche Buchgesellschaft, 1985.
Alan D. Schrift, 'Nietzsche's Contest: Nietzsche and the Culture Wars', in: *Why Nietzsche Still?
Reflections on Drama, Culture, and Politics*. Ed. Alan D. Schrift. Berkeley/Los Angeles/
London: University of California Press, 2000, pp. 184–204.
Gerhard Schulz, 'Goethes *Italienische Reise*', in: Gerhart Hoffmeister (ed.), *Goethe in Italy, 1786–
1986*. Amsterdam: Rodopi 1988, pp. 5–20.
Ingrid Schulze, "Nietzsche und Claude Lorrain", in: Volker Gerhardt and Renate Reschke (eds.),
Nietzscheforschung 4. Berlin: Akademie Verlag, 1998, pp. 217–225.
Roger Scruton, *Modern Culture*. London: Continuum, 1998.
Hans-Gerd von Seggern, 'Nietzsches (anti-)naturalistische Ästhetik in der *Geburt der Tragödie*',
in: Nicholas Martin (ed.), *Nietzsche and the German Tradition*. Oxford/Bern/Berlin: Peter
Lang, 2003, pp. 187–203.
Hans-Gerd von Seggern, *Nietzsche und die Weimarer Klassik*. Tübingen: Francke Verlag, 2004.
Harald Seubert, "Der schwierige Weg zum guten Europäer: Europäische Visionen bei Hegel und
Nietzsche", in: Wulf Segebrecht (ed.), *Europavisionen im 19. Jahrhundert: Vorstellungen von
Europa in Literatur und Kunst, Geschichte & Philosophie*. Würzburg: Ergon, 1999, pp. 80–97.
Gary Shapiro, *Archeologies of Vision, Foucault and Nietzsche on Seeing and Saying*. Chicago/
London: The University of Chicago Press, 2003.
Gary Shapiro, 'Nietzsche on Geophilosophy and Geoaesthetics', in: Keith Ansell Pearson (ed.), *A
Companion to Nietzsche*. Malden/Oxford/Carlton: Blackwell, 2006, pp. 477–494.
Herman Siemens, 'Agonale configuraties in de *Unzeitgemässe Betrachtungen*. Duitsers, Grieken
en de *Übertragung* van culturen in het vroege denken van Nietzsche', in: Gerard Visser
(ed.), *Nietzsches Cultuurkritiek in de Unzeitgemässe Betrachtungen*. Leiden: MD Publishers,
2000, pp. 55–84.
Herman Siemens, 'Nietzsche *contra* Liberalism on Freedom', in: Keith Ansell Pearson (ed.), *A
Companion to Nietzsche*. Malden/Oxford/Carlton: Blackwell, 2006, pp. 437–454.
M.S. Silk, J.P. and Stern, *Nietzsche on Tragedy*. Cambridge, London, New York: Cambridge Uni-
versity Press, 1981.
Josef Simon, 'Nietzsche on Judaism and Europe', in: Jacob Golomb (ed.), *Nietzsche and Jewish
Culture*. London/New York: Routledge, 1997, pp. 101–116.
Peter Sloterdijk, *Falls Europa erwacht*. Frankfurt am Main: Suhrkamp, 1994.
Bruno Snell, *Die Entdeckung des Geistes*. Göttingen: Vandenhoeck & Ruprecht, 1980[5].
Stefan Lorenz Sorgner, H. James Brix, Nikolaus Knoepffler (eds.), *Wagner und Nietzsche. Kultur –
Werk – Wirkung. Ein Handbuch*. Reinbek: Rowohlt, 2008.

Roderick Stackelberg, 'The Role of Heinrich von Stein in Nietzsche's Emergence as a Critic of Wagnerian Idealism and Cultural Nationalism', in: *Nietzsche-Studien* 5 (1976). Berlin/New York: Walter de Gruyter, pp. 178–193.

Werner Stegmaier, *Nietzsche's Befreiung der Philosophie. Eine kontekstuelle Interpretation des V. Buchs der Fröhlichen Wissenschaft*. Berlin/New York: De Gruyter, 2012.

Werner Stegmaier, '"Philosophischer Idealismus" und die "Musik des Lebens". Zu Nietzsches Umgang mit Paradoxien', in: *Nietzsche-Studien* 33 (2004). Berlin/New York: De Gruyter, pp. 90–128.

Werner Stegmaier, 'Nietzsche, die Juden und Europa', in: Werner Stegmaier (ed.), *Europa-Philosophie*. Berlin/New York: Walter de Gruyter, pp. 67–91.

George Steiner, *The Idea of Europe*. [Tenth Nexus Lecture] Tilburg: Nexus Institute, 2004.

R.H. Stephenson, 'Die Aneignung des "Fremden" durch ästhetische Gestaltung – anhand von Goethes "Faust"', in: Bernd Thum and Gonthier-Louis Fink (eds.), *Praxis interkultureller Germanistik, Forschung-Bildung-Politik*. Munich: Iudicium Verlag, 1993, pp. 789–795.

R.H. Stephenson, *Goethe's Conception of Knowledge and Science*. Edinburgh: Edinburgh University Press, 1995.

R.H. Stephenson, 'The Proper Object of Cultural Study: Ernst Cassirer and the Aesthetic Theory of Weimar Classicism', in: Paul Bishop and R.H. Stephenson (eds.), *Cultural Studies and the Symbolic* 1. Leeds: Northern UP, 2003, pp. 82–114.

R.H. Stephenson, '"Binary Synthesis": Goethe's Aesthetic Intuition in Literature and Science', in: Science in Context 18–4. Cambridge: Cambridge University Press, 2005, pp. 553–581.

R.H. Stephenson, 'Schiller's "Concrete" Theory of Culture: Reflections on the 200th Anniversary of his Death', in: Paul Bishop and R.H. Stephenson (eds.), *Cultural Studies and the Symbolic* 1. Leeds: Maney Publishing, 2006, pp. 92–117.

R.H. Stephenson, 'What's Wrong With Cultural Studies? A Modest Proposal', in: Minnesota Review 44, 2003, pp. 195–206.

Tracy B. Strong, 'Nietzsche's Political Aesthetics', in: *Michael Allen Gillespie and Tracy B. Strong* (eds.), *Nietzsche's New Seas. Explorations in Philosophy, Aesthetics, and Politics*. Chicago and London: The University of Chicago Press,1988, pp. 153–174.

Tom Sutcliffe, 'Schiller and the Revolution in Opera', in: *Friedrich Schiller, Five Plays*. Transl. Robert David Mac Donald. London: Oberon, 1998, pp. 53–64.

Paul van Tongeren, 'Nietzsche's Symptomatology of Skepticism', in: Babette Babich and Robert C. Cohen (eds.), *Nietzsche's Epistemology and Philosophy of Science*. Dordrecht: Kluwer, 1999, pp. 61–72.

Paul van Tongeren, 'Nietzsches boodschap van de dood van God', in: G. Grunt, P. Leenhouwers, and D. Losse (eds.), *De weerbarstige werkelijkheid: essays over metafysiek*. Tilburg: Tilburg University Press, 1989, pp. 195–210.

Paul van Tongeren (ed.), *Nietzsche als arts van de cultuur, Diagnoses en prognoses*. Kampen: Kok Agora, 1990.

Paul van Tongeren, 'Die Kunst der Transfiguration', in: R. Duhamel and E. Oger (eds.), *Die Kunst der Sprache und die Sprache der Kunst*. Würzburg: Königshausen & Neumann, 1994, pp. 84–104.

Paul van Tongeren, *Reinterpreting Modern Culture. An Introduction to Friedrich Nietzsche's Philosophy*. West Lafayette, Ind.: Purdue University Press, 2000.

Paul van Tongeren, 'Nietzsche and Ethics', in: Keith Ansell Pearson (ed.), *A Companion to Nietzsche*. Malden/Oxford/Carlton: Blackwell, 2006, pp. 389–403.

Paul van Tongeren, 'Vom "Arzt der Cultur" zum "Arzt und Kranken in einer Person", Eine Hypothese zur Entwicklung Nietzsches als Philosoph der Kultur(en)'. Unpublished paper for the International Nietzsche-Gesellschaft Conference 'Nietzsche – Philosoph der Kultur?' 2007.

Bart Vandenabeele, 'Schopenhauer, Nietzsche, and the Aesthetically Sublime', in: *The Journal of Aesthetic Education* 37–1 (2003). Illinois: University of Illinois, pp. 90–106.

Gianni Vattimo, *Dialogue with Nietzsche*. New York: Columbia University Press, 2006.

H. L. Visser, *De goede Europeaan*. Zutphen: Thieme, 1933.

Aldo Venturelli, *Kunst, Wissenschaft und Geschichte bei Nietzsche. Quellenkritische Untersuchungen*. Berlin/New York: Walter de Gruyter, 2003.

Aldo Venturelli, 'Die *Gaya Scienza* der "Guten Europäer". Einige Anmerkungen zum Aphorismus Nr. 377 des V. Buchs der *Fröhlichen Wissenschaft*', in: *Nietzsche-Studien* 39 (2010), Berlin/New York: De Gruyter pp. 180–200.

Aldo Venturelli, 'Das Klassische als Vollendung des Sentimentalischen. Der junge Nietzsche als Leser des Briefwechsels zwischen Goethe und Schiller', in: *Nietzsche-Studien* 18 (1989). Berlin/New York: Walter de Gruyter, pp. 182–202.

Vivetta Vivarelli, '"Vorschule des Sehens" und "Stilisierte Natur" in der *Morgenröthe* und der *Fröhlichen Wissenschaft*', in: *Nietzsche-Studien* 20 (1991). Berlin/New York: Walter de Gruyter, pp. 134–151.

Vivetta Vivarelli, 'Nietzsche, Goethe und der historische Sinn', in: Tilman Borsche, Federico Gerratana, and Aldo Venturelli (eds.), *Centauren-Geburten. Wissenschaft, Kunst und Philosophie beim jungen Nietzsche*. Berlin/New York: Walter de Gruyter, 1994, pp. 276–291.

Vivetta Vivarelli, 'Nietzsche als guter Europäer', in: Georges Goedert and Uschi Nussbaumer-Benz (eds.), *Nietzsche und die Kultur – ein Beitrag zu Europa?* Hildesheim, Zürich, New York: Georg Olms, 2002, pp. 112–123.

Martin Vogel, *Apollinisch und Dionysisch*. Regensburg: Bosse, 1966.

Friedrich Voßkühler, *Kunst als Mythos der Moderne*. Würzburg: Königshausen & Neumann, 2004.

Cosima Wagner, *Wagner's Diaries. An Abridgement*. Ed. Geoffrey Skelton. New Haven/London: Yale University Press, 1994.

Cosima Wagner, *Die Tagebücher*. Vol. I (1869–1877), Vol. II (1878–1883). Eds. Martin Gregor-Dellin and Dieter Mack. Munich/Zürich: Piper, 1976/1977.

Gustav Friedrich Wagner, *Schopenhauer-Register*. Ed. Arthur Hübscher. Stuttgart/Bad: Frommann (Holzboog), 1960 (new ed.).

Hedwig Walwei-Wiegelmann, *Goethes Gedanken über Musik (eine Sammlung aus seinen Werken, Briefen, Gesprächen und Tagebücher)*. Frankfurt am Main: Insel, 1985.

M.L. West, *Ancient Greek Music*. Oxford: Clarendon University Press, 1992.

Armin Wildermuth (ed.), *Nietzsche und Wagner. Geschichte und Aktualität eines Kulturkonflikts*. Zürich, 2008.

Elizabeth M. Wilkinson, L.A. Willoughby, *Models of Wholeness: Some Attitudes to Language, Art, and Life in the Age of Goethe*. Ed. Jeremy Adler, Martin Swales and Ann Weaver. Oxford/Bern/Berlin: Peter Lang, 2002.

Mariëtte Willemsen, *Kluizenaar zonder God*. Amsterdam: Duna, 1996.

Johann Joachim Winckelmann, *Gedanken über die Nachahmung der griechischen Werke in Malerei und Bildhauerkunst*. Stuttgart: Göschen, 1885 [1750].

Johann Joachim Winckelmann, *Geschichte der Kunst des Alterthums*. Weimar: Böhlaus, 1964 [1764].

Ralf Witzler, *Europa im Denken Nietzsches*. Würzburg: Königshausen & Neumann, 2001.

Ralph-Rainer Wuthenow, 'Süden als Metapher: Zu Nietzsches Italien-Bild', in: Italienisch, Zeitschrift für italienische Sprache und Literatur in Wissenschaft 27 (1992). Frankfurt am Main: Diesterweg, pp. 2–17.

Hester IJsseling, *Over voorwoorden*. Amsterdam: Boom, 1997.

Julian Young, *Friedrich Nietzsche. A Philosophical Biography*. Cambridge: Cambridge University Press, 2010.

Julian Young, *Nietzsche's Philosophy of Art*. Cambridge/New York/Melbourne: Cambridge University Press, 1994.
Yirmiyahu Yovel, 'Nietzsche contra Wagner on the Jews', in: Jacob Golomb, Robert S. Wistrich (eds.), *Nietzsche, Godfather of Fascism? On the Uses and Abuses of a Philosophy*. Princeton/Oxford: Princeton University Press, 2002, pp. 126–143.
Carsten Zeller, *Die doppelte Ästhetik der Moderne. Revisionen des Schönen von Boileau bis Nietzsche*. Stuttgart/Weimar: Metzler, 1995.
Massimo Ferrari-Zumbini, *Untergänge und Morgenröten. Nietzsche-Spengler-Antisemitismus*. Würzburg: Königshausen & Neumann, 1999.

Websites

www.europe.com.
www.europe.eu.
http://www.eurotreaties.com/messina.pdf.
http://www.europarl.europa.eu/summits/lis1_en.htm.
www.nietzschesource.org.
www.degruyter.com/view/db/nietzsche.

Index

Adorno, Th. W. 267, 268, 274

Aestheticization 13, 19

Africa 3, 248, 257

America 247, 257

Andreas-Salomé, Lou 189, 224

Apollo 111, 116, 130, 137, 152, 153, 156, 157, 159

Appiah, Kwame Anthony 267

Aristotle 123, 125, 261, 267

Art 46, 108, 162, 163, 169, 175, 190, 219, 229, 233, 235, 237, 238, 267–270, 275, 283

Assorted Opinions and Maxims vi, 16, 145, 178

Bach, J.S. 75, 83, 125, 129, 151, 153, 183

Beethoven vii, 14, 42, 46, 51–54, 57, 60, 63–67, 70–73, 75–79, 81–89, 91–93, 95, 96, 99–101, 103, 104, 106, 107, 114, 119, 123, 125, 127–130, 133, 139, 140, 150, 151, 153, 155, 159, 161–163, 183, 201, 202, 224, 225, 255, 265, 270, 273–275, 278

'Beethoven' essay vii, 14, 42, 51–53, 63–65, 67, 95, 96, 163, 225, 278

Benjamin, Walter 69, 136, 268

Berlioz, Hector 76, 91, 92, 99, 279

Binary Synthesis 281

Bishop, Paul 74, 93, 132, 133, 141, 229, 267–269, 278, 279, 281

Bizet, Georges 15, 200, 205, 208, 209, 211, 213–215

Bizetismus 211

Bowie, Andrew 135, 269

Brobjer, Thomas 269

Brusotti, Marco 6, 248, 249, 252, 269

Carmen 15, 200, 205–207, 209, 211, 214, 215, 270, 276, 277

Chorus 88, 89, 107

Cosmopolitanism 169, 267, 268, 272, 279

Culture 8, 52, 136, 237, 267, 268, 270, 272, 275, 278–281

De-Germanization 13, 167, 188

Democracy 263, 271

Derrida, Jacques 262, 268, 271, 276

Dionysos 16, 18, 111, 155, 156, 241, 272

Dionysus 17, 111, 116, 130, 137–139, 142, 151, 153, 155–157, 241, 272, 277

Docherty, Thomas 260, 271

Dynamic interculturalism 13, 167

East 3, 247–249, 257

Economy 4

Epicurus 213, 230, 233, 239, 245

Europe 3–7, 10, 13–16, 19, 42, 52, 64, 68, 69, 72, 75, 77, 83, 84, 88, 92, 93, 128, 130, 131, 133, 136, 153, 163, 164, 171, 187, 188, 196, 198, 199, 224, 236, 247–251, 253–261, 263, 267–272, 274, 276–279, 281

European Union 3, 53, 66, 198, 260–262, 270, 272, 277, 278

Europeanism 5, 165, 169, 247–249, 252, 268

Faust 88, 144, 147, 148, 150, 218, 222, 281

Florence 148

Foucault, Michel 272, 276, 280

France 3, 43, 45, 54, 64, 66, 67, 77, 83, 84, 92, 103, 132, 133, 209, 212, 220, 271

Gast, Peter 15, 17, 200, 204, 205, 214–216, 219, 223, 224, 248, 274

Genoa 206, 207, 211, 226, 231, 235, 236, 248, 268

German Classicism 74, 138, 145, 146, 150, 176

Germanization 13, 167, 173, 188, 197, 198, 206, 223, 224, 226

Gersdorff 43–45, 52, 133, 181, 185

Gluck 92

God 6, 67, 229, 255, 281, 282

Goethe vii, 1, 14, 15, 17, 46, 56, 57, 63, 66, 68, 70, 72–77, 79, 83–85, 88, 89, 94, 96, 98, 103, 104, 107–109, 111, 115, 116, 122, 127, 134, 137, 139–141, 144–147, 150, 152, 153, 160, 164, 165, 170–173, 175, 176, 179, 181, 182, 185, 192, 193, 196, 200, 202, 205, 206, 212, 213, 215–221, 223–225, 228, 229, 231–234, 236, 247, 253, 255, 258, 261, 266–270, 272–282

Good European 167, 228, 254, 271, 276

Graecization 13, 129, 131, 132, 138, 140, 144, 164, 171, 175, 176, 197, 223, 225, 256, 258

Graecize 14, 131, 145, 164

Greece 53, 63, 75, 112, 122, 125, 148, 156, 173, 193, 205, 247, 256

Hanslick, Eduard 34, 65, 79, 89, 97–99, 101, 129, 181, 271, 273
Health 208, 211
Hegel 280
Herder 212, 256, 273, 279
Higgins, K.M. 221, 222, 224, 273
History vi, 152, 174, 268, 270, 272, 275, 276, 278
Hoffmann, E.T.A. 99, 273
Homer vii, 46, 77, 85, 130, 136, 137, 140, 148, 157–159, 172, 193, 217, 273, 278
Hüffer, Franz 31–34, 50

Idyll 115, 120, 213, 275, 278
Idyllen aus Messina 241, 270
Idyllic tendency 121
Idylls from Messina vi, 213, 241
Im Süden 242, 244, 254
In the South 223, 241, 244, 254
International 275
Introduction 3
Italian opera 12, 13, 53, 62, 63, 66, 71, 74, 100, 103, 111, 116–119, 122, 124, 127, 137, 145, 148–150, 153, 155, 160, 197, 198, 200, 204, 205, 213–215, 217, 218, 220, 225, 226
Italy 3, 13, 45, 46, 54, 64, 76, 77, 79, 83, 93, 102, 103, 133, 148, 163, 176, 195, 209, 212, 218, 220, 223, 231–233, 240, 272, 273, 275, 280

Joke, Cunning, and Revenge vi, 15, 200, 205, 215, 216, 218–221, 223, 224, 228, 241
Joy 52, 86, 87, 104, 106, 139, 140, 150–153, 155

Kant 54, 74, 105, 144, 145, 150, 153, 268, 274
Köselitz, Heinrich 178, 179, 200, 204, 207, 214–216, 268
Kropfinger, Karl 53, 58, 78, 98, 275
Krug, Gustav 46
Kulturkampf 68, 72, 74, 96

Liszt, Franz 45, 76, 89, 92, 97, 99, 129, 180, 279
Lorrain, Claude 211–213, 226, 280
Love, Frederick 101, 215, 216, 219, 276
Lyotard, J.-F. 3, 276

Marbach, Oswald 34, 276
Mediterranean 13, 209, 214, 223
Mérimée, P. 277

Messina vi, 66, 213, 241, 259, 266, 270
Meyerbeer 42
Meysenbug, Malwida von 181
Mittmann, Thomas 42, 44, 277
Modernism 270
Modernity 118, 143, 183, 198, 238, 269, 279
Morgenland 249
Mozart, W.A. 57, 83, 87, 92, 118, 125, 182, 205, 213, 216, 217, 219, 220, 247, 267, 268
Müller-Warden 6, 7, 277
Music 42, 52, 59, 70, 73, 76, 81, 90, 98, 99, 103, 115, 129, 199, 206, 215, 219, 267, 269–275, 277, 282
Music drama 12, 27, 28, 30, 33, 34, 43, 50, 53, 58, 65, 67, 70, 81, 89, 91, 92, 97, 99–101, 105, 107, 111, 113, 124, 125, 128, 130, 140, 146, 152, 153, 157, 163, 164, 170, 177, 210, 220, 225
Myth 114, 136

National 177, 277
News 68
Nizza 248
Nussbaum, Martha 277

Ode to Joy 52, 104, 106, 139, 140, 150, 151, 153, 155

Pagden, Anthony 3, 4, 259, 260, 262, 270, 272, 277, 278
Paradise 86, 152, 248
Pätzold, Detlev 115, 277, 278
Peri, Jacopo 92, 148
Periodenbau 67, 89, 90
Pessimism 273
Plato 54, 79, 130, 164, 165, 260, 261, 278
Play 107, 218
Pocock, J.G.A. 259, 260, 278
Politics 46, 267, 271, 274, 280, 281
Poussin, Nicolas 212, 213, 226
Prange, Martine 214, 221, 223, 278, 279
Prince Vogelfrei vi, 189, 223, 224, 241, 246
Prinz Vogelfrei 223, 246
Provencalism 256

Rafael 79, 85, 142
Raphael 71, 79, 152
Recoaro 215
Rée, Paul 207
Reformation 65, 83, 84, 256, 275

Renaissance 5, 65, 70, 71, 73, 83, 85, 92, 114, 117, 131, 151, 163, 164, 196, 203, 256
Representation vii, 54, 55, 60–63, 101, 123, 266, 271
Reschke, Renate 10, 273, 275–280
Rhythm 125
Ritschl 34, 44, 129
Rohde, Erwin 5, 44–46, 52, 124, 129, 160, 163, 181, 185, 187, 221, 273
Romanticism 58, 63, 76, 157, 160, 190, 199, 206, 269, 270, 274
Rome 71, 92, 148, 212, 218, 219
Rousseau 76, 93, 120, 133, 140, 157–160, 163, 183, 208, 219, 267, 271, 279

Sanctus Januarius 229, 231, 233, 235
Satyr 141
Scherz, List und Rache 200, 215, 216, 218
Schiller vii, 14, 52, 57, 59, 62–64, 66–68, 70, 72–76, 83–85, 88, 94, 96, 98, 103–111, 114, 116, 121, 122, 127, 135, 139, 140, 142, 145–154, 156–159, 161, 163–165, 170, 173, 176, 181, 192, 206, 213, 216, 218–220, 224, 266, 268, 270, 273, 274, 276, 278, 281, 282
Schopenhauer vii, 46, 54–67, 72–75, 77, 78, 86, 90, 92–94, 96, 100, 101, 105, 107, 108, 110, 116, 123, 125, 132, 137, 139–142, 144, 145, 150, 152, 153, 156, 160, 162, 192, 255, 277, 278, 282
Schubert, Franz 80, 129, 182, 218
Sentimental 68, 116, 121, 266
South 195, 209, 212, 214–216, 223, 229, 232, 241, 245, 247, 249, 254, 257
Southern 233, 249
Southernization 164
Spirit of Bizet 211
Stephenson, R.H. 56, 74, 93, 132, 133, 141, 177, 229, 267, 268, 278, 281
Stoic 231
Style vii, 56, 108, 150, 239
Supra-European 248
Supra-Europeanism 248
Symbol 136, 277
Symbolization 278

Takt 123, 125, 126, 205
The Antichrist vi, 18
The Birth of Tragedy vi, 6, 10, 13–16, 42, 52, 59, 62, 67, 68, 74, 79, 85, 90, 93, 96, 97, 101–103, 106, 108, 109, 111, 113, 114, 116–118, 120, 122, 124, 127, 129–132, 134, 135, 137, 140, 145–147, 151, 153, 154, 156, 157, 160, 163–165, 169–171, 173, 176, 185, 191, 199, 200, 204, 211, 223, 228, 233, 239, 254, 265, 270, 278
The Gay Science vi, 15–17, 189, 200, 209, 216, 221–224, 226, 228–233, 236, 237, 239, 241, 251, 253–257, 265
Thus Spoke Zarathustra vi, vii, 16, 43, 247–250, 256, 265, 269
Tongeren, Paul van 127, 189, 281
Tragic vii, 172, 173
Travel 195
Truth vii, 98, 219, 274

Venturelli, Aldo 98, 229, 270, 282

Wagner vi, vii, 12–14, 16, 34, 42–46, 51–53, 55–57, 59, 61–93, 95–107, 109–116, 118, 119, 121–133, 135–140, 144–157, 159–165, 169–173, 176, 178–182, 184–187, 191, 192, 194, 196–202, 204–207, 209, 210, 213–217, 219–221, 223–225, 230, 254, 255, 258, 268, 269, 271–273, 275, 277–279, 282, 283
Wagner, Cosima 43, 45, 46, 65, 95, 101, 172, 178, 181, 185, 213, 255, 282
Wagner, Richard vii, 12, 13, 43, 45, 52, 97, 112, 114, 120, 129, 131, 132, 163, 171, 173, 178, 181, 182, 258, 268, 272, 273, 275, 277
Weimar Classicism 63, 74, 95, 256, 268, 281
West 15, 247, 273, 281, 282
Will to Power 17, 18, 272
Wille 8, 17, 18, 54, 57, 65, 236, 241, 266
Winckelmann, J.J. 63, 74, 138, 146, 150, 170, 172, 176, 247, 279, 282
Witzler, Ralph 6, 282

Zeitfolge 67, 89, 90, 123, 124

www.ingramcontent.com/pod-product-compliance
Lightning Source LLC
Chambersburg PA
CBHW081042110426
42740CB00052B/3163